American-African Gandhis

An Analytical Synthesis of Three Gandhis

Dr. Martin Luther King, Jr.: 1929-1968

American-African Gandhis

An Analytical Synthesis of Three Gandhis

Col. M N Gulati

Manas Publications
New Delhi - 110 002 (India)

MANAS PUBLICATIONS
(Publishers, Distributors, Importers & Exporters)
4858, Prahlad Street,
24, Ansari Road, Darya Ganj,
New Delhi - 110 002 (INDIA)
Ph.: 23260783, 23265523 (O); 23842660
Fax: 011-23272766
E-mail: manaspublications@vsnl.com

2005

ISBN 81-7049-217-3
Rs. 795/-

Typeset at
Manas Publications

Printed in India at
Nice Printing Press, Delhi
and Published by Mrs Suman Lata
for **Manas Publications,** 4858, Prahlad Street,
24, Ansari Road, Darya Ganj,
New Delhi - 110 002 (INDIA)

Preface

Times do move fast. Barely four decades ago America was an altogether a different nation. Indeed, it was not one nation. And it was at war. No, not the Vietnam War whose negative momentum was propelling itself to a self-destructive end; instead, the super-power of the world was at war with its own self. It was a nation torn asunder by its inability to reconcile itself with its own intrinsic self, fighting to find its own true identity. It was struggling to establish peace at the global level but unable to do so back at home. The world at large was unable to make out: Whither America? No fault of the outside observers of the world scene of course; it was the kaleidoscope of colors of America that distinguished the various sections of the American people themselves whose mutual antipathy was the root cause of centuries of internal conflict, dissention, contradictions and bloodshed, earning for itself the epithet of the nation of murderers — a people who murdered their own President, shot its own Nobel Laureate who was trying to pull it out of the morass of self-deception and to build it into a cohesive one single nation at peace with its own self, killed its budding presidential candidate, and a host of Black Nationalists who were discriminated against because of the color of their skin, lynched, castrated, murdered in cold blood, and hung on trees as a lesson to others of the same hue. And the irony of fate was that those Blacks were faithful Christians imbued with a deep sense of spiritualism, and treated in so evil a manner by none others but Christians themselves.

Could a civilized people of the twentieth century who were on a trajectory to conquer outer space be as weird, cruel and merciless as to treat a section of their own populace as sub-human? Who preached democracy, human rights, equality, rule of law and justice to the world at large, possibly deny the same to a big chunk of its own people, all because they were the black descendents of African slaves? Who drafted a master piece bill of rights in the form of 'Declaration of Independence' could be on a fast-forward mode to deny the same to a large section of its own people? Who proclaimed that "All Men are Created Equal" could possibly practice total negation of this principle in their own land? Who preached the virtues of democratic polity to the world at large could deny the same at home? The list of intrinsic contradictions in the American 'white psyche' was indeed endless, and one could go on and on in this vein: But to what purpose!

The inventive spirit of the New World, the will to survive and to expand beyond visible horizons, the assembly-line technology, the debt-oriented economy giving rise to consumer-society — again the list is endless — turned America into the proverbial ever-expanding universe of products and services that totally transformed the concept of living in the modern world of science and technology, harnessing the immense potential of nature's bounty. And along came the concept of social engineering and reconstruction, reviving the couple of centuries old idea of 'Reconstruction' that was unfortunately discarded prematurely during its first avatar.

A new awakening came like a gust of fresh cool breeze in the hot summer of racial disharmony, discrimination, segregation, violence, denial of equal opportunities, jobs and income, *et al.* The oppression and revolting cruelties inflicted on Black Christians by the White Christians, painted a bright red blemish on the face of white Christianity, that paled into insignificance the treatment meted out by Brahmanical India to the 'Untouchables' class of that nation. Mohandas Karamchand Gandhi having experienced the humiliations of second-class citizenship in South Africa because of the color of his skin returned to India as a messiah not only for the emancipation of the low-caste Hindus but also to establish the might of nonviolent Satyagraha as a powerful tool to set the sun on the mighty British Empire, which in turn took large chunks of rest of the colonial world in its spate to free them from foreign domination. If Indians and a host of African countries could achieve that, why not the Negroes of America? But they had to find a Gandhi! And the Indian Gandhi, the 'Brown Gandhi', the proponent of "Soul-Force", could not possibly come to Black America.

So Black America did find its own brand of Gandhi —'Mahatma' and the 'Frontier' Gandhis of India — in their own country, amongst their own community: **Dr. Martin Luther King, Jr.** Even South Africa, in its struggle for racial equality and democracy, was well on its way to find their own Gandhi in the image of the Indian Gandhis, but then Dr. Nelson R. Mandela went off on a tangent but still succeeded in his life's mission.

India got rid of British colonialism through the powerful weapon of nonviolence. Many African and Asian countries followed suit. So did the 'Niggers' of America who found their heritage, their centuries-old legacy, and came to be called Afro-Americans with rights, privileges and responsibilities at par with their White compatriots.

This book is the geo-politico-historical review of their struggle against color-discrimination under the leadership of Dr. Martin Luther King, Jr., following in the footsteps of Indian Gandhis.

Col. M N Gulati

Acknowledgements

A biographical work through turbulent times has of necessity to rely on what the subject(s) and his immediate circle of associates have written about the person and the events as perceived by them at that point of time, without the benefit of hindsight-developments. Fortunately for the posterity Dr. Martin Luther King, Jr. and his wife, Mrs. Coretta Scott King, as well as the leadership of the Movement for Emancipation of the Negro of America, have left ample record of personalities and events surrounding them. I have therefore relied on the writings of Dr. King and Mrs. Coretta King and the leadership for the basic facts. I am indebted to all of them, one and all, as well as the *Time* Magazine. However, there is a pitfall in such a situation. An element of subjectivity is bound to creep in such works, besides the hero-worship-syndrome. The historian has therefore to sift the chaff from the grain, and place on record his critical comments, howsoever bitter the truth might be. I trust I have not been unduly harsh in my remarks.

- The magnitude of available literature directly connected with the Civil Rights Movement, its leadership and cadres is immense; and the indirect one is still greater. Rev. Ralph David Abernathy, Taylor Branch, Professor Lawrence D. Reddick, and a host of others have filled volumes. Rev. Abernathy was King's closest associate and the standard-bearer after him while Taylor was his first biographer. I have made use of their material and have liberally acknowledged the same, together with the very large number of other writers and historians whose writings provided the basic material to construct the story of Dr. King and his martyrdom. The historical background as in the first few chapters is of course a different matter altogether. The excellent libraries — oceans of knowledge if I may say so — of Universities of California at Berkley and Stanford proved to be of immense help. I am grateful to their staff for their patience and cooperation. Again, I have taken pains to acknowledge their works, of one and all; and in the process if I have inadvertently missed out some, my apologies to them, please. The basic matter is not mine, but its interpretations, presentation and comments thereon are mine, so are the errors therein; and I alone am responsible for the same.

- When one is covering a vast panorama of events over an equally vast country spread over a long time-span, repetitions are the bane of the author. I am grateful to Ms. Vijay Suda for her painstaking efforts to identify and rectify the repetitions. Ms. Raj Dar of St. Thomas College, Dehradun, gladly undertook the onerous task of correcting the typescript.
- The pictures of the contemporary period add luster to the text. I am grateful to Ms. Veena Chawla and Mr. Asok K. Samanta of American Information Resource Center, New Delhi, for their invaluable assistance in providing the prints of the bygone period. My thanks are also due to Mr. Bhatt and Ms. Pervesh of Ministry of Information and Broadcasting, Government of India, for providing the pictures of Gandhis and others out of the 'vaults' of their archives. Above all, it was Maj. Gen. K.N. Singh, AVSM, VSM & Bar, who was instrumental in resolving the frustrating bureaucratic part of the assignment.

And last, but not the least, I am indebted to my wife Nirmala for leaving me free by treating me as a 'paying guest' so that I could devote full time to this task!

Col. M N Gulati

Glossary

ACMHR	Alabama Christian Movement for Human Rights.
AFDC	Aid Families with Dependent Children.
Agapé	Greek word for love in general; like love of God, love for one's country, people; a non-demanding type of love as distinct from love for ones wife, kith and kin, property, etc.
Ahimsa	Nonviolence, non-injury to other beings in thought, word or act; absence of hostility or even thought to kill or cause harm.
ACMHR	Alabama Christian Movement for Human Rights.
AME	American Methodist Episcopal Church
BPP	Black Panther Party.
BSCP	Brotherhood of Sleeping Car Porters and Maids: A labor union of Black workers employed as porters and maids on passenger rail services.
Civil Disobedience	Non-compliance with laws or directive of an authority as an act of defiance to achieve one's political or social or economic objective.
COFO	Council of Federal Organizations.
COME	Community on the Move for Equality. (Based on the spiritual exhortation, "Come, let us reason together."
COHAR	Committee on Appeal for Human Rights.
CORE	Congress of Racial Equality.
Dharna	"Sit-in"; an act of civil resistance or deliberate defiance, and disobedience. Gandhi used this form of mass protest as a political weapon against unjust laws. This technique of nonviolent protest was first used in the United States in

	1940 by CORE against racial segregation. It came into prominence at Greensboro, North Carolina, with the 'sit-in' on February 1, 1960 when four young black students remained seated at a lunch counter when they were refused service, and continued to do so when asked to leave the premises.
FOR	Fellowship of Reconciliation.
Freedom Rides	An act of civil disobedience to defy local segregation laws while traveling inter-state.
FNP	Freedom Now Party.
Harijan	Children of God. Gandhi gave this name to Indian outcastes, 'untouchables'.
Hartal	Suspension of working activity, business, offices etc. to press the authorities to meet specific demands.
Hijrat	Migration or self imposed exile. Genesis of the word lies in Prophet Muhammad's migration from Mecca to Medina in 622 A.D.
Jim Crow	Rules and regulations governing conduct of Negroes regarding segregation, housing, social-conduct, etc. Essentially a pejorative term denoting racial segregation and discrimination.
Koran	Also Quran. Holy Book of Islam.
Lathi	About five feet long wooden stick, generally tipped with metal.
Mahatma	Great pious soul.
Mandir	A Hindu Temple.
MCCR	Memphis Committee on Community Relations.
MFDP	Mississippi Freedom Democratic Party, as an alternative to Mississippi "Jim Crow" Democratic Party. Also Movement for Depressed People.
MIA	Montgomery Improvement Association.
NAACP	National Association for Advancement of Colored People formed in 1909 by a group of Northern social workers. W.E.B. DuBois took a leading part in its formation. It was a premier civil rights litigation organization till Dr. Martin Luther King Jr. came on the scene.

NGRLC	Northern Grass Roots Leadership Conference.
NWRO	National Welfare Rights Organization.
NNPA	National Negro Press Association.
PPC	Poor Peoples' Campaign.
Sarvodaya	Universal general welfare.
Satyagraha	Nonviolent resistance, particularly to unjust laws. "Truth-Force". Truth is God.
SCLC	Southern Christian Leadership Conference formed by sixty Negro leaders, mostly clergymen, meeting at Ebenezer Baptist Church in Atlanta, Georgia, January 10-11, 1957, about three weeks after the successful end of Montgomery Bus Boycott. Dr. Martin Luther King was unanimously selected as its first president and continued in that position till his assassination in 1968. It had branches all over the South and was the coordinating body for various marches, demonstrations and protests.
Sit-in	Same as Dharna, as above.
SNCC	Students Nonviolent Coordinating Committee formed by regional leaders of 'sit-in' movement at their meeting in Shaw University in Raleigh, North Carolina, April 15-17, 1960. Ella J. Baker and Rev. James M. Lawson Jr. provided basic leadership. This was a sort of sister-organization to SCLC.
Swadeshi	A form of patriotism in which products made in one's country are given preference.
Swarj or Swarajya	Self rule, independence.
UNIA	Universal Negro Improvement Association.
VEP	Voter Education Project.

List of Photographs

Photo Credits

- * American Information Center, New Delhi
- ** Ministry of Information and Broadcasting, Govt. of India, New Delhi.
- *** Time Magazine (Cuttings from Personal Collection), Personal collection (Stamp issued by Government of India)
- @ These high quality pictures are through kind courtesy of Mr. Asok K. Samanta of Embassy of the United States of America, New Delhi.

Contents

1

The White Man Ate Alone

The two elements that are still most responsible for active segregationist sentiment are the newspapers and the politicians. When the white man argues that segregation should continue because of the Negro's lagging standards, he fails to see that the standards lag behind because of segregation. Segregation has placed the whole of the South socially, educationally, and economically behind the rest of the nation. It is as harmful to the Whites as it is to the Blacks.

Notwithstanding the various legal safeguards that were legislated from time to time extending over a period of three, if not four centuries, segregation of races as a way of life was a fact of American Life, more so in the Southern States. It permeated all facets of social, cultural and intellectual life, including the religious institutions. Segregation of races, Blacks and Whites, was practiced openly, without fear of God or law. It was an intrinsic part of the American system. There was no social interaction between the two racial communities. Even till as late as the late 1930's, if not the early 1950's, there was no social mixing of the Negroes and the Whites. Racial segregation permeated every facet of American society; it was the single most important guiding principle of social etiquette and behavior.

It so happened that some time during 1937, the Scott family — Coretta, wife of Dr. Martin Luther King Jr. belonged to the Scott family — moved to a new and much bigger house. But the pattern of segregation was strong enough to come into their fine new house also. "I remember the time my Father asked a white man to a meal. He was a friend, as well as a business acquaintance." There was long drawn argument about whether Daddy should eat with this man. The Father thought he should not, but Mother said: "Obie, this is your own house. He is coming as your guest. You should sit and eat with him." Coretta and her sister strongly supported the Mother, but the Father insisted that he should not. "No, I wouldn't feel right doing it."

The white man ate alone![1]

1. King, Coretta Scott: *My Life With Martin Luther King. Jr.*; New York, 1969, p. 49.

2

Founding of America

Abused and scorned though we the Blacks may be, our destiny is tied up with America's destiny. Before the Pilgrims landed at Plymouth, we were here. Before the pen of Jefferson etched the majestic words of the Declaration of Independence across the pages of history, we were here.

Neither Christopher Columbus discovered the American continent, nor did he give it that name. The three ships which discovered this continent in 1565 sailed under the Spanish flag. An Italian sea captain commanded this flotilla and had amongst its crews an Englishman, an Irishman, a Jew and a Negro. It was a German mapmaker, Martin Waldseemüller, who named this continent as "America" in honour of an Italian explorer, Amerigo Vespucci. The first wave of settlers, who were predominantly English in origin, came in 1607 and founded the Colony of Jamestown[1] at the mouth of James River. The Colony was held together largely through the valiant efforts of Captain John Smith. However, of the 120 Englishmen who founded the Colony, only 35 survived by the end of the year. The survival rate was so low that of the settlers who followed in the next decade, about half to two-thirds died within a year of settlement. The next English venture was by the Plymouth Company established in 1606, but their first two attempts to establish a colony at Plymouth at the mouth of Kennebec River ended in failure. However, a group of 'Pilgrims' left England aboard the Mayflower arriving at Cape Cod in November 1620. They established the Mayflower Compact with John Carver as their Governor and selected Plymouth as the site of the new settlement, which was independent of the English Crown. But the English were not the first settlers on the American East

1. The year 1607 marked the founding of Virginia by English colonists, to "fetch treasure" and enjoy religious and happy government.

coast; it was the Spaniards[2] who founded the oldest American city, St. Augustine, as early as in 1565. Spain basked in the vain glory of a Spanish Empire in the Western Hemisphere, howsoever brief it might have been, but enough to loot and steal tons of gold and silver for shipment back home to the King(s). During the late sixteenth and early seventeenth centuries, a good number of African Negroes frequently took part in the Portuguese and Spanish expeditions to the American continent, and were part of the colonial American settlements.

The above is the historically accepted version of establishment of slavery in North America; but it is not necessarily the correct one. This aspect is clarified in Chapter 24 where the 1965-Quadricentennial celebrations of St. Augustine established in 1565 by Catholic Spaniards have been discussed. Here it will suffice to say that the Catholic Spaniards took possession of Fort Mose just off St. Augustine, and established the first armed independent settlement of Free Blacks in North America. This caused deep consternation amongst the Protestant colonists of South Carolina. They were so enraged that they prescribed the punishment of castration for any Negro who tried to escape to take refuge in the Spanish St. Augustine. This cruel punishment was even actually carried out in a number of cases. The original Governor of colonial Georgia, James Oglethorpe, led a number of violent expeditions against the catholic St. Augustine to wipe out a sanctuary for the run-away slaves. Ultimately, the British did succeed to throw out the Spaniards and took charge of Florida in 1763. The Spaniards along with the entire population of Fort Mose, whites and blacks alike, evacuated to Cuba.

The colonists were now in a tight situation. They were extremely short of working hands. Of sheer necessity, they welcomed one and all to meet the labor requirements of opening up a wild new vast expanse of land. When Great Britain conquered Nieuw Amsterdam in 1664, they offered citizenship to eighteen different nationalities. One enterprising Scotsman, Andrew Turnbull had a bright idea. He imported the largest mass of white indentured servants ever assembled in North America. They were known as "Turnbull's Niggers" and came from Greece, Italy and about three hundred families from the island of Minorca off the coast of Spain.[3] As the indigo plantations started failing, they took refuge in nearby St. Augustine. Thousands of these unfortunate, unemployed, homeless human beings sold away their freedom, may be temporarily for a few years, in exchange for transportation. They came to America

2. Zinn Howard: *People's History of the United States, 1492-Present.*. New York, 1922/95, pp. 17-18.
3. Branch Taylor: *Pillar of Fire.* New York, 1998, p. 34.

as indentured servants to work without wages. Such indentured servants from Europe were in turn sold for a price in the American markets. The same holds good for the slaves brought from Black Africa to provide a bank of labor force for developing the new colonies, as well as for the personal comforts of their white masters. The story of white indentured labor to America has its parallel in another continent. Many Indians left their homes and hearths and went over to South Africa as indentured labor to work on the white man's plantations. But for those indentured forced laborers and the terrible atrocities inflicted on them, there would have been no Gandhi!

However, the English themselves, the Spanish and the French constituted three major segments of the new population. "At one time it seemed the continent might ultimately divide into three language sections: English, Spanish and French."[4] Fortunately for the world and the coming generations, after 1763 the English victories over the French in the 'Seven Years War' — known in America as the French and Indian War expelling the French from North America — and the purchase of territories held by the French and the Spanish prevented such a catastrophic division. The colonists were now left with two rivals only: the British and the Red Indians. Thus America remained a united country with the English as the predominant community whose language, culture, customs, system of government, *et al,* laid the foundations of the new continent, giving birth to a new nation of mixed genes, a nation of immigrants indeed, many of whom did not come as free men.

But the Red Indian was tough, resourceful, defiant and self-supporting. He was at home in the jungles but the neo-colonists were strangers to that soil and environment and totally misfit to survive on their own. The white colonists had no option but to get outside help. Just twelve years after the founding of Jamestown in the colony of Virginia, the first shipload ot twenty Negro slaves ("Twenty Negars") was brought to Jamestown from Africa in August 1619 by the Dutch ship Jesus. She did her trading and was gone.[5] This marked the beginning of mass migration of Africans to the North American shores.[6] The Mayflower came a few

4. Kennedy F. John: *A Nation of Immigrants.* Hamish Hamilton, London, 1964; p. 11. Also Zinn: op.cit. p. 59.
5. Zinn Howard: op.cit. p. 23.
6. The initial waves of African migrants were not treated as slaves; they were like the indentured servants like the Indians who went to South Africa in pursuit of jobs and better like. In fact, one of the first African Blacks was Anthony Johnson who received his freedom in a few years, became wealthy, and he owned Negro slaves! It was only after 1661 that the African migrants cam to be treated as slaves or life rather than as indentured servants.

months later. The traffic in human beings as cargo had started. It continued as a roaring trade for a couple of centuries. These immigrants and their immediate successors were the first indentured bond-servants as a source of labor supply in the new America. The next logical development was legal slavery. It took hardly fifty years for it to make its first appearance in the new colonies. The next two centuries saw a deluge of African Negroes imported to meet the ever increasing demand for agricultural, industrial and domestic labor for the white colonizers. In the process Negro population in the new Colonies increased manifold, and in 1790 they constituted almost twenty per cent of the total population — 757,208 out of total U.S. population of 3,929,214. Thereafter the proportion of Negro population started declining with the increasing influx of the Caucasians. By the end of the nineteenth century it stabilized at around ten per cent of the total.

Declaration of Independence

The intervening events like the 'Boston Massacre' of 5th March 1770, the 'impressments riots' through the 1760's in New York and Rhode Island, the 'Boston Tea Party' of December 1773, *et al*, leading to ultimate defeat of British troops at the hands of the colonists, are not within the purview of this work. What matters is the founding of America as an independent sovereign nation through the Declaration of Independence written by Thomas Jefferson, adopted by the Congress on 2nd July and officially proclaimed from the town hall balcony in Boston on 4th July 1776 by Thomas Crafts — a member of the Loyal Nine Group — embodying the principles that 'all men are created equal' endowed by the Creator with unalienable Rights of 'Life, Liberty and pursuit of Happiness'. The Women, the Blacks and the 'Red Indians' were not even mentioned in this Declaration, which remained an empty rhetoric for the next couple of centuries till Dr. Martin Luther King Jr. and other leaders came on the scene to remove the scourge of 'segregation' and restored 'equality'.

The evil practice of slavery was officially outlawed by vote of the American Congress in 1807.[7] But this did not lead to freedom for the slaves. That had to wait for the Emancipation Proclamation of 1863,[8]

7. Initially, the Royal African Company had a monopoly of slave trade. The business of sale-purchase of human beings as if they were cattle expanded rapidly. Since the New Englanders found this a highly profitable business, the monopoly of the Royal African was soon brought to an end.
8. The preliminary Proclamation was issued on September 22, 1862 while the final one came into effect on 1st January 1863.

the War between the North and South, and finally the adoption of the Thirteenth Amendment[9] to the Constitution two years later in 1865. That is when the slaves got their freedom. But that freedom was a bad cheque issued by the whites to the Negroes! The Black people had to wait another century before segregation, racial discrimination, equality before the law, et al, became realities. The immigrants were predominantly of European stock. Most of them came over voluntarily either due to economic distress or on account of political upheavals caused by defeat of democratic forces in their own lands. For instance, just because of these two developments during the period 1830 to 1848, more than one million Germans migrated to America in the fifteen years before 1860. No doubt some were attracted by bold ads for sale of land at the throw away price of $8 to $12 per acre in what was then known as the Garden State of America, the State of Illinois, while others were attracted by the tablet mounted on the pedestal of Statute of Liberty reproducing the poem "The New Colossus" written in 1883 by Emma Lazarus. "Give me your tired, your poor, your huddled masses yearning to be free".[10]

The African ancestors of the American Negro came from a variety of tribes from all over the vast lands of the African continent. They had their roots in a variety of countries and regions in Central and West Africa, like the vast Niger Valley, the Cameroon and the Congo, French West Africa, Guinea, Ivory, Slave and Gold Coast. A few who were captured into slave trade belonged to the Moors and Arabs to the north, while a small number came from the East and South African tribes including Hottentots and Madagascans. They were taken to the African slave ports from where they were transported to American slave marts in overcrowded ships whose sanitary conditions were revolting, more like a cargo of animals than as human beings. Be that as it may, once on the job in the plantations a certain degree of fusion of racial groups was part of the natural process. There was admixture of white and American-Indian blood through casual sex, concubines, etc. Inter-marriage

---

9. The Thirteenth Amendment read: Neither slavery nor involuntary servitude except as punishment for a crime whereof the party shall have been duly convicted shall exist within the United States nor any place subject to their jurisdiction.
10. James A. Garfield, a Republican and twentieth President of the United States was assassinated by Charles Guiteau, a disappointed office seeker, in 1881 after a very short term in office. He was the last President born in log-cabin, and the second to be assassinated while in office. He was shot on July 02 and died on September 19, 1881.

between American-Indians and the slave Africans, albeit on a small scale, was an accepted pattern of the social phenomenon. While this process added to the available labor force, for which there was always a great demand in the plantations, over a period of time a new race, a distinct biological and cultural product, started taking shape. As time went on, there was gradual increase in direct and compounded intermixture with various strains of white blood so much so that the present Negro population of pure or unmixed African descent is less than twenty percent. The bulk of the American Negro population at present is a mixed group of brown or brownish-yellow "mulattoes". The intermixing of White and non-White blood strains has gone so far that a few mulattoes might even be mistaken for Caucasians. No wonder therefore those traditional racial distinctions make little sense in the present scenario. Nevertheless, traditional Negro music, art forms, and emotional religious expression continue to play a significant role in their cultural life. Over a period of time, a refreshingly peculiar cultural blend has taken form adding to the fusion and variety in the overall relationship between the traditional racial groups, notwithstanding the enormous strength of 'White Power', which reigned supreme during the early formative years of the nation-in-making. The Black resurgence had to face the all-pervading White Power — the Government was white, and so was its entire machinery; judiciary was white, so were the schools and colleges; the Congress was white, so were the industrial and business corporations; even the labor unions were controlled by the whites. Thus all the three engines that propel the Government of United States of America — executive, legislative and the judiciary — were white. White was the color of early America until the huge manpower demands of the Second World War partially transformed the psychological and physical attitudes towards racialism. Nonetheless, in so far as the Civil Rights movement was concerned, its sole sustenance came from the judiciary. Litigation was the only channel open to the black minority till as late as the early 1960's.

The United States of America

The aforesaid evolutionary development in turn led to the formation of "The United States of America", a term borrowed from the Dutch — 'The United States of the Netherlands.' Various nationalities and races have jointly contributed to what has come to be the most powerful nation in the world. Its economic and military strength remains unmatched, while its citizens enjoy the highest living standards. America has freely imbibed whatever good came from the rest of the world. The

Jews too made immense contribution towards development of the new Continent, particularly in the intellectual field, primarily because the Jews were better educated. They provided their newly adopted country with a nucleus of scholars, lawyers, judges, journalists, writers and literary figures, besides of course world famous scientists of the calibre of Albert Einstein and Edward Teller. The contribution of the Dutch was not limited only to the name of the new country; they brought golf (kolf in Dutch) to America along with ice skating, bowling, boating as a sport, waffles, cookies, and of course the American staple of the menu, the doughnuts (kruller in Dutch). And last, but not the least, Santa Claus and his reindeer came from Holland![11]

The early waves of slaves were primarily employed on plantations for cultivation of rice, indigo and tobacco. Soon these products lost their profitability, and but for the sudden upsurge of cotton-culture, perhaps, the slave trade would have died a natural death. It was the invention of cotton-gin in 1793 that saved the economy of the Colonies, and kept alive the institution of slavery in the United States. In fact, the Southern States had such a boom in cotton industry, from cultivation to the end product, that the demand for slave labor increased manifold. Despite legal barriers, import of slaves increased. The demand for labor was so high that even reproduction of slaves became an 'industry' by itself! This resulted in substantial increase in Negro population in the U.S. It increased by 200,000 by the end of the last decade of the 18th century, by 300,000 in the end of the following decade, and by 500,000 by the close of the year 1830. It will thus be seen that slavery became the very foundation of the economy of the Southern States. Their very survival depended on the continuation of the institution of slavery. While a certain degree of humanization of slavery had occurred when slaves were working directly for the master, that human touch completely disappeared and gave rise to cruelty when the absentee landowners had their plantations and industry managed by professional white supervisors. Expansion of plantations and increased production gave rise to absentee landlordism. In turn, this ultimately led to the end of the slavery itself.

Around the middle of the 20th century, the population of American Negroes was about fifteen million, constituting about one tenth of the total American population. They formed the largest minority group in the United States of America and their classification was based on ethnic and/or social basis. Their common ancestral origin from hundreds and thousands of Africans legally imported mainly as slaves from Africa during

---

11. Kennedy, op.cit., p.12.

1619 to 1808 forms the basis of their ethnic or social classification. Although slave trade was declared illegal and abolished in 1808, a large number continued to be imported clandestinely until 1848, just a few years before declaration of general amnesty in 1863. However, any person with recognizable Negro blood admixture, howsoever slight it may have been, was classified as Negro. Thus the basis of classification became social to that extent, and such persons were victims of color prejudice like any other totally Negro person. The extent of social and economic discrimination that the Negroes in America suffered was related to the region as well as the period of history. It was far more intense in the southern states and the adjacent areas than up in the north. The seeds of racial minority problems and consequent social tensions were there to germinate, sooner or later, and grow into rich fertilizer for political bonanza, ultimately leading to 'Poor Peoples March' unifying all the depressed and oppressed classes of America irrespective of the color of their skin — Blacks, Whites, Browns, and the Reds.

Abraham Lincoln

Abraham Lincoln's early life was in rough soil. May be he was coarse in speech but he was pure in life. He was patient by nature and sympathetic in his concern for other human beings. A lawyer by profession, he was fair in his dealings. In politics his integrity was above board. These qualities earned him the nickname "Honest Abe". His attitude on slavery was typical of the men of the North who were at once humane and regardful of "the established order".[12] He strongly believed in freedom for the slaves. But it did not mean equality of the Negro with the white man. Lincoln had no intention of giving voting rights to the freed slaves, nor to make them jurors. In fact, Lincoln's anti-slavery position was very moderate. Nevertheless, the Civil War began on April 12, 1861 and Lincoln made the famous Gettysburg address.[13] He presented the Emancipation Proclamation to his Cabinet in July 1862. "The Cabinet was amazed — and divided."[14] Seward suggested that in view of the recent military reverses in McClellan's Peninsula, it was not the appropriate time to put forward such a farreaching reform. Lincoln agreed and postponed the issue for a later

12. Merriam S. George: *Negro And The Nation*; pp. 176-78.
13. Vice President Johnson too made an equally significant address at Gettysburg after the Memorial Day service when he said: "One hundred years ago the slave was freed. One hundred years later the Negro remains in bondage to the color of his skin. In the process, he endorsed Martin King's theme, "neutrality of time" and declared: "We must not lose that soul in dishonor on the fields of hate."
14. Merriam S. George: op.cit. p. 257.

date. This was on 22 July 1862. However, when Lee took the offensive after a yearlong defensive, and entered Maryland, he was beaten and turned back at Antietam, the singlemost bloodiest day of the Civil War, even though it was indecisive — total deaths during the Battle or as a result thereof reached 7,800 with another 15,500 wounded. Lee began to fall back into Virginia. Now Lincoln got his opportunity. He summoned the Cabinet again on 22 September 1862 and placed the proposed Proclamation of Emancipation before them for approval. It was more of a military move than a mere act of anti-slavery campaign, more so since Lincoln's 'ultimatum' promised that the States that returned to the Northern fold would be left alone with their slaves in place. The proclamation itself was issued the next day giving the South four months to end the rebellion. The American nation was thus "inexorably committed to emancipation, — compensated if possible; forcible if necessary; partial at first, but moving inevitably, swiftly, toward universal freedom."[15] The Proclamation came into effect on 1st January 1863, whereby slaves still fighting the Union were deemed to have been freed for ever. It resulted in freeing of some and 'left others alone'.

The above imperfect state could not be allowed indefinitely. Meanwhile, Lincoln won the Presidential election of 1864. Every state supported him except the States of New Jersey, Kentucky and Delaware. While Grant and Lee were locked in the last desperate struggle at Petersburg, and with final victory well in sight, Lincoln 'spoke his second inaugural'. His election for another term gave the anti-slavery lobby a big boost. It was therefore decided to grant universal freedom to all slaves through a constitutional amendment. The Thirteenth Amendment was brought forward in April 1864 but it did not receive the requisite majority vote. The same amendment was put up again next year when it received the necessary majority and was declared adopted on 18 December 1865. On that day the evil of slavery in the United States came to the end, albeit on paper only. Moreover, the American Constitution had a built-in contradiction in Article 1 inasmuch as a Negro slave was to be counted as three-fifths of a person while computing the number of representatives a state could send to the Congress.

Lincoln had already fulfilled his life's mission, but he was not destined to bask for long in the warmth of its full glory. On 14th April 1865, Good Friday, while he sat in the Ford's theatre he was mortally shot by John Wilkes Booth and died the next day.[16] A life of heroic glorious

---

15. Ibid. p. 259.
16. Stearns N. Peter: *The Encyclopedia of World History.* New York, p. 610.

service was thus crowned by a martyr's death through an assassin's bullet. The Vice President, Andrew Johnson succeeded to the Presidency.[17]

Blacks-Whites Conflict

During those early days there were hardly any blacks in the American urban centres. The two World Wars, recruitment of the Blacks in the defence services at whatever level, the economic depression of the 30's, industrial development, the preponderance of the automobile, *et al*, altered the old pattern, besides awakening the Negroes to the realities of racial discrimination and inequality in the eyes of the law. A large number of Negroes moved out of the plantations to the ghettoes in the urban centres, thereby ending decades of isolation. Here they came face to face with the realities of two sets of rules: one for the Whites and the other for the Blacks. The former were the superior beings, supreme in the land they had grabbed from the American-Indians way back. The Negro was a second, if not the lowest class of citizen. His inferiority complex nurtured over a couple of centuries of slavery, segregation and racial discrimination, deprivation and denial of education, etc., erupted on the surface of social platform. He came to realize that he too was somebody, a part of the vast panorama of American kaleidoscope. His religion came to his rescue inasmuch as his belief that God loves all His children irrespective of the color of their skin, or the texture of their hair. In the ultimate analysis what mattered was his intrinsic and eternal worth as a person before God. The Negroes were thus inspired, determined to achieve parity with their white countrymen insofar as Civil Rights and equality before the law were concerned. At the same time, the Negroes must be honest enough to accept that their standards often did lag behind. It is altogether a different matter that they fell short of the standards primarily on account of segregation. For instance, the Negro crime rate was much higher than the rest of the population. The blame for this lies entirely at the doorsteps of the Negroes themselves. The parents should give their children love, attention and a sense of belonging so that they may adjust to urban environment and maintain high moral standards. Concurrently, the authorities perpetuating violence need to realize: "All who take the sword will perish by the sword." Be

---

17. Sixteen attempts to kill U.S. Presidents had been made in the Twentieth Century. Only two were successful—the 25th President William McKinley on September 14, 1901, and the 35th President John F. Kennedy on 22 November 1963. President Reagan was wounded and President Ford escaped unhurt in two attempts, both in 1974, and both, curiously, by females.

that as it may, the records show that whites seldom attacked the Blacks, except of course when the Blacks demanded equal rights.

Similarly, immigration from the Orient in the later part of the nineteenth century was a blemish on the otherwise good name of the new democracy, as it was also the shameful treatment of White America against the Black America. Indeed, the latter aspect of American attitude proved beyond any doubt that commonality of religion could not be considered a unifying factor amongst different racial groups. Above all, white America's treatment of the Oriental immigrants[18] represented a shameful episode in the history of the United States. The Chinese suffered the worst indignities at the hands of the native-Americans, and the Chinese Exclusion Act of 1882 was a disgraceful piece of legislation enacted by a proud democracy which shouted at the top of its voice: "All Men are Created Equal'. It was Jefferson, the slaveholder, who had written those pompous words without the least intention of putting them into practice. Concurrently, they also proved that some are more equal than others, depending upon the color of their skin. The 'Black Scourge' and 'Yellow Peril' were an enigma to the White America. A campaign of organized violence against Chinese communities and subsequent hysteria reached a level that President Hayes could not ignore without serious damage to his political standing. Although the President vetoed an act of Congress restricting Chinese immigration, he made sure that the Burlingame Treaty[19] was renegotiated. Their treatment of the American citizens of Japanese origin, the Nisei, during the War days proved to the rest of the world that America is a white nation, highly discriminatory on racial grounds. Does the white America really consider the Puerto Ricans as equal citizens of the United States? The equality of all citizens before the law, irrespective of caste, color and creed, was a mere facade, an exercise in futility in the field of public relations. All that the American concept of equality justified was what was enshrined in the words of the Declaration of Independence which Thomas Jefferson made: "All men are created equal ... are endowed by their Creator with certain unalienable rights." In practical terms, its application was restricted to a certain segment of society; and for all practical purposes the dogma of equality remained a mere joke for

18. According to the US Census 2000, people of Indian origin number 1.7 million constituting 0.6 per cent of the total population, the fourth largest immigrant community. However, in England they number 1.5 million but represent 1.8 per cent of the total population.
19. Under the Burlingame Treaty the Government of China had agreed to restrict emigration voluntarily.

more than two centuries when great personalities like Dr. Martin Luther King Jr. applied the principle of equality to all sections of American society in line with the philosophy of Mahatma Gandhi.

It is worth recalling that well before Dr. Martin Luther King Jr. came on the scene, a form of nonviolent resistance, 'not to work so hard', had been conceived and preached by the famous Black philosopher-intellectual-writer, W.E.B. Du Bois. In 1905, he gathered twentynine black leaders, mostly professionals like doctors, lawyers and teachers, at Niagara Falls, Canada, and formed the Niagara Movement whose mission was 'Black Equality' in real terms. Through this organization, he inaugurated a program of agitations for black rights. But in 1910 it came to a premature end due to financial stringency since most of the funds for advancement of colored people were going to Booker T. Washington. The demise of Niagara Movement gave birth to the most important inter-racial civil rights organization, the National Association for the Advancement of Colored People (NAACP) founded in 1909. The famous Boston lawyer, Moorefield Storey, a white man, was its first President with W.E.B. Du Bois as its Director of Publicity and Research. Once again, the mission of NAACP was "to achieve, through peaceful and lawful means, equal citizenship rights for all American citizens by eliminating segregation and discrimination in housing, employment, voting, schools, the courts, transportation, recreation." The very first crusade of NAACP was for enacting federal anti-lynching legislation[20] which, though twice passed by the House, was killed in the Senate by Southern senators.

Around the same time a parallel organizational setup came up amongst the Blacks of South Africa too. It started with the founding of Natal Indian Congress in 1894 by M.K. Gandhi giving rise to African Peoples' Organization (APO) in 1902 and the African National Congress in 1912. The two African national organizations were considerably influenced by Gandhi's philosophy of militant Satyagraha which took birth in South Africa in 1907.

While delving on the subject of racism in trade union movement, Du Bois pointed out in 1913 that the greatest enemy of the American Negro is not the employer, but 'his fellow white workingman', also a member of the American Federation of Labor (AFL). He was one of the first militant black leaders and was responsible for breaking the pattern of 'patience' set by black nationalists like George Washington Carver and Booker T. Washington. Indeed, Du Bois[21] was a hero for the Black

20. NAACP: *Thirty Years of Lynching in the United States, 1889-1918.*
21. 23rd February 1968 was observed as the centennial ceremony honoring the memory of Dr. W.E.B. Du Bois.

people of America. He taught at the Atlanta University and, in his book, *Black Reconstruction* written in 1935, he exposed the brutalities to which the Negro was subjected as a matter of routine. He wrote in *The Gift of Black Folk*:

> The Negro was not "as easily reduced to mechanical draft-horse which the European laborer became. He tended to work as the results pleased him and refused to work or sought to refuse when he did not find the spiritual returns adequate; thus he was easily accused of laziness and driven as a slave when in truth he brought manual labor a renewed valuation of life".

The First World War witnessed yet another outbreak of White Americanism. Ku Klux Klan appeared on the scene with a totally irrational philosophy denouncing everything that had anything to do with the Negroes, Jews, Catholics, liberalism of any hue, pacifists, internationalism, *et al.* They propagated their clannish fundamentalist views in the name of what they called as 'True Americanism' and 'Nordic Superiority'[22]. Even though the American Government and the people in general did not subscribe to these racist ideas, the fact remained that "a qualified person born in England or Ireland who wanted to immigrate to the United States could do so at any time. A person born in Italy, Hungry, Poland or the Baltic States may have to wait for many years before his turn is reached".[23] And regarding the Asians, Yellow or the Brown races, the less said the better. However, in a 'remarkably perceptive article' titled *The African Roots of War,* W.E.B. Du Bois pointed out that the First World War was primarily a struggle for empire-building in Africa by Germany on the one hand and the Allied Powers on the other. "Africa is the land of the Twentieth Century" because of the gold and diamond of South Africa, the cocoa of Angola and Nigeria, the rubber and ivory of the Congo, and the palm oil of the West Coast.[24]

Successive American administrations were reluctant to grant equal rights and privileges to the Negroes lest that might endanger national security — national security from the perspective of the Whites. However, a close study of American history shows that the constituent units of the Union, the States themselves were the real culprits. It is the States which posed real danger to American freedom, and not the American-Indians or the Negroes. If and when it was not the States, the Federal Government itself curtailed the freedom of its own people. Glaring examples of the

---

22. Kennedy: *op.cit.,* p. 71
23. Ibid., p. 75.
24. Zinn Howard: *op.cit.,* p. 354.

latter danger may be cited as the Alien and Sedition Acts of 1798, the draconian legislation enacted during the First World War leading to large scale repression and trampling over rights of the individual, and above all, the McCarthyism of the 50's. Indeed, there is no explanation for the paradoxical behavior of the whites of America for their treatment of the colored citizens of their country. They preached one doctrine to the rest of the world; but they themselves contravened the same in their treatment of their own minorities. Perhaps, it was their inherent belief in the superiority of the Whites over the Blacks. While ninety percent of the Americans the Whites were proud of their heritage, generosity, democratic traditions and equal rights for all, they refused to concede the same to the remainder ten per cent of the population. However, once the Negroes got back some of their rights, they wanted all of them, the whole lot of them, without any further delay.

3

Martin Luther King, Jr.: The Early Years

Who are we? We are the descendents of slaves. We are the heirs of a past of rope, fire and murder. I for one am not ashamed of this past. My shame is for those who became so inhuman that they could inflict this torture upon us.

James King, a prosperous minister of one of the largest and richest Baptist congregations in the country, had ten children. Martin was the second child, and first son, borne at Atlanta, Georgia, on 15 January 1929.[1] The King family was the proverbial middle class outfit with all the advantages such background confers. But these advantages did not come easily. Daddy King used to say: "I have a mule complex. I vowed when I left the country: I'm not going to be a slave, and I'm not going to plough another mule." On the other hand, Martin had a sociological outlook. When his father told him to wash his own car, he responded: "Daddy, you know society is based on the division of labor, and if I wash my own car it means someone else doesn't have a job."[2]

Martin had a strong unbendable formidable sense of conscience. It kept him throughout on the path that he thought was right one. And if he did slip up sometime, he made it a point to apologize and seek

1. Martin's was baptized as Michael, as was his Father, the son of a sharecropper. Since King Sr. had experienced racial brutalities at first hand, he led the fight for equal salaries for teachers and was instrumental in the elimination of 'Jim Crow' elevators in the courthouse. A reformist at heart, he decided to take on for himself and his son the full name of the Protestant reformer. "Both Father and I have fought all our lives for reform, and perhaps we have earned our right to the name." — *Time,* February 18, 1957.
2. King Scott Coretta: *op. cit.* p. 93.

forgiveness. No wonder therefore that Martin did feel that many an honor heaped on him in later life did not belong to him alone; his colleagues and the organizations he represented deserved an equal, if not larger, share of those honors. Indeed, Martin was a humble man by nature, a man of high moral fibre and totally honest. Humility was sort of inborn in Martin. He was blessed with a deep rich voice and soloed hymns at church services and conventions. When he was barely six, his mother played the piano and Martin — popularly known as M.L. at that tender age — sang his favorite gospel song, *'I Want To Be More and More Like Jesus.'* There was all-round thunderous applause. "But the boy didn't get puffed up; he just went and sat down, very quiet and humble."[3] On the other hand, M.K. Gandhi continued to be extremely shy. While traveling by ship to England for higher studies, he would not mix or talk to other passengers, nor eat in the dining room. He had reasonable knowledge of English but the accent and the slangs were a problem, so were the knife and fork! So the young Gandhi ate all his meals in his cabin from the food he had brought with him, to make sure that he did not violate his vows about wine, women and meat. As for Martin, it was at this tender age of six when M.L. first experienced, and understood the meaning of segregation. He saw plenty of "Whites Only" signs all over the place in his hometown. These made him feel awfully bad. But his understanding Mother told him not to worry about these signs: "You are as good as anyone". However, a bigger shock was to come soon. — He used to play with some white children who lived near King's home in Atlanta. Martin went to Negro elementary school but his friends went to the white school which was obviously much better looking and furnished. The white youngsters told M.L. that he could not come to play with them any more, "because we are white and you are colored."[4] Nonetheless, M.L. was very fortunate as compared to other Negro boys and girls. He did not have to suffer many of the humiliations and cruelties of segregation, all because of the fortuitous circumstances of his family. Moreover, Daddy King had set an example for his children by fighting 'Jim Crow'[5] from an early age.

3. Coretta: op. cit. p. 94.
4. Ibid., pp. 94-95.
5. The series of laws passed by the states were called the Black Codes. These came to be known as "Jim Crow" laws. The name 'Jim Crow' came from a comic black character that was portrayed by a white performer in an early nineteenth century variety act.

Segregated Facilities: "Whites Only"

Signs like this were posted all over the place in most urban areas, particularly in the Southern States. These were humiliating eye sores to the Black People.

King Sr.'s strong dynamic personality went a long way in moulding Martin's character qualities. "Daddy" King was indeed proud of his prodigious son who had imbibed his Father's intense dislike of segregation and all the humiliation that it entailed. 'Jim Crow' laws passed by white legislatures were designed to impress on the Blacks that they were an inferior people. A Negro was never referred to as a 'mister'; he was always a 'boy' or a 'girl'. However, Daddy King would not accept this nonsense. One day while driving his car with Martin in the other front seat, a policeman told King Sr., "Boy, show me your license." Pointing towards Martin, he retorted in his powerful voice: "Do you see this child here. He's a boy. I'm a man." They were supposed to always say "yes, sir" or "yes, ma'am", even to teen age whites. Aim of the exercise? — To instill a 'slave mentality'. On any complaint by a white woman against a Negro, the latter was invariably lynched, and often strung up a tree to use the body for target practice.

Martin grew up in Atlanta, capital of the State of Georgia, the so-called 'gateway to the South', about 150 miles northeast of Montgomery, Alabama. Atlanta was by far the most forwardlooking city in the South. It was Martin's home base and was blessed with a university, Morehouse College, Spellman College, Morris Brown College and Clark College. These institutions produced the cream of black middle class. There was so much black potential in this Southern city that it was a matter of considerable surprise and regret that Atlanta had not been desegregated. Be that as it may, Martin had a happy comfortable childhood, notwithstanding the vagaries of segregation, denial of swimming pool, public parks, theatres or lunch-counters in stores. He was an intelligent, gifted, self-confident and an extraordinarily healthy child who did well in studies, sports, debates and oratory, and whatever else was the school activity. He went through the public schools of Atlanta for his early education followed by two years in the Atlanta University Laboratory High School, from where he entered Brook T. Washington High School, skipped a year and passed the entrance examination for (Negroes') Morehouse College, almost equivalent of Whites' Harvard in prestige. Martin passed his matriculation in 1944. He was a graduate student at Columbia University when Eisenhower was President of the University. He was confident, self-possessed and his oratorical skills were of a high order having a high sense of humour sharpened with some quick wit. Now, he looked forward to becoming a lawyer or a doctor so that he could do his bit in improving the lot of black masses. However, to be able to do that sort of thing, it was essential to understand in depth the social, economic and family problems of the under-privileged and oppressed people, as well as to 'feel their feelings'. He therefore did not take the usual white collar jobs during the summer; instead, he chose a manually hard job of handling baggage for the Railway Express Agency, after which he shifted to the loading platform of the Southern Bedspring Mattress Company — both physically exhausting hard manual jobs. In the process he not only came to be intimately acquainted with his fellow labourers, but also found what it was like to work under supervision of white bosses. The black 'boys' were 'niggers' and personal humiliations were heaped on one and all as a matter of routine. One day when M.L. went to have a meal in the dining car, "the waiter ushered him to a rear seat and pulled a curtain down in front of him" as if he was a non-entity.[6] Martin felt as if a curtain had come down across his whole life. "The insult of it I will never forget." The second instance of deep humiliation that left a permanent scar on King's psyche also happened during an impressionable age. He was traveling by bus with his school teacher from Macon to Atlanta when the driver ordered them to give their seats to white passengers. When they did not move, the driver started cursing and abusing them on which the teacher prevailed upon Martin to surrender the seats to the whites. They stood in the aisle and traveled the entire remaining ninety-miles standing, all the way to Atlanta. Within a week of Gandhi's arrival in the African Continent, he too was subjected to a series of racial humiliations. Thus both Martin and Gandhi suffered racial humiliations during the very early part of their professional lives. So did Nelson Mandela in his own country. He said: "I detest racialism because I regard it as a barbaric thing, whether it comes from a black man or a white man." The scars left behind by these acts of injustice and racial-humiliations were to mould the future career of these men who ended up as world leaders, each in his own way. Their paths were different but the destinations coincided, more by accident than by deliberation.

Crozer Seminary

As an undergraduate student he was interested in medicine and law, later changed to enter the seminary as his father had been trying to persuade him for a career in the Ministry. The King-family was steeped in traditions of Southern Negro ministry. His Father and maternal grandfather, the Reverend Adam Daniel Williams[7] , were Baptist preachers, so was his great-grandfather. This was the traditional family vocation. Thus Martin hardly had a choice. Next, Martin managed to convince his father

---

6. King Scott Coretta: pp. 98-99.
7. Daniel Williams had taken over the pastorate of Ebenezer in 1894.

to let him go to Crozer. At the age of nineteen, he joined the Crozer Theological Seminary in Chester, Pennsylvania, in 1948, the year Gandhi was assassinated. He spent the next three years at Crozer and was elected president of the student body. While there, he attended lectures on philosophy at the University of Pennsylvania, and above all, he devoured through the life and works of Mahatma Gandhi, the apostle of peace, non-violent resistance and civil disobedience as a means of ameliorating the lot of the oppressed classes as well as to cut the shackles of servitude and slavery. It had a profound effect on M.L. His 'intellectual quest' for a method to eliminate evil continued unabated. In 1951, he graduated with the highest 'academic average' in his class earning the Degree of Bachelor of Divinity from Crozer. He won the Pearl Plafker Award as the most outstanding student and was awarded the J. Lewis Crozer Fellowship for graduate studies. Yale and Boston both accepted him; he chose Boston. It was a lucky coincidence that Coretta Scott also went to New England Conservatory of Music that very year.

Martin was a brilliant student alright but as a leader of nearly twenty-million Negroes he lacked the quiet brilliance and sharp administrative capabilities of NAACP's Roy Wilkins. His lieutenant Whitney Young Jr. of National Urban League made up for Martin's deficiency in sophistication and experience in handling high echelons of US business community. King lacked the inventiveness of CORE's James Farmer or the raw militancy of SNICK's John Lewis. To cap it all, King barely earned $10,000 a year — a paltry sum that even a plumber would make.[8] And above all, he had very little personal possessions. It will thus be seen that King was lucky in having a team of senior workers who complemented him in many respects.

Dr. Benjamin E. Mays, the President of the Morehouse College, was a graduate of Bates College and a member of Phi Beta Kappa. Having earned his Ph.D., he came to occupy the most prestigious academic position a Negro could aspire to. At that time Martin was still undecided and had hardly any intention of joining the ministry. But it was the personal example of Dr. Mays that guided M.L. on the path to the ministry. Another factor that might have influenced Martin's decision was, perhaps, close friendship between Dr. Mays and 'Daddy King' since the latter was also a trustee of the Morehouse. Since Dr. Mays preached more of social justice, or 'social gospel' that went right to the heart of Martin, in course of time Dr. Mays became Martin's 'spiritual mentor'. Supplementing Mays with another brilliant minister, Dr. George D. Kelsey,

8. *Time* Magazine, January 3, 1964; p.13.

head of the Theological Department, "Martin came to see that the ministry could be intellectually respectable as well as emotionally satisfying". This, in turn, led to his acceptance of the church as a professional assignment. "The balance between mind and soul, intellect and emotion" would be his objective in the church. On the suggestion of Daddy King, a trial sermon proved such a great success that night, that King Sr. "got down to his knees and thanked the Lord for giving him such a son." On the other hand, on return to India from England as a Barrister, Gandhi remained in India for about two years during which period he was professionally a total failure. After the successful trial-sermon, M.L. turned into a highly religious man whose sole interest in life became the Bible and the Lord. So it was with Gandhi — daily prayers, often twice a day, and regular recitation of some *shlokas*[9] too, inculcated a sense of religion in the young Mohandas Karamchand Gandhi in his early formative years. He was profoundly impressed with the Gita which became his life's guiding light and the law of his life. The Bible played the same role for Martin. He was ordained in 1947 at the tender age of eighteen, and made assistant pastor of Ebenezer Church. His theme for his sermons often used to be: 'God is Love' like Gandhi's perception of 'God as Truth'. The idea of Truth as the supreme characteristic was thus implanted in Gandhi's young mind, and remained for all time to come as the central idea governing every facet of his life and philosophy.

It was Dr. Mays who first introduced Martin to Gandhian philosophy of nonviolent Satyagraha. Dr. Benjamin E. Mays had traveled to India at the end of 1936, and returned greatly impressed by the course of Indian independence movement through non-violent struggle. During this period of student days, Martin read Henry David Thoreau's essay *"On Civil Disobedience"*[10] which greatly fascinated him, particularly the idea of refusing to cooperate with an evil system. This was how Gandhi had reposed his faith in the Bhagvad Gita, New Testament, Tolstoy, Ruskin or Thoreau, *et al,* which provided him with reinforcements for the ideas that had already germinated in his fertile mind. In developing his political philosophy both in South Africa and India, Gandhi was particularly influenced by the writings of Tolstoy, albeit, it took quite some time for the non-violence to take shape as the fundamental creed. Martin's political philosophy was also greatly influenced by Henry David Thoreau's work *On Civil Disobedience,* which taught him the value of non-cooperation with an evil system. This

9. Stanzas from Bhagvad-Gita and other scriptures.

10. Thoreau, a courageous New Englander, had refused to pay his taxes as a protest against the unjust war that was to spread slavery to Mexico. He chose to go to jail to uphold his personal conviction and principles.

was his first 'intellectual contact with the theory of non-violent resistance'.[11] However, ultimately it was the Gandhian philosophy as it unfolded in India that provided the beacon of light for subsequent development of the Negroes' Freedom Movement in the United States.

Martin received his BA degree in 1948. He was awarded a scholarship of $1,200, which enabled him to go to the School of Theology at Boston University.[12] This institution was deeply under the pacifist influence of Dean Walter Muelder and Dr. Chalmers, both strong proponents of nonviolent methods to attain social justice for the masses. This is exactly what Gandhi also taught: "Truth is God" and non-violence was the force created out of Truth and Love. He was convinced that the non-violence preached by the Brahmins was a sham, a mere passivity. Martin studied philosophy and theology, in the shadow of Gandhi, under the guidance of Drs. Edgar S. Brightman and L. Harold DeWolf. It was under these teachers, the embodiments of evangelical liberalism, that Martin studied the 'personalistic philosophy'— "the theory that the clue to the ultimate reality is found in personality", finite or infinite, leading Martin to the idea of a personal God thereby instilling in him the metaphysical basis for the 'dignity and worth of all human personality'. Martin studied under the guidance of these distinguished teachers. Dr. Brightman died in February 1953 when Dr. DeWolf took over as Martin's Guide under whom Martin earned his Ph.D. He was awarded the Doctorate in 'Systematic Theology'[13] from Boston on June 05, 1955. While studying for his Doctorate, he also undertook a grueling study in 'comparative religions' that included Hinduism, Jainism, Shintoism, Taoism, Confucianism and, of course, Islam, besides some other faiths. Martin was encouraged in his research by George Davis who was a pacifist and an admirer of Gandhi. Here he focused his attention on concepts of relationship of man to God. Martin's own concept of God was "an active personal entity. In his view, Man's salvation was to be found neither in the quest for social progress nor in the unaided power of reason. Faith in God's Guidance was the essential thing."[14] As far as Mohandas was concerned, "morality is the basis of things, and that truth is the substance of all morality. Truth became my

---

11. King, Martin Luther Jr.: *Stride Toward Freedom*; p. 91.
12. Martin encountered racial discrimination at first hand (certainly not for the first time) when he tried to rent some place to live in Boston. Rooms were for rent till the landlord discovered that Martin was a Negro when they suddenly became already rented out!
13. The topic for Martin's doctoral thesis was: "A Comparison of the Conception of God in the Thinking of Paul Tillich and Henry Nelson Wieman." It was an interesting exercise since Martin did not agree with either of them.
14. *Encyclopedia*: op. cit. p. 472.

sole objective" since there is no religion higher than Truth. His religion had always been morality. There were differences in expression; but in essence both Gandhi and Martin had identical concepts about God, Truth, morality and religion, even though they belonged to different religions. God is One, irrespective of the name of the religion.

Martin was also influenced strongly by Howard Thurman who was a Professor at the School of Theology in Boston University, and had led a delegation of four American Negroes, including his wife, to India in the fall of 1935 to meet with Gandhi. That is where he was first acquainted with Gandhian Philosophy of non-violence as well as with contemporary thought of Protestant Theologians. Dr. King claimed: "What was new about Mahatma Gandhi's movement in India was that he mounted a revolution on hope and love, hope and non-violence."[15] Martin was not satisfied with Social Gospel of Walter Rauschenbusch. Since Reinold Niebuhr in his 1932 *Moral Man and Immoral Society* saw no moral difference between violent and non-violent resistance, Martin could not accept this pessimistic thought process of neo-orthodoxy, which, in fact, was tantamount to reverting to basic theological principles of the 16th century. Unfortunately, the psychological and physiological complexities of human beings makes them liable to commit 'colossal collective evils' as was evident from Niebuhr's native Nazi Germany. Martin synthesized Gandhi's philosophy with Christian dogmas preached by Niebuhr and Rausbuschchen, and came to the firm conclusion that "any religion which professes to be concerned about the souls of men and is not concerned about the social and economic conditions that scar the soul is spiritually a moribund religion."

During that period of early 1930s, communist ideology was finding roots in the United States. A nineteen-year old black young man in Georgia took a leading part in 'Unemployment Council' organized by the Communist Party in Birmingham while another Negro leader, Angelo Herndon, organized the Communist party in Atlanta. He along with fellow-travelers organized a demonstration on behalf of the Unemployment Council. The whites took a prominent part and next day the City voted $6,000 as a relief for the jobless. But soon after that, Herndon was arrested and convicted of insurrection in violation of a statute of Georgia. The White Establishment felt that the new movement and its ideology was a threat to the stability of the established order, more so when men like Benjamin Davis — the lawyer who had defended Herndon — the famous singer and actor Paul Robeson, and last but not the least, the well known Negro intellectual-writer W.E.B. Du Bois lent support to the nascent Party.

---

15. King, Martin Luther Jr.: *Where Do We Go From Here,* p. 44.

These Black leaders were admired by the downtrodden community, which further enhanced the fears arising out of militancy in political affairs. The last straw was cast in 1945 when Du Bois said: "The problem of the 20th century is the problem of the color line."[16]

Eventually, it was Gandhian philosophy as dissected by noted Pacifist A.J. Muste and Howard University's then President, Dr. Mordecai Johnson during their lectures[17] on Gandhi in the spring of 1950 that cleared the cobwebs and resolved this dilemma for Martin, since Gandhi would not acquiesce to evil, individual or collective, and instead would resist evil with love rather than hatred and violence. The power of love overpowered the evil and bitterness perpetuated by the powerful oppressor. "Gandhi was probably the first person in history to lift the love ethic of Jesus above mere interaction between individuals to a powerful and effective social force on a large scale." Martin was particularly moved by Gandhi's 'Salt March' to the Sea and his numerous fasts. This philosophy and attitude were in line with the traditions of Martin's family background, more so since for Gandhi Love was a 'potent instrument for social and collective transformation'. In short, Gandhi restored Martin's original faith in the power of love.

Love at First Sight

One cannot say that Martin was born with a silver spoon; nevertheless he was lucky that his family enjoyed the luxuries of a good middle class black family in an otherwise white racial segregationist ocean of hatred and exploitation. He was lucky in his marriage too. Mary Powel, a friend from Atlanta and a student in New England Conservatory of Music, was instrumental in Martin and Coretta Scott[18] getting together while at Boston. She too was studying music in the same Conservatory. The first time they met their discussion was centered on the question of racial and economic injustice. He had met Coretta barely a couple of times when, while driving back to the conservatory in the car, he suddenly became very quiet.

"Very quietly but intensely he said: You have everything that I ever wanted in a wife. There are only four things and you have them all."

16. Zinn Howard: op. cit. pp. 439-40.
17. Martin had traveled to Philadelphia specially to hear the sermon by Dr. Mordecai Johnson who had just returned from a trip to India. "His message was so profound and electrifying" that, after leaving the meeting, Martin bought whatever books on Gandhi he could lay his hands on.
18. Coretta Scott was born at Heiberger, Alabama, on April 27, 1927.

"I don't know how you can say that. You don't even know me."

"Yes, I can tell. The four things that I look in a wife are character, intelligence, personality and beauty. And you have them all. I want to see you again. When can I?" Of course, Martin did not at that time mention that he expected his wife to be the 'mother for his children'[19], and be home waiting for him! Coretta has written: "Martin had all through his life an ambivalent attitude towards the role of women. ... he did believe that women are just as capable and competent as men." But sometime after their marriage, Martin dropped a brick by remarking: "I want my wife to respect me as the head of the family. I *am* the head of the family." Coretta laughed at his pomposity but relented when Martin, realizing the absurdity of his statement, said: "Of course, I don't really mean that. I think marriage should be a shared relationship." Agreed: Martin made this remark off the cuff. But it also shows that Martin was unable to see the connection between racism and sexism. Both he and Malcolm X challenged white values regarding race, but they accepted black male privileges like any other white American. They shared much of the typical American male's view of women. Like of the rest of the Americans, white or black, they too believed that the woman's place was in the home, the private sphere, and the man's place was in society, the public arena.

They were married on 18th June 1953, perhaps against the unexpressed wishes of Daddy King who would have preferred to bring in bride from one of Atlanta's leading Negro families, rather than a singer from a town in the backward Black Belt of Alabama. But destiny had cast Martin for an altogether different role, an immortal place in history, not only of the United States of America but of the world at large too. Be that as it may, the ceremony was conducted by 'Daddy King' on the spacious lawns of Coretta's parents' home in Marion. Mrs. Coretta Scott King inherited a talent for music from her mother, Bernice Scott, and was a gifted singer. She was a mezzo-soprano and wanted to be a concert-singer, but gave up the musical career to marry Martin and stood shoulder to shoulder with him in his political-racial career. It may sound unbelievable that in those days there were no hotels with bridal suites for Negroes in that part of the country and, therefore, they spent their first night at the home of family friends who were undertakers for Coretta's family!

---

19. They had four children. The eldest, a girl was born on November 17, 1954, and the youngest also a girl, Bernice Albertine, came on 28 March 1963.

4

Three Dimensions of A Complete Life

Dexter Avenue Baptist Church

It really boils down to this: that all life is inter-related. We are all caught in an inescapable network of mutuality, tied into a single garment of destiny. Whatever affects one directly, affects al indirectly.

Martin finished writing his thesis in the winter of 1954. It was time to start looking for a job. He was invited to the Dexter Avenue Baptist Church to preach a trial sermon. He was nervous. So in good humor he told himself: "Keep Martin Luther King in the background and God in the foreground and everything will be alright. Remember you're a channel of the gospel, not the source."[1] Martin started his career in the ministry with a bang! He delivered his first sermon, a trial sermon, at Dexter Avenue Baptist Church in Montgomery, Alabama, on January 24, 1954. A large gathering had turned up that morning to hear the person who was being considered for the pastorate of their Church. The topic of his sermon was: "The Three Dimensions of a Complete Life". — The Length of Life is the forward push to its personal ends and ambitions. The Breadth of Life is the 'outward concern for the welfare of others'. The Height of Life is the 'upward reach toward God'. "Life at its best is a great triangle. At one angle stands the individual person, at the other angle stand other persons, and at the top stands God."[2] Life remains incomplete unless all three work harmoniously together. The session was a great success and the congregation was greatly impressed by the pastor-designate.

---

1. Coretta: op. cit. p. 109.
2. King, Martin Luther: op. cit. (Autobiography), p. 43.

Ebenezer Baptist Church at Atlanta, Georgia

The above trial sermon was followed by a guest-sermon at Second Baptist Church in Detroit, Michigan, on February 28, 1954. The Kings had a number of points in favour of accepting an appointment at Detroit, most important of which was escape from racialviolence and segregation that was intrinsic part of life and work in Montgomery. However, both Martin and Coretta felt that it was their moral duty, an obligation indeed, to work for the congregation in the South to which they essentially belonged to. It meant a degree of inevitable sacrifice on their part, besides voluntary acceptance of all the disadvantages of living and working in the South. His intense interest in the upliftment of Negroes in the South left the couple hardly any choice. "He most certainly felt that his place was as pastor of a Negro church in the South." Therefore, Martin accepted the call to Dexter's pastorate on April 14 and delivered his first sermon as Dexter's minister on 2nd May 1954. Martin took up the pastorate officially in September 1954 and the couple moved into the parsonage. He was officially confirmed as Pastor of Dexter on 31st October and the installation sermon was delivered by Martin's Father, Martin Luther King Sr., who came down from Atlanta with a large contingent of Ebenezer Baptists who, besides contributing liberally, boosted Martin's morale in his new difficult assignment.

When they came to Montgomery they found very little church activity amongst the members of the congregation. Martin immediately immersed himself in socio-political activities in his pastorate. He exhorted the church members to join NAACP[3] and become registered voters. In August 1955, he was elected to the executive committee of NAACP. Although Martin did not possess an impressive figure — he was 5 feet 7 inches in height, heavy chested, weight about 173 lbs. — his sermons-lectures in resonant confident voice made up for the shortcoming in his physical appearance, if at all that was so. He always dressed conservatively, 'funeral conservatism' so to say, since his five or six suits were all black, and he usually wore black ties only. He was a serious type of person with little sense of humour, if at all. Yet he was witty alright. Thoreau, Hegel, Kant and Gandhi were the usual subjects in which he excelled. And he preached endlessly, particularly about Ahimsa and non-violence. Thus the young couple took upon themselves an extremely busy schedule — he to finalize the text of his dissertation and she to do her secretarial duties! By this time, Coretta had assumed the role of Martin's secretary;

3. NAACP was a noble organization inasmuch as it was organized by the Whites for the benefit of the Blacks.

rather, the role was thrust on her, albeit with her voluntary consent. Besides having to type out the 350 page-dissertation, she was a member of a number of committees, sang in the choir as well as the solo parts of the anthems or oratories, et al. And let's not forget Coretta's main job — keeping house for Martin! Meanwhile Martin was deeply involved in church duties like counselling, marriages, funerals, comforting sick parishioners, personally calling on, one by one, every one of the three hundred-odd members, and so on. In the midst of all these activities,[4] Martin took two weeks off in October to go to Boston to give finishing touches to his dissertation, and to present it to the University.

In the spring of 1955, Martin was awarded his degree of Doctor of Philosophy in Systematic Theology. In November of the same year, Martin was appointed president of the local NAACP. Concurrently, they worked out a series of new programs for presentation to the board of deacons at their meeting in January next.

To cap it all, Martin had to spend considerable time in writing his usual Sunday sermon, and then memorizing it. "The congregation always marveled that he could speak, apparently extemporaneously" for about half an hour, and speak with such intensity and fluency, combining social and religious message.[5] The Reverend Martin Luther King Jr. was an eloquent Black Baptist Minister. From mid 1950s to his assassination in April 1968, Dr. King led the first mass civil rights movement in US history. He rigorously followed the teachings of Gandhi and applied the principles of non-violent resistance patterned after Mahatma Gandhi. His primary objective was struggle for racial equality in the US.

---

4. How many Hindu priests in India perform even one-tenth of these onerous duties!
5. Coretta: op. cit. p. 117.

5

Mahatma Gandhi

Nations are born out of travail and suffering. The powerless do have power, since the force of arms cannot prevail for ever against the force of spirit.

Mohandas Karamchand Gandhi was born on 2nd October 1869 in a very small princely state, Porbandar, otherwise known as Sudamapuri — the youngest son of Karamchand Gandhi, alias Kaba Gandhi, who was the Prime Minister of the state like his grandfather had been. Sounds grand, but was not all that exalted since it was a tiny little state, more like an estate. Kaba Gandhi married four times in succession, having lost his wife each time by death. His last wife, Putlibai, was a saintly lady. She bore him a daughter and three sons. Mohandas was the youngest. Not a wealthy family — 'Gandhi' means grocer — Bania by caste, and devout Vaishnava Hindus by religious practice. Population of Porbandar included many who belonged to Jain sect for whom taking of any life was a sin. The Gandhi family was therefore considerably influenced by Jain precepts. His father used to read the *Gita*.[1] Notwithstanding the sacrosanctity of religion, Christianity was strongly associated with British colonialism in India, particularly during the nineteenth century. In fact, it was rather difficult to separate one from the other. The Christian missionaries saw their work as part and parcel of the Empire, the colonial rule with all its evils and atrocities. It was unfortunate that in their enthusiasm for proselytizing they ignored the humanitarian angle and did not demur over the large scale violations of human rights perpetuated

---

1. *Gita*, or Song, is short for *Bhagavad-Gita*, the Song of God, or Song of Heaven. It is an exquisite poem of seven hundred stanzas, as sacred to Hinduism as the Koran is to Islam, the Old Testament to Judaism and the New Testament to Christianity.

by the colonizing powers. To them, Imperial expansionism was more important than the humane aspect. They saw their work through colored glasses, as acts of civilizing the heathens. Even C.F. Andrews[2] fell a prey to this stratagem in the initial stages. Only later, when he became a close associate of Gandhi did he become a strong critic of British rule in India. "Although Gandhi was brought up in an atmosphere of religious tolerance, he developed an early antipathy to Christianity, which he experienced as a colonial subject. When still a boy in Rajkot, he had paused to hear a missionary who was preaching in the street and was disgusted by the way he poured abuse on the Hindus and their gods."[3]

Mohandas was extremely shy, so much so that he ran to and from school to avoid talking to other boys. He was greatly influenced by the play, *Harishchandra* based on the great epic *Mahabharata* wherein the great king suffers many agonizing ordeals, and sacrifices everything for the sake of truth.

To England

Mavji Dave had been a lifelong friend of Gandhi's father. He was a Brahmin whose advice was valued by the Gandhi family. He suggested that Mohandas Karamchand should study in England. The young man leaped at the idea. His first reaction was to go in for medicine. But the old man suggested that a medical doctor could never be the Prime Minister of his State for which law was a more appropriate subject of study. Although the idea caught the family's fancy, it was also a serious matter inasmuch as Hindu young men seldom went overseas in the 1880's for fear of contamination through eating and living with foreigners. The usual punishment for this aberration was excommunication from the caste. Those who had gone abroad were considered to be lost to their own religion and society, to be contaminated. They wore foreign clothes which were indecent since they enhanced the contours of their body. Wearing of trousers was not at all acceptable in the conservative Hindu society of those days. Gandhi's elders were therefore against the idea, particularly his mother and uncles. The old woman was afraid that the young eighteen-years old might fall a prey to wine, women and meat-eating. She sorrowfully consented to the proposal after the young

2. C.F. Andrews popularly known as Charlie was an Englishman, an Anglican priest like the rest of his fraternity. He was greatly influenced by the Indian people as well as by Gandhian thought and philosophy, so much so that he left the Church and became a lay person in the service of Indian nationalism.
3. Hardiman David: GANDHI in his time and ours; Delhi, 2003, p. 177.

Gandhi pledged that he would abstain from all such evil things. He took his vows before a Jain monk that he would abjure meat, liquor and women while in England. But that was not the end of his travails. When he reached Bombay he ran into more caste-complications. In a solemn meeting of his caste elders, he was officially expelled from his Bania caste and remained so for the rest of his life. Fortunately, his elder brother who had accompanied him to Bombay supported the young Gandhi and he set sail for England on 4th September 1888. Meanwhile, his brother had arranged for his English clothing, tie, shoes, and all; but there is nothing he could do for his ears which stuck out almost at right angles from his head. While in England, the vegetarian vow was to make his life particularly difficult, all the more so since English cooking of vegetables made them sodden and tasteless, virtually impossible to savour. A book, "*A Plea for Vegetarianism*", together with his chance discovery of a vegetarian restaurant finally gave him a full meal, the book being an authority for his vegetarianism.

In his early days in London vegetarianism took much of his time and attention. In his younger years, Gandhi was invariably on the lookout for written "authority", some book or pamphlet which could provide rationalization for his simple natural ideas. Gita, New Testament, Tolstoy, Ruskin or Thoreau, *et al,* provided him with reinforcements for the ideas which had already germinated in his fertile mind. In developing his political philosophy both in South Africa and India, he was particularly influenced by the writings of Tolstoy, albeit it took quite some time for the non-violence to take shape as the fundamental creed.[4] Since his Indian friends were somewhat embarrassed by his non-conformity with the English way of life, he tried all sorts of things to "play the English gentleman" by wearing evening clothes, taking dancing lessons, learning to play violin, etc. In short, he made every effort to look funny through artificially imbibing English culture and mannerisms. However, he soon realized that he had come to London to study law, and not to make a 'joker' of himself. Since it did not require much hard work to be "called to the bar", he devoted his spare time in learning Latin as well as preparing for the London matriculation examination, besides seriously reading the *Bhagavad-Gita* and the New Testament. He was profoundly impressed with the Gita which became his life's guiding light and the law of his life. However, he did not neglect his prescribed studies. He studied Roman law seriously. As for the official purpose of his life in London,

4. Green Martin: *The Origins of Non-violence: Tolstoy and Gandhi in their Historical Settings;* New Delhi, 1998; p.3.

he passed his examinations easily, was called to the bar on 10th June 1891, enrolled in the High Court the next day, and sailed for India the day after that. Indeed, he did not stay in England even for a single day more than was absolutely obligatory.

The showy temples displeased Mohandas. As a youngster, he could never understand why it was sinful to come in contact with the scavenger who used to come to the house to clean the latrines. His father's modest library included the Hindu law book of Manu which he read carefully, but found its mythology pointless and its logic lacking in coherent rationale. He found nothing divine about the text, although it was claimed to be so.

As far as Mohandas was concerned, "morality is the basis of things, and that truth is the substance of all morality. Truth became my sole objective" since there is no religion higher than Truth. His religion had always been morality. While in Kensington he had taken lodgings with a landlady. Often, he used to take her daughters out for dinner and had no qualms of conscience about Kasturbai back in India with his infant son. He had not let it be known that he was already married and was the father of a son back in India. Similar circumstances overtook Mohandas in 1889 while he was visiting Brighton. An elderly widow who had a girl staying with her invited him for dinner on Sundays. She used to leave the two young people alone and the acquaintance ripened. However, before the affair could go too far, he confessed to the widow about his marital status. His sole motive in doing so was an overpowering need to be truthful. To Gandhi: "Truth was God" and nonviolence was the force created out of Truth and Love. He was convinced that the non-violence preached by the Brahmins was mere passivity.

Gandhi in South Africa

Civil war, often referred to as the 'Zulu War', broke out in South Africa in 1883-84. In May 1884 Dinizulu, son of Cetewayo was declared as the King. However, the war ended with the British annexation of Zululand on 21st June 1887. The same year it was incorporated into Britain's Natal colony and Dinizulu, the King of Zulus, was banished to St. Helena.[5] The Indian immigration to South Africa started in 1890 when the White settlers there recruited indentured Indian labour, mainly from South India, to work on their sugar plantations. They and their descendents were mostly uneducated and had practically no knowledge of English. The merchant class that followed the plantation workers was

5. Peter N. Stearns: op. cit. pp. 597-98.

mostly Muslims from Gujarat, and they too had practically no knowledge of English. The Indians suffered racial discrimination and humiliation but they had come to accept that as a way of life.

During his absence from India, Gandhi's mother had died while he was in England. This was a terrible blow to him. His elder brother did not want to distract him and therefore did not inform him of this tragic loss. He remained in India for about two years during which period he was professionally a total failure since he was not at all conversant with the Indian law, and how the justice system worked in Indian courts. To cap it all, his extremely shy nature was a serious handicap so much so that in the very first case he took up in Bombay as a barrister, he just could not even utter a word. This was his first and the last brief as a barrister in India, and brought his career to an end insofar as India was concerned. However, soon he had another chance to earn his living, perhaps through some discreet work done by his devoted brother. Dada Abdullah & Co., a Moslem Indian firm in South Africa, had a claim for some thousands of pounds dragging through the courts for years. M.K. Gandhi was invited as a guest of the firm for one year, all expenses paid, to advise them about the conduct of the case. In addition, he was to be paid £105 in cash. Destiny had cast Gandhi for a role which he, or any body else for that matter, could hardly even imagine in their wildest dreams. It was not a planned evolution to greatness but merely a series of improvisations to meet the needs of the circumstances. Greatness was thrust on Gandhi, so to say; he did not aspire for it, nor did he endeavor to achieve the same. While describing Gandhi as a 'Statesman of Peace', Frederick Bohn Fisher wrote: "The man may be right or the moment may be right; but it is only when the two conjoin that an hour of history is struck." On the contrary, Dr. Martin Luther King Jr. reached the zenith of life and leadership as a gradual evolutionary process.

Mohandas Karamchand, the twenty-four years old English educated Barrister, landed in Durban in 1893. He was the first highly educated Indian to come to South Africa. He was not the type to accept racial insults and discriminations, more so since he was an English educated Barrister. But during his journey from Durban to Pretoria which he undertook within a week of his arrival in the African Continent, Gandhi was subjected to a series of racial humiliations. It was an entirely a new and unexpected experience for him. Although he bought a first class ticket, he was bundled out from the first class compartment because of the colour of his skin and left behind to spend the night shivering in the station waiting room. Again, while he had a first class ticket by coach, he was made to travel in the driver's box. As if that was not humiliation enough, he was ordered by the coach leader to vacate even that seat and to sit on the footboard. On his refusal to comply, he was soundly thrashed. On reaching Johannesburg, no hotel would give him a room to spend the night. At first he was denied a first class train ticket from there to his destination, Pretoria; but after he quoted extensively from the rail-regulations, he managed to get the ticket and was almost once again pushed out of the first class compartment but for the kind intervention of a European passenger.

During his first week in Pretoria, Mohandas called on Tyeb Sheth who, in fact, was the opposite party to the suit that Gandhi was deputed to defend. The handicaps faced by the Indian community were the main topic which attracted the two persons to each other. Tyeb, a prosperous Muslim businessman proposed to bring the City's Indians together to discuss their common problems. The meeting was well attended, mostly by Muslims. In any case, there were very few Hindus in Pretoria. This meeting transformed Gandhi inasmuch as it not only launched him on to a political career, but also got rid of his shyness in public speaking. He laid emphasis on truth and honesty in all dealings, including business. The Indians should cultivate clean habits and avoid sectarian or regional feuds. Since language was a stumbling block, he offered to teach them English. They decided to fight against racial discrimination. Gandhi represented them in the courts and won some cases in favor of the Indians. It was a small start, but certainly worth all the trouble. Gandhi's fight was against authority that wielded power: And possession of power corrupts men. What is more important is 'inner perfection, truth and love', in self-abnegating closeness to God who is the source of all life. Christ must be obeyed not for fear of hell, or sin, but because he teaches Truth. For Gandhi, it was alright to hate sin, but not the sinner; to fight aggression, but not the aggressor.[6] And that holds good for the prophets of other religions too. After all, religion and morality are mere two facets of the same coin. No wonder therefore that Gandhi offered his services to go round inspecting latrines when there was a scare of outbreak of plague in Rajkot. Latrines, sanitation and cleanliness were Gandhi's lifelong interests turned into personal fads. He took pride in performing this public service for the good of the public.

---

6. Arne Naess: Gandhi and Group Conflict; An Exploration of Satyagraha; Oslo, 1974, p. 127.

Abolition of Indentured Emigration

The abolition of the system of indentured emigration from India to South Africa — that is, labour destined for South Africa bound by contract written in iron clad terms and conditions — was of prime importance to Gandhi. The Government of India had been dilly-dallying on the subject for quite some time. Now, Gandhi wanted a definite date to be fixed for discontinuation of this abominable system of bonded Indian labour exported to a foreign land. In desperation Gandhi fixed the date for abolition of such emigration as 31st May 1917. Gandhi's work in South Africa had earned him such reputation that the Government abolished indentured emigration well before that date.

One day a Tamil workman entered his office. His mouth was bleeding and two front teeth were knocked out. With his turban in his hands, he poured out his story, but Gandhi did not understand Tamil; his clerk did and he explained the poor man's tale of woe. He had been severely beaten by his master, a well known European. Gandhi sent the man to a doctor for a certificate of the injuries and then took him to a magistrate who issued summons for the master. The laws governing indentured labor were quite severe. A man could not leave his employment. Criminal proceedings and imprisonment was the usual fate of those who did. For all practical purposes it was a form of slavery, albeit for a limited time. But the man had no rights or liberty. Gandhi knew the law well but he did not want the master to be punished. All he wanted was that the victim be released from the particular indenture and transferred to another. The erring master agreed to the proposal and Gandhi approached the Protector of Indentured Labourers who released the man to another indenture. This episode made Gandhi famous all over South India, particularly the Tamil areas. The succeeding waves of indentured labor were told even before they left the home shores that Gandhi was their friend. The Tamilians, the South Indians would not recognize Gandhi, face to face, but they knew that Gandhi was their friend and well wisher on whom they could bank on in case of need. He was the friend of the poor, depressed classes of people. "The pathos of the headgear struck him more particularly because he had gone through such a series of incidents concerned with his own. The humiliation to which he had objected was accepted as natural by the stricken man, the defenceless. Gandhi had asked him at once to resume his scarf, and Balasundaram had done so hesitantly, but with a glow of pleasure. Such small things were Gandhi's secret power."

Gandhi had spent three years in South Africa and it was high time that he saw his family again. His Moslem friends in Durban agreed to let him go to India to collect his family on the condition that he would return within six months, on the same terms as before. M.K. Gandhi was 'fighting' the white people, the British in particular. But "at all stages of his life British people indistinctively liked him. ... The British never had in their wondrous history a more loyal and loving rebel than Gandhi." Back in Bombay he got a cablegram from Durban informing him that Joseph Chamberlain was coming to South Africa. The Indians there needed him urgently. Gandhi must return immediately.

Back to South Africa

The return journey to South Africa had its usual ordeals in store for him and now his family too. In the first place, he had to find the right way to dress his family. The boys had to be in coat, trousers and shoes — all foreign to their body comfort — while Kasturbai had to wear Parsee sari, shoes and stockings. And to cap it all, they had to get used to fork and knife to eat while on board the ship, which belonged to Abdullah Sheth. The white people of Natal decided that since Gandhi was the trouble-maker, he and his family would not be permitted to disembark. On Christmas-eve an ultimatum was served on all the passengers that they must return to India, or face the risk of death. After all legal hurdles had been exhausted, the authorities allowed the ship to anchor in the harbour and disembark the passengers. An English lawyer for Abdullah advised that Gandhi and his family should disembark only after dark to which he agreed. The family was put in a carriage and taken straight to a friend's house while Gandhi took his chance to quietly walk out and go on foot. He disembarked with Mr. Laughton, one of Abdullah's lawyers, and soon some ruffians recognized Gandhi and shouted "Gandhi! Gandhi!" A crowd soon collected. Gandhi was badly beaten up by the crowd but Mrs. Alexander, wife of the Superintendent of Police happened to pass by and saved Gandhi from further lynching. Alexander soon came by and escorted Gandhi to Rustom's house where his family had been taken. But here too a crowd collected and Alexander escorted Gandhi out of the house disguised as a police constable. He was kept in the police station under guard for a few days during which all accusations against him were proved false, and the white people were pacified. This episode proved a blessing in disguise for hereafter he was more esteemed than ever amongst the whites of Natal.

Mohandas Karamchand Gandhi with wife Kasturba Gandhi on their return to India from South Africa: 1914

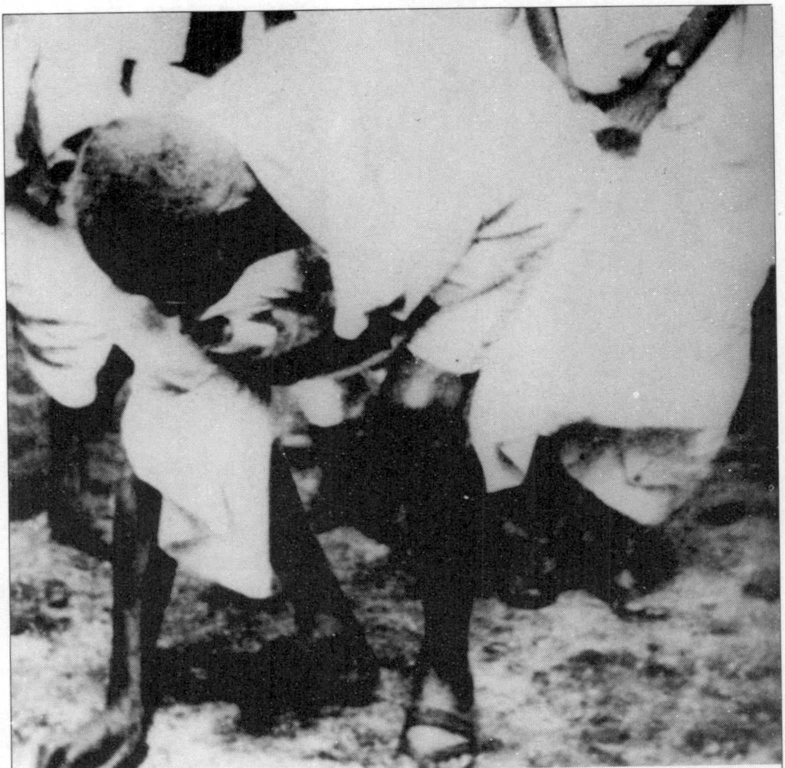

The Salt March, December 1928: Mahatma Gandhi
picking up salt on the sea shore

Cripps' Mission to India: 1942
Sir Stafford Cripps with Mahatma Gandhi

Mahatma Gandhi with British Parliamentary Delegation at Madras: Professor Richard, leader of the Delegation is second from left

Mahatma Gandhi leaving Manorilla at Simla for his evening prayers: Early 1947

Mahatma Gandhi with Lord and Lady Mountbatten
March 31, 1947

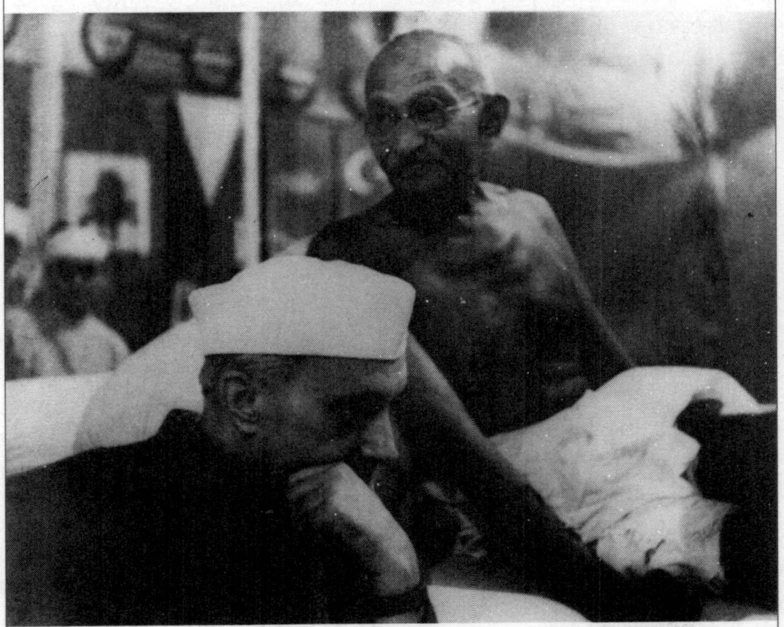

Mahatma Gandhi with Jawaharlal Nehru, April 1947

This time he took a few young men with him who could help him in his work. Among them was his second cousin Maganlal Gandhi who was to prove one of the most useful lieutenants in the forthcoming struggle. He reached just in time to draw up the paper and present it. From Natal he had to go to Transvaal where Chamberlain was due next. Transvaal was a much rougher and tougher country for an Indian than Natal. He was not allowed to present the paper to Chamberlain, but he arranged for the petition to be read to Chamberlain by an Indian Christian barrister. A number of Indians had left Transvaal in the wake of the war. With the war having ended they were returning to what had become their second home. Gandhi's immediate task was to expose the shameless manner in which the Indians were being fleeced for re-entry permits. They were being compelled to pay very large sums as bribe to get the permit. Gandhi carefully collected the evidence and presented it to the Police Commissioner. A trial ensued. The jury acquitted the accused officers. But the evidence was so overwhelmingly against them that they were dismissed from their jobs. Gandhi's prestige again went sky high. In the process, Gandhi became the lawyer for every Indian dispossessed of his land or just payment. He took up some seventy cases of dispossession of land and lost only one. The Indian labourers, all illiterate, regarded Gandhi as their greatest friend and started calling him 'bhai' (Brother). He liked this appellation which remained in common use as long as he was in South Africa, later to be transformed to 'Mahatma' or 'Bapu'.

Trustee of Indians' Money

During 1899-1902 the British were involved in the South African War also known as the Anglo-Boer War. Although Gandhi's sympathies were with the Zulus, his loyalty to the British Empire took precedence. He organized a group of twenty-four Indians who served through the war looking after the wounded, including the Zulus. The war came to an end after the Boers accepted British sovereignty under the Treaty of Vereeniging (31 May 1901). By the end of the War, the British had 300,000 troops against sixty to seventy thousand Zulu soldiers.

In 1904 Gandhi started the weekly journal, Indian Opinion, in which he gave wide publicity to his ideas on various problems of, and subjects of interest to, the Indian community in South Africa. The theory and practice of *Satyagraha*, i.e. "Truth- Force", or voluntary sacrifice, received special attention in this Journal. While Gandhi was busy with litigation work regarding the Indian quarters, there was an outbreak of pneumonic plague in the gold mines area.[7] Most of the workers employed on mining gold were African Negroes with a sprinkling of Indians, twenty-three of whom were stricken with the deadly disease. Gandhi moved into the overcrowded coolie location at once. He took the four young men he had brought from India, and together they set up a quarantine camp for the patients where all of them were brought in. Gandhi tried his own 'earth and water' treatment on three patients while the other twenty got the 'brandy' treatment officially prescribed by the physician, Dr. William Godfrey. Two of the patients undergoing Gandhi's treatment survived; all the rest died. In order to ensure the safety of the urban area, the municipal authorities decided to burn down the entire coolie location. The Indians were moved to a tented camp about thirteen miles away. Unfortunately for the Indians, they had all their monetary savings buried in the ground under their huts. The workers secretly excavated all this treasure and handed over the same to one person they all could trust. Thus Gandhi became the trustee of nearly £60,000/-Meanwhile the Indian Opinion was moved to a farm where they had to resort to hand-printing. Gandhi seemed to enjoy this victory of human power over the machine, and hereafter printing by hand-wheel became the routine.

From South African Jail to Ashram in India

The Government of Transvaal had announced its intention to introduce a bill making it obligatory for all Indians above the age of eight to be finger printed, registered, and to carry the registration certificate with them at all times. Contravention of this order was made an offence punishable by imprisonment, or deportation, or both. A mass meeting was called to protest against this proposed draconian law when Gandhi delivered an impassioned speech calling upon all to take a vow to defy this law when passed. This was the beginning of Satyagraha — non-violent 'passive resistance' and 'civil disobedience — on 11th September 1906. A number of prominent Indians from Natal crossed the frontier into Transvaal to defy the new immigration laws. A large number of Indians were jailed. They were all arrested. Gandhi was the first to be produced before a magistrate for defying the law that became effective on 31 July 1907. He pleaded guilty and requested the magistrate to impose on him the heaviest sentence since he had deliberately acted against the law. The magistrate imposed the lightest punishment — two months simple imprisonment, specifying that it shall be without hard labour. Thus M.K. Gandhi landed

7. Pneumonic plague is what is called 'black plague' in general parlance. It is worse than bubonic plague

himself in South African jail in October 1908. While in jail, Gandhi used to cook for about seventy-five Indian prisoners, and when volunteers were required for latrine-duty, Gandhi immediately volunteered to clean the latrines. "A jailor is as much a prisoner as his prisoners. There is no doubt a difference. From my point of view he is worse."

Around this time Gandhi's German-Jewish friend and follower, Kallenbach, purchased a large tract of land, about twenty-one miles from Johannesburg, and presented the same to Gandhi to establish a settlement to house the families of Satyagrahis and to provide them with some work to sustain themselves. Contributions also poured in from India — Sir Ratan Tata sent Rs. 25,000, the Indian National Congress and the Indian Muslim League as well as the Nizam of Hyderabad also gave a helping hand. It was named 'Tolstoy Farm', a precursor of the later Gandhian ashrams. Here Gandhi took a vow not to drink cow or buffalo milk since cruelty was used to increase their production. His austerity reached its climax when he vowed to live on fruits and nuts alone with some olive oil.[8] It goes without saying that Martin Luther King did not believe in Gandhian self-imposed poverty and austerity. But the 'Frontier Gandhi' did follow in the footsteps of Mahatma Gandhi.

Gandhi's routine in the Ashram included two short walks during the day and a prayer meeting before sunset when friends from other faiths would sit with him cross-legged singing hymns and reading from the scriptures, chiefly Gita.[9] He used to get up at four and go to bed at half past nine. Most of the time he spent on tours involving extensive traveling. He traveled by third class only. The villagers en-route gave him a thunderous and overwhelming welcome. They would wait for hours to have his darshan, 'that blessing from his mere presence which made his Mahatmaship a dynamic force'. Unscheduled halts by the train he was traveling by were a common occurrence since the villagers would lie on the track to prevent the train from moving forward till they had his darshan. As soon as Gandhi appeared at carriage-door, it was suddenly all quiet. Since there were no microphones, the people could not hear him. He preferred to speak sitting down and he always sounded 'fervently sincere'; a mere glimpse of the Mahatma was enough. "The crowd knelt on the platform, weeping."[10] They considered him an '*avatar*', a Mahatma — Mahatma Gandhi or Gandhiji, and not mere M.K. Gandhi. Unity amongst all Indians was his constant refrain;

8. Gandhi M.K.: *Autobiography*, pp. 302 and 418.
9. Ashe Geoffrey: *Gandhi; A Study in Revolution*; New Delhi, 1968, p. 216.
10. Ibid. p. 219.

not mere Hindu-Muslim monolithic unity but true secular rapprochement was the constant theme.

When Gandhi could not sleep, millions did not sleep. When Gandhi fasted which was quite often, millions of his countrymen also fasted. With the passage of time, the frequency of his undertaking fasts increased manifold. He fasted as a penance, against the sins of others, against communal riots and injustice, for the benefit of depressed classes or untouchables, as a prayer, for self-discipline and selfpurification, *et al.* "He had the unparalleled misfortune to become a public saint in the twentieth century, canonized alive in the glare of flashlights and the relentless gaze of cameras." He altered the course of history and the fate of the great British Empire. "We cannot satisfactorily explain the phenomenon of Gandhi." For him, goodness was synonymous with innocence. He was extremely lustful and subjugation of lust was his biggest personal agony, and a cause for conflict with his wife.[11]

Meetings with Viceroy

Lord Reading arrived in India on 2nd April 1921. Soon after taking over as the Viceroy of India, he held six meetings with Gandhi who came to the Viceroys Palace dressed, as usual, in loincloth and dhoti, with bare legs and feet, and a hand woven cap. The Viceroy summed up his impressions of Gandhi: "When he talks, the impression is different. He is direct, and expresses himself well in excellent English with a fine appreciation of value of the words he uses. There is no hesitation about him and there is a ring of sincerity in all that he utters, save when discussing some political questions. His religious views are, I believe, genuinely held, and he is convinced to a point almost bordering on fanaticism that non-violence and love will give India its independence and enable it to withstand the British Government. His religious and moral views are admirable and indeed are on a remarkably high altitude, though I must confess that I find it difficult to understand his practice of them in politics. ... Our conversations were of the frankest; he was supremely courteous with manners of distinction. ... He held in every way to his word in various discussions we had."[12]

Champaran

The Benares Hindu University incident or the abolition of indentured labour to South Africa did not create any worthwhile impression on the

---

11. While discussing civil disobedience with Margaret Sanger, Gandhi agreed that the women of India could adopt 'marital disobedience' if the 'wife did not want it'.
12. Fischer Louis: *The Life of Mahatma Gandhi,* Part II, pp. 195-96.

masses of India. Nor did these episodes create headlines. The opportunity to make a mark in public life of India came Gandhi's way, just by the way only. In fact he tried to spurn it away but the peasant sharecroppers Rajkumar Shukla from the Champaran district of Bihar was a strong minded person who would not take no for an answer. He turned up at the annual convention of Indian National Conference at Lucknow in December 1916. Gandhi and Nehru met at this Conference for the first time, and were greatly impressed with each other. While Shukla wanted Gandhi to come to Champaran to see for himself how abominably the indigo-cultivators were being treated,6 Gandhi was much too busy with other mundane matters to spare the time for this trip. But Shukla was obstinate, determined to do what he wanted to. He not only waited but followed Gandhi wherever he went. He followed him to his Ashram too, and stayed there for a few weeks. Finally, Gandhi gave in and they reached Patna on 10th April 1917, the capital of Bihar Province. Here he met a number of members of the Indian National Congress and lawyers who had some sympathy for the sharecropper and had taken up their court-cases, of course for a fee. Gandhi recruited a number of voluntary fellow workers who pledged to give their time and services for free, including being prepared to go to jail if it came to that. This sort of proposal came out of the blues as far as the Bihar politicians and lawyers were concerned. Gandhi had not yet used Satyagraha as a full scale revolutionary strategy. It therefore took some time and persuasion, but ultimately Gandhi did succeed in recruiting a large enough team.

Champaran, the land of King Janaka, covering an area of about 3,500 square miles lies beside Nepal and the Himalayas, a countryside of mango groves, having a population of about two millions at that time. In 1917 Champaran was controlled by British planters who owned most of the arable land and imposed a totally feudal system. Special levies were imposed even on weddings, or when the Sahib wanted a new car! The planters could hire labour at will. A man was paid 2½ d. a day, a woman 1½ d and children, when they were big enough to handle a hoe, ¾ d. Tenancy was based on a contract system known as tinkathia under which the tenant had to plant three-twentieths of his holdings with indigo and hand over the indigo harvest to the Englishman as part of the rent. It went into dye factories owned by the English. When indigo crop was no longer profitable due to synthetic dyes capturing the market, the tenancy contracts were revised in favour of the English and the tenants were literally forced into accepting unequal contracts.

In the characteristic Gandhian style of conducting public agitations, the next step for Gandhi was to inform the head of the Indigo Planters

Association and the Commissioner of the area that he intended to investigate the grievances of the sharecroppers. "When I called on the Commissioner, he bullied me and advised me to leave immediately."[13] Although the response from these two quarters was somewhat threatening, but Gandhi went ahead all the same, recording the peasants' deposition en-route. The crowds became unmanageable. Gandhi realized that a campaign of this type could be upgraded to compel the British to hand over power to Indians — the road to *Purna Swaraj* (Total Self Rule). But at this point of time it was a mere pipe dream only. "This was my first act of civil disobedience against the British. However, he was now convinced that the Truth-Force could be expanded for a national uprising with unlimited aims. The peasants were not deterred by flogging either. The civil authorities therefore ordered Gandhi out of the district, which, of course, he refused pointblank. He was therefore summoned to stand trial the next day. The magistrate was completely flabbergasted by Gandhi's attitude. Gandhi simply declared that he was guilty as charged, and requested for legal punishment. The magistrate was at his wits' end. The judgment was postponed. Meanwhile, the Government at Delhi was rather disturbed by the adverse publicity, and Sir Edward Gait, the Lieutenant-Governor of Bihar ordered the case as withdrawn. Gandhi's act of defiance had succeeded, not through retaliation, but through the power of Ahimsa, civil resistance without resorting to offensive conduct or language. Nevertheless, Gandhi proceeded with his work of recording the deposition of thousands who came forward. His reasoning was that if the peasants talked freely of the indignities and cruelties inflicted on them, they would no longer be afraid. They will thus conquer their internal fear. More than ten thousand depositions were taken and filed. "It is no exaggeration, but the literal truth, to say that in this meeting with the peasants I was face to face with God, Ahimsa and Truth."[14]

On 29th April W.A. Lewis, a civil servant at Bettiah, wrote to the District Magistrate about Gandhi's activities vis-à-vis the peasants as follows:

> "They credit him with extraordinary powers. He moves about in the villages asking them to lay their grievances before him, and he is transfiguring the imagination of masses of ignorant men with visions of an early millennium. I put the danger of this before Mr. Gandhi,

13. Fischer Louis: *A Week with Gandhi*, p.97.
14. Ibid. p. 98

and he assured me that his utterances are so carefully guarded that they could not be construed as an incitement to revolt. I am willing to believe Mr. Gandhi, whose sincerity is, I think, above suspicion: but he cannot control the tongues of all his followers"

Gandhi was again asked, and not ordered, to leave but he declined. Sir Gait sent for Gandhi. After four hours of talks, the Lieutenant Governor, at the instance of the Viceroy, agreed to appoint an Inquiry Commission with Gandhi as spokesman for the peasants. To cut the long story short, the Commission recommended abolition of the tinkathia and the planters to refund a percentage of the money they had collected from the peasants. Consequently, most of the planters sold their holdings piecemeal to the tenants. Hereafter, he was no longer a mere Gandhi: now onwards he was Gandhiji, or Mahatma Gandhi. "Civil Disobedience had won. It became the method by which India could be made free. What I did was a very ordinary thing. I declared that the British could not order me around in my own country."[15]

During all this period, the gentry from Patna had their own servants to look after their creature-comforts. Separate food was cooked for them and they ate all their meals away from the peasants. Gandhi managed to convince them to have a common kitchen and have their meals together. Totally vegetarian of course.

As usual, Gandhi's next dictum was hygiene and sanitation. The peasants' villages were squalid with filth. Extreme poverty and lack of resources were the basic problems. Gandhi started his customary routine of scavenging, cleansing, washing, sweeping etc. in the first six villages selected for attention. He had to get volunteers from other parts of India to do this work. Mahadev Desai from Bombay came as a volunteer and was chosen as his secretary. Kasturbai and the almost illiterate womenfolk from the Ashram in Gujarat interacted with peasants' wives and daughters. A school was started in each of these six villages. The Truth-Force grew stronger and village welfare programme got a big boost. Meanwhile the Government got weary of this campaign and enquired as to when Gandhi would go back. He did so soon after the Commission's recommendations were implemented. Good riddance for the Government of Bihar!

The Champaran episode may be taken as the first triumph of Satyagraha movement in India. In fact, Champaran was the introduction of Satyagraha as well as of village-culture in Indian politics.

15. Fischer Louis: *A Week with Gandhi*; pp. 98-99.

So was the Montgomery Bus Boycott for the Negroes in America about four decades later — their hour of triumph against the white segregationist regime.

Dandi Salt Satyagraha

Rabindranath Tagore, India's great novelist and poet laureate, who won the Nobel Prize for Literature in 1913, and M.K. Gandhi, revered each other. It was Tagore, apparently, who conferred on Gandhi the title of Mahatma — "The Great Soul in a beggar's garb," Gandhi called Tagore "The Great Sentinel" and "the Poet."[16] Gandhi was arrested on the night of 4th May 1930 while he was sleeping on a cot under a mango tree at a village near Dandi in the course of the famous 'Salt March'. His arrest set off a general strike popularly called hartal. Numerous workshops and mills stood idle. There was a riot in Sholapur in which some policemen were killed. The Government declared martial law and twenty-five people were mowed down. In this movement altogether 60,000 persons were jailed, 103 killed and 420 were injured in police firings all over the country. Gandhi was released from prison on 26 January 1931 and the Civil Disobedience Movement was called off by Gandhi on 4th March as a result of the Delhi Pact between Gandhi and Lord Irwin. The tragedy of Chauri Chaura[17] was almost repeated, but some congressmen rescued the imprisoned policemen. While in prison his scheduled fast from 20th September as a protest against separate electorate was postponed. The Sabramati Ashram came to be known as the Satyagraha Ashram — 'School of Truth-Seekers'. "The Satyagraha Ashram was the birth place of modern India."[18] And Gandhi was not an ancient man! He was as modern as 'each new morning'. It was a rule in the Ashram that food and water should always be handled, and therefore polluted, by 'Untouchables'. Beggars were not at all permitted to enter the Ashram. When some one was admitted as full member of the Ashram, that person had to take fourteen vows — Truth; Ahimsa; Chastity; Control of the Palate; Non-Thieving; Non-Attachment; Poverty, Swadeshi; Fearlessness;

---

16. Fischer Louis: *The Essential Gandhi*, London, 1962; p. 125.
17. It is a small village near Gorakhpur in U.P. In the course of mob violence, a police station was burnt down killing twenty-two policemen. Consequentially, as a protest against eruption of violence, Gandhi suspended the popular mass movement towards national struggle for independence launched in the early 1920s. — R.C. Majumdar, *et al*: *An Advanced History of India*; New Delhi, 1946/1999, p. 972.
18. Ashe Geoffrey: op. cit. p. 176.

Rejection of Untouchability; Use of Vernaculars; Manual Labour; Khadi; and Study of Politics in the light of Religion. "I can say without the slightest hesitation and yet in all humility, that those who said that religion has nothing to do with politics do not know what religion means."[19] A daunting list indeed! It is noteworthy that "chastity to Gandhi meant abstinence: not repression, which he never approved, but sublimation."[20] In this context Gandhi wrote:

> "A man whose activities are wholly consecrated to the realization of Truth, which requires utter selflessness, can have no time for the selfish purpose of begetting children and running a household. ... If a man gives his love to one woman, or a woman to one man, what is there left for the entire world besides?" By implication, it means that the one hundred per cent Satyagrahi must be above sex.

On the occasion of opening ceremonies of the Benares Hindu University founded by Mrs. Annie Besant, Gandhi openly spoke against India and the Indians for their practice of untouchability, extravagance by the princes, rajas, maharajas and the rich who were quite prominent with their rich gaudy garments. He spoke against Indian lack of hygiene and sanitation; filthy garbage along streets, roads and railway lines; the intolerably dirty conditions of third class compartments of the railways; the dirty habit of spitting all over, particularly by the paan chewers; all this and a lot more. Gandhi had a critical intelligence and he spoke with pungent criticism. This was anathema to the rich and the royalty as well as to the British themselves, even though the criticism was voiced against India and the Indians. It was fashionable to praise Indian culture and the way of life. Gandhi had broken the rules of the game: 'You scratch my back and I scratch your back'. A holy man living like the poor had spoken for the poor, but critically against the rich. For all practical purposes, the opening of Benares Hindu University was thus the beginning of Gandhi's public life and political career in India.

Gandhi was in the Agha Khan Palace-prison from August 1942 to May 1944. Only the liberal minded British would put their arch enemy into a Palace as a prison camp (!) as opposed to what the white Americans did to Dr. Martin Luther King Jr. who was put into dungeon like prison-cell, more than once, whose condition was most disgustingly abominable. Gandhi was extremely unhappy during this period, besides the painful

---

19. Gandhi M.K.: *The Story of My Experiments with Truth*; London, 1949; p.420.
20. Ashe Geoffrey: op. cit. p. 180.

ordeal of his fast from February 10 to March 02, 1943.[21] During this period Gandhi suffered two great personal griefs, one after the other. The first was the death of his devoted Personal Secretary Mahadev Desai; and the second, the death of his life-long companion and the wife of his youth, Kasturbai. Gandhi's sorrow in both cases was extreme. Meanwhile the Great Bengal Famine of 1943 had come and gone. It was obvious that if Gandhi died in prison, it would amount to a catastrophe. The new Viceroy, Lord Wavell, therefore released Gandhi, Patel, Mrs. Naidu and their associates on May 06, 1944. By then Gandhi had spent 249 days in South African jails and 2089 days in Indian prisons.[22] Notwithstanding all his efforts and personal sacrifices, events during the last two decades had amply proved that the non-violence, which he assumed that the masses had learnt from him, was indeed superficial. It was an outcome of weakness rather than strength of character. The last few months of British rule over India were a black blemish on the character and human nature of the Indian nation — Hindus and Muslims alike — as well as the British. The Great Killings all over India, particularly North India, went unchecked by the police and the civil administration. The perpetrators of this genocide were well prepared, well armed and went unchecked by the police. Direct Action Day, 16th August 1946, fixed by Jinnah dawned in Calcutta bringing in its wake a prolonged massacre of Hindus, a crime against humanity to which the Muslim Chief Minister of Bengal was also a party. The murderous riots spread all over India and Jawaharlal Nehru who took over as Prime Minister of an Interim Government found himself at his wits' ends. Indeed, he was powerless to control the situation. Nobody else could either. Counter-massacres in Calcutta and Delhi and many other towns were the Hindus' answer to the Muslim challenge. "Madness answered with madness simply deepens, it never dispels it. Hinduism will be sorry stuff if it has to exist on cowardly vengeance that pursues those who can offer no effective resistance."[23] The humanity had gone off its head in those heady days. Gandhi was morally defeated. He could not prevent the massacres, or the birth of a fragmented India. After his death, Gandhi, "the whole man seemed to have gone through a prism and come out divided into various beams: the pacifist Gandhi, the ascetic Gandhi, the vegetarian and faddist Gandhi, the religious Gandhi, the political Gandhi."[24]

---

21. Gandhi's first fast was in the Phoenix settlement near Durban in South Africa while his last one was at Delhi, 13-17 January 1948, just a couple of weeks before the assassin's bullet extinguished that noble life.
22. Fischer Louis: op. cit. p. 34.
23. Bose N.K.: *Studies in Gandhism*; Calcutta, 1947.
24. Wofford Harris: *Of Kennedys and Kings*; New York, 1980, p. 117.

6

'Frontier Gandhi'

The Frontier Gandhi reminded the Muslims that the freedom movement was a fight for liberation of both Hindus and Muslims. The Hindus were not obliging any one by taking part in the struggle, nor would the Muslims be obliging any one by joining the Hindus. All were creatures of God. And to serve the creatures of God was to serve God. That was the motto of Khudai Khidmatgars, the Servants of God. Love is the key to the problems of the world. Sooner or later, all the people of the world will have to discover a way to live together.

Khan Abdul Ghaffar Khan was borne in 1890 to a rich and respectable landlord family of Muhammadzai clan in the village of Utmanzai Ashtanagar in the house of Khan Behram Khan, as the fourth child of the family. It was small village situated in Charsadda tehsil of Peshawar district, about forty kms from Peshawar. He was 'a man of God', a nationalist to the core and a shrewd politician. Freedom for the Pathans from British yoke was *sine qua non* for any meaningful economic and educational progress for his people. He was pragmatic enough, and had the political acumen to appreciate, that freedom for the Pathans would come only by aligning himself and his people with the Indian Nationalist movement under the leadership of Gandhi. "Once you compromise a principle, you not only compromise truth but also your self-respect." Thus, non-violence was imbibed by him whole heartedly as a weapon of peaceful liberation, as much as it was Gandhi's creed. "Indeed, the gulf between Mr. Gandhi's philosophy and the outlook of an average Pathan could scarcely be wider. The principle of 'non-violence' is almost un-intelligible on the Frontier where most men carry firearms and the maintenance of the blood-feud is still regarded as a sacred duty." Nor did the Muslim Pathan have a concept of *Ahimsa* or the tradition of *Tapasya* or self-suffering. "The Pathan is trained to defend himself and to establish his position in his society through skillful and ruthless use of violence."[1] On the other hand, Gandhi categorically rejected the concept of nationalism that sought freedom through violence. Gandhi insisted that terrorist methods were alien to Indian religion and culture. This is precisely the line that was adopted by Dr. Martin Luther King Jr. down the road of history. The Blacks of America were racially exploited by the white people; so were the Pathans exploited and kept in ignorance by the White rulers of the Indian sub-continent.

The correct designation for the Pathans is Pakhtuns. They are of Aryan stock and their language is known as Pakhtu or Pashtu, an Indo-Iranian Aryan language closely related to Sanskrit and Zend. In Pakhtu language a river is called 'sind'; that is the genesis of 'sindhu' or 'Hindu'. This tall handsome young man, who stood out feet above any crowd of Indians, was attracted, rather mesmerized, by Gandhi's magnetic personality. His respect for Gandhi and his principles, the simple ascetic life led by the Master, service before self and non-compromising attitude towards the principles of socio-political emancipation of India, irrespective of caste, color or creed, were the true reflection of his belief that "All Men are Created Equal". What impressed Khan Abdul Ghaffar Khan most was not Gandhi's high flown rhetoric, but putting these principles into actual practice in the day to day life of the Ashram where every one had to follow the basic tenets in a voluntary spirit. Nonviolence was the essence of his life and work — the British were indeed totally flabbergasted by a person with Pathan blood falling in the 'trap' of non-violence. They did not believe that official reports to that effect could ever be correct and taken on their face value. In essence, the war-like Pathan and non-violence were mutually incompatible, as repelling each other as fire and water. The Pathans inhabited a big chunk of difficult perpetually turbulent terrain; it therefore suited the British to keep them uneducated, but in a highly volatile frame of mind, since that provided additional cross-border security. Should the Pathans adopt an attitude of non-violence, the defence commitment on the international frontier would make ever increasing demands on the British Empire.[2]

Khudai Khidmatgar Movement

The Khudai Khidmatgar movement was founded by Khan Abdul Ghaffar Khan in September 1929. Its activities were restricted to the Frontier Province

1. Coupland, Sir Reginald: *The Constitutional Problem in India, Part I, The Indian Problem, 1833-1935*, Oxford University Press, Madras, 1944, pp. 75-76.
2. The Simon Commission reported: "The North-West Frontier is not only the frontier of India; it is an international frontier of the first importance from the military point of view. It is the gateway of India."

only. This designation meant the 'Servants of God'. He had not called them Satyagrahis, but servants of God. Since God does not require any service from his creatures, the Khidmatgars were essentially meant to serve the people. It was something like the 'Servants of India Society, which was lying dormant in the rest of India. He adopted the red colour for his workers' dress, and hence the name "Red Shirts"[3] stuck on to the members. It was a nationalist organization whose basic aim was freedom for India, and their motive: service of the people. Keeping in view the defense aspect of the turbulent Frontier region, the Chief Commissioner of the Province demanded dissolution of the Khudai Khidmatgar movement, which was refused point blank by Khan Abdul Ghaffar Khan. The British demand for dissolution of the Movement provided added momentum for expansion and strengthening of the Khudai Khidmatgars. The British efforts at suppression led to its popularity all over India. Gandhi saw the hand of God in the name that Badshah Khan had given them.

Any person desirous of becoming a Khudai Khidmatgar had to take the following vow, like the ten commandments of Black Liberation Movement of Dr. Martin Luther King Jr.:

> "I am a Khudai Khidmatgar, and as God needs no service I shall serve Him by serving His creation selflessly. I promise to serve humanity in the name of God.
>
> I shall never use violence. — In the words of Gandhi: "People laugh at me at the idea of Khudai Khidmatgars becoming full-fledged non-violent soldiers of Swaraj. But their mockery does not affect me. Non-violence is a quality not of the body, but for the soul." I shall not retaliate or take revenge; and I shall forgive any one who indulges in oppression and excesses against me.
>
> I shall not be a party to any intrigue, family feuds and enmity, and I shall treat every Pathan as my brother and comrade.
>
> I shall give up evil customs and practices. I shall develop good character and cultivate good habits. I shall not lead an idle life.
>
> I shall expect no reward for my services. I shall be fearless and be prepared for any sacrifice. I promise to refrain from anti-social customs and practices.

---

3. While Ghaffar moved in the rural areas, white clothes of the group soon got dusty and dirty. There was a local tannery nearby. One of the members took off his clothes and dyed them in the pine-bark solution generally used for hides. Soon every worker was wearing dark-brown red colored clothes. The color and the name stuck!

I promise to live a simple life, to practice virtue and to refrain from evil."[4]

Educating the Pathans was the first priority task before the Khan. Such muscular well built tall men having an unmatched reservoir of energy were good for nothing to man or beast without the attribute of literacy. The primary task of Khudai Khidmatgar was to make up for this deficiency of education. When Gandhi returned to Bombay, empty-handed, on 28th December 1931, Nehru, Khan Abdul Ghaffar Khan and Dr. Khan Sahib and many other leaders of NWFP were behind bars. The same year the 'Red Shirts' had merged into the Indian National Congress, thereby both the organizations gained in strength. The genius of Ghaffar was amazing inasmuch as he managed to transform a war-like tribe, the Pathans, having a strong tradition of blood-feuds and violence into a disciplined non-violent freedom-fighters. That is why Gandhi used to say: "Non-violence is always for the brave and not for the weak." And the Pathan was certainly not a weak person. While on the march, the 'Red Shirts' sang:

We are the army of God,
By death or wealth unmoved.
We march, our leader and we,
Ready to die.
We serve and we love
Our people and our cause,
Freedom is our goal,
Our lives the price we pay.

Abdul Ghaffar Khan noted that to attain freedom, two types of movements had been launched in the Frontier Province: violent and non-violent. ... The British crushed the violent movement in no time; but the nonviolent movement launched in 1929 flourished in spite of intense repression. The former generated fear and cowardice while the latter made the Pathans brave and raised their moral. This is precisely what took place a couple of decades later to the movement led by Dr. Martin Luther King Jr. in the United States. The British considered a non-violent Pathan more dangerous than a violent Pathan. The atrocities and cruelties to which the Pathans were subjected to are mentally so revolting that one might as well skip them at this point of time in history. Ghaffar, popularly known as Badshah Khan at that time, called himself

4. Tendulkar D.G.: *Abdul Ghaffar Khan; Faith is a Battle*; Bombay, 1967, p. 59, and *Frontier Gandhi*: p. 51.

"Khudai Khidmatgar": 'a servant of God' for the North West Frontier Province (NWFP) in particular.[5] The essence of this organization was the element of saintliness which the Khan imbibed from Gandhi. It was this attribute together with non-violence as a politico-social creed that gave him the nickname of "Frontier Gandhi", which stuck to him all his life and thereafter. Above all, it was the Khan's educational background that made a vast difference, in that practically every single Pathan of those days was illiterate. But "My education had created in me that spirit of dedicated service to my community and country. I made up my mind to serve the creatures of God and particularly my people who, at that time, due to their stupidity and backwardness, were heading towards disaster and chaos".

Young Ghaffar was greatly influenced by the Headmaster of the Edward Memorial Mission High School, Rev. E.F.E. Wigram who enthused him with the spirit of 'service to the creatures of God'.[6] For Ghaffar, this was also the beginning of close contact with the so-called untouchables —children of sweepers, dry or wet. Ghaffar spent more time playing with these tabooed children belonging to oppressed classes, than with those of his own.

Oppressed & Exploited

On the one hand the Pathans from Peshawar district had contributed 12,000 recruits for the Army to fight in the First World War, on the other, the British did not deem it fit to let them even run their own school. The people were very much disenchanted with this attitude. The Pathans at large resented being treated in this manner. In 1914 a small group of *maulvis* and Ghaffar Khan met at Deoband in the then United Provinces and decided to establish a center in NWFP devoted to achieving freedom for India. Since the First World War had broken out, this move was a dangerous development from the British point of view. They closed all schools, arrested Ghaffar Khan and all the teachers. To add to Ghaffar's miseries, his wife died in December 1915. When the nationalist leaders of the liberation movement gave a call for All India

5. The NWFP came to have two boundaries: the international boundary represented by the Durand Line which separated British India from Afghanistan, and the administrative boundary, demarcating the zone actually held by the British. The Tract between these two was known as the Tribal Belt, and that constituted a no man's land.

6. Ghaffar's elder brother, later known as Dr. Khan Sahib, was the first in the whole district to be sent to school. Later, he went to England to study medicine and become a Doctor.

total hartal on 6th April 1919, the Pathans from the NWFP whole heartedly joined their compatriots in the rest of India. The point to note is that the people of the Frontier under the leadership of Ghaffar had thrown their lot with Gandhi and other Indian nationalist leaders of the time for the liberation movement of their homeland. The British administration came down on the local leaders with a heavy hand. Collective fines were imposed. The amount collected far exceeded the fine imposed. Large scale arrests were made and the leaders of the liberation movement in Peshawar area were put in fetters. Since the available fetters did not fit the big feet and ankles of Khan Abdul Ghaffar Khan, the "authorities strangulated his feet even beyond the point of cuts and abrasion and placed him in fetters, his strong feet bleeding but never yielding."[7] After his release Abdul Ghaffar Khan travelled to Delhi during early 1920 to participate in the Khilafat Conference. It was attended by a large number of Indian Muslim leaders besides Maulana Abul Kalam Azad and Mahatma Gandhi. The Conference was organized to bring to the notice of the British Government the depth of anguish and resentment felt by Indian Muslims, amongst others, against the treatment being meted out to the Caliph — the Sultan of Turkey. In order to show solidarity with the Muslims, Gandhi had also given a call for non-cooperation. As a protest against the British policy, many Indian Muslims left India and moved to Kabul. Khan Abdul Ghaffar Khan also left his home and moved to Kabul where King Amanullah provided the necessary facilities to the migrants. This part of the protests was called *Hijrat*. Meanwhile, the King convinced Ghaffar as the leader of the Indian Khilafat Movement that running away from ones homeland is not going to resolve the problem, which should be 'faced squarely in their own place'. Consequentially, Ghaffar and his compatriots returned to India. The schools were reopened. Ghaffar's village Utmanzai had the school going full swing again. Indeed, spread of education amongst his people was a pre-requisite for liberation in-so-far as Ghaffar was concerned. With that aim in view, Ghaffar had earlier founded *Dar-ul-Ulum* under the patronage of Haji Sahib of Turangzai. This organization was required to set up new schools as well as superintend the existing ones. Abdul Ghaffar developed contacts with senior leaders of progressive and revolutionary movements in India. He was well aware of the political and socio-economic developments in the rest of India through the medium of the Urdu daily *Zamindar* and the weekly, *Al Hilal* — the latter became extremely popular amongst the Urdu knowing people, and proved to be a turning-point in the history of Urdu journalism.

---

7. Zutshi G.L.: *Frontier Gandhi*; Delhi, 1970, p. 29.

While Mahatma Gandhi was in prison, the death of his wife came to him as the saddest blow, amongst some others. And that is what happened to Ghaffar too. Like Gandhi, he too was told the sad news much after the incident. Gandhi was honoured so much that he was almost idolized much against his wishes. And that is what happened to Ghaffar too. On the occasion of annual function of Azad School, Ghaffar too was honoured with the title Fakhr-e-Afghan — Pride of the Pathan — which was later upgraded to Fakhre-e-Hind — Pride of India.[8] This was the stepping stone for Khan Abdul Ghaffar Khan rising to the exalted title of "Frontier Gandhi". Unfortunately, the Frontier Province witnessed one of the worst communal riots in September 1924. The seeds of discord had been broadcast far and wide by the interested foreign rulers, with the connivance of the Indian Muslim League, who was easily won over by the British as one of their accomplices in their evil design of perpetuating the foreign rule. By and large, the Muslim community was not enthusiastic about the freedom struggle. They were generally aloof except in parts of Punjab and most of the NWFP where Khan Abdul Ghaffar Khan and his 'Red Shirts', the nationalist Congress-oriented 'Servants of God', were deeply and totally committed to the freedom movement. The Khan was totally opposed to the partition of India. "On the whole, the enthusiasm of 1920 was lacking amongst the Muslims of 1930". For all practical purposes, the Muslim League was non-existent in the Frontier Province. However, the League's fortunes took an upward trend in 1934 when the U.P. politician, Liaqat Ali Khan managed to persuade Jinnah, then permanently resident in England, to return home to take charge of the Muslim League as a counter-balance to the nationalist Congress.[9]

While Ghaffar was in Hazaribagh Central Jail in Bihar a couple of thousand miles away, the highly repressive measures resorted to by the British Government against the Red Shirts, which included even bombardment from the air, had its repercussions in the tribal territory north of the Kabul River. The hostile activities indulged in by the Haji of Turangzai and his sons, as well as the Fakir of Alingar, were perhaps instigated by the Red Shirts refugees from the NWFP leading to the closure of the Chitral road. The air action was therefore probably justified from the military stand-point. It continued on the 10th and 11th of January 1932 and the Turangzai House was bombed on the 12th. The situation was restored to normalcy — from the British point of view — by that evening and the road to Chitral reopened.

8. Zutshi G.L.: op. cit. p. 37.
9. Masselos Jim: *Indian Nationalism,* New Delhi, 1985; pp. 182, 193.

Meanwhile, the atrocities inflicted on the Red Shirts had reached the depth of savage treatment of human beings by a class of rulers who took pride in their democratic values, human rights, and the so called civilized behavior. They stripped the Pathans naked and whipped them on their naked bodies. They tied their testicles with ropes to turn and twist till the non-violent Red Shirts groaned in agony. Some of the civil disobedience volunteers were thrown into the icy waters while others were thrown into pits full of human excreta. The less said the better ... Physical and mental torture had reached the limit of human degradation.[10] The Englishman's treatment of Pathans was comparable to lynching, cutting off of testicles and using the black-human body for target practice by the white man in America against their own Black minority was a disgrace on the so called white western civilization.

Both Gandhi and Ghaffar toured the country preaching unity, peace and nonviolence; but the British continued to have an upper hand. Meanwhile, the British maneuvered to get King Amanullah of Afghanistan out of the way lest he became a pain in the neck through his otherwise well intentioned humanitarian work amongst the sturdy Pathans. Soon after Gandhi had finished tour of the Frontier, Badshah Khan and his bands of Khudai Khidmatgars started wok to get the Hindus and Sikhs back to their ancestral villages. The Muslims of the localities waited in deputation to receive the uprooted families back home assuring them of safety of their lives and property. Concurrently, he requested Gandhi to send Mirabehn and Bibi Abdus Salam to come over to assist him in the work of social reforms and education amongst the Muslim women, who were otherwise reluctant to join any educational classes and social-work activities. He also encouraged the Muslim women to put forward their ideas and grievances through the columns of the *Pakhtun*. On the eve of his departure, he addressed a public meeting at Abottabad in which he laid emphasis on communal harmony and the evil acts of divisive forces who caused divisions and hatred amongst the various classes of Indian population for their own selfish ends. The British found it hard to flare up communal passions in the Frontier Province. Severe lack of education and poverty of the Frontier masses was his constant refrain to improve the general condition of the people at large. Of course, he let the Congress have it too for its internal squabbles. But it was the Badshah who had the last word in the Congress Working Committee meeting at Wardha in 1939. He asserted that communal amity could not be brought about by mere tall talk by the top leaders; only "prolonged

10. Zutshi G.L.: op. cit. p. 99.

and patient work right in the midst of the masses can bring about this unity."[11]

Our Gandhi of the Frontier Province started his sort of journalistic career with the launching of his monthly journal called '*Pakhtun*'. It was edited by Ghaffar himself and was printed in Pakhtun language, first in Rawalpindi, then shifted to Amritsar and finally to Peshawar.

In order to control the activities of Red Shirts, Colonel Smith — a quick tempered deeply prejudiced against the Khudai Khidmatgars type of officer — was specially selected as the Frontier-Province Inspector General of Prisons. He came on a visit to Haripur prison where Ghaffar Khan was lodged. "I had reared some poultry in my yard. The birds used to come and sit on my lap. Sometimes, they perched on my back and head and shoulders. Colonel Smith witnessed all this from behind me unobserved. ..." After some time the Colonel confronted the Khan who replied to his query with the remark that this little episode held a rich lesson for the British in India: "These feathered friends knew that they were to be eaten, that we would slaughter them, and therefore, as a rule were afraid of man. But see how they respond to a little affection!" ... After this incident, Colonel Smith appeared to be a different moody man. "The Britishers are patriotic and brave, and they admire these qualities in others. He had a soft corner for me. Although haughty, he was a man of character. ..." He wanted to serve in India till Pakistan was created, and retired and returned home as soon as it was formed.[12]

The Governor wanted to remove Dr. Khan Sahib from power, by hook or crook. He created a situation whereby he dismissed the Congress Ministry and in May 1943 installed Aurangzeb Khan as the Chief Minister. This was a corrupt, inefficient and unpopular set of ministers who were soon thrown out of power. In March 1945, Dr. Khan Sahib once again assumed the reins of power, and ordered release of Ghaffar and his Khudai Khidmatgars. In May 1945 the Germans surrendered, and on 25th June Simla Conference was held to pave the way for settlement of Indian imbroglio. Lord Wavell, the Viceroy inaugurated the Conference attended by the Congress and the Muslim League amongst others. Jinnah and Dr. Khan Sahib were both present when Jinnah made off the cuff remark: "We have met here as communities and the Congress does not represent anybody but the Hindus." Dr. Khan Sahib retorted: "What does Mr. Jinnah mean? I am a Congressman. Am I a Hindu or a Muslim?"[13]

---

11. Tendulkar: op. cit. p. 298.
12. Ibid: p. 358.
13. Tendulkar op. cit.; p. 361.

Ghaffar Khan returned to Wardha from his Bengal tour on 4th December 1934 and was arrested on the 7th, convicted and sentenced to two years rigorous imprisonment, after exactly one hundred days of so called freedom. He was put in solitary confinement. His reaction to the entire episode: "It is all God's doing; He kept me out just for the time he wanted to use me outside. Now it is His will that I must serve from inside. What pleases Him pleases me." With the grant of various remissions totaling to about four months, Ghaffar was released on 1st August 1936.

Soon after returning from *Hijrat*, Ghaffar was arrested and sentenced to three years imprisonment. His crimes: Going to Afghanistan on *Hijrat* and establishing the Azad High School at Utmanzai. He was lodged in the jails at Dera Ismail Khan and Dera Ghazi Khan. As a prisoner undergoing hard labour, he was required to grind twenty seers of corn in the *chakki* allotted to him. The Pathan officer in charge got ground atta given to Ghaffar along with a small quantity of corn — *atta* to save him hard labour and corn to show to the British officers that he was indeed doing hard labour. Ghaffar declined the offer made in good faith: he would not like to tell a lie, nor be a party to the jailer losing his job. A typical Gandhian approach. So the deputy jailer conspired and got Ghaffar transferred to another jail. While in the two jails, Ghaffar devoted a lot of time in reading the Bible and Guru Granth Sahib. Yet another Gandhian trait. He did not like Hindus and Muslims reading the scriptures in a language of which they did not understand a word, and appreciated the Sikhs and the Christians praying in their own language which they understood. For obvious reasons, Arabic and Sanskrit were not the right medium to pray in. These languages were foreign to the masses.

While Ghaffar was in jail, the Administration went out of its way to make life miserable for the Khidmatgars. His village Utmanzai was the worst victim which was looted by the British troops and subjected to collective fine.[14] The tales of atrocities perpetrated by the British reached Ghaffar in the jail. He therefore approached the Muslim League to give a helping hand to the Pathans. Since the League was pro-British for their own selfish communal interests, they did not wish to annoy the British, and hence did nothing whatsoever in the matter. If anything, they made the Pathans' life all the more difficult. When the

14. A punitive fine of rupees thirty-thousand was imposed but the actual collection exceeded rupees one lac. Over one hundred and fifty persons were kept in jail as hostages till the fine was collected — Tendulkar; p.30.

Indian National Congress was approached in the matter, they readily agreed. The Provincial *Jirga*[15] of Khudai Khidmatgars held a meeting and decided to join the Congress to liberate their land from the British yoke. Thus, the British themselves were responsible for transforming a purely social reformist movement into a political movement. After that, much as the British tried to incite communal passions in NWFP, the Khudai Khidmatgars just did not fall a prey to their machinations. In fact, when the notorious Rowlatt Acts were passed, Swami Shradhanand, the celebrated leader of the Arya Samaj, addressed a huge audience in the famous Jumma Masjid in Delhi. The Pathans came to realize that the division of India will result in an all round weakness. However, by the time the Partition of India came in 1947, Abdul Ghaffar was already popularly known as 'Badshah Khan' or 'Frontier Gandhi'. He told Gandhi that Indians were leaving Pathans to the wolves.[16]

Failure of Gandhi and his Politics

As a consequence of Partition of India, the unfortunate fate of the Pathans under the leadership of Abdul Ghaffar Khan, the "Frontier Gandhi", was M.K. Gandhi's most distressing political defeat, so was the holocaust that resulted in death and destruction leading to trans-migration of populations on a scale unheard of in the annals of civilization. The Frontier Referendum sealed the fate of the Pakhtuns. It began on 6th July and was completed on the 18th. The result was already a foregone conclusion since the Khudai Khidmatgars boycotted the uncalled for referendum whose terms of reference were totally one sided in favour of Pakistan. Barely fifty per cent of the total electorate of the Province voted for Pakistan; 2, 89,244 for Pakistan and 2,874 for India. The Frontier Gandhi remarked: "I regret to say that not we but the Congress deserted us. Our people have been greatly disappointed by the weakness shown by the Congress. ... Jinnah sent us messages time and again to make common cause with him, in which case he would concede to us whatever we wanted. ..." Mahatma Gandhi totally failed the Frontier Gandhi. For M.K. Gandhi, it was a political defeat of horrendous proportions. So were the Partition and its aftermath. After the referendum

15. A *Jirga* is a sort of peoples' assembly and is perhaps the most important Pathan institution.

16. After 1947, Badshah Khan spent fifteen years in solitary confinement in Pakistani jails — These were the fruits of Independence for the Pathans! Nonetheless, Abdul Ghaffar Khan celebrated Pakhtunistan Day in Kabul on 31st August 1965.

and the Partition of India, the Frontier Gandhi did not correspond with any of his colleagues in India. While in Pakistan, he was a victim of a vilification campaign, besides being persecuted. In fact he was in Pakistani jails most of the time.

His life's labours had gone down the drain. He was a broken man, who did not know if he had any place at all in the India of the 'morrow. He was dubbed anti-Hindu and pro-Muslim. Mahatma or no mahatma, a Hindu gang broke into the Calcutta house he was staying in. He was profusely abused. Some one threw a brick at him, another brandished a *lathi.* Although Calcutta returned to sanity after Gandhi resorted to yet another fast, he knew he and his philosophy had totally failed. About five hundred policemen and their English officers observed one day fast in sympathy with Gandhiji. As it is, Hindus had grown bitter against Gandhi. His insistence that India pay five hundred and fifty million rupees to Pakistan as its share of assets of undivided India further embittered the Hindus against him. They regarded him as a traitor to Hinduism.

Khan Abdul Ghaffar Khan: The "Frontier Gandhi"

Post-Partition/Independence

After the formation of Pakistan, the Frontier Gandhi was back to his original role as Abdul Ghaffar Khan, a Khudai Khidmatgar, a citizen of Pakistan, a member of the Pakistan Constituent Assembly. He founded a new political party, Jamiat-ul-Awam, the Pakistan People's Party, with the Khudai Khidmatgars as the volunteer corps and extended the movement to the whole of Pakistan. On the conclusion of the Constituent Assembly session at Karachi, he returned to NWFP in the third week of May to announce: "We will not rest content till we succeed in establishing Pakhtunistan — rule of the Pakhtuns, by the Pakhtuns, and for the Pakhtuns. On the morning of 15th June 1948 he was arrested near Kohat along with his son, Wali, and two other companions. He was charged with sedition and "intended collaboration with the hostile Fakir of Ipi". A summary trial was held by the Deputy Commissioner of Kohat. Ghaffar was awarded three years rigorous imprisonment and sent to Montgomery jail in West Punjab.

The Khudai Khidmatgars gathered for a protest demonstration. The police opened fire on the peaceful gathering killing hundreds and wounding thousands. One eye witness swore on the Koran that at least two thousand were killed that day, 12th August 1948. It was a pre-planned massacre since a large contingent of additional police had arrived in the village. The villagers who had gathered to offer *namaz* were fired at when they approached the village mosque. The villagers were told that they had no right to offer namaz since they were 'Hindus' coming to a 'Hindu mosque'! That is how the Khudai Khidmatgars were treated by the Muslim government of Pakistan. Soon after that, Dr. Khan Sahib and Ghani were also arrested. After the expiry of three years' sentence, Abdul Ghaffar Khan was held as a detenue under the archaic Bengal Regulation of 1818, his period of detention being extended for six months each time.

After spending about six years in Pakistani jails, Abdul Ghaffar was released from Rawalpindi Central Prison, but he was not a free man since he was kept under house-arrest, confined to the Circuit House. However, he was allowed to attend the budget session of Pakistan Parliament held in Karachi in March 1954. While at Lahore, he bluntly criticized the proposed integration of West Pakistan into one single administrative unit. On this issue, he totally disagreed with his elder brother, Dr. Khan Sahib who, as leader of the Republican Party, had taken over as the Chief Minister of West Pakistan. He enjoyed a sort of freedom for barely two years when he was arrested again on 16th June 1956 from near his village, Utmanzai. The charge: actions prejudicial to the safety and territorial integrity of Pakistan. He was tried in the High Court of West Pakistan at Lahore. Just about a year after his arrest and conviction, Dr. Khan Sahib was dismissed as the Chief Minister of West Pakistan on 7th July 1957 indicating signs of a deepening crisis in the top echelons of Pakistan Government. To cap it all, Dr. Khan Sahib was murdered on 9th May 1958 — a sure sign of tense and unstable political situation in Pakistan in general and West Pakistan in particular.

A coup d'etat by the President, General Iskander Mirza and the Defence Minister General Ayub Khan took place in Pakistan in October 1958. Martial Law was proclaimed in the country.[17] Ayub was sworn in as the Prime Minister under President Iskander Mirza. However, within a couple of hours of the swearing in ceremony, Ayub dethroned the President and packed him off to Quetta to be interned in the Circuit House there. Thus Ayub assumed full powers as the President and Supreme Commander of the Armed Forces. Abdul Ghaffar along with Maulana Bhashani and eight prominent leaders of East Pakistan was arrested on October 11, 1958. In jail once again! For the good old Frontier Gandhi Pakistan itself was a big vast jail. However, he was released on 4th April 1959 on health grounds, but was debarred from membership of any elective body until the end of 1966. Just about two years after being released from jail, Abdul Ghaffar was arrested again under the Maintenance of Public Order Ordinance and lodged in Hyderabad jail in Sind. His period of detention was extended every six months. Since the birth of Pakistan, out of eighteen years Abdul Ghaffar Khan had spent fifteen years in various prisons, mostly in solitary confinement. Amnesty International interceded on his behalf, but in vain. Meanwhile his health deteriorated considerably causing serious concern He was therefore released from jail on 30th January 1964, but placed under strictly controlled house-arrest. However, in September he was allowed to go to Great Britain for treatment. At Kabul airport in December, he was accorded an enthusiastic welcome and was received by the Afghan Prime Minister and his Cabinet colleagues.[18]

While at Kabul, Abdul Ghaffar was deeply touched by the observance of Pakhtunistan Day on 31st August 1965. It was inaugurated by the Mayor of Kabul who said that they will continue to celebrate that Day every year till their Pakhtun brethren achieve independence. The flag of Pakhtunistan was hoisted by the Mayor. The entire Afghan Cabinet was present to mark the occasion.

---

17. Martial Law was first declared in Pakistan in 1950.

18. The Pakistan Government prevailed upon the United States not to issue a visa to Abdul Ghaffar Khan.

The "Frontier Gandhi" speaking at a gathering of Tribal People during Jawaharlal Nehru's visit to tribal areas of North West Frontier Province of undivided India: 1946, while Nehru was the Interim Prime Minister

Jawaharlal Nehru, the Interim Prime Minister, with Dr. Khan Sahib, Premier of North West Frontier Province of undivided India, and the "Frontier Gandhi", 1946

7

The Slave Trade

Exploitation of the Weak

Since the institution of slavery was so important to the economic development of America, it had a profound impact on shaping the social-political-legal structure of the nation. Land and the slaves were the chief forms of property. In the service of this system, human beings were reduced to propertyless property.

Around the middle of the 20th century the population of American Negroes was about fifteen million, constituting about one-tenth of the total American population. They formed the largest minority group in the United States of America and their classification was based on ethnic and/or social criteria. Their common ancestral origin from hundreds and thousands of Africans legally imported mainly as slaves from Africa during 1619 to 1808 forms the basis of their ethnic or social classification. Although slave trade was declared illegal and abolished in 1808, a large number continued to be imported clandestinely until 1848, just a few years before declaration of general amnesty in 1863. In fact, the 1850- Fugitive Slave Act signed by President Fillmore was a concession to the Southern States in return for California and adjoining Mexican war-territories into the Union as non-slave states. The act facilitated recapture of slave by their masters, and sometimes even those blacks who were not slaves were taken away on the false declaration that they were run-away slaves. This complicated the matters since any person with recognizable Negro blood admixture, howsoever slight it may have been, was classified as Negro. Thus the basis of classification became social to that extent, and such persons were victims of color prejudice like any other totally Negro person. The extent of social and economic discrimination that the Negroes in America suffered was related to the region as well as the period of history. It was far more intense in the Southern States and the adjacent areas than up in the north. The seeds of racial minority problems and consequent social tensions were there to germinate, sooner or later, and grow into rich fertilizer for political bonanza, ultimately leading to 'Poor Peoples March' unifying all the depressed and oppressed classes of America irrespective of the colour of their skin — Blacks, Whites, Browns, and the Reds.

The original inhabitants of the North American continent were the 'Red Indians'. They were on their own land. The white colonists were in their own European culture. It was the unfortunate Blacks who had been torn from their land and culture. They had been forced into a situation where the heritage of language, dress, custom and family relations were completely shattered. Here it should not be forgotten that in that distant past the "African civilization was as advanced in its own way as that of Europe. In certain ways it was more admirable ..." While the practice of slavery existed in Africa itself too, the American slavery was the cruelest form of slavery in history, primarily on account of greed for excessive profit from capitalistic agriculture where the slave was reduced to less than a human being. The White man was the master, the black was the slave.[1]

The African ancestors of the American Negro came from a variety of tribes from all over the vast lands of the African continent. They had their roots in a variety of countries and regions in Central and West Africa, like the vast Niger Valley, the Cameroon and the Congo, French West Africa, Guinea, Ivory, Slave and Gold Coast. A few who were captured into slave trade belonged to the Moors and Arabs to the north, while a small number came from the East and South African tribes including Hottentots and Madagascans. They were taken to the African slave ports from where they were transported to American slave marts in overcrowded ships whose sanitary conditions were revolting, more like a cargo of animals than as human beings. No wonder therefore that resistance to slavery had started on the slave ships during the very early stages of slave-trade in the early seventeenth century. Be that as it may, once on the job in the plantations a certain degree of fusion of racial groups was part of the natural process. There was admixture of white and American-Indian blood through casual sex, concubines, etc. Inter-marriage between American-Indians and the slave Africans, *albeit* on a small scale, was also an accepted pattern of the social phenomenon. While this process added to the available labour force for which there

1. Zinn Howard: op. cit. pp. 26, 28.

was always a great demand in the plantations, over a period of time, a new race, a distinct biological and cultural product, started taking shape. As time went on, there was gradual increase in direct and compounded intermixture with various strains of white blood so much so that the present Negro population of pure or unmixed African descent is less than twenty percent. The bulk of the American Negro population at present is a mixed group of brown or brownish-yellow "mulattoes". The inter-mixing of White and non-White blood strains has gone so far that a few mulattoes might even be mistaken for Caucasians. No wonder therefore that those traditional racial distinctions make little sense in the present scenario. Nevertheless, traditional Negro music, art forms, and emotional religious expression continue to play a significant role in their cultural life. Over a period of time, a refreshingly peculiar cultural blend has taken form adding to the fusion and variety in the overall relationship between the traditional racial groups, notwithstanding the enormous strength of 'White Power', which reigned supreme during the early formative years of the nation in making. The Black resurgence had to face the all pervading White Power — the Government was white, and so was its entire machinery; judiciary was white, so were the schools and colleges; the Congress was white, so were the industrial and business corporations; even the labour unions were controlled by the whites. White was the colour of early America until the huge manpower demands of the Second World War made a dent in the psychological and physical attitudes towards racialism.

At first the Dutch dominated the slave trade. They ruled New York in the 1600's.Then the English, the traders of the world, took over. By 1795 Liverpool had more than a hundred slave-carrying ships. The English accounted for more than half of all European slave trade. The white American colonist in New England saw immense profits in the human cargo and they too entered in this business. In 1637 the first American slave-ship, the *Desire*, sailed from Marblehead. "Its holds were partitioned into racks, two feet by six feet, with leg irons and bars." By the end of the nineteenth century, about ten to fifteen million blacks had been transported to the Americas. It is roughly estimated that Africa lost nearly fifty million human beings to slavery (and consequential incidental death) during the period called the 'beginnings of modern western civilization' to slave traders and plantation owners in Western Europe and America, that part of the globe 'deemed most advanced in the world'.[2]

---

2. Ibid. pp. 29 and 206.

Christianity Blesses Slave-Trade

There are three major religions in the U.S. — Protestants, Catholics and Jews. All three are politically and economically powerful entities, in their own peculiar way. Martin Luther King Jr. soon found out that all those who claimed to be true Christians were far from being Christians in true sense of the word. It is the Catholic community that started slave-trade in Africa, and in course of time, that is what has been the basic cause of racial problems in the U.S. "From the beginning Catholicism has had an exploitative and dehumanizing relationship to black people. Priests went on the journeys to Africa, waiting beside the sandy, windswept barracoons of Badagry in Nigeria and Cape Coast in Ghana, blessed the slaves bound in chains for the New World."[3] Similar developments followed in Santo Domingo (Haiti). However, it would be wrong to lay the entire blame at the feet of the Catholics; the Protestants soon followed in their footsteps. Extra money and free labour was as welcome to Protestants as it was to the early Catholics. It would therefore not be wrong to conclude that practically the entire wealth of the New World was indeed Catholic wealth.

Insofar as the Jews were concerned, anti-Semitism was a dominant sentiment all over the world. Notwithstanding that negative downward drag, the poor immigrant Jewish community prospered and attained the middle class status. They became an influential segment of society socially, economically, academically and politically, all within a single generation wielding influence much beyond their numbers. The Jews had attained such power and influence that if the Anglo-Saxon America found it necessary to rid itself of a minority group, it would be the Blacks and certainly not the Jews. However, Martin King's humanitarianism was a positive factor that immensely appealed to the U.S. Jews. As opposed to the Jews, the King's forefathers were way behind in education. And an uneducated or partially educated Black was held in contempt, especially so if he tried to move in a circle dominated by college graduates.

Negro intellectuals all over America had come to realize that the so-called 'Christian Love' as propagated and preached by the whites was a pure and simple sham. They preached one thing; and that was applicable to the Caucasians. But that concept of Christian Love was not applicable to the non-whites, who were treated more like animals than human beings. Humane treatment of blacks was not in the dictionary of Christian doctrine, not even for those blacks who had embraced

3. Williams A. John: *The King God Didn't Save*; London, 1971, pp. 123-24.

Christianity as their abiding faith. This contradiction in theory and practice of Christian love was paradoxical, and its double-standards were degrading, not only to American Christians but to all Christians all over the world. The Americans rhetoric to the world was equality irrespective of the three C's — caste, color and creed. But at home, to its own people, it was segregation, racial discrimination, oppression, revolting cruelty, and lynching beyond description. How the so-called 'Pilgrims' could possibly stoop so low is beyond imagination. No wonder therefore that Martin Luther King Jr. could not reconcile to this contradictory distinction between theory and practice of Christian love and justice. Malcolm X, a Christian Baptist priest also turned away from Christianity to Islam in disgust over the double standards applied by the practitioners of Christian religion. "All men are created equal" is the principle applicable according to the color of one's skin, the region and income-level. Malcolm saw through the "kind condescension" of the whites as well as the violent hate of white Christians who burnt down his mother's house all because the colour of their skin was black. "Malcolm's rejection of Christianity did not arise so much from intellectual doubt as from his personal experience of being treated as less than human by white Christians."[4] The racial factor in human exploitation was, and perhaps still is in many parts of the world, that caused extensive distress to the collective psyche of the exploited. "The whites have always been an unjust, jealous, unmerciful, avaricious and blood-thirsty set of beings, always seeking after power and authority."[5] Much too strong an indictment, but largely true too!

Absentee Landlordism

The early waves of slaves were primarily employed on plantations for cultivation of rice, indigo and tobacco. Soon these products lost their profitability, and but for the sudden upsurge of cotton-culture, perhaps, the slave trade would have died a natural death. It was the invention of cotton-gin in 1793 that saved the economy of the Colonies, and kept alive the institution of slavery in the United States. In fact, the Southern States had such a boom in cotton industry, from cultivation to the end product, that the demand for slave labour increased manifold. Despite legal barriers, import of slaves increased. The demand for labour was so high that even reproduction of slaves became an 'industry' by itself! This resulted in substantial increase in Negro population in the U.S. It increased

---

4. Cone H. James: *Martin & Malcolm & America*; New York, 1991, p. 153
5. Stuckey Sterling: *The Ideological Origins of Black Nationalism*; Boston, 1972, pp.55-56, 97, 99.

by 200,000 by the end of the last decade of the 18th century, by 300,000 in the end of the following decade, and by 500,000 by the close of the year1830. It will thus be seen that slavery became the very foundation of the economy of the Southern States. Their very survival depended on the continuation of the institution of slavery. While a certain degree of humanization of slavery had occurred when slaves were working directly for the master, that human touch completely disappeared and gave rise to cruelty when the absentee landowners had their plantations and industry managed by professional white supervisors. Expansion of plantations and increased production gave rise to absentee landlordism. In turn, this led ultimately to the end of slavery itself.

In the Northern States sentiment against slave holding had been on the rise, slowly but steadily. The members of the Congress were divided on this issue on predictable lines. Religion also came to be involved inasmuch as many people held the view that slavery was against God's wish. They formed anti-slavery societies with the objective of ending the obnoxious practice, slowly and peacefully. Run-away slaves escaped to the North, and some went up as far as Canada.[6] The crusade to declare slavery and holding of slaves as an illegal activity came to be known as 'Abolitionist Movement'. It caused considerable emotional bitterness and ill-will amongst the people. While the Northern whites were proud of helping a human being escape the bondage, the Southern owners of slaves called it stealing, since it involved a loss of their property. The abolitionist movement got a big boost in the areas of Northwest Territory where slavery had been prohibited through an Ordinance promulgated in 1787. The debates in the Congress on the subject got more and more acrimonious. Much as the Negro-slaves wished to be free of white shackles, they could not possibly match the strength and organizational ability of the neo-colonists. Non-violent crusade to gain the rights guaranteed under the American Law appeared to be the only viable course open to the Slaves.

The 'slave trade' was outlawed in 1808, but slavery continued to exist in the South.[7] Existence of slavery was a blot on the democratic tradition of the United States. The betrayal of Reconstruction, the enactment of cruel and revolting laws, lynching and other atrocities, re-enslavement, and political disenfranchisement led to the formation in 1816 of the American Colonization Society in Washington D.C. in order

6. Slavery was declared illegal in the British Empire in 1833.
7. France abolished the slave trade in 1815; other European countries, notably Spain and Portugal soon followed suit.

to promote the repatriation of freed American slaves back to Africa, and to settle them on the west coast of Africa. Nat Turner became an ardent advocate of emigration back to Africa so that the progeny of slaves could lead a free life in their own land. In 1822 the first batch of freed Negroes was sent to the new colony named Liberia, the "Land of the Free" — nominally a free entity, but economically its umbilical cord remained intact with the United States.[8] They first landed at Freetown in Sierra Leone from where they made their way to Liberia in January 1822. Incidentally, Liberia was a mere private colony; it was not an official territory of the United States, even though its capital, Monrovia was named after the fifth President of the U.S., James Monroe. In this way about twelve thousand Negroes were settled in Liberia. However, it was soon evident that colonization would not solve the problem of Negro slaves due to various reasons, including financial and the long distance involved. The situation was further aggravated when in 1831 a Negro preacher, Nat Turner, led a band of sixty fellow slaves on some Virginia[9] plantations killing fifty-seven whites and about one hundred blacks. Nat was captured and hanged. Panic spread in the Southern States. All reforms of the slave system suddenly came to an end. Severe restrictions were placed on all activities and propaganda against slave trade.

The Kansas-Nebraska Act and the violence in Kansas gave an idea to the Northerner leaders to form a separate Party. It was born at Jackson, Michigan on 6th July 1854 and christened The Republican Party. The strength of the new Party was on the rise and by the end of the year it spread its tentacles all over the North. The Supreme Court of the United States tried to settle the slavery issue. In the Dred Scot case, it gave judgment which was in favour of continuation of slavery. The North would not accept the 'Dred Scot' decision.[10] The Lincoln-Douglas debate on the subject further widened the gap and anti-slavery feelings

---

8. Liberia declared war on Germany on August 04, 1917.
   It may be recalled that on December 20, 2000, the U.N. Security Council implicated Liberian President Taylor, amongst other West African countries, in the diamond trade imbroglio.
9. There were 6,000 slaves in Virginia in !700 A.D. By 1763 the number had increased to 170,000.
10. On March 07, 1857, the U.S. Supreme Court handed down the decision that the Missouri Compromise was unconstitutional since the Congress had no right to enact a law that deprived a person of his property. Since a slave was considered a personal property, the Negro slave Dred Scot was not deemed to have secured his freedom by being taken to a territory where slavery was illegal.

reached a high pitch in the North. The strict Fugitive Slave Act proved a failure and the Northerners would not accept the proposition that run-away slaves be returned to their masters. Harriet Beecher Stowe's novel *Uncle Tom's Cabin* added fuel to the fire. The emotional upheaval was a sure sign of clash between the North and South. The 1860 Presidential election was the most exciting and significant in the history of the United States. It was won by Abraham Lincoln as the Republican candidate. The South had already given notice that they would quit the Union if a Republican became the President. As soon as the election result was known, the South Carolina legislature met at Columbia, the State capital, and passed a resolution declaring that: "... the Union now subsisting between South Carolina and other states under the name of the United States of America is hereby dissolved." Nothing worse could have happened. Six more states followed suit immediately. The delegates from the seven states met in February 1861 at Montgomery, Alabama, and formed a new nation to be called the Confederate States of America, or the Confederacy. Jefferson Davis of Mississippi resigned from the US Senate to become its first President.

It is wrong to assume that extension of the war towards Mexico was for acquisition of new territories and thereby add to the area of control of the United States of America. The American Anti-Slavery Society was quite emphatic in their statement: the war was being waged solely for the 'detestable and horrible purpose of extending and perpetuating American slavery throughout the vast territory of Mexico'. So the split did take place after all! But Lincoln neither wanted separation, nor did he want to abolish slavery in the Southern States. All that he wanted to ensure was that slavery was not introduced in the new territories. And he certainly did not want to initiate any military action against the South. But the South was not prepared to concede even that much. A fratricidal War became inevitable. Lincoln assumed the Presidency on 4th March 1861. Before that date, the Confederate States took over most of the forts of the Union in the South. The Commander of Fort Sumter in Charleston Harbour refused to give in. He was low on supplies. The Confederates refused Lincoln's request for a supply column, sans armaments. The first shots of the bloody war were fired by the Southerners when their guns on the mainland blasted Fort Sumter for two days. Major Robert Anderson, commander of the Fort, surrendered on 13th April 1861. Mobilization by the North was started immediately thereafter. Meanwhile four more States seceded from the Union making a total of eleven in the Confederacy. The Capital of the Confederacy was then shifted to Richmond in Virginia.

8

American & Indian Revolutions

The Emancipation Proclamation of 1863 did not bring full freedom to the Negro. Four million newly liberated slaves found themselves with no bread to eat, no land to cultivate, no shelter to cover their heads. In 1863 he was given abstract freedom expressed in luminous rhetoric; but he was given no land to make his liberation concrete.

The people of Boston were ill at ease with the presence of large number of English soldiers patrolling their streets and enforcing their orders. Feelings between the two sides had become extremely harsh and fist-fights between the towns' people and the Redcoats were common occurrence. So far so good. But unfortunately on March 05, 1770, the popular hatred towards British troops erupted into a serious brawl between the colonists and the soldiers who resorted to firing their muskets resulting in atleast five deaths and injuries to several citizens. Preston, the commander of British contingent was acquitted. This incident came to be called the 'Boston Massacre' and, perhaps, it represented the opening shots of the War of Independence.

The British Parliament passed an act repealing customs-duties on paper, glass and a few more items, but retained duties on tea. It came to be popularly called the new 'Tea Act', which was designed to help the failing British East India Company by allowing it to ship tea direct to America and to sell the same to retail merchants there. While full duty was payable in the Colonies, a system of duty-drawback was introduced under which the duty was to be reimbursed in England. The shippers and importers in the Colonies were unhappy inasmuch as they would almost go out of business since the East India Company was not obliged to sell stock through them, besides selling the tea at a lower price than what the Colonial importers were charging by importing tea from other sources. Protest demonstrations were held in Charleston, Philadelphia and New York against landing of tea in those ports. Three tea-ships of British East India Company arrived in Boston harbour in 1773. These shipments were to be sold by two sons and a nephew of Governor Thomas Hutchinson of Massachusetts. The people of Boston were determined that these ships would not be allowed to unload in Boston. However, the Governor did not pay heed to their pleadings. The angry citizens of Boston organized themselves under Samuel Adams as their leader. On the evening of 16th December 1773 they, dressed as Indians, climbed aboard the three ships and dumped the entire cargo worth more than ninety thousand dollars into the sea. London was extremely angry over this incident and adopted a punitive policy. The British Parliament passed laws to punish the people of Boston and Massachusetts. These laws were so draconian that the Americans called them the 'Intolerable Acts', the 'Coercive Acts' — the Boston Port Act closing the Port after June 01; Massachusetts Government Act depriving the people of most of their chartered rights thereby substantially enlarging the Governor's powers; the Administration of Justice Act under which certain capital offences were to be tried only in England; the Quartering Act, the Quebec Act, *et al.* The Colonies took a united stand and resolved that these coercive legislations be rejected in toto since these were insidious attempts to enslave the American Colonies. The reaction of the Colonies came to be known as the 'Suffolk Resolve'. It was a united stand, particularly to help the Bostonians.

American War of Independence

Fifty men representing every Colony except Georgia met in Philadelphia on September 05, 1774. This was the First Continental Congress. The members were divided into the 'Radicals' under Samuel Adams and the 'Conservatives' under Joseph Galloway Pennsylvania. The Radicals got approval for the 'Suffolk Resolve' much against the wishes of the Conservatives. They drew up a Declaration of Rights and Grievances', which, *inter alia,* was a list of complaints and grievances against King George III and the British Government in London. The Resolutions passed by the Congress were sent to the thirteen Colonies as well as to the King in England. London responded by sending more troops and warships to the Colonies with orders to crush the rebellion. The writing on the wall was loud and clear — a long drawn conflict between the colonists and the British Crown. The first in the series of battles was fought on April 19, 1775. The British troops ordered to destroy military stores at Concord got embroiled with the local militia men at Lexington. However, after destroying the store-dump at Concord they were forced to retreat to Lexington and thereafter back to Boston. Meanwhile the Second Continental Congress also organized some sort of an army to carry on the fight. On 10-12 May 1775 Ethan Allen led his eighty-two freshly trained men known as 'Green Mountain Boys' against Fort Ticonderoga. They surprised the sleepy British troops who surrendered without a fight. This British Fort was selected as the target since a number of guns and a large quantity of ammunition was stored therein. The booty fell to the Americans and soon the guns and ammunition was on its way to Boston, the site of the main battle. Concurrently, the Crown Point was captured by Seth Warner.

On that very day the Second Continental Congress met at Philadelphia. The building in which the meeting was held came to be known as the Independence Hall. Notwithstanding all the jubilation around, the delegates to the new Congress were in a somber mood; they had a war on their hands. They had strong leaders like Benjamin Franklin, John Hancock, John Adams, George Washington and Thomas Jefferson. They decided to raise a Continental Army and asked each Colony to send companies of riflemen to Boston. They recruited young poor working-class white men, slaves, free blacks. They also got into their ranks some women who served as cooks, nurses and laundresses, and sometimes as grave diggers too. George Washington was selected to command the Continental Army.

After the Battle of Bunker Hill opposite Boston on June 17, 1775, the Continental Army laid siege to Boston that lasted from July to March 17, 1776 when the British were forced out of Boston. Consequentially, the urge amongst the Colonies for complete independence became stronger leading to the Declaration of Independence on 4th July 1776. The British forces captured New York in the autumn of 1776 but were soon surprised by the Colonists when they captured Trenton and Princeton in the beginning of 1777. The Battle of Saratoga proved to be the turning point of the War for Independence when the British troops surrendered there on 17 October 1777. However, Washington's army remained in Pennsylvania to counter the much awaited British offensive in that sector and had to go through a terrible winter at Valley Forge. Meanwhile, John Paul Jones won a great victory at sea in 1779 and the fighting ended with the surrender by General Cornwallis at New York on 19 October 1781 when eight thousand British soldiers under Cornwallis surrendered to the American and French troops, with the band playing a lively tune called "The World Turned Upside Down". Negotiations for restoration of peace were long and frustrating. The formal end of the

American War of Independence came on September 03, 1783, with the signing at Paris of a 'Definitive Treaty of Peace' between Great Britain and the United States under which "His Britannic Majesty acknowledged the United States to be free, sovereign, and independent". George Washington became the first President of the United States of America, with John Adams as the Vice-President.

The Treaty did not make any mention of the Native Americans. As for the 'Thirteen", the Founding Fathers had come to a tacit agreement to ignore the thorny question of slavery as well as the status of the slaves. In fact, the new Constitution did not restrict the 'human traffic' along the 'Great Triangle' — Africa, America and Great Britain. It continued without let or hindrance as heretofore, keeping up the tobacco plantations in Virginia.[1] However, the period 1783-87 was the most critical in American History, more so since the nascent Country was almost friendless in entire Europe. The economic situation was quite distressing with shipping, and consequentially, import-export trade at a standstill. Large scale English immigration to Canada with financial aid provided by the British Government added to the complexity of the situation. The Northwest Ordinance enacted in 1787 laid down a gestation period as 'colonial stage' before ultimate statehood would be granted. This 'principle of coordinancy' set the pattern for admission of new territories into the Union in the 19th century going through a process of colonial system. The same year, discontented and indebted farmers in western Massachusetts blocked the courts from executing foreclosures on farms. Under the leadership of Daniel Shays, they broke into local jails and released the prisoners. The Governor, James Bowdoin was constrained to deploy 4,000 troops to end the revolt. Again, in May of the same year a Constitutional Convention was convened at Philadelphia. It was attended by all the States of the Union except Rhode Island. After four months of hard work and negotiations to achieve consensus, the Constitution was signed by the delegates present. The document was sent to the States for ratification with the proviso that it would become effective as soon as nine States have ratified it. In June 1788, ratification by New Hampshire, the ninth state, placed the new Constitution into operation. However, the ratification incorporated a number of conditions and restrictive provisions to make it acceptable to anti-federalists in some of the states. It was a Constitution made operative after a number of compromises, the more important of which were:

---

1. Later on, tobacco replaced cotton.

- States were prohibited from issuing their own currency.
- Slaves were counted as three-fifths of a person towards Southern representation in the Congress.
- The Congress was prohibited from enacting export duties on cash-staples produced by the Southern States.
- The Congress would not legislate against the international slave-trade for twenty years.

After Washington's farewell address on September 18, 1796, John Adams became the President on March 04, 1797, with Thomas Jefferson as the Vice President. The conclusion of Jay's Treaty on November 19, 1794, whose provisions were to become effective in 1796, was considered as pro-British and anti-France by the French Government. This attitude on the part of France created some difficulties for Adam's Administration so much so that, during Adam's Presidency, the United States fought an undeclared war against France. Normalcy was restored in the relations between the two countries through a treaty signed in 1800, thereby preventing a full scale war between the two countries. Nevertheless, Adam's Administration was severely criticized for its real and imaginary failings, which in turn led to passage of four laws known as the Aliens and Sedition Acts. These laws conferred unfettered powers in the Presidency to deal with foreigners as well as the domestic press whose freedom was considerably curtailed.

Negro-Slave Labour

The institution of slavery met the labour needs of the Southern States. Whenever there was a shortage of slaves or labour, raiding parties were sent to Africa to capture the Blacks and bring them over to America. In fact, slavery was known and practised even before Columbus 'discovered' America. Spaniards tried to force the local Indians work for them but this did not succeed. The Negroes proved more enduring thereby giving a boost to slave trade which soon spread to the Southern English colonies also. However, sentiment against slavery was pretty strong in the North and the Northerners found various ways to help the Negro slaves escape from captivity and get shelter in the North.

In 1820 a compromise (The Missouri Compromise) was reached between the North and South over this pernicious question but it raised its head again in 1848 when the United States won the Southwest in the Mexican War. The American settlers in California were rebelling against Mexican rule. In 1846 John C. Frémont helped them set up what they called the Bear Flag Republic.[2] The Southerners expected the area to be open to slave trade, but David Wilmot, a Pennsylvania congressman, proposed that slavery should be forbidden in all land captured from Mexico. Once again there was fear of secession, but the compromise of 1850 saved the Union. It postponed the War between the States by ten years but the balance between the 'free' and the 'slave states' in the Union now stood at a slender sixteen to fifteen in favour of the North. Meanwhile, many people wanted to settle in the Kansas-Nebraska region, and they demanded popular sovereignty for that area insofar as the question of slavery was concerned. In May 1854 Senator Stephen A. Douglas of Illinois managed to persuade the Congress to repeal the Missouri Compromise of 1820 by passing the Kansas-Nebraska Act. This legislative action opened Nebraska to settlement on the basis of 'popular sovereignty'. Groups of Northerners rushed to Kansas to increase the vote against slavery while hordes of Southerners came over to do the same for introduction of slavery. There was bloodshed galore. Arson, shooting and looting went on for five years. The pro-slavery and the anti-slavery elements fought pitched battles. Extreme violence was the order of the day. Free and fair elections under these conditions were virtually impossible.

A period of over-expansion and speculation followed the economic panic of 1857. The economic downturn was especially hard on the poor working-class families, white or black, so much so that by 1860, five per cent of all families owned fifty per cent of the nation's wealth.[3] The same year Jefferson Davis introduced a resolution in Congress demanding a federal slave-code for the protection of property owned in the form of slaves. It came to be known as the Davis Resolution. The seeds of a civil war on the question of slavery were getting ready to germinate. The 1860-Presidential Election turned out to be the catalyst.

American Civil War

Abraham Lincoln's early life was in rough soil. May be he was coarse in speech but he was pure in life. He was patient by nature and sympathetic in his concern for other human beings. A lawyer by profession, he was fair in his dealings. In politics his integrity was above board. These qualities earned him the nickname "Honest Abe". His attitude on slavery was typical of the men of the North who were at

2. The 'Republic of California' had a grizzly bear on its flag.
3. Stearns: op. cit. p. 606.

once humane and regardful of the established order".[4] He strongly believed in freedom for the slaves. But it did not mean equality of the Negro with the white man. Lincoln had no intention of giving voting rights to the freed slaves, nor to make them jurors. In fact, Lincoln's anti-slavery position was very moderate. Nonetheless, in the Northern States sentiment against slave holding had been on the rise, slowly but steadily. The members of the Congress were divided on this issue on predictable lines. Religion also came to be involved in as much as many people held the view that slavery was against God's wish. It was a question of principle on which North was not prepared to compromise. They formed anti-slavery societies with the objective of ending the obnoxious practice, slowly and peacefully. Runaway slaves escaped to the North, and some went up as far as Canada.[5] The crusade to declare slavery and holding of slaves as illegal activity came to be known as 'Abolitionist Movement'. It caused considerable emotional bitterness and ill will amongst the people. While the Northern whites were proud of helping a human being escape the bondage, the Southern States called it stealing since it involved a loss of their 'property'. The abolitionist movement got a big boost in the areas of Northwest Territory where slavery had been prohibited through an Ordinance promulgated in 1787. The debates in the Congress on the subject got more and more acrimonious. Much as the Negro-slaves wished to be free of white shackles, they could not possibly match the strength and organizational ability of the neo-colonists. Non-violent crusade to gain the rights guaranteed under the American Law appeared to be the only viable course open to the Slaves.

The Civil War therefore got protracted beyond early expectations; it was costly, bitter and woeful.

The 1860-Presidential election was the most exciting and significant in the history of the United States. The Republican Party's electoral-platform was moderate inasmuch as it opposed further extension of slavery in the new territories acquired from Mexico, or whatever. The Party also supported homestead and tariff. The Republicans therefore nominated Abraham Lincoln as their candidate. On the other hand, the Democratic Party was itself split on the fundamental question. They drew up two electoral-platforms: one was demanding passage of Davis Resolution on a federal slave-code, the other supporting the 'Freeport Doctrine' of Douglas. The Southern Democrats nominated John C.

4. Merriam S. George: op. cit. pp. 176-78.
5. Slavery was declared illegal in the British Empire in 1833.

Breckinridge while the Union Party's candidate was John Bell. Abraham Lincoln won the Presidency as the Republican candidate purely on a sectional basis in that he did not receive any electoral support from the slave states. The South had already given notice that they would quit the Union if a Republican became the President. As soon as the election result was known, the South Carolina legislature met at Columbia, the State capital, and passed an ordinance of secession on December 20, 1860, declaring that: "... the Union now subsisting between South Carolina and other states under the name of the United States of America is hereby dissolved." Nothing worse could have happened. All efforts to save the Union, including the Peace Convention held at Washington D.C. on February 04, 1861, proved futile. Six more states followed suit immediately. The delegates from the seven states met in February 1861 at Montgomery, Alabama, and formed a new nation to be called the Confederate States of America, or the Confederacy. Jefferson Davis of Mississippi resigned from the US Senate to become its first President, and Alexander H. Stephens the Vice President. During the period January to May 1861 the strength of the Confederacy had swelled up to eleven — South Carolina, Mississippi, Florida, Alabama, Georgia, Louisiana, Texas, Virginia, Arkansas, Tennessee and North Carolina — the last named having joined the Confederacy on May 20, 1861.

Notwithstanding the secession, Lincoln's first inaugural address in March 1861 was conciliatory towards the South and the seceded states: "I have no purpose, directly or indirectly, to interfere with the institution of slavery in the States where it exists. ..." Lincoln neither wanted separation, nor did he want to abolish slavery in the Southern States.[6] All that he wanted to ensure was that slavery was not introduced in the new territories. And he certainly did not want to initiate any military action against the South. But the South was not prepared to concede even that much. A fratricidal War became inevitable. The first shots of the bloody war were fired by the Southerners' battery at Charleston on January 09, 1861, on the ship *Star of the West*. Lincoln assumed the Presidency on 4th March 1861. Before that date, the Confederate States took over most of the forts of the Union in the South. The Commander of Fort Sumter in Charleston Harbour refused to give in. He was low on supplies. The Confederates refused Lincoln's request for a supply column, sans armaments. The Confederacy, having seized all property and funds

---

6. Vajpayee, Atal Bihari: "History can remind us, guide us, teach us or warn us. It should not shackle us." —
SARC Summit: *India Today*, January 19, 2004.

of the Union in the South, blasted Fort Sumter for two days, 12-13 April using their guns deployed on the mainland. Major Robert Anderson, commander of the Fort, surrendered on 13th April 1861. Mobilization by the North was started immediately thereafter. By the time the number of states in the Confederacy had risen to ten, the Capital of the Confederacy was shifted to Richmond in Virginia, the northern most limit of the Confederacy. This move indirectly hastened the secession of North Carolina, May 20, 1861, besides reflecting the confidence of Confederate leadership in their ability to defend the new nation.

The Civil War had started in earnestness. Right from the beginning, the North had immense advantage inasmuch as it had twenty-three states with a population of almost 23 million, whereas the South had eleven states with a population of only five million, besides other advantages by way of rail communications, manufacturing facilities, etc. A blockade of Confederate ports was proclaimed on 19 April 1861. Thus right from the beginning, the South was on the defensive. The first major battle of the War was fought at Bull Run on 21st July 1861. The Federal forces under overall command of General Winfield Scott were routed. He was replaced by General George B. McClellan on 1st November 1861. He was a cautious general who believed in meticulous planning and preparation. He devoted the winter in training his command — 200,000 men known as the Army of the Potomac for march on Richmond, the capital of the Confederacy. Concurrently, naval operations were undertaken. However, McClellan's advance on Richmond over the sea route was a failure and the Federal army withdrew from the Peninsula. The initiative was wrested by the Confederate commander, General Robert E. Lee, who commenced advance towards Washington. The Federal forces were again defeated in the Second Battle of Bull Run fought on 30th August 1862. Lee crossed the Potomac on 4th September and invaded Maryland.

The bloodiest day of the entire War happened at Antietam on 17th September 1862. It was the single most bloody-day in American military history, but the battle was indecisive despite very heavy casualties — 7,800 killed and 15,500 wounded. The conduct of the Civil War in its early stages was under the joint control of the Congress and the President. Leading members of the Congress interfered with day to day operational plans, besides creating favouritism in command and control. This arrangement proved most unsatisfactory. "Chronic hostility between President and Congress is partly psychological, mainly institutional".[7]

7. Dishman B. Robert: op. cit. p. 95.

And the Civil War was fought over constitutional doctrine rather than over the abolition of slavery alone. Indeed it would be an oversimplification to attribute to slavery the prime position amongst the causes of the Civil War. In fact, Lincoln did not propose to abolish slavery wherever it was being practiced. "The controversy was over the power of the Federal Government to control the spread of slavery into new territory, and over the voluntary or compulsory character of the federal compact". The conflict between the judiciary and the executive branches of the government is inherent in the democratic system; only its intensity varies from time to time depending on the personalities involved. Whenever America had a strong man at the helm of affairs, the conflict became more pronounced and open — for example, during the presidencies of Jefferson, Jackson, Lincoln and Franklin Roosevelt. As long as these two branches kept within the bounds of their respective domains, there was no conflict. But whenever the Supreme Court tried to enter the political realms through the indirect route of private litigation, the conflict assumed serious proportions. The source of funds for the presidential campaign contributions often proved to be fertile ground for mud-slinging.

While the Civil War was on, a number of slaves managed to escape and took shelter in the camps of the Northern armies. Their owners, the masters of the slaves claimed them back as their rightful property. The local commanders used their discretion and some restored the slaves to their masters while others did not. In order to maintain uniformity of policy, in March 1862 the Congress forbade the army and the navy to return the fugitives. The anti-slavery sentiment was exceptionally strong in the North. It was a question of principle on which North was not prepared to compromise. Thus the War therefore got protracted beyond early expectations. Meanwhile, Lincoln presented the Emancipation Proclamation to his Cabinet in July 1862. "The Cabinet was amazed — and divided."[8] Seward suggested that in view of the recent military reverses in McClellan's peninsula-campaign, it was not the appropriate time to put forward such a far-reaching reform. Lincoln agreed and postponed the issue for a later date. This was on 22 July 1862. However, when Lee took the offensive after a yearlong defensive, and entered Maryland, he was beaten and turned back at Antietam, Lincoln got his opportunity. He summoned the Cabinet again on 22 September 1862 and placed the proposed Proclamation of Emancipation before them for approval. The proclamation was issued the next day giving the South four months to end the rebellion. It was thus more of a military move,

8. Merriam S. George: op. cit. p.257.

than a mere act of anti-slavery, more so since his 'ultimatum' promised that the States that returned to Northern fold would be left alone with their slaves in place. Nonetheless, the American nation was "inexorably committed to emancipation, — compensated if possible; forcible if necessary; partial at first, but moving inevitably, swiftly, toward universal freedom." The Proclamation came into effect on 1st January 1863, whereby slaves belonging to the States still fighting the Union were deemed to have been freed for ever. Thus, "the principle is not that a human being cannot justly own another, but that he cannot own him unless he is loyal to the United States.[9] The Proclamation, *inter alia*, opened the Union Army to blacks who were thus fighting for their own liberation. However, the draft law enforced in the North applied to the poor whites only since the rich could buy their way out for $300. This discrimination led to draft riots in the North. The irony of the situation was that the rich whites were not the victims of the riots; it was the blacks at hand — men, women and children — who were butchered by angry white mobs. In this respect, the Northern-Whites were no better than the Southern-Blacks. Racism was ingrained in the white psyche — north or south was merely incidental. The vestiges of that psychological blemish may be perceived there even now, in the first decade of the twenty-first century.

Following the Battle of Antietam, General Ambrose E. Burnside was appointed to succeed McClellan, but he too was badly defeated by Lee on December 13 in the Battle of Fredericksburg. He was replaced by General Joseph Hooker on 25th January 1863. In the Western Theatre of operations, Brigadier General Ulysses S. Grant serving under General Henry W. Halleck captured Fort Henry on 6th February followed by surrender of Fort Donelson on the 16th. The Confederate counter-attacks on Grant resulted in heavy casualties on both sides totaling to about 20,000 killed or wounded in the Battle of Shiloh which ultimately ended in favor of Grant. This was followed by fall of strategic Confederate positions in Vicksburg and Port Hudson in early July thereby giving the Federal forces command of the entire Mississippi River, thus conferring a major strategic advantage to the Federal forces. By the time Grant won the Battle of Chattanooga during November 1863, he was a rising star, more like a meteorite on the upward trajectory. He was promoted to Lieutenant General and commander-in-chief of all armies. His next notable success was the Battle of Wilderness, 5-6 May 1864. Meanwhile Sherman in the West neutralized Atlanta. The Confederate armies

9. A comment by the London Spectator.

withdrew from Savannah on December 20, and Sherman overran South Carolina. He captured Columbia on 17 February 1865 and continued his advance into North Carolina. In the process, the Confederate armies were caught in the Federal pincer movement — Grant in the north and Sherman from the south. That was virtually the end of Confederacy. Lee capitulated at Appomattox Court House on 9th April 1865. The President of the Confederacy, Jefferson Davis, fled to Georgia but was captured on 10th May and imprisoned.

Lincoln's Assassination

Meanwhile, Lincoln had won the Presidential election of 1864. Every State supported him except the States of New Jersey, Kentucky and Delaware. While Grant and Lee were locked in the last desperate struggle at Petersburg, and final victory was well in sight, Lincoln 'spoke his second inaugural'. His election for another term had given the anti-slavery lobby a big boost. It was therefore decided to grant universal freedom to all slaves through a constitutional amendment. The Thirteenth Amendment was brought forward in April 1864 but it did not receive the requisite majority vote. However, Lincoln had already fulfilled his life's mission, but he was not destined to bask for long in the warmth of its full glory. On 14th April 1865 while he sat in the Ford's theatre he was mortally shot by John Wilkes Booth and died the next day.[10] A life of heroic glorious service was thus crowned by a martyr's death through an assassin's bullet. The Vice President, Andrew Johnson succeeded to the Presidency. The same amendment was put up again next year when it received the necessary majority and was declared adopted on 18 December 1865. On that day the evil of slavery in the United States came to the end, albeit on paper only. It was the US Supreme Court that started negating the positive aspects of the new law; instead of protecting the rights of the Negroes which the Amendments conferred on them, the highest judicial forum of the land developed the law into a protection for the corporations. The law is invariably on the side of the rich!

Reconstruction After the Civil War

Although the Civil War officially came to an end on April 9, 1865, when Robert E. Lee surrendered at Appomattox Court House in Virginia, the Thirteenth Constitutional Amendment prohibiting slavery everywhere in America had already been passed by the House. The Negroes were now permitted for the first time to enter Congressional Chambers, The

10. Stearns N. Peter: op. cit.; p. 610.

White House, be accredited to the Supreme Court,[11] and so on. The War itself had been extremely expensive, both in terms of money and human lives — 620,000 Americans of whom 360,000 were Northerners and at least 260,000 were southerners had lost their lives. About 180,000 Blacks served in the Union Army and more than one-third of them, 68,178, were killed in action. It was a fratricidal war whose sole purpose and gain was the unified existence of the United States of America, destined to be the richest and most powerful nation on planet earth. Emancipation of Negro-slaves, though made out to be the prime objective was, in fact, a mere side issue. Nonetheless, while some whites were skeptical about war-aims, the Blacks knew that the War was their own cause. The four million blacks in the South were now legally free. Instead of being called 'slaves', they were now being called 'freemen', but their struggle for true equality had just begun since the Southern politicians concurrently enacted a series of vicious regulations known as the 'Black Codes', later as 'Jim Crow'. For all practical purposes, it was 'revival of slavery in disguise'. Meanwhile, with the passage of the Fourteenth Amendment guaranteeing civil liberties, the South had been divided into five military districts under the Army, which in turn imposed Martial Law. However, the 'Freedmen's Bureau' was continued as a permanent organization in the South.

After peace was restored, Mississippi sent two Negroes to the Senate while the other eight Southern States sent twenty blacks to the Congress. This representation came to a dramatic end after 1876, and in 1901 there was not a single black man in the Congress.[12] During this period, the Congress legislated in favour of civil rights, and the Supreme Court applied the reverse gear. "Bands of hooded white men — Jaywalkers, Black Horse, Cavalrymen and the infamous Ku Klux Klan (KKK) — roamed the South at night terrorizing blacks and white Northerners."[13] In the process, KKK murdered thousands of blacks. Many other thousands were evicted from their homes and hearths after they were severely beaten up. The cap-stone was placed in position with the election of Rutherford Hayes as the President who got himself elected on the plank of promised-withdrawal of federal troops from the South thereby bringing the 'Reconstruction' to an end in 1877.[14] Thus, the beginning of the

11. John Rock was the first Black to be accredited to the Supreme Court of the United States.
12. The Black representation in the Congress started again in 1928.
13. Wexler Sanford: *The Civil Rights Movement*, New York, 1993, p. 4.
14. This election compromise which snuffed out "Reconstruction" came to be known as the "Great Swap".

20th century witnessed the rise of conflict between the Negroes and the Whites. While the White majority was not willing to accept the Negro as their equal, the Blacks were not prepared for anything less than that. This was particularly true for the southern States who were determined to delay, if not completely negate, the full implementation of Negro's legal and political rights.[15] Although the Supreme Court of the United States of America had given a historic judgment in May 1954 for integration of public schools, the southern States were loath to implement the same. Racial segregation in public schools in the South continued as heretofore. The Whites in the South were against the very idea of close, intimate, personal or prolonged relationship between the two races, like school children sitting side by side in a class room, or using the same restrooms (toilets). The Negroes as a race were considered inferior in social and moral standards. For all practical purposes the Negroes were considered second-class citizens in the Southern States. But the twenty million Negroes in America were not prepared to accept second-class citizenship at any price and demanded equal protection of the laws to which they were naturally entitled under the US Constitution. The Supreme Court had accepted that "In view of the Constitution, in the eyes of the law, there is in this country no superior, dominant, ruling class of citizens. There is no caste here. Our Constitution is color-blind, and neither knows nor tolerates classes among citizens."[16]

The legal victory was significant, but it was only a paper victory. Racial and political equality was the aim of the movement. After all, three-fourths of the world's population is coloured. It therefore stands to reason that the coloured peoples — black, brown or yellow — should occupy the pride of place rather than the whites usurping the rights of the coloured. This certainly does not imply that the coloured people should dominate or humiliate the whites. Far from it; however, it does mean that the coloured people must have their rights and privileges, no less than those of the whites. The economic front was equally important. So the Negro leadership transferred their attention to these vital sectors. This took the form of boycott, 'picket-lines', 'sit-ins' (dharnas), demonstrations, 'freedom rides', etc. Even before Martin Luther King Jr. was born, the concept of non-violence as a pacifist theory to be applied in the United States had been developed by Richard Gregg, a

15. The United States Constitution which became effective in 1789 had a serious deficiency in that it did not guarantee personal liberty. A Bill of Rights was therefore added in 1791 through ten amendments passed simultaneous.

16. Dishman B. Robert: Supreme Court case. p. 404.

white Southerner and a Quaker, a lawyer by profession, who was active in the local labour movement in the 1920s. He was greatly impressed by the Gandhian movement against the British domination in India so much so that he spent four years in India studying Gandhi's methods, the principles and practice of non-violence at first hand, when the Mahatma was alive and active. Martin was greatly influenced by his book, *The Power of Non-violence,* which he re-read. He wrote extensively on the subject and helped in popularizing the Gandhian philosophy in America. As a result of his untiring efforts to establish non-violence as the principal means of attaining freedom for the Blacks, a Committee for Non-violent Revolution was founded there in 1946. This Committee opposed the expansion of armament industry as well as development of nuclear weapons, and encouraged the people to refuse to serve in the armed forces, or in the armament industries.[17] Finally, non-violent civil resistance-cum-disobedience movement was the outcome of all these efforts as described by Ostergaard in his book, *Non-violent Revolution in India*. Another book that made a significant impression on Martin's mind was *War Without Violence* by Krishnalal Shridharani, a close associate of Gandhi, who had participated in the famous Dandi Salt March.

The Indian Scene

A more or less similar situation prevailed in the Indian socio-political milieu. The Lahore-Congress met in a tense atmosphere in the Christmas week of 1929. There were about 30,000 delegates and spectators. The Frontier Province was well represented under the leadership of Abdul Ghaffar Khan. This was the first time that the Pathans were present in a Congress session in such large numbers as to stand out as if in a majority. While Gandhi had been so far opposing Nehru's demand for complete independence, in this session he himself sponsored the resolution for "*Poorna Swaraj*" — total independence. "At the stroke of midnight on December 31, 1929, the resolution was declared carried, and as 1930 ushered in, the flag of Indian independence, the Tricolor, was unfurled, to the deafening shouts of 'Inquilab Zindabad', 'Long Live Revolution'." The Pathans were ecstatic with joy. They danced their tribal dances ansd were enthusiastically joined by Jawaharlal Nehru donning a Pathan turban. This session, and its outcome, gave a big boost to the "Red Shirts" whose strength shot up to 50,000 from a mere

17. Bregg B. Richard: *The Psychology and Strategy of Gandhi's Non-violent Resistance*, Madras, 1929; *Gandhism and Socialism*, Madras, 1931; *The Power of Non-violence*, Philadelphia, 1934.

500 a few months earlier. And India observed its first 'Independence Day' on 26th January 1930, even though independence was nowhere in sight, still a couple of decades away.

The next historic event was the 'Salt March'. Thousands of people took part in the civil disobedience movement. In Bombay alone, about a million people went to the beach to defy the 'slat law'. Calcutta witnessed about 80,000 volunteers while 50,000 in Madras and 20,000 in Lahore broke the slat law. As for the Frontier, almost the entire population of Peshawar city joined in the protest. The climax of this series of protests came in Kabuli Gate Thana in Peshawar where, in April 1930, armored cars rushed into a peaceful crowd, crushed a number of persons, and shot dead many more. A rough estimate given by some witnesses put the number of those killed at two to three hundred with many more wounded. In Peshawar the demonstrations took a tragic turn when Khudai Khidmatgars (non-violent Servants of God) challenged armoured cars to protest against the arrest of their leader Khan Abdul Ghaffar Khan. One British motorcycle dispatch rider in the interval between the two armored cars was attacked and killed. Petrol was thrown over the motorcycle and one armoured car, setting them on fire. The Deputy Commissioner who had by then reached the site gave orders to open fire. Two bursts of ten rounds were fired by one gun. The crowd dispersed, but re-formed. The armoured car fired ten rounds and the British troops twentyfour rounds. A significant feature of Peshawar disturbances was a defiant refusal by the Hindu troops of two platoons of Second Battalion Royal Garhwal Rifles to fire on the Muslim demonstrators.[18] During April 1930 severe rioting broke out in Peshawar City. The Battalion was deployed in the City on the 23rd to restore law and order. During the general briefing it was impressed on all ranks that there was to be no firing, nor offensive action, except on a direct order from a British officer or to save their own lives or unless authorized by a magistrate in writing — 'A' Company reached Kabuli Gate at 11:25 a.m. 23rd April. Two platoons of the 2nd Battalion, The King's Own Yorkshire Light Infantry were also dropped at Kabuli Gate. The Garhwalis then moved over to Kacheri Gate, about a mile away, where they were in direct contact with the mob that was throwing stones, bricks and soda-water bottles, etc. The Company Commander, Captain G.A. Mc G. Ricketts, MC, was hit by a brick. The next day the whole Battalion was ordered to move to the City. Nos. 1 and 4 Platoons of 'A' Company

18. Leaving Lansdowne on 16th November 1927 for the Khyber, the 2nd Battalion moved to Landi Kotal in July 1928 and to Peshawar on 26th October 1929.

refused to embuss. Several men stated that they wanted to be discharged from service. The Commanding Officer was given orders for the whole Battalion to be disarmed, and move to Abbottabad, where a Court of Inquiry found that only the NCOs of Nos. 1 and 4 Platoons were involved but no Garhwali Officer was involved, which indeed was totally incorrect.[19] These troops were otherwise distinguished by their discipline and loyalty to the British. All of them were promptly arrested, and all NCOs were court-martialed. Their plea: "We will not shoot our unarmed brethren, because India's army is to fight India's enemies without. You may blow us from the guns, if you like. Seventeen men were sentenced — one to transportation for life, another to fifteen years imprisonment and the rest to varying terms of rigorous imprisonment. The remaining personnel of the two platoons were dismissed from service under orders of the Brigade Commander.[20]

In the ensuing confusion the people took charge of the city of Peshawar. The British had to resort to air supply and support to be able to re-establish control over the city by 4th May, the day Gandhi was arrested for contravening the Salt Tax laws. On 27th May 1930, Lieutenant Colonel C.C. Walker was replaced by Lieutenant Colonel Mainwaring, DSO, as the new Commanding Officer.[21] It was during this period, 1930-31, that the Afridi tribesmen from across the border showed an exceptional characteristic. Normally, when they used to pass through the 'Settled Districts' they used to indulge in looting the villages en-route. But now they stopped indulging in this pastime, and instead, leaving the villagers alone, they gave an ultimatum to the British administration to "Release Badshah Khan and 'Malang Baba' (the naked fakir, Gandhi); release the Khudai Khidmatgars and stop the atrocities and repression against the Pakhtuns. If you don't, we shall declare war on you." They also demanded the release of "Inquilab" thinking that it was a person in whose honour they used to shout the slogan, '*Inquilab Zindabad*'! The name "Frontier Gandhi" affectionately used by his admirers and slightingly by his adversaries would seem to derive from this period.

---

19. In those days GO was the designation for Garhwali VCOs (Viceroy's Commissioned Officers as distinct from the King's Commissioned Officers) and JCOs (Junior Commissioned Officers)..
20. Deedes B. Ralph, Lieutenant General, Sir, KCB, OBE, MC.: *Historical Record of The Royal Garhwal Rifles*, Vol. II, 1923-1947; Dehradun, 1962.
21. The British were so paranoid about law and order in the Frontier region that, in the Geneva Air Disarmament Conference, they were the only ones to have put forward a stupid proposal requesting for exemption of air-bombing for policing purposes. Naturally, it was turned down.

While confined to the Gujarat jail in the Punjab, he used to keep fast for one day a week and also observe "*maun vrat*" (vow of silence) for one day in a week.[22] However, as a result of Gandhi-Irwin Pact signed on 5th March 1931, various Congress leaders were released from prison. Badshah Khan was released from Gujarat jail on 11th March 1931 and his surprise-appearance at Peshawar was a signal for spontaneous celebration, receptions and welcoming speeches after which he left for Karachi to attend the Congress session.[23] The Khudai Khidmatgars under Badshah Khan, in their bright impressive uniforms and band, were special invitees. They were represented at the Session in such large numbers that they were allotted a separate camp in the Congress Nagar. Badshah Khan had indeed succeeded in making the Pakhtuns the friends of India and the Indians. On the other hand the Muslim League did not have any grass-roots organization in the Frontier Province. The British were in dire need of some agency to counter the social and constructive work of Khudai Khidmatgars. With that end in view, they recruited Inayatullah Mashriqi, the headmaster of the Government High School at Peshawar and helped him in founding the Khaksar movement. However, due to the great popularity of the Khudai Khidmatgars and the good work they had been doing over a period of time, the Khaksar movement did not make much headway in the Frontier Province. The crux of British policy was 'to regard the Frontier Province as the gateway of India', and they intended 'to keep the gatekeeper aloof from the rest of India'.

Destiny Casts Leaders

Like Gandhi and Nehru, Martin too was catapulted to top leadership position by the prevailing circumstances. Destiny had cast Martin to be the stalwart to lead and guide the mass movement. Significantly, between the Montgomery Bus Boycott that commenced in December 1955 in Alabama and the passage of Voting Rights Act of 1965[24], the fight for

22. Tendulkar: op. cit. pp. 74-75.
23. The national hero, Bhagat Singh, was executed just as the delegates for the Session were assembling. The atmosphere was all the more tense due to the recent communal riots which also took the life of Ganesh Shankar Vidyarthi... Incidentally, Bhagat Singh, with complicity of Azad and Rajguru, assassinated a British police officer, Saunders, on 17 December 1928 as an act of revenge against police lathi-charge in which the old venerated nationalist leader, Lajpat Rai, was fatally wounded.
24. The Southern States disenfranchised the Negroes through some insidious legal measures, e.g.; payment of a poll tax, ability to read and explain some obscure provisions of the State Constitution, *et al.* These were tests that were generally applied to blacks only.

racial equality created history for non-violent resistance to American apartheid and oppression. It is noteworthy that Montgomery Bus Boycott was not the first bus boycott as is often erroneously believed: Baton Rouge in Louisiana, Mobile in Alabama and Atlanta in Georgia had already successfully desegregated city bus seating on the basis of first-come, first-served.[25]

The Twentieth Century saw the United States successfully fight two World Wars, and at the threshold of a severe 'cold war' involving two super-powers, poised to destroy not only each other, but the entire world. On balance, the US was the stronger of the two but it was a question of mutually destructive balance of terror in which none would come out unscathed, and perhaps neither would survive. However, the US had an upper hand insofar as economic strength, industrial development and consumerism were concerned. From that point of view, there was none to challenge the Americans. They were the richest and most prosperous nation on planet earth. The beginning of the 1960's brought the standard of living of the average American to its highest level ever. It was also the highest in their own history too. Their prosperity was boundless. The variety, quality and availability of consumer goods exceeded all expectations, and further improvements were the order of the day. The market economy of the United States was the envy of the rest of the world, including the rival super power. This exceptional rise in the standard of living was not confined to whites only; it spilled over to the Negroes and American-Indians as well, albeit the Black communities, comparatively speaking, were not as well off as the whites. The rise in per capita income resulted in increased purchasing power of all the three racial groups. They spent the additional funds to provide for luxuries, comforts and conveniences. Abundance of electric power made life more comfortable, and the car-industry made it more mobile. Three-fourths of the population of the United States had at least one automobile, and many had more than one. The supermarkets and grocery stores throughout the country were overflowing with a variety of goods and food products. The people of the United States were better housed, better clothed and better fed than at any time in their history. And they were better off than the rest of the people all over the world. However, notwithstanding the high degree of prosperity, during the second half of the twentieth century the American nation faced serious domestic problems and severe internal challenges as never before in the past.

25. Fairclough Adam: *To Redeem the Soul of America; The Southern Christian Leadership Conference and Martin Luther King Jr.*; University of Georgia, Athens, 1987; p. 12.

The two World Wars, recruitment of the Blacks in the defence services at whatever level, the economic depression of the 30's, the preponderance of the automobile, etc., altered the old pattern white-black relationship, besides awakening the Negroes to the realities of racial discrimination and inequality in the eyes of the law. A large number of Negroes moved out of the plantations to the ghettoes in the urban centres, thereby ending decades of isolation. The migration was spurred by the two wars which created new jobs in the defence industries, largely in the North, but also in the Southern States too. This influx of cheap black labour gave rise to new socio-economic problems. In turn, the Whites were alarmed at the rising rate of unemployment caused by the end of the Second World War, leading to urban riots. Here the Blacks came face to face with the realities of two sets of rules: one for the Whites and the other for the Blacks. The former were the superior beings, supreme in the land they had grabbed from the American-Indians way back. The Negro was a second, if not the lowest class citizen. His inferiority complex nurtured over a couple of centuries of slavery, segregation and racial discrimination, deprivation and denial of education, *et al*, erupted on the surface of social platform. He came to realize that he too was somebody, a part of the vast panorama of American kaleidoscope. His religion came to his rescue inasmuch as his belief that God loves all His children irrespective of the colour of their skin or the texture of their hair. In the ultimate analysis what mattered was his intrinsic and eternal worth as a person before God. The Negroes were thus inspired, determined to achieve parity with their white countrymen insofar as citizenship rights were concerned. At the same time the Negroes must be honest enough to accept that their standards often lagged behind. It is altogether a different matter that they fell short of the standards primarily on account of segregation. For instance: the Negro crime rate was much higher than the rest of the population. The blame for this lay entirely at the doorsteps of the Negroes themselves. The parents should give their children love, attention and a sense of belonging so that they may adjust to urban environment and maintain high moral standards. Concurrently, the authorities perpetuating violence need to realize: "All who take the sword will perish by the sword." Be that as it may, the records show that whites seldom attacked the Blacks.

In 1901, the population of the United States was a mere seventysix millions. Large scale immigration added to the numbers, but it was the post Second World War baby boom, better health care and improved medical facilities which resulted in a population explosion so much so that by 1963 it reached an estimated 189 millions. By mid-1990s, it jumped to 265 million, the third most populous country in the world after China and India. The increased population required more homes, education, health care facilities, jobs, governance, *et al,* thereby increasing the pressure on available resources. The movement of population from rural areas to urban centres added to the complexities. While 18 per cent of Americans lived on the farms at the end of the War, by 1963 their number came down to a mere eight percent. Congestion and pollution in the urban environment were additional complications, besides the deterioration in law and order situation. The westward migration of population for more opportunities and better life was an additional complicating factor. California bore the brunt and became the nation's fastest growing State, as well as the richest. During this phase of westward migration, the population of California was reported to have increased by 1,700 persons per day. The rising cost of governance caused additional burden on local and state finances necessitating increased federal financial aid and consequent tax burden at all levels. Social security requirements skyrocketed, and so did the unemployment benefits leading to the evil of some citizens finding it more convenient to live on state charity rather than do useful work.

The Presidency of the United States is, by itself, a unique institution demanding the highest standard of personal leadership, devotion and integrity. From about the mid 1950's onwards, the Civil Rights issue was the most pressing thorny problem for the Administration. The word Negro was an anathema to the Black community of America who were not prepared to accept segregation in public places, particularly segregation in schools, and the 'second class citizenship' to which they had been reduced by the majority community. Soon they were to be called Afro-Americans and segregation in schools was abolished. The acceptance speech was the last essential pre-election item of the nomination-campaign process. On Friday, 15th July 1960 John F. Kennedy addressed eighty thousand people in Los Angeles Coliseum:[26]

> We stand today at the edge of a New Frontier — the frontier of the 1960's — a frontier of unknown opportunities and perils, a frontier of unfulfilled hopes and threats. ... The New Frontier of which I speak is not a set of promises — it is a set of challenges. It sums up not what I intend to offer the American people but what I intend to ask of them. ..."

In the election campaign Kennedy incorporated the plight of the Negroes with a tilt towards emotionalism and rational statistics. "The

26. The Associated Press: *Triumph and Tragedy*, p. 144.

Negro baby has one-half, regardless of his talents, statistically has one-half as much chance of finishing high school as the white-baby, one-third as much chance of finishing college, one-fourth as much chance of becoming a professional man or woman, four time as much chance of being out of work. ... Only a President willing to use all the resources of his office can provide the leadership, determination and the direction ... to eliminate racial and religious discrimination from American society."[27] John Kennedy also advocated more vigorous measures to win the Negro the right to vote, the right to employment, and the right to federal appointments, especially in the Foreign Service where there were only twenty six Negro officers at that point of time. In 1960 when the Cold War was at its coldest and man's achievements in outer space exceeded all expectations, the Americans elected John Fitzgerald Kennedy, a Democratic Senator from Massachusetts, as their 35th President with Senate majority leader Lyndon B. Johnson of Texas as the Vice President. Although the Negroes overwhelmingly voted[28] for Kennedy, he won against the Republican candidate Richard M. Nixon by an extremely narrow margin of one half of one per cent. In other words it was the Negro vote that placed JFK in the White House.

President Kennedy was the youngest ever to be elected to this most powerful job in the world — he was barely fortythree years old when he assumed the Presidency. Unfortunately he could serve for just two years and ten months when, on 22nd November 1963, he was shot and killed by a sniper in Dallas, Texas, while riding in an open car.[29]

The King never dies. And that holds good for the Presidency of the United States too. The American Revolution continued on course.

---

27. Schlesinger M. Arthur Jr.: op. cit. p.792.
28. Both the Gallup and Harris Polls assessed the Negro vote in favor of Kennedy to be around 68 to 70 percent.
29. Kennedy was the fourth President of the United States to be assassinated while in office; the other three were: Abraham Lincoln on Good Friday, 14th April 1865, James A. Garfield, the 20th President in 1881 and the 25th President, William McKinley in 1901.

9

Satyagraha and Ahimsa

"Ahimsa Paramo Dharmah" — Non-violence is the Greatest Religion or Duty. We can conquer our enemy without hating him. Moral force is stronger than the strongest of all the modern weaponry of our times. I must reduce myself to zero. So long as man does not of his own free will put himself as last among his fellow creatures, there is no salvation for him. Ahimsa is the farthest limit of humility.

The Black masses in the American North started imbibing the Gandhian political philosophy. The initial modus operandi to gain freedom and justice was non-cooperation. It was soon transformed into non-violence, and then the basic doctrine of Satyagraha. The latter is a means to an end, to secure the rights of the oppressed; those who are made to suffer by the authority of the State. Satyagraha believes that the authority of the State is not unlimited. The tyranny of the majority is not necessarily to be tolerated merely because it is imposed by the majority. In fact, the State invariably tends to trample on the rights and privileges of the people, the minorities in particular. According to Raghavan N. Iyer: "In essence Satyagraha emphasizes that social and political conflicts can be handled best in an atmosphere in which the contestants respect the moral worth of each other, distinguish between measures and persons, conduct their battles in a spirit of self-criticism, and abstain from the cruder forms of coercion."[1]

Satyagraha[2]

The chief legacy of M.K. Gandhi to the rest of the world has been his innovative style of conducting the struggle for Indian Independence,

1. Williams A. John: op. cit. p. 174.
2. Based on M.K. Gandhi: *Autobiography*, pp. 276, 292-93, 318, 437.

and ultimately pushing the British out of their Indian Empire without causing any bitterness in its aftermath. Gandhi believed that self-discipline, self-purification and self-control were essential prerequisites not only for his own release from the vice-like grip of the senses, "but also for the birth of Satyagraha, his distinctive creation, the idea that changed the world." Martin maintained that he had discovered a profound significance in Gandhi's central concept of Satyagraha as a way of life. No doubt, the concept of *Satyagraha*: *sat*=truth and *agraha*=firmness or force, already existed in Hindu philosophy; but not as Satyagraha but as *Sadagraha*. Since the latter Sanskrit phrase would not make much sense to the general public, Gandhi adopted the version Satyagraha. The notions of purification of the self (mind), self-sacrifice, sacrifice for truth, voluntary abnegation, self surrender in the service of the community at large, *et al*, were inherent in the basic concept of Sadagraha, now Satyagraha ... that is to say, the Force which is born of Truth and Love or Non-violence. Satyagraha is based on self-help, self sacrifice and faith in God,[3] meaning 'Firmness in Truth' or 'Truth-Force'[4]. For Gandhi, and Martin after him, Truth was perhaps the most important name of God. Satyagraha has been widely translated as the 'Truth-Force'[5]. Its most appropriate translation is 'voluntary sacrifice' rather than 'civil disobedience' or 'passive resistance' — a form of mass civil protest of non-violent type by a large section of the populace in order to check the excesses committed by the State machinery. In turn, the State bureaucracy took undue advantage of criminal terrorist activities and prevailing unrest to abrogate to itself excessive powers through legislative action, or police powers in the garb of maintenance of law and order. The net result was increase in police powers, surveillance operations, detention without trial, summary form of dispensing (in)justice, *et al*. Those who followed Gandhi's line of action were called 'satyagrahis'. Gandhian ideas of non-violent protest have imparted a new light to civil resistance in the twentieth century. In order to be a worthy person to offer sacrifice, a satyagrahi had to struggle towards self abstinence, purity of thought and action, and self restraint. It is noteworthy that Gandhi's concept of 'Satyagraha' precluded 'dharnas', meaning 'sit-ins', which together with 'kneel-ins' and 'pray-ins' formed one of the vital constituents of the Black-American scene. The latter was tantamount to causing obstruction, which Gandhi totally rejected as a political weapon. According

3. Gandhi M.K.: *Satyagraha in South Africa*; pp. 172-73, and p. 282.
4. Ashe Geoffrey: op. cit. p. 41.
5. Dennis Dalton: *Mahatma Gandhi; Non-violent Power in Action*; Columbia University Press, New York, 1993, p.8.

to Gandhi, a true satyagrahi must observe non-violence of the mind, getting rid of hate, passion and prejudice. He must seek Truth in a spirit of love. Truth and Non-violence were the cornerstones of Gandhi's philosophy of 'Satyagraha' — total renunciation of violence in word, thought and deed.[6] He believed that violence could be effective in suppressing evil for a short period, but then it would emerge with renewed vigour; only non-violence could put a definite end to evil since it transforms an opponent into an ally. "Ahimsa and Truth are so intertwined that it is practically impossible to disentangle and separate them. They are like two sides of a coin ... But Ahimsa is not the goal; Truth is the goal."[7] A satyagrahi may resort to boycotts and strikes, but must not retaliate against the government-authority; instead he must submit to the authority in total non-violence, without rancour, indeed with joy and courtesy, like a true 'soldier of non-violence'.[8] Gandhi's movement of disobedience did not imply resorting to anarchy. Gandhi's movement of Satyagraha was a success partly also due to the self-restraint exercised by the British authorities. The British reaction, more often than not, was rather civilized than would have been the case if Indian Truth-Force — Force of Truth would be more appropriate — had to face other nations like the Russians, Germans or the Japanese of that period. However, Gandhi never admitted that![9]

During his youth, Gandhi was physically exceedingly lustful. He realized that his sex-life interfered with the mission of his life. He started thinking in terms of *Brahmacharya*: — Brahmacharya means control of the senses in thought, word and deed —- which implies self control and voluntary denial of sex, self-abnegation in its purest form. He started experimenting brahmacharya in 1901 but did not feel strong enough to take the plunge through formal vows. He did so, after all, in 1906. He was a transformed man thereafter. Since his wife Kasturba had suffered enough through the excesses of his lust, she readily agreed to her husband taking the vows of brahmacharya. She became his most devoted friend and helper. The quarrels and disturbances of the past between

6. Morgan Kenneth: *The Religion of the Hindus*, New York. Ronald Press, 1953; pp. 31-32.
7. Gandhi M.K.: *From Yervada Mandir — Ashram Observances*, 1935, Ahmedabad; p. 13.
8. Ashe Geoffrey: op. cit. pp. 100-101
9. Gandhi may not agree: But, having lived through that period and taken a very limited part in the freedom movement to the extent possible for a 12-16 years old youngster, I have no doubt about the veracity of that statement — The Author.

husband and wife which were primarily due to Gandhi's extreme lust now faded away. He came to the realization that this self-purification was essential not only for his own release but also for the birth of Satyagraha.

The essential ingredients of Satyagraha are:

- Sacrifice for Truth;
- Voluntary abnegation;
- Self-surrender in the service of the community;
- Challenge to unrighteous law;
- Unjust application of law(s);
- Ahimsa as the basic guiding principle of life;
- Non-violent struggle to achieve the collective mission;
- Fasting as a form of penance, prayer, self-discipline, self purification.

At the end of the Boer War in South Africa, Gandhi again returned to India. He was loaded with expensive gifts during the various farewells to which he vehemently objected. Much against his wife's wishes, he put the valuables in a bank as a trust to support public works for the welfare of Indians. The Natal Indian Congress also made him pledge that he would return to them if they needed him again, which of course he did. While in India Gandhi wished to attend the session of Indian National Congress at Calcutta. The Indian National Congress had been founded by Allen Octavian Hume who remained its secretary until 1907. The then Viceroy, Lord Dufferin wished to strengthen the Congress by making it more Indian and let the Indians preside over it. In view of universal illiteracy, the organization primarily catered to the middle class Indian intelligentsia.

When Gandhi had to go to Bombay he decided to experience rail travel by third class. He found it incredibly filthy, unsanitary and overcrowded. By now he had switched over to Indian clothing, the shirt and dhoti. While en-route to Bombay, he stopped at Benares. The famous sacrosanct pilgrimage centre was filthy beyond description. The dirt and money grabbing by the agents of God Almighty around the famous Kashi Vishvanath Temple was nauseating to Gandhi. The narrow dirty lanes with all their rubbish disgusted him. Indeed, Benares repelled him.

Satyagraha in South Africa

General Smuts was determined to eradicate what he called as the 'Asiatic Cancer' while Botha, the other prominent Boer soldier-politician, proposed to "drive the coolies[10] out of the country within four years". The agitation against the 'Black Law' was perhaps the first Satyagraha. The actual date of beginning of Satyagraha as a movement to achieve a common aim may therefore be taken as 11th September 1906, the fateful year of Gandhi's final renunciation. The phrase and the idea originated in South Africa whence it grew into a gigantic movement to shake the very foundations of the British Empire. The passage and implementation of Asiatic Act which enjoined all Indians, amongst other brown or yellow foreigners, to compulsorily register, get finger-printed, and carry the registration certificate on their person at all times, made the Indian community furious over this badge of inferiority. They defied this obnoxious law by mass burning of the certificates, which by itself was an offence. Gandhi was arrested again on 10th October 1908.[11] This was Gandhi's second prison sentence. He continued his Satyagraha movement resulting in his third prison term for three months commencing on 25 February 1909.[12] While in prison, he cooked food for about seventy-five Indian prisoners and frequently volunteered for 'latrine duty'. Soon after completing his third jail term, Gandhi went to London where he stayed from July to November 1909. During this period he kept up the tempo for removal of disabilities and indignities which the Indians had to suffer. Both Smuts and Botha had gone to London in connection with formation of the Union of South Africa. Gandhi was able to persuade a number of influential Englishmen to make General Smuts agree, albeit reluctantly, to repeal the objectionable Asiatic Act, besides permitting immigration of some specially selected Indians to Transvaal. Both the Boer generals agreed to this simple arrangement. Meanwhile, the Supreme Court in the Cape Colony decreed that only Christian marriages would be valid in South Africa. In other words, all Indian wives were reduced to the status of concubines, and their children as bastards. This was a cruel blow to the Indian community. The time for large scale Satyagraha had arrived.

---

10. In those days, Indians in South Africa were called 'coolies'.
11. In 1907 Gandhi discovered the American essay on Civil Disobedience by Henry Thoreau. That was act of defiance by a single individual — Satyagraha on a much smaller scale — when he had refused to pay his taxes as a protest against the institution of slavery and the Mexican War — Ashe: op. cit. p. 117.
12. Gandhi's first jail-term was for two months in January 1908.

The new marriage laws aroused the women no end; they were all out to fight for justice. A group of women crossed from the Transvaal to Natal without permission, while another group did the same in the other direction, again without permission. Then they proceeded to the coal mines at Newcastle and instigated the indentured Indian labour to strike work. About five thousand coal miners struck work. Now the Transvaal police arrested the women-group from Natal. They were tried, convicted and all of them were sentenced to three months imprisonment. Gandhi himself went over to Newcastle where he found that the coal-miners were determined to continue the strike. He took care to see that the striking miners were properly housed in clean hygienic camp conditions. 'Hygiene and Sanitation' were always the first priority in his arrangements. The strike was totally nonviolent. Gandhi was arrested. So were thousands others. The strike movement spread. More than fifty thousand indentured Indian laborers had walked off their jobs bringing the entire industrial set-up to a halt.[13] The coal-miners were taken to the mines under escort, flogged and starved; but they refused to work. The jails were filled with Indians. Lord Hardinge, the Viceroy of India, demanded a commission of enquiry. London agreed. Generals Smuts and Botha were in a tight situation. They released Gandhi on 18 December 1913. But this was not what Gandhi wanted. He threatened to court arrest again. Smuts invited Gandhi to Pretoria for talks. The negotiations were painfully long and frustrating. An agreement was finally reached on 30 June 1914 and legalized through Indian Relief Bill, which was passed by the Union Parliament and became law in July 1914. Indian women were no longer concubines, and their children were no longer bastards!

Satyagraha as a non-violent weapon had proved its worth. It was indeed a novel idea in the techniques of human struggle to safeguard human rights, and to obtain justice. The 'Indian Relief Bill' brought to end Gandhi's work in South Africa. On 18th July 1914 he along with his wife and friend Mr. Kallenbach sailed for England.

Weapons of Peace

The concept of Satyagraha was a weapon of peaceful non-violent agitation to claim justice and establish human rights. Fasting was an important part of his personal armoury. His capacity to undergo the rigours of fasting was indeed phenomenal. He had imbibed this trait from his saintly mother who never missed rigorous observance of

13. Gandhi M.K.: *Autobiography*, op. cit. pp. 367-69.

Chaturmas and *Chandrayan*[14]. Paradoxically, loyalty to the opponent occupied a high pedestal in his concept of Satyagraha, in that the opposite party must know in advance your intentions and intended course of action. "We see in him a man of no possessions or appetites, a true *sannyasin*, and yet from the depths of his renunciation he dictates to empires and models the course of history." He had achieved all this, and a lot more, at age forty-five. And that was true of Dr. Martin Luther King's political career too — he had become a national leader and achieved world fame by the time he was barely thirty.

The opening shots of the First World War were fired on 4th August 1914[15] when the British declared war on Germany, just two days before Gandhi and party landed in England. A couple of months later when Germany defeated France, Subhash Chandra Bose talked to him for the last time suggesting a militant revolution. But Gandhi's response was: "We do not seek our independence out of Britain's ruin". Meanwhile, the attempted revolution in Ireland and the actual revolution in Russia ignited the flames of self-government amongst Indians too. In order to curb the same, the British Government in India enacted obnoxious legislation, the Rowlatt Acts, in February 1919. By then the First World War had ended. The prices of essential commodities had sky-rocketed. Unchecked profiteering made life all the more miserable. Extortion of taxes, forced loans, *et al*, added to the burdens of the populace, bringing in its wake the world-influenza and a pneumonia epidemic exclusive to India resulting in nearly thirteen million deaths comparable to the battle losses of all Europe put together.[16] In desperation, the mill workers of Bombay resorted to mass strike in December 1918. The strike spread involving more than 125,000 workers. The Rowlatt Bills added oil to the fire. The stage had reached when Satyagraha was inevitable. A Satyagraha Sabha (means chapter) was formed in Bombay with Gandhi as the president.

---

14. Chaturmas was a period of four months of fasting and semi-fasting, a sort of long *Lent*. Chandrayana was a sort of fast in which the daily intake of food was increased or decreased as the moon waxes and wanes. Gandhi undertook his first fast in India in 1917 in Ahmedabad in connection with certain grievances of mill workers of the textile town.

15. The War started on 28th July 1914 when Austria declared War on Serbia. Thereafter, Germany declared War on Russia on 1st August, against France on 3rd August and on Belgium the next day. Various countries of Europe, American continent and Eurasia kept up the momentum of War Declarations, the last one being by Honduras against Germany on 19th July 1918 — Stearns N. Peters: op. cit. p. 650.

16. Ashe Geoffrey: op. cit. p. 184-85.

Hartal — complete cessation of work in the entire country bringing every thing to total stoppage — was Gandhi's weapon to fight the British through non-violent means. It was a notch ahead of 'civil disobedience' and perhaps a couple of more places ahead of non-cooperation. Hartal as the means to achieve the goal was first tried by Gandhi against the Rowlatt Acts, which were placed on the statute book on 21 March 1919. Gandhi called this "a farce of legal formality". The people at large distilled the essence of the obnoxious legislation as "*Na vakil, na appeal, na dalil*" (No Lawyer, no appeal, no argument). As a protest against this draconian legislation, the day for the first All India Hartal was fixed: 6th April. The Hartal was Gandhi's first political act against the British Government of India. From now onwards, Gandhi became a political force in India. Hartal means a day off from work, a day of abstention from economic activity. It is not a holiday *per se*. It was a day of fasting and prayer, and not an unearned holiday. "The concupiscence of the mind cannot be rooted out except by intense self-examination, surrender to God and lastly, grace." It is a curious coincidence of history that the American Revolution also began in much the same way — the "day of fasting and prayer" which Thomas Jefferson and his friends proclaimed for Virginia on 1st June 1774.[17] The British were completely bewildered by this total cessation of all work all over the country. Copies of the proscribed book *Hind Swaraj* by Gandhi and his translation of Ruskin's *Unto This Last* were distributed.

The All India *Hartal* (Strike) led to large scale rioting and violence. The news of Gandhi's alleged arrest inspired a wave of arson, sabotage and hooliganism. The rioters were obstructing traffic, throwing stones and assaulting Englishmen. As penance for the evil acts of his disciples, Gandhi undertook a fast for three days. Meanwhile, he was forbidden to enter Punjab. This only aggravated the situation in Amritsar. The marching-crowd murdered several English bankers and assaulted Miss Sherwood, a schoolmistress. Stray cases of arson and terrorism occurred all over Punjab. Brigadier-General Dyer decided to 'teach a lesson to Indians'. Result: the infamous Jallianwala Bagh massacre in which the army fired on a peaceful gathering inflicting over 1500 casualties including 379 dead. Prisoners and women were tortured. "Peasants were bombed from the air." Tagore wrote to Lord Chelmsford to renounce his knighthood. On 1st August 1920 the Nationalist Congress launched the Non-Cooperation Movement. The same day, Gandhi returned his Kaiser-i-Hind Medal to the Viceroy. Among numerous other measures adopted

---

17. Sheean Vincent: *Mahatma Gandhi*; New Delhi, 1954, p.98.

under Gandhi's guidance to further the non-cooperation movement, abolition of salt tax was the 'weirdest and most brilliant challenge of modern times'.

Concurrently, the Sikhs of Punjab launched a Gandhian style nonviolent Satyagraha to take charge of administration of their gurudwaras (Sikh Temples). Despite the Sikhs being from a highly martial class like the Pathans of North West Frontier Province, they observed the rule of non-violence to a remarkable degree.[18] Thus Satyagraha was not confined to political resistance only; it started spreading its tentacles in the socio-economic and religious fields as well, besides providing the so called Untouchables with a broom to sweep clean the stigma of untouchability.

Fasting was yet another weapon in Gandhi's armoury. According to Gandhi, 'fasting was supposed to prod the consciences of friends, not to coerce opponents. ... It was an appeal to the Highest Tribunal' — prodding the conscience of the Almighty. Totally unconvincing indeed!

Another weapon in the arsenal of non-violent Satyagraha was the 'No Rent Campaign'. It had its beginning in the United Provinces and Jawaharlal Nehru was the force behind this innovative protest. Dr. Martin Luther King Jr. made excellent use of this non-violent economic weapon in Chicago and other North American slums.

Satyagraha had taken roots in India. Soon Gandhi and his Ashrams in India turned into pilgrimage centers for Black American leaders to learn the fine points of Gandhian technique of non-violent mass movement to obtain justice and equal rights. It was a one way traffic that led to moral resurgence amongst the oppressed Black minority of America to fight for equal rights and desegregation in all spheres of life giving birth to the 'Civil Rights' movement. India achieved independence. The Negroes of America became Afro-Americans enjoying full freedom and end of oppression by the white majority. A number of countries in Asia and Africa broke the shackles of foreign rule. The world-map was redrawn during the ensuing couple of decades — all this, and a lot more — all through the power of Satyagraha, a potent non-violent socio-political weapon.

Ahimsa

The concept of Ahimsa, of doing no harm to any living being, of self-suffering, is as ancient as Hinduism and Buddhism. It was the principal tenet of Jain religion that originated in India in the sixth century B.C. and

18. Mohinder Singh: *The Akali Movement*, Delhi, 1978, p. 52.

was widely accepted as a way of life in Gandhi's home state of Gujarat. His mother was particularly committed to Jainism. But that ancient ideology was primarily negative in its application. What Gandhi preached as Ahimsa was a positive force, an aggressive political weapon to free India from foreign domination without resorting to armed conflict or bloody revolution. Strict moral discipline of Ahimsa which Gandhi called "the highest religion" of ancient India was the basis of Gandhi's Satyagraha. When some person was admitted in Gandhi's Ashram one of the vows he had to take was *Ahimsa*, *Satya* and *Brahmacharya* — Truth, Nonviolence and self control over sex. Brahmacharya had become the hall mark of his personal character. Throwing bricks to break shop windows and heads, such violence 'stinks in my nostrils'. His 'sovereign remedy' was *'Ahimsa'*= non-retaliation. He was not after "fusion on the American model but synthesis, a co-existence of cultures. It should be a co-existence of classes and races also. Society should flourish without conflict or oppression, rooted in *Ahimsa*."[19] Ahimsa is synonymous with non-violence. It is a synthesis of various traditional philosophies of what is so eloquently expressed in Mahabharata as "*Ahimsa Paramo Dharmah*" — nonviolence is the greatest religion or duty. And this aphorism was well known in every village in India, notwithstanding the prevalent illiteracy, particularly so in the household environment of Mohandas where Jainism had a strong presence.[20]

Jainism is a religious sect, an offshoot of Hinduism. To give expression to his social and political philosophy, Gandhi took recourse to Jain vocabulary, at least partly — *ahimsa* and *Satyagraha*. They followed the rules of Ahimsa most rigorously inasmuch as they would go out of their way not to cause any harm even to an insignificant insect. No doubt Gandhi was influenced by the Jains in his belief in Ahimsa. But it must be appreciated that Gandhi's concept of ahimsa was very much different from that of the Jain community. And it was that concept that got exported to the United States to be rigorously followed as a religious precept by the Black people under the leadership of Dr. Martin Luther King, Jr. Gandhi's, and thereby Dr. King's non-violence, was rooted in "altruism and compassion towards human beings", as opposed to that of the Jain *Baniya* community who were scrupulous about not causing any harm even to an insect, but had no qualms whatsoever about mal-

---

19. Ashe Geoffrey: op. cit. p. 221.

20. Jain servant in the family, Rajchandbhai, was primarily responsible for Jain influence on Gandhi right from his early childhood. The former's purity of character and desire for self-realization deeply impressed Mohandas — *Encyclopedia of Religion*; Macmillan, New York, 1987; p. 482.

treating their fellow human beings in matters of money and business. This type of non-violence did not find a place in the thoughts and practices of Gandhi, "Frontier Gandhi" and later the "American Gandhi"; one could perhaps include Dr. Nelson Mandela too in this august company, albeit to a limited extent only since Mandela, as he explained at his Rivonia trial: "At the beginning of June 1961, after long and anxious assessment of the South African situation ... it would be wrong and unrealistic for African leaders to continue preaching peace and non-violence at a time when the Government met our peaceful demands with force ...". It will thus be seen that while Dr. King was steadfast in his belief and practice of non-violence, the South African struggle took recourse to armed resistance when the African National Congress formed "Umkhonto we Sizwe (MK)' as a military wing of the ANC for violent political struggle. Mandela went the way of Malcolm X!

A Marwari proverb vividly describes the above facet of Jain character: "Oh Baniya! Nobody knows your doings. Although you do not drink water without straining and sifting it, you sap the blood of your clients without reserve."[21] The general thrust of Gandhi's injunction was that Ahimsa involved qualities of respect and sympathy for the opponent, freedom from anger, and a desire for peace. *Daya* was the crux of his concept of *Ahimsa* — pity, compassion, commiseration, mercy, clemency, sympathy, tenderness.[22] These qualities were the foundation stone of Gandhi's exposition of *Ahimsa*. In fairness to Gandhi and his respect for other religions, it should be noted that Gandhi's von-violence was influenced, albeit to a limited extent, by Jesus and other Christian traditions. However, non-violence certainly did not embrace cowardice. It was not a weapon of the weak. Gandhi also appreciated that non-violence could not be practiced under *all* circumstances; people had to resort to violence under exceptional circumstances like those imposed by totalitarian regimes. In those days Nazi Germany was a glaring example of such an exceptional circumstance, even though the Nazi officers admitted that they had found it much harder to deal with non-violent civilian resistance than the guerrilla warfare.[23]

---

21. The Marwari original goes something like this: "*Baniya thari bań koi ar jane nahin. Pani piye chhan lohi unchhalneopiye.*" — as quoted by David Hardiman in *GANDHI*, p. 58, from Report on the Census of 1891, Vol. II, *The Castes of Marwar*, Marwar State, Jodhpur 1894, p. 130.
22. Hardiman David: op. cit. p. 58.
23. Randle Michael: *Civil Resistance*; London, 1994, pp.122-123 and 169.

10

Militant Nonviolent Mass-Movement

Non-violence is the greatest force at the disposal of mankind. It is mightier than the mightiest weapon of destruction devised by the ingenuity of man. It is not an expedient of a moment; ultimately it is a way of life that men live by because of the sheer morality of its claim. It does not seek to defeat or humiliate an opponent, but to win his friendship and understanding. From my background, I gained my regulating Christian ideals. From Gandhi, I learned my operational technique.

The fundamental principle of Martin King's mass-movement was militant non-violence. Martin was conscious of the obvious contradiction in 'militant non-violence'. The two are more or less self-contradictory. Some of his critics have called it "The Violence of Non-violence" while others felt that King's non-violence had the 'essence of violence' since it 'provoked violence'. Again, while the Whites were pleased with Martin's policy of non-violence, there was an obvious incongruity in their approach to domestic and foreign issues. On the one hand, the Whites desired non-violence in their dealings with the Blacks and other non-white — one way non-violence only, since the Whites retained the option to use violence against the Blacks, Yellows and Browns — on the other they were fighting a full scale war in South-East Asia. In any case the white people had been making full use of white ethnic power from the day they landed on the shores of the 'New World'; but they called it immoral if the Blacks, the aborigines used their ethnic power in retaliation. This was the crux of white morality since the ages. "Heads I win; tails you lose"! Martin King was a man of morality, more or less pristine, and he spoke against the white morality. He was rather mild in his chastisement in the initial stages, but later came out strongly against this one way morality. Martin's views on the subject were moulded, at least partially, by Bayard Rustin. The latter generally remained in the background but still had a subtle influence on King's ideas regarding morality of violence and war. Rustin was a Quaker and believed: "... the law of violence is such that each side becomes equally vicious. To try to distinguish between which is more vicious is to fail to recognize the logic of war. It is war that is evil, not the Viet Cong, not the United States."[1]

Non-violence is a way of humility and self-restraint. It is a quality not of the body, but for the soul. "I shall not retaliate or take revenge; and I shall forgive anyone who indulges in oppression and excesses against me." Its three ingredients — militant, non-violent and mass movement — were inseparable one from the other. While all three had their respective places in the struggle, non-violence was the absolute imperative. If the movement is devoid of non-violence, the militant shall engulf the entire community in bloodshed. The fears of the white community could be neutralized only through non-violence. And those fears were real in as much as the Whites, having treated the Blacks with brutality and injustice, were afraid that should the Blacks attain power, they would resort to revenge for years of injustices done to them, and seek retribution. Dr. King was, therefore, particularly anxious to ensure that the mass movement remained totally non-violent. Dr. King wished to assure the Whites that the Negro understands and was ready to forgive and forget the past; all he sought was justice for his Black brethren as well as for the white man.

The Negro, or any oppressed community for that matter, had three options, the first was acquiescence — to resign oneself to one's fate, good, bad or indifferent. This was obviously unacceptable besides being cowardly and immoral, although this was the easiest way out. Resistance would lead to retaliation by the white man thereby adding to the suffering of the Negro families. Dr. King would not accept the *status quo* which meant continuation of second-class citizenship.

The second course open to the Negro was to resort to physical violence to free him from the chains of slavery and injustice. This required equal or superior physical force. Since the Negro could possibly never match the physical and military strength of the white man, this was not a practical proposition, besides involving lot of bloodshed. Moreover, violence cannot possibly bring lasting peace. 'An eye for an eye' approach would leave everybody blind! After all, violence is basically self-defeating. Under the circumstances, violence was not only impractical but it was

1. Williams A. John: op. cit. p. 101.

also immoral. In fact, as Gandhi perceived it: nonviolent struggle demanded greater courage than a violent one.

The above left non-violent resistance as the only practical option for an oppressed community to get justice. However, non-violence certainly does not imply fear-complex, and this ideology is not for the coward. Only the strong and the brave can withstand the attendant adversities that are the inherent consequences of non-violent methodology. The principle of non-violent resistance seeks to reconcile the truths of two mutually contradictory notions — acquiescence and violence — while bypassing the extremes and immoralities of both. "The non-violent resister agrees with the person who acquiesces that one should not be physically aggressive toward his opponent; but he balances the equation by agreeing with the person of violence that evil must be resisted. He avoids the non-resistance of the former and the violent resistance of the latter. With nonviolent resistance no person or group need to submit to any wrong, nor any one need to resort to violence in order to right a wrong." Dr. King strongly believed that through "non-violent resistance the Negro would be able to rise to the noble height of opposing the unjust system while loving the perpetrators of the system". If the Negro followed the path of non-violent resistance, there would accrue an added advantage in that he would be able to continue to live in the South and also continue to struggle for his rights. His problems cannot possibly be solved by running away, or migrating to the North; by following the path of non-violence he would also earn the goodwill and sympathy of other persons who believe in justice and equality. The point at issue is not merely racial in character, nor it is a struggle between two communities or sets of people; it is the question of justice against injustice, and the tension arising from the clash thereof. Since any advantage gained by the Black minority was likely to generate a fear complex amongst the white majority, leading to white-backlash, that was all the more reason to avoid violence and consequent bloodshed. In fact, a number of white men in the South were so conscious of the injustices inflicted by them on the Negroes that they were afraid of severe black-backlash. The genius of 'Frontier Gandhi' was amazing in as much as he managed to transform a war-like tribe, the Pathans, having a strong tradition of blood-feuds and violence into a disciplined non-violent freedom-fighters. That is why Gandhi used to say: "Nonviolence is always for the brave and not for the weak."

A comparative study of the Negroes' struggle for freedom in the two continents, oceans apart, brings out some interesting similarities and contradictions. The two Movements were not only oceans apart, they were also generations apart. While Martin was born January 15, 1929, at 501 Auburn Avenue in the city of Atlanta in the United States, Nelson was borne on 18th July 1918 at Qunu, a remote village near Umtata in the Transkei region of South Africa. However, both families were reasonably well off middle class type, each in its own way. Mandela joined the African National Congress in 1942 and transformed the organization into a veritable mass movement. At that point of time, Martin's movement was in barely embryonic stage. Both Movements had Gandhian philosophy of non-violent Satyagraha for their initial start. While the Mass Movement in the Southern States of the United States was in its early stages of development, the Blacks of South Africa, when they found that constitutional means and polite petitioning were of no avail, in early 1950's they took the plunge to an armed militant struggle. Thus, the African National Congress came to have a military wing of which Mandela was the Volunteer-in-Chief. In 1962 Nelson Mandela went to Algeria for military training, and also arranged for the 'MK' cadres to be trained in Algeria for active military style campaign against the white regime. On the other hand, Martin prescribed "militant" nonviolent mass movement as a panacea for emancipation of the Negroes. He did not deviate from the path of non-violence and continued to follow the Gandhian technique. But how does militancy fit in with non-violence?

Non-violence in itself is a powerful weapon within the bounds of discipline. It did not seek revenge. Non-violence touches men where the law cannot. The law can order desegregation of the public schools system but it cannot mitigate the hatred and irrationality surrounding the system; only nonviolence can overcome the ill effects of implementation of unpopular laws. Till the middle of the 20th century "the Blacks were far behind the Whites in jobs, income, housing, education and health."[2] In 1954 the Supreme Court reversed its 1896 "separate but (normally) equal" doctrine, and ordered the desegregation of public schools. It was accepted that 'separate educational facilities are inherently unequal'. The Little Rock High School in Arkansas assumed menacing proportions of a test case in which nine children of Little Rock[3], and their counterparts in Nashville, Clinton and Sturges stood their ground with dignity and courage, notwithstanding the suffering involved. Unfortunately, President Eisenhower refused to 'lend his

2. Charles Sellers *et al*: op. cit. p. 407.
3. Little Rock, Arkansas, had a population of 105,000 of which 82,000 were white and 25,000 were black.

considerable moral authority to the crusade against racism'. It was a mere repetition of the Proclamation of Emancipation: the announcements had been made but implementation was sadly lacking. However, in 1957 when the Arkansas Governor, Orval Fanbus attempted to obstruct court-ordered desegregation by calling out the state national guard to prevent black children from entering the Central High School, the President ordered one thousand troops from the 101st Airborne Division to enforce the decree, and also federalized the 10,000 members of the Arkansas National Guard. By 5:00 a.m. September 24, 1957, the paratroopers had ringed the school with 'fixed bayonets'. They provided protection to the black children for the next two months after which the federalized National Guard continued to do so for the rest of the year.

Although the President signed the Civil Rights Acts of 1957[4] and 1960, Eisenhower provided little moral or executive support. These were essentially the result of the strategy of the NAACP. The school desegregation and the Montgomery boycott leading to the "Brown decision" provoked fierce opposition in the South. In this context non-violence is the ultimate weapon to persuade those who would refuse to accept the law they do not like to obey. Just laws can be implemented only through non-violent persuasion by appealing to the conscience of the public at large so that they start accepting the Negro as a partner in nation building, and not as a hostile intruder. Disobeying the unjust laws is not a crime; on the contrary it is the sacred duty of the oppressed people not to submit to unjust practices. Dr. King told his people that they should do so peacefully, cheerfully and openly. "We adopt the means of non-violence because our end is a community at peace with itself. We will try to persuade through our words; but if our words fail, we would try to persuade through our actions." Dialogue and fair compromise are the essence of non-violent movement. So is willingness to suffer and to sacrifice for the cause. The non-violent resisters were prepared to go to jail for their fair cause. They were ready to fill the jail houses of the Southern States, and even face death if it came to that. Around the same time, black-violence had taken a wild turn in Congo, which ran a chill through the American white spine. The Americans were therefore lucky that they had a man like Martin Luther King, a follower of Gandhian philosophy of non-violence, at the helm of Black affairs in the U.S.

Lest it might be construed that all Negroes were positively inclined to struggle for justice and equal rights, it needs to be emphatically stated

4. The Civil Rights Act of 1957 was the first Congressional enactment on civil rights for eighty-seven years, since the 19th century.

that there was an up and coming middle-class amongst the Negroes too, struggling for status and prestige. In fact, Martin himself came from a middle class well to do family. The point is that there were a large number of Blacks who were not prepared to sacrifice their comfortable way of life, and the road to further prosperity, for the cause of justice, racial equality and civil rights. Again, it would be wrong to label them as black sheep; after all, personal interests do play a significant role in social and political matters. Come to think of it, even Mahatma Gandhi had barely one hundred persons absolutely committed to his philosophy of non-violence; even some of his close colleagues had sharp differences with him on the subject. Gandhi himself admitted to this deficiency. It is a different matter altogether that Gandhi succeeded beyond all expectations through the support of such a small number of devoted workers. However, the Indian masses were with him even though most of them did not understand the implications of his non-violent techniques, and all that it involved. Above all, the Indian struggle was against the British who were essentially liberal minded notwithstanding certain glaring exceptions, and not against the Nazis or the Japanese of the 1930-40's.

Racial Harmony

The Rev. Martin Luther King Jr. was an eloquent Black Baptist Minister. He preached non-violence *ad infinitum*, but his non-violent movements often led to violence, albeit more often than not, from the opposite side by the whites. He himself had been stabbed in the chest, and physically assaulted three more times. His home had been bombed three times, and he was sent to jail fourteen times — the latter was considered an honor, something to be proud of. From mid 1950s to his assassination in April 1968, he led the first mass civil rights movement in US history. He rigorously followed the teachings of Gandhi and applied the principles of non-violent resistance patterned after Mahatma Gandhi. His primary objective was struggle for racial equality in the U.S. The immediate outcome of the bus-boycott movement was abandonment of segregation in seating arrangement in public transport, wherever it was in force. He wrote: "If the Negro is to achieve the goal of integration, he must organize himself into a militant non-violent mass-movement. ... The movement must have a mass base and a militant character to overcome the barriers to equality and justice. ..." His emphasis was on non-violence as the principal consideration in the conduct of the movement so that, in the final analysis, the two races could live together in the same community in complete harmony, without fear of each other, or resentment by one against the other. His aim was to 'break down the legal barriers' which kept the two races physically apart. He wanted to achieve genuine integration of American society leading to 'inter-group and inter-personal' living. Dr. King was convinced that "The problem is not purely a racial one, with Negroes set against the whites. In the end, it is not a struggle between the people at all, but a tension between justice and injustice."

"In appealing for justice, Dr King and the other Negro leaders have shown a shrewd understanding of the national character."[5] They seek democracy and not the substitution of one tyranny for another. God is not interested in the colour of skin; He is for all humanity, to be free and to have equal rights. But the Negroes were too slow to participate in the democratic practices even though they had the legal rights to do so. Many Negroes did not exercise their voting privileges. It was tantamount to political and moral suicide. But the Negroes alone were not to blame for this lapse. "The advocacy of free elections in Europe by American officials is hypocrisy when free elections are not held in great sections of America."[6] President Kennedy never had any illusions about the political advantages — if at all any — of 'equal rights'. But it was the ominous tendencies amongst the Negroes — like throwing eggs on Dr. Martin Luther King Jr. in Harlem, booing of Mayor Richard Daley and even of James Meredith — that worried the President. However, the signs of awakening of the conscience of white middle class were certainly heartening. In a meeting with the Black leaders in the Cabinet Room, the President seemed to prefer to shift from the streets to the courts. A. Philip Randolph, speaking in his usual dignified manner, pointed out that the Negroes were already in the streets, and it would be virtually impossible to get them back at that point of time. Therefore, "is it not better that they be led by organizations dedicated to civil rights and disciplined by struggle rather than to leave them to other leaders who care neither about civil rights nor about nonviolence? If the civil rights leadership were to call the Negroes off the streets, it is problematic if they would come."[7]

Harlem was indeed in the throes of a crisis. The malady was deep-rooted. The so-called 'New Deal' reforms had not made any impression in that sprawling ghetto. 350,000 people cramped in there at the rate of 233 per acre. And Manhattan? 133 per acre. The population of Harlem had multiplied six times in twenty-five years due to Negroes'

5. Dishman: op. cit p. 404.
6. Ibid. p. 431.
7. Schlen: op. cit. pp. 824-25.

from the South migrating to urban North to escape the police and white brutalities. There were ten thousand families in rat-infested cellars. In 1932 the fatality rate in the black Harlem Hospital was twice as high as in the white Bellevue Hospital. Most women worked as domestics. And to find work, these females used to gather at street corners which came to be known as 'slave markets'. The conditions were just ripe for spread of prostitution as the standard profession, the only means of getting a job and some money for the family. Like poor living conditions, medicare was equally bad. So was the crime rate. Poverty and crime keep pace together; so they did in Harlem. In 1935 it exploded. On March 19, ten thousand Blacks swept through the streets destroying white property. Seven hundred policemen had to be deployed to restore a semblance of order. Two Blacks were killed in the process.

Amongst the numerous complications faced by President Kennedy in tackling the racial problems, the tussle for leadership within the black organizations themselves was an unnecessary additional complicating factor. For instance: When the June 22 meeting with the Black leaders in the Cabinet Room broke up, Dr. Martin Luther King Jr. gave newspapermen the impression that the President had asked the Group to call off demonstrations and that he had boldly refused. In the light of the foregoing, this was obviously misconstruing the course of discussions. No doubt, this posture was calculated to improve his standing among Negroes at the cost of other black leaders.

The average American is not a cynic. In the opinion of Gunnar Myrdal: "He is on the average more of a believer and defender of the faith in humanity than the rest of the Occidentals.[8] It is a relatively important matter to him to be true to his own ideals and to carry them out in actual life." He believes in explicit statement made in the American Declaration of Independence that 'all men are created equal'. To enunciate a principle, or believe in a principle is altogether a different matter; what matters is putting the same in practice in daily life. Unfortunately, the white America merely believed in that lofty ideal but was reluctant to put that into practice insofar as the Black population was concerned, or the American Indians for that matter. Both Mahatma Gandhi and the 'Frontier Gandhi' led simple ascetic life. They practised service before self and followed a non-compromising attitude towards the principles of socio-political emancipation of India, irrespective of caste, color or creed — true reflection of the principle that "All Men are

---

8. His comparison of American character with that of Occidentals is without any basis or rationale. However, this argument is not relevant to this work.

Created Equal". That is precisely what the Negro leaders like Rev. Dr. Luther King Jr. were fighting for. Nevertheless, fighting for freedom and equal rights by Blacks alone was not likely to yield the desired results in the face of fierce and powerful resistance by the Southern Whites. Gunnar Myrdal put forth this point of view "with such overwhelming intellectual authority, philosophical imagination, and analytical skill as a Swedish scholar who had so immersed himself in the American racial dilemma as to become a citizen in thought if not in law."[9] In a similar forthright manner, Gunnar cut down to size the rural socio-economic ideas of Jayaprakash Narain and Ram Manohar Lohia as archaic, outmoded and stagnant.

The Supreme Court had already declared segregation of bus-terminals as illegal. So James Farmer and other CORE leaders decided in early May 1961 to put the 'movement on wheels'. Thirteen activists, half white and half black, boarded two Greyhound buses in Washington D.C. to traverse every Deep South state ending the 'freedom ride' in New Orleans. They managed to get to Rock Hill, South Carolina where SNCC organizer John Lewis and Albert Bigelow, a white former navy commander, were set upon by white toughs as they entered the waiting rooms. However, they managed to get back into the buses and carried on. Their intention was to refuse bail and stay in jail so as to attract the nation's attention. They drove through Georgia and entered Alabama. Here in Anniston a white mob armed with iron bars attacked one of the buses, smashed windows, slashed tyres, and forced the bus to stop outside the town where a firebomb turned the bus into a blazing inferno. There was blood and smell of burning flesh all over the place. Needless to say: the local police remained mere spectators. No arrests or attempt to restrain the holocaust was made. Meanwhile, a second bus was fetched in. As the brave thirteen got into the bus, the white-toughs made the Blacks and White riders sit separately. Thus the 'Ride' continued to Birmingham where a bigger and more vicious mob awaited. As the riders entered the white waiting rooms, everyone of them was severely beaten up so much so that all one could see was blood, and more blood, all over the place. Several FBI men took pictures of the beatings but no arrests were made. The riders were taken into 'protective custody'. The next day, they were deported three hundred miles to the Tennessee border where they were again bloodied by violent white mobs.

In Washington, the Attorney-General urged Alabama Governor John Patterson to give the 'Freedom Riders' safe passage across his State, but

9. Burns M. James: op. cit. p. 359.

in vain. He simply refused to take the calls from White House. The Freedom Riders were badly beaten up by a white mob of more than one thousand persons. In desperation, the Attorney-General dispatched five hundred marshals under command of Byron White to the Alabama capital.[10] Concurrently, a mass meeting was held in Ralph Abernathy's church in Montgomery to lend moral support to the 'freedom riders'. The meeting, surrounded by menacing white crowds, was addressed by King. Rocks smashed the stained-glass windows showering people in the pews with glass. To cut the long story short, the beleaguered church goers were driven away to their homes early next morning in army trucks. But that was not to be the end of the episode. The Federal Government had to establish its authority. A few days later, therefore, two bus loads of freedom riders escorted by National Guardsmen and highway patrolmen drove to Jackson, Mississippi, where the local police arrested them and put them behind bars for nearly two months. While the Attorney-general wanted to get the protesters out of jail to defuse the situation, Dr. King, following in the footsteps of Gandhi, insisted that they would stay in jail to 'right a wrong': "It is a matter of conscience and morality." However, before the year ended, the Department of Justice made sure that travel terminals of all sorts throughout the South were open on equal terms to whites and blacks.

Truth, Love and Soul-Force

Love was the core of King's philosophy of non-violence. Dr. King exhorted the Negroes to rise to the level when they could tell their white brethren, paraphrasing the words of Gandhi: "We will match your capacity to inflict suffering with our capacity to endure suffering. We will meet your physical force with our soul force. We will not hate you, but we cannot in all good conscience obey your unjust laws. Do to us what you will and we will still love you. Bomb our homes and threaten our children; send your hooded perpetrators of violence into our communities and drag us out on some wayside road, beating us and leaving us half dead, and we will still love you. But we will soon wear you down by our capacity to suffer. And in winning our freedom we will so appeal to your heart and conscience that we will win you in the process." It will thus be seen that, for King, freedom became a synthesis of various nuances that went with this term — freedom from fear and hunger; freedom from racism; freedom from segregation and inequality; freedom under the law to enjoy equal civil rights, and so on. In a speech at a rally at

---

10. Schlesinger M. Arthur: *A Thousand Days; Kennedy in the White House*, London, 1965; p. 798.

Gadsden, Alabama, on 21 June 1963, he went on to add: freedom from fear of death was the most difficult to attain. In that state of mind a man becomes totally and eternally free.

In short, non-violence as perceived by Martin comprised of five elements:

- Non-violence is not an easy way out for cowards; it is the way of the strong.
- It does not seek the humiliation, defeat or destruction of the opponent.
- It targets evil, and not the person perpetuating evil.
- The willingness to suffer is transformational.
- The non-violent resister rejects even inward violence; instead chooses the path of love.

Dr. King was a practical man. He was realistic enough to admit that many of the Negroes will find it difficult to follow the highly spiritual path of nonviolence as outlined by him. Some of them may even consider it senseless while others might argue that they don't have the strength nor the courage to join such a mass movement in which violence is only one-sided, and suffering is the prerogative of the other. After all, all Negroes were not down and under. A good many of them were going up the economic ladder thereby creating a niche for themselves in the American middle class. They saw no rational basis to give up what they had achieved through their hard work. Fortunately, total unanimity is not *sine qua non* for success of every non-violent mass movement but total faith in its righteousness is.

Non-violent mass movement does not produce miracles overnight. It is essentially a positive concept. It cannot aim at the 'bull's eye' only; it needs a broad range of goals. Non-violence requires non-cooperation with evil and simultaneously, cooperation with the positive constructive forces of the good. Love and sacrifice are its core elements. Gandhi's concept was based on the premise that popular cooperation can be withdrawn through non-violent techniques of resistance. Obviously, no government can possibly exist for any length of time if people cease to obey its dictates. That is what Gandhi preached as the non-cooperation movement. Truth-Force was the basis of Gandhi's technique. For Gandhi, Truth and God were synonymous terms, more or less. "Truth is God." The crux of non-violent resistance was to face superior physical force, howsoever brutal, in a disciplined manner. Truth-Force would impart courage and willingness to bear all the consequences cheerfully. Similarly,

King focused on Love (*agape*) and emphasized that cooperation can be withheld from a government, its laws and dictates that treat a part of its own population as inferior: Blacks in case of America and the 'Untouchables' in case of India. For King, non-violent struggle was grounded in divine theology and philosophy and it was that basic characteristic which imparted the believers the dignity and courage to face the ill consequences. But the underlying approach in both cases was the same. No wonder therefore that 'non-violent struggle has been described as the political equivalent of war'.[11] Gandhi and King thus shared the 16th century French wisdom: 'you can refuse to be governed by those who dominate you even if you are in bondage or servitude'. King adopted this line of thought when he wrote:

> "Admittedly, nonviolence in the truest sense is not a strategy that one uses simply because it is expedient at the moment; nonviolence is ultimately a way of life that men live by because of the sheer morality of its claim ..."[12]

Since King believed that it was the "Jesus of Nazareth that stirred the Negroes to protest with the creative weapon of love", in the initial stages the Montgomery Movement was given the generic name of "Christian Love". Soon thereafter, the Movement got inspired by the influence of Gandhi. By this time King had come to the realization that the 'Christian doctrine of love operating through the Gandhian method of nonviolence was one of the most potent weapons available to the Negro in his struggle for freedom'. Thus, in due course the protests came to be classified under the generic term of 'Militant Nonviolent Mass Movement'.

'Black Power'

Malcolm X was what was known at the time as a "Black Nationalist". He denounced Gandhi's and King's ideas as 'fool's dreams', a set of pipe dreams. The Blacks in the North felt that their problems were different from those of the South, inasmuch as they already had the vote and there was no segregation by law. He did not subscribe to the philosophy and methodology propounded by Gandhi. It is a different matter altogether that he respected Gandhi for his leadership of Indian people that got them freedom from British colonial rule. Gandhi was

11. Gene Sharp: *The Political Equivalent of War* — Civil Defence, No. 555 of *International Conciliation*, New York, 1965.
12. King: op. cit. (*Stride Towards Freedom*), pp 87-89.

assassinated, and so were Malcolm X and Martin Luther King Jr. — all three lost their lives for holding on to views that were not popular with some of their own people even though they worked for the long term good of their people. While a strain of deep inner spirituality ran through Gandhi and Dr. King, Malcolm X and spirituality repelled each other like poles having similar polarity. The major problem was poverty. The vast majority of the Blacks in the North lived in deplorable poverty, in squalid ghettos ruled by the slum-lords. Unemployment rate was high, much higher than that amongst the whites. The police treated every Negro as a criminal and they were victims of frequent exceptional police-brutality. Race-riots were a common feature. Dr. King therefore decided in 1966 to extend his movement to the North. He held meetings with youth gang-leaders of Chicago to persuade them to abjure violence, and adopt the path of non-violence as propounded by India's Mohandas Karamchand Gandhi, who had succeeded in freeing his country from the British yoke. The Mayor of Chicago, Richard Daley, had strong local support. He mobilized his forces against the propaganda let loose by King, and by mid-1966 the Chicago campaign appeared to be petering out. "Black Power" was on a rising crescendo. King had therefore no option but to devote major part of his efforts to counter the gross errors inherent in the philosophy of 'Black Power', and the immense damage it could do to the otherwise non-violent movement, for King knew very well that the Blacks could never hope to defeat white America in an open show of force. White America was indeed a great power, perhaps the greatest on Planet Earth. No doubt, Gandhi's philosophy is a frustratingly slow process. It does not immediately change the heart of the oppressor. Nonviolence recognizes that social change cannot come overnight. Both Gandhi and King held the view that 'oppressors can be held down by their own practices of cruelty to others'. Only in the final analysis does it reach the opponent and stirs his conscience to such an extent that reconciliation becomes a reality. In fact, after his visit to India, King wrote a letter dated 19 May 1959 to G. Ramachandran:

> I left India more convinced than ever before that the method of non-violent resistance is the most potent weapon available to oppressed people in their struggle for freedom and dignity. In fact, there is no other lasting way. I have returned to America with a greater determination to achieve freedom for my people through non-violent means.[13]

13. King Mary: op. cit., p.212.

Just about thirty years before the above letter was written by King, Gandhi had sent a message "To the American Negro":

> Let not the twelve million Negroes be ashamed of the fact that they are the grandchildren of the slaves. There is no dishonour in being slaves. There is dishonour in being slave owners. But let us not think of honour or dishonour in connection with the past. Let us realize that the future is with those who would be truthful, pure and loving. For, as the old wise men have said, 'truth ever is, untruth never was'. Love alone binds and truth and love accrue only to the truly humble.

During the period when the above message was sent, a number of black leaders had been visiting India simply because they were aware of the analogous nature of their respective political and social problems. They had been meeting Gandhi and seeking his advice. Some did go so far as to express the need for raising a "Negro Gandhi' who could lead the black people to attain social and racial equality. And ultimately one did arise, in the person of Dr. Martin Luther King Jr. who filled the void for leadership.[14]

"When the under privileged demand freedom, the privileged first react with bitterness and resistance. ..." Nehru once remarked that the British were never so angry as when the Indians resisted them with non-violence, that he never saw eyes so full of hate as those of the British troops to whom he turned the other cheek when they beat him with *lathis* (sticks). But non-violent resistance at least changed the minds and hearts of Indians, however impervious the British may have appeared. 'We cast away our fears', said Gandhi's disciple, Jawaharlal Nehru. And in the end the British not only granted freedom to India but came to have new respect for the Indians. Today a mutual friendship based on complete equality exists between these two peoples within the Commonwealth. ..."[15] It has been accepted the world over that Gandhian-style non-violent civil resistance has had a much greater global impact on world politics than armed struggle and violent resistance. The

---

14. While ending his law paper in 1952, Harris Wofford had written, rather presumptuously, that what the Black Belt needed was "a Negro with some Gandhi in him." — Harris Wofford in *Of Kennedys and Kings*, New York, 1980, p. 113. However, every one including William Stuart Nelson who had known and revered Gandhi seemed to be of the opinion that "the American Negro did not have the Gandhian dimension in him." Of course, Dr. Martin Luther King Jr. proved them all wrong.

15. Dishman B. Robert: op. cit. pp.429-30.

large number of colonial countries that achieved their independence in the aftermath of Indian Independence is proof enough of the success of this methodology to fight the Imperialist powers. King continued to justify the use of non-violent resistance, based on *agape,* love. Racial justice, desegregation and equal opportunity were the cardinal points of his Movement.[16] Both Malcolm X and Martin Luther King died as "they attempted to mount programs involving not only blacks, but the oppressed of every race and kind."[17] Thus for King, non-violence became a globally unifying ideology. He maintained that international relations could be managed far more wisely and peacefully if non-violence was pursued by the nations of the world as an instrument of mutual diplomatic relationships.

Gandhi's philosophy of non-violence followed by its total acceptance and practice by King displayed out its global impact in the world arena well after both of them, and the 'Frontier Gandhi', had departed from Planet Earth. In the extraordinary year of 1989 the world scene underwent an unimaginable metamorphosis. As it was, a number of nations of Asia had already gained independence in the wake of break-up of the Dutch and British Empires. And in 1989, just within that year, Eastern Europe witnessed successful culmination of popular resistance movements resulting in the map of Eastern Europe being redrawn all over again. The collapse of Warsaw Pact and corresponding extension of NATO, the break up of the erstwhile Soviet Union and the Berlin Wall, South African revolution, agitations in Philippines and Burma — all these and a lot more are not within the scope of this work. Suffice to say that non-violence as a weapon of resistance had actually attained a global status.

The views expressed by Gandhi were re-echoed over and over again. Marcus Garvey of Jamaica came to the United States on March 23, 1916. It was about one year after Turner's death. While Turner had worked in the South, Garvey worked in the North and made Harlem his base. Garvey knew the pain of segregation and discrimination since he had personally experienced it. Garvey had appreciated that no people could survive without racial pride. This

16. This has been openly corroborated by *Time* magazine dated 31 December 1999, pp. 24-26. Incidentally, *Time* magazine selected Gandhi as joint runner-up with Franklin Roosevelt and Albert Einstein as 'person of the twentieth century'. The Magazine singled out Gandhi as the century's foremost representative of the 'crusade for Civil Rights and individual liberties'. *Time* magazine had already declared Gandhi as 'Man of the Year' for 1930.

17. Williams A. John: op. cit. p. 78.

particularly true of black Americans who had been enslaved for more than three hundred years. He said: "To be a Negro is no disgrace, but an honour, and we of the Universal Negro Improvement Association do not want to become white." As Whites ruled Europe and America, Garvey was certain Blacks would rule Africa. The crux of his message was "Africa for Africans". In 1920 Garvey called the first International Convention of the Negro People of the World. It was held at New York and was attended by more than 25,000 delegates from twenty-five countries.[18] It is noteworthy that well before Martin Luther King Jr. came on the scene, the struggle for freedom by Negroes had made a fairly good start.

Garvey's approach to Negro-problems had close resemblance to that of Malcolm, so was his criticism of what he alleged as pseudo-intellectual in which category he roped in integrationist philosophy, W.E.B. Du Bois, Roy Wilkins, NAACP. His criticism of liberalism, liberal capitalism and co-existence with whites even on equal terms was often intemperate. His brand of Black Nationalism had the stamp of exclusiveness and separatism. In 1920 UNIA claimed a membership of nearly four million.

In addition to UNIA, Moorish Science Temple founded by Noble Drew Ali in Newark, New Jersey, and the 'Nation of Islam' ('Black Muslims') founded by Wallace D. Fard in Detroit in 1930 made substantial contribution towards defining and encouraging black nationalism. However, both these organizations were primarily religious in character with a sprinkling of politics thrown in. The 'Nation of Islam' soon developed into a significant organization, more so after the Baptist minister from Georgia, Elijah Poole (later Elijah Muhammad), became its virtual head, more like some sort of a prophet. Both organizations totally rejected Christianity and its white protagonists. Religion of Islam was the savior of the world. Afro-Asians were to be the dominant force in global affairs. The Moorish Science Temple soon disintegrated and its members joined the Nation of Islam, which achieved considerable success after Malcolm X became its hyper-active member, a virtual head. In fact, Malcolm was totally carried away by the philosophy of 'Nation of Islam'. He spread the new cult amongst Black Muslims of America as the only viable proposition for the emancipation of American Negroes. Allah was certainly not white, nor was the Christian God whom the Nation of Islam discarded outright.

---

18. Cone H. James: *Martin Malcolm & America*; New York, 1991, p. 13.

Traditional Indian Methods of Protest

From times immemorial the Indian polity had suffered under the dictatorial rule of various rajas, nawabs and, of course, many foreign rulers and invaders. In order to redress their individual or collective grievances they had evolved various forms of protests, generally non-violent. In case the ruler or his agent was not amenable to dialogue and used brute force to enforce his will, insurgency and counter-violence were invariably the consequence. Sometimes an erring official was caught hold of, his head and moustaches were shaven and face blackened. He was then paraded through the village mounted backwards on a donkey — a highly effective non-violent form of protest against an oppressive official. However, where dialogue was an option, the aggrieved people would march to the capital city and demand an audience with the ruler to put forward their grievances. In the Himalayan states, this practice was known as *dhandhak.*[19] Mass migration known as *hijrat* — departure from one's country and friends — was another form of non-violent resistance.[20] While the *hijrat* of the twentieth century as a symbol of nonviolent protest was a recent occurrence, the tradition goes back to much earlier times when, in 1669, about eight thousand *Baniyas* left Surat and sought refuge in Bharuch to escape the atrocities inflicted on the community by Aurangzeb's *qazi.* In the first case the protest did not bear fruit while the second ended in victory for the *Baniya.* In the same vein, *Hijrat* for the Negro in the South to migrate to the North was no solution to the problems of racial injustice and segregation. The Negro of the South had to remain in the South to solve his problems, which would not be resolved by running away from them.[21]

Another form of non-violent protest is mentioned in *Manusmriti.* It is called *carita* and involves recovery of debt by the lender by putting the debtor to shame through a 'sit-in' at the front door of the debtor.

---

19. Hardiman: op. cit. p. 42.
20. The *Hijrat* movement of 1920s was an offshoot of the *Khilafat* agitation when a large number of Indian Muslims, particularly the Pathans, left their homes and hearths as a protest against the British policy towards the Caliph. Their contention was that India had become *Dar-ul-harb,* land of war; "it was their duty to give up everything and go on pilgrimage, *hijrat,* to a *Dar-ul-salam,* the land of peace. As a result about 18,000 Pathans sold all their possessions and moved to Kabul. The Frontier Gandhi led a large party and his ninety-year old father was eager to join the emigrants — *Abdul Ghaffar Khan* by D.G. Tendulkar, Bombay, 1967, pp. 32-33.
21. Coretta Scott King: The Martin Luther King, Jr., *Companion*; New York, 1993, p. 44.

This practice was generally known as *dharna*[22] or *tukaza*. The British Government in India declared dharna a criminal offence under the Indian Penal Code punishable with imprisonment upto one year or fine, or both. Yet another form of application of moral pressure exerted by the wronged party used to be the threat of self immolation or suicide. The well known Champaran protest led by Gandhi in 1917 is an excellent example of success of totally non-violent agitation. Thus Gandhi forged a new weapon, or a set of weapons, to offer non-violent resistance to British oppressive rule. He modified ancient forms of protest and made use of the same to achieve his political and social objectives. "Part of their efficacy lay in the strong theoretical underpinning that Gandhi gave to this form of protest through his doctrine of Satyagraha."[23] Gandhi's nonviolent resistance was an active and not a passive force.

By the time the American Negroes' delegation visited India in 1936 and after, Gandhi had severed his official relations with the Congress Party so that he was not tied down to the organizational structure.[24] Thus Gandhi was in close touch with the depressed people of the United States. By virtue of Gandhi's experience and personal contacts with the black community of South Africa, he had a special affinity and sympathy for the Negroes. He was of the view that "A civilization is to be judged by its treatment of its minorities." ... "The tendency of Indian civilization is to elevate the moral being that of the Western civilization is to propagate immorality. ..."[25] Although Dr. Martin Luther King Jr. had not yet appeared on the political scene of America, Gandhi did suggest that the future generation(s) of Negroes might as well be the standard-bearers of non-violence as a political weapon. In April 1945 when the United Nations Organization was formed at San Francisco, Mahatma Gandhi commented: "India's nationalism spells internationalism. Freedom of India will demonstrate to all the exploited races of the earth that their freedom is near. ... In my opinion, there is no place on earth and no race, which is not capable of producing the finest types of humanity, given suitable opportunities and education..."[26]

---

22. The word dharna is derived from the Sanskrit *dhri* which means to hold out.
23. Hardiman David: op. cit. p. 51.
24. 28th October 1934 was the last day of the Bombay Congress when Gandhi made a personal announcement to this effect. He was now free to devote himself to rural development work.
25. Gandhi M.K.: *Hind Swaraj*: pp. 43-46.
26. Gandhi M.K.: *Satyagraha in South Africa*; pp. 19-20.

Violence has to be met with deliberate non-violence. By doing so, the oppressor's counter-measures are seen in a harsher light. If the oppressed people use violence, they would only strengthen the opponent's determination and give him the pretext for harsher crackdown, thereby defeating the very purpose of non-violent resistance. "When a ruler is opposed by the populace, and attempts to secure his position through brutality, the greater his cruelty, the weaker does his regime become."[27]

Wherever Gandhi went, the crowds were delirious to have his '*darshan*'. Lahore went overboard with ecstasy although its population was largely Muslims. Thousands of Punjabis met him to tell him their tales of woe. He rejected whatever could not be substantiated or corroborated. Nonetheless, the indictment against the British administration was quite strong and convincing. On the other hand, the British inquiry had been boycotted by most Indians who could have testified and brought out the truth, with the result that the British inquiry report was a mere white-wash. Since the inquiry by Gandhi was thorough and carried out painstakingly, Gandhi was now in the Indian politics up to his neck. He could neither avoid the annual meeting of the Indian National Congress, nor refuse the invitation to the Moslem Conference on the subject of Caliphates and the British treatment of Turkey. In fact, the Muslims were so eager for Gandhi's support on the Caliphate question that they offered to place the question of cow protection on the agenda of their Conference. Gandhi saw through the artificiality of the proposal and declined the *quid pro quo* approach on what was essentially a politico-military question.

Non-Cooperation

On the question of the Caliphate and involvement of Indian Muslims in the vexed issue, Gandhi was in a quandary. His philosophy of Satyagraha was not in the Muslim lexicon. It was not in their tradition or character. They would not understand its fine points either, nor was a Sanskrit phrase the right terminology for a purely Muslim question. In a flash Gandhi hit upon one single momentous word: "Non-Cooperation". That was it. — The Moslem Conference had proposed boycott of English textiles. Gandhi told them that that was not at all enough. He suggested firm non-cooperation in all other fields — refusal of all British honours and awards; refusal of British employment, schools or courts; non-payment of taxes. All this would involve lot of personal sacrifice and loss.

27. Gene Sharp: *The Dynamics of Non-violent Action*; p. 696.

Such grave measures should be taken only after the terms offered to Turkey were fully known. If the same were as severe as expected, then non-cooperation was the right answer. The word 'non-cooperation' became a key phrase, a universal panacea for re-dressing of all grievances and agitations. And soon it was put to use. — A ruthless and thoroughly humiliating peace treaty was dictated to Turkey. Muslims all over the world, in India in particular were seething with resentment. As for the Hindus: General Dyer's[28] pension was continued after his retirement to England, and to rub salt on deep wounds on Indian psyche, the pension was paid from India. To cap it all, a large purse was collected through donations and presented to Dyer for the good work he had done in India! — The Amritsar-Massacre. Nothing could have been more tactless, or humiliating to the people of Punjab, to hurt the Punjabi sentiments. It was just the right time to launch the Non-Cooperation Movement. As was his practice, Gandhi gave advance notice to the Viceroy by writing to him that he had advised the Muslims and Hindus "to withdraw their support from Your Excellency's Government." While the Viceroy characterized this as "the most foolish of all the foolish schemes", Gandhi asked the people of India to fast and pray on 31st July 1920. The launching of Non-Cooperation Movement was scheduled for the next day. Hindu and Muslim committees worked together raising the slogan of Self-Rule, *Swaraj*, which instantly caught the imagination of the people at large. Foreign (read English) goods and clothing were discarded and consigned to public bonfires which swept the entire country. *Charkha* (spinning wheel) was adopted as the symbol of unity[29] and self-sufficiency in clothing. Gandhi exhorted the people of India to switch over to home-spun clothing as early as possible. A white cap made of home-spun cloth, later known as 'Gandhi cap', became the symbol of nationalism. Money poured in thousands. Women donated their golden jewelry to the National Fund. Self-sacrifice was the order of the day. On 5th October 1920 Gandhi requested the Congress Working Committee to pass a resolution declaring it the duty of every Indian soldier or civilian to quit government service. That was the acid test of non-

---

28. The Butcher of Jalianwala — a massacre ordered by a British Army officer in Amritsar in Punjab, India.

29. The Government had in its possession a subtle weapon to scout all notions of Indian unity. Besides the usual ethnic divisions, it included a table of 222 distinct languages allegedly spoken in the sub-continent. Compared to the 1901 Census, the official census machinery had somehow invented seventy five more languages. Out of the dialects spoken in the border areas, one was spoken by three persons only, another by two, and yet another one by one person only. But who did this one talk to!

cooperation. Around this time, Gandhi adopted the loincloth, the garment of the poor, with a spun-yarn shawl as his personal dress — extreme in simplicity and poverty.

The Prince of Wales (Later King Edward VIII) was scheduled to arrive in India on 17th November 1921 on a State visit at the height of the non-cooperation movement. It was a tactless move by London and Delhi who, erroneously assumed that the popularity of the Prince would cool down the temperature in Indian political scene. But the contrary happened. The Congress Working Committee declared a national hartal that day. They boycotted all ceremonies connected with the Prince's visit. In Bombay six donkeys were decked in foreign dress including hats. They were paraded in all the main streets of the great city; otherwise the streets bore a deserted look during parades of the Prince. However, some pro-British elements led by wealthy Parsees staged a welcome. The opponents attacked them. Riots broke out. When the police tried to separate the two factions, several policemen were killed. Gandhi tried to restore the situation, but in vain. He therefore resorted to his usual weapon of fasting. A deputation persuaded him to break his fast and assured him of good conduct by all and sundry. But the unfortunate fact was that fifty-eight citizens of Bombay had been killed and four hundred injured.[30] The "Chauri Chaura" episode in Gorakhpur also confirmed in a most brutal manner that civil-disobedience movement was bound to lead to violent disturbances — Gandhi or no Mahatma Gandhi, fasting or no fasting; the inevitable sequel had to be brutal violence. It was therefore decided that, henceforth, milder form of protests like non-cooperation, Swadeshi and other constructive programs alone would be permitted by the Congress. Nevertheless, Gandhi was arrested on 10th March and sent to Sabramati jail. The Indian Government reacted in a typical stereotype fashion by arresting thousands who obeyed Gandhi's call. Police opened fire on protesting crowds at Calcutta, Madras and Karachi. Surprisingly, the Government did not arrest Gandhi who was the main 'culprit' for whatever the people were resorting to — sedition was the word used for such activities, and even then Gandhi was not arrested for preaching 'sedition'. "Yet it is curious how unimaginative so many Britishers are. What they recognize as a virtue in themselves is an appalling vice in others, else we should never hear of alleged sedition in Ireland, Egypt or India." The Viceroy continued to resist pressure in this regard both from the Governors of provinces as well as His Majesty's Government in London. The arrests of members of the public continued till practically all political leaders were behind

30. Ashe Geoffrey: op. cit. p. 225.

bars, except Gandhi who was the real instigator of all the trouble. The Indian public was puzzled by the attitude of the Government in that they refrained from arresting Gandhi, but everyone else who mattered. However, Gandhi offered himself for arrest. About an hour or so past midnight the District Magistrate came with a contingent of two police officers and thirty policemen. Gandhi requested a fellow Satayagrahi to recite his favourite hymn, '*Vaishnavajan*'. He listened with head bent and eyes shut. After this he was ready to go. He was then driven to Yervada Central Jail.

Since a large number of people were out for violent rebellion and were angry with Gandhi that he would not permit them to infringe the basic principle of Satyagraha viz., peaceful non-violent agitation, they dare not resort to violence: And this puzzled the Government too. Thus both the British and the Indian nationalists faced a situation which was so novel, so new, that neither of them could evaluate it properly nor take a decision in the matter. However, in August 1920 Gandhi did clarify that Satyagraha never meant total pacifism, and certainly not passivity.

- The first principle of Gandhi's technique of non-violent mass movement: "Where there is a choice only between cowardice and violence, I would advise violence."[31]
- The second principle: non-violence is not to defeat or humiliate an opponent; on the contrary, it must aim at seeking his understanding and friendship.
- The third characteristic of non-violent mass movement was that it was directed against the forces of evil and certainly not against the persons perpetuating those evil.
- The fourth component of Gandhi's technique was non-retaliation — the oppressed must be willing to accept blows and abuse without striking back, the principle of the 'other cheek'.
- And last but not the least, non-violent resistance is not confined to mere external physical force but also encompasses spiritualism inasmuch as the resister not only refrains from retaliating physically, but also refuses to hate the oppressor. Instead, he continues to follow the ethics of love as propounded by Jesus in the first place, and elaborated by Gandhi in his philosophy for attaining independence for India.

---

31. Ibid. p. 112.

This concept of love — *agape in Greek* — was further elaborated by Dr. King. "*Agape* means understanding, redeeming goodwill for all men. It is an overflowing love which is purely spontaneous, unmotivated, groundless and creative. It is the love of God operating in the human heart." Indeed, *agape* is totally disinterested love for humanity — good, bad or indifferent.

"Our non-cooperation is neither with the English nor with the West. Our Non-cooperation is with the system the English have established with the material civilization and its attendant greed and exploitation of the weak." Dr. Martin Luther King's sermon at the Dexter Avenue Church reading a fictional letter from the Apostle Paul to American Christians of the mid-twentieth century delivered in Montgomery, Alabama, on 4th November 1946 notes the gap between the nation's scientific progress and its ethical and spiritual development. Like Gandhi, he too deplored the exploitive tendencies of capitalism, and of course added the evils of racial segregation and egotism. He also emphasized that fair means be used in their struggle against evil, when he exhorted his people to ensure that only Christian methods and Christian weapons are used. He strongly advocated that non-cooperation with evil was as much a moral obligation as was cooperation with the good. It was in line with the Gandhian concept: our non-cooperation is a retirement within ourselves. Our non-cooperation is a refusal to cooperate with the English administration on their terms. We say to them: "Come and cooperate and it will be well for us, for you and the world. ... Every good deed has its own advertisement. ... In my humble opinion, rejection is as much an ideal as the acceptance of a thing. It is as necessary to reject untruth as it is to accept truth."[32]

---

32. Quoted from *Young India* by Louis Fischer: op. cit. pp 165-66.

11

Civil Rights

Noncooperation & Civil Disobedience

'All Men are Created Equal'. Non-cooperation is an attempt to awaken the masses, to a sense of their dignity and power. This can only be done by enabling them to realize that they need not fear brute force, if they would but know the soul within.

Successive American administrations were reluctant to implement equal rights and privileges to the Negroes — even if the same were legally granted — lest that might endanger national security as perceived from the perspective of the Whites. However, a close study of American history shows that the constituent units of the Union, the States themselves were the real culprits. It is the States which posed real danger to American freedom, and not the American-Indians or the Negroes. If and when it was not the States, the Federal Government itself curtailed the freedom of its own people. Glaring examples of the latter danger may be cited as the Alien and Sedition Acts of 1798, the draconian legislation enacted during the First World War leading to large scale repression and trampling over rights of the individual, and above all, the McCarthyism of the 50's. Indeed, there is no explanation for the paradoxical behaviour of the whites of America for their treatment of the coloured citizens of their country. They preached one doctrine to the rest of the world; but they themselves contravened the same in their treatment of their own minorities. The contradiction in fighting the racist philosophy of Nazism in Europe while practising severe racial discrimination at home was much too pronounced to be missed by the educated elite of America, as well as by the world at large. Perhaps, it was their inherent belief in the superiority of the Whites over the Blacks. While ninety percent of the Americans, the Whites, were proud of their heritage, generosity, democratic traditions and equal rights for all, they refused to concede the same to the remainder ten per cent of the population. However, once the Negroes got back *some* of their rights, they wanted all of them, the whole lot of them, without any further delay. Consequentially, the Civil Rights movement made the United States as a whole more democratic. And it is Gandhian non-violence which made true democracy flourish in the United States.

There is no doubt that the American Supreme Court and the White House have played a significant role in upward move of the Negroes to improve their standards, and to enable them attain the status of first-class citizenship. In this respect the First Amendment went a long way in protecting the rights of the people on an equal footing — freedom of speech, free press, freedom of peaceful assembly, freedom of religion, *et al.* Such rights had been enshrined in the Magna Charta and the Bill of Rights. A Bill of Rights was therefore added to the American Constitution in 1791 through ten amendments passed simultaneously. The ten Rights guaranteed by the Constitution were:

- Freedom of Religion;
- Freedom of Speech;
- Right to assemble;
- Right to petition;
- Freedom from unreasonable searches;
- No illegal loss of liberty;
- Just compensation for property;
- Right to a public trial by jury;
- No excessive bail or fines;
- Right to summon witnesses.

The same holds good for the Fourteenth Amendment also. However, insofar as the Black minority was concerned, the above rights were observed more by denial than by implementation. This was particularly so in the Southern States which had founded the Confederacy. For instance: The Civil Rights Act of 1866 guaranteeing property rights to the Negroes and the 1875-Act outlawing racial discrimination in public facilities were nullified in 1883 under a ruling by the Federal Supreme Court. Nevertheless, the Federal Government did seek to broaden the Negro rights and opportunities, albeit rather late in the day. The first step in

The Civil Rights
Movement
in the U.S.
during 1950's-60's

this direction was taken on 5th December 1946 when President Harry S. Truman[1] appointed the 'President's Committee on Civil Rights'. It was comprised of a group of distinguished citizens and its report made far reaching recommendations towards racial equality and justice. However, implementation of the Report was fraught with many dangers and obstacles with the result that the Negro struggle had to go for many more years before a reasonable level of racial equality and desegregation could be achieved. Nonetheless, as a result of work of this Committee, the armed forces of America were completely desegregated during the Truman and Eisenhower Administrations. But it should be noted that this was more to meet the demands of the War(s) than through any sense of justice or generosity towards the Black minority.

The next notable milestone was reached on 17th May 1954 when the U.S. Supreme Court ruled that "Separate educational facilities are inherently unequal."[2] For all practical purposes, this legal victory was a paper-victory only, devoid of positive integration in the classrooms, particularly in the Southern States who made every effort to ensure that there was no real integration. The Kennedy Presidency witnessed a leap forward when a comprehensive Civil Rights bill was sent to the Congress. A number of measures to eliminate discrimination including end of segregation in hotels, other places of public accommodation, use of federal action to ensure registration of Negro voters, promoting better educational facilities, housing and job opportunities, *et al.* However, all these changes were coming in much too slowly, in driblets, since the Congressmen from the Southern States resorted to filibuster tactics to stall the passage of crucial provisions. It was typical case of "too little too late". The Blacks were totally dissatisfied, particularly in the South. While Negro leaders like the Lawyer Thurgood Marshall fought their battles in the courts, men like Martin Luther King Jr. organized programs like "sit-ins", "freedom rides" demonstrations, boycotts, etc., not only in the Southern States but all over the country. The sit-ins led to kneel-ins, prays-ins and other forms of nonviolent protests. There were some isolated incidents involving violence but, by and large, the protests were

---

1. President Truman was the first president to appoint a permanent Civil Rights Commission.

2. The ruling came as a result of a case, *Brown v. Board of Education of Topeka, Kansas,* filed by the attorneys of the Legal Defence Fund of the NAACP. The Organization had earlier won a similar case, Missouri v. Canada (S.W. Canada, Registrar of University of Missouri), involving admission of a 25-year-old black man, Lloyd Lionel Gaines, seeking admission to the all-white law school at the University of Missouri. Charles Houston and Thurgood Marshall represented the NAACP.

peaceful. The civic and business officials worked with Negro leaders to resolve the differences peacefully. Besides the racial problems, the Administration had to deal with some "problems of plenty". Surplus farm and dairy production had been constantly nagging the American economy simply because improved farming techniques, new and improved farm machinery, better quality seeds and fertilizers have all made American farming among the most efficient in the world resulting in huge surpluses, which in turn implies low prices causing hardships to the rural communities. Above all, the 'cold war' and super power rivalry constantly hovered over the horizon with the result that international issues like communism, Red China,[3] end of colonialism and consequent freedom to a number of African and Asian countries, took precedence over domestic problems which were pushed to the back seat. The Berlin Wall, aggressive designs of Red China in Asia, unrest in the Middle East with its vast reserves of oil and natural gas, development of more powerful and advanced nuclear weapons with equally advanced delivery systems — the list is indeed endless — occupied the world leaders' time and imagination. One bright star in the midst of dark clouds of hostility and war-mongering was the introduction of Peace Corps in 1961 by President Kennedy. The first batch of trained volunteers was sent to Africa in 1961, and by 1963 Peace Corps units were deployed on humanitarian work in forty-two countries around the world.

Assassination of President JFK

Before the year was out, President John Fitzgerald Kennedy (JFK) was assassinated in Dallas, Texas, on 22nd November 1963. The middle of next year, July 18 to 21 1964 to be more precise, marked the first of those several "long hot summers" during which Blacks expressed their growing dissatisfaction with life in the urban North. The Civil Rights Movement was gaining ground. Its birth and progress at a fast pace could not be explained "without a divine dimension". The MIA was delighted to note that "Montgomery, the cradle of Confederacy, was being transformed into Montgomery, the cradle of freedom and justice".[4] The City ghettos remained almost unaffected. By now it was obvious that a large number of Blacks were getting frustrated, and losing their patience with their moderate leadership. Militant non-violence was on its

3. After his first tour as Vice President, Nixon addressed the Nation on radio and TV: "China is the basic cause of all our troubles in Asia. If China had not gone Communist, we would not have had a war in Korea." — Wicker Tom: *One of Us*, p. 17. Nixon's focus at the time was to make himself indispensable to the Republicans. — p. 280.

4. King Scott Coretta: op. cit. p. 133.

way to turning into real militancy. Racial violence soon erupted. It soon spread to Harlem, New Jersey, Chicago and Philadelphia. According to the February-1968 National Advisory Commission Report on Civil Disorders, "the riots were spontaneous upheavals, chiefly caused by white racism and 'explosive mixture' it fostered, police brutality, slum housing, poverty and welfare dependency, job discrimination, unemployment and blighted opportunity. ... The Whites wanted not additional reforms but repression."[5] In the same vein the National Council of Churches claimed that "America was seen as a predominantly white nation using our overwhelming strength to kill more Asians".

A similar story was repeated when King was reported missing on 12th April, Good Friday, 1963 along with his perennial companion, Ralph Abernathy. They had been arrested and put in jail in Birmingham. Eight days after their arrest, both came out on $300 cash bond. William Robert Miller compiled a list of all that went on during the year 1963: Nine hundred and thirty eight demonstrations occurred in atleast 115 Southern cities in eleven Southern States in which 20,083 arrests were made, one of which was Martin King. On the positive side of the balance sheet, 'some progress towards integration' in 186 localities had been made and negotiations in 102 bi-racial communities were in progress.

Council of Federated Organizations (COFO) was composed of SCLC, CORE, NAACP, and SNCC and a number of local groups and small unions. Students were put through short orientation courses in non-violence and sent southwards. These youngsters were required to organize black communities and persuade them to register to vote. The SNCC were already familiar with the police and 'crackers' and knew what they were up against. By the end of June these youngsters, blacks and whites, were familiar with the brutal methods employed by the Southern racists to suppress the deprived classes. They were beaten, harassed and humiliated during the mini-marches. Although the US District Court had issued an injunction against Sheriff David, it had no effect and the marchers were prevented from proceeding further through the use of physical force. Concurrently, President Johnson, in consultation with the Congressional leaders was giving finishing touches to the Civil Rights Act of 1964. Incredibly, Johnson was ahead of the Negro leaders. What he proposed to the Congress was certainly more liberal and far reaching than what the black leaders themselves had aspired for. Just as the Act was ready for Presidential signature, three prominent COFO leaders of the Movement were found missing. Later, their mutilated chain-whipped bodies were discovered sending shock waves throughout the nation.

5. Sellers Charles, et al: op. cit. p. 422.

As for Martin Luther King, he was truly pragmatic and said that he could no longer disapprove acts of violence by his own people without speaking out against the greatest purveyors of violence in the world today — my own Government.[6] Segregation is as bad for the Negroes as it is for the Whites. "The system that has banished personality and scarred the soul of the Negro has also damaged the white man's personality" inasmuch as it has given the white man a false sense of superiority and to the black man an undeserved sense of inferiority. Segregation has ill consequences on the Whites as well as the Blacks. Thus the year 1968 proved to be a turning point in the history of race relations in the U.S.

The atrocities and cruelties inflicted on the Negroes by the white police and administration were something that was in any case expected more so in the light of desegregation movement launched by King. However, in so far as the white church was concerned, the black clergymen had high hopes of sympathy and cooperation, passive if not active. King was distressed to say: "Let me take note of my other major disappointments. I have been so greatly disappointed with the white church and its leadership. Of course there are some notable exceptions .... When I was suddenly catapulted into the leadership of bus protest in Montgomery, Alabama, a few years ago, I felt we would be supported by the white church. I felt that the white ministers, priests and rabbis of the South would be amongst our strongest allies. Instead, some have been outright opponents, refusing to understand the freedom movement and misrepresenting its leaders ..." Unfortunately, 1963 was a year of murders in the United States, the major casualty being The President himself. Edgar Evers in Jackson, Mississippi, William Moore in Alabama, and last but not the least, four Negro children in Birmingham. No doubt all these murders were politically motivated.

In March 1964, Martin King and Dr. Hayling, a dental surgeon and local leader of NAACP in St. Augustine, had to suffer terribly under the Klan who ruled the countryside without fear of man or God, more so since it was Hayling who had encouraged the sit-ins of 1961. On Easter Sunday of 1964 an inter-racial group of eminent ladies including Mrs. Malcolm Peabody, the mother of Governor Endicott "Chub" Peabody of Massachusetts and Mrs. John Burgess whose husband was the first black bishop in the Episcopal Church, attempted to take communion at St. Augustine's Trinity Episcopal Church. They were not allowed to enter

6. Tuchman W Barbara: *The March of Folly from Troy to Vietnam*; London, 1984, p. 340.

the Church and were arrested. Mrs. Peabody was then seventy-two. Naturally, tension mounted, and King arrived on the scene in May. The Sheriff and the local police chief, sporting a glove and hand relationship, informed that the marchers would be in serious danger if they tried to march through Klansmen land. While the leaders of the marchers obtained an injunction against the Sheriff and the police chief, but that did not help at all. The marchers were beaten up as never before. The two leaders were arrested and confined in the local jail for two days. Meanwhile, the Civil Rights Act of 1964 was signed into law; but it had no effect on the situation in St. Augustine. However, when the Voting Rights Bill was signed on 6th August 1965, the two pieces of legislation were certainly a great advance in as much as they provided a high degree of basic legal protection for the Negroes. It was well known that the Southern States directly obstructed the Blacks from exercising their franchise. Even in areas where the Blacks outnumbered the whites, there was no black representation. It had been almost a century of white terrorism at the polls. So King undertook tour of the area to bolster support for the MFDP.

That is alright as far as it goes; but laws do not fill a stomach. The real issue before the public, mostly the Blacks but some whites too, was suffering the agony of poverty. Economic and political equality had to go hand in hand to achieve any degree of tangible progress. It was high time that the Black leadership faced the question of bread and butter, squarely and seriously to ameliorate the economic conditions of the oppressed classes.

While the Selma march was underway, the President addressed the Congress: "The real hero in the struggle for equality was the Negro American. His actions and protests — his courage to risk safety and even life — have awakened the conscience of the Nation. His demonstrations have been designed to call attention to injustice. ... To ignore the Negro vote and Negro insistence on civil rights must be either an act of absolute folly — or one of absolute miscalculation."[7]

Nixon had learnt his lesson in the 1960-election. In 1968 he had decided not to risk suburban votes or indebtedness to any single community. One major issue during 1966-67 election campaign was 'civil rights', more so in the Southern States. The Republicans could not afford to openly play to white segregationist stand for fear of losing the Black votes elsewhere. Nixon therefore laid down the following policy line:[8]

---

7. Franklin John Hope: *From Slavery to Freedom: A History of the Negro Americans;* Chicago, 1961, p. 625.

8. Wicker Tom: op. cit. p. 281.

"Southern Republicans must not climb aboard the sinking ship of racial injustice. Any Republican victory that would come from courting racists, black or white, would be a defeat for our future in the South and our party in the nation."

Civil Disobedience Movement

The very idea of mass civil resistance was the by-product of post-French Revolution in Europe. It had the same ingredients as Gandhi's concept of Civil Disobedience (C.D.): non-violent, disciplined, no cutting of telephone/telegraph wires, no disruption of rail traffic. People not to take the law into their own hands. Peaceful agitations. Rebellion without the element of violence. "A violent man's activity is most visible, while it lasts. But it is always transitory." It is virtually impossible to establish whether Gandhi's concept was the original idea, or the Europeans gave birth to the basic concept. Either way, the basic aim was: Equality and Liberty within the bounds of state system concurrently correcting the excesses, which may be committed by the all-pervading governmental machinery and state power.

A Leaf out of Indian Independence Movement

The Federal Government of the United States was left with no option but to negotiate with the Black leaders. That is precisely what had happened to Gandhi's movement of Civil Disobedience in India in the 1930s and 40s. The British had no option but to hold talks with Gandhi. So he was released on 26th January 1931 and invited to the Viceregal Palace for talks with the Viceroy, Lord Irwin, who along with Churchill was of the view that Gandhi dressed like a coolie. In London, Churchill thundered:

> It is alarming and also nauseating to see Mr. Gandhi, a seditious Middle Temple lawyer, now posing as a fakir of a type well known in the East, striding half-naked up the steps of Viceregal Palace while he is still organizing and conducting a defiant campaign of civil disobedience, to parley on equal terms with the representative of the King-Emperor.[9]

Terrorism has evolved into a universal phenomenon all over the world, which in turn provides the state mechanism with opportunities to acquire unprecedented powers to curb the violence let loose by the terrorist. The more the activities indulged in by the terrorists, the more severe the retaliation by the state, leading to large scale violation of

---

9. Quoted by Akbar: op. cit. p. 233.

human rights. And mind you: the concept of human rights is not a one way street. The victims of terrorists' nefarious activities have as much claim over human rights as the terrorists themselves when they are caught, placed in custody and dealt with severely. But the self-appointed guardians of human rights shout 'State Terrorism' without caring for the victims of terrorists. They can't have the cake and eat it too!

The state mechanism finds it quite convenient to deal with violent terrorism: But when it came to the so-called terrorist activities of a purely non-violent nature, the state mechanism was totally at a loss to tackle this new form of disorder. The Satyagrahis would just not retaliate. They would not even put up their hands to protect their skulls. The Black minority of America also followed the same principle of non-retaliation in the face of atrocities inflicted by the White Administrations and the Klansmen.

The Indian Government amended the relevant provisions of the obnoxious Rowlatt Acts passed in 1919.[10] Gandhi met the new Viceroy, Lord Irwin, in October 1927. He was informed that Sir John Simon would soon arrive in India at the head of a British Parliamentary Commission to enquire into conditions in India and to make recommendations for reforms. London constituted a seven-member Commission of British MPs headed by Sir John Simon, sans Indian representation. India refused to have its fate decided by the British alone. The All-Parties conference held on 15 Jan 1928 under the chairmanship of Dr. Ansari decided to observe *Hartal* on 3rd Feb, the day Simon Commission was to land at Bombay, and to boycott the Simon Commission. In May, Ansari appointed a Committee with Motilal Nehru as Chairman and Jawaharlal Nehru as the Secretary — a Father and Son team —- to work out a constitution that would ultimately lead to complete independence. Jinnah did not cooperate with the Nehru Committee which recommended joint electorate. Meanwhile, on 8th April 1929 Bhagat Singh and B.K. Dutt threw bombs into the Legislative Assembly. The inevitable violent reaction occurred after all. Concurrently, the Simon Commission continued its study tour and got a Black-flag reception at Lahore on 30th October. The crowd kept shouting "Simon! Go back". Police action on the front row of the procession resulted in serious injuries to a senior venerated leader, Lala Lajpat Rai who died on 17th November as a result of the injuries he sustained. The fatal casualties were as much a part of the Indian non-violent movement as they were of the Negroes in America.

10. Rowlatt was the chairman of the Committee that recommended a series of repressive measures to contain the Indian agitation for independence. The Acts came to known after his name.

When the Simon Commission visited Lucknow as part of their tour, a massive procession came out in the streets in protest. Mounted Police charged the crowd resulting in many injuries. But the crowd stood its ground after initial failure. The *hartal* in Lucknow was a complete success and Jawaharlal became a hero in the process. The younger generation was unhappy with the passive resistance policy of Gandhi. They were impatient for action. However, Gandhi did not subscribe to the idea that non-violence meant meek submission to the oppressor. Far from it. The term 'passive resistance' was therefore a misnomer. Martin King too faced similar opposition to non-violence from leaders like Malcolm X and his votaries who were in favour of violent retaliation in self defence against the whites. A schism was perceptible in the Congress organization. But Gandhi stuck to his guns and made sure that violence was abjured. In his younger days, while in South Africa, Gandhi was influenced by the writings of Thoreau. So was King while he was at Crozer. Consequentially, Gandhi's South African movement came to be known as 'Civil Disobedience'. So was Martin's protest movement. However, Gandhi found that the phrase 'civil disobedience' failed to convey the full meaning of the struggle, both in South Africa and later in India. He therefore took recourse to the term 'Civil Resistance' which was equally acceptable in the United States also. First Gandhi, and then Martin, read the American Transcendentalist Henry Thoreau's essay on 'Civil Disobedience'. Martin was particularly impressed by this intellectually stimulating work while Gandhi often quoted Thoreau's maxim: "That Government is the best which governs the least". Non-violent protests continued as a matter of policy. This technique of protests soon caught the imagination of the Indian public.[11] It became the central feature of Indian political system, a strong base in its own right to counter the illegitimate power of the colonial state.

During early 1930's the Indian Government made liberal use of the "Civil Disobedience Manual" and convicted 32,600 persons of political offences connected with tax strikes, forest laws, Salt Law, foreign-cloth boycott, etc. The Satyagrahis could stand a lot, but when it came to the prison lavatories — 'rows of holes so close together that each user touched the next, who might be a criminal or pervert' — caused a high degree of revulsion against the British Raj. It was during this period that Gandhi revived the proposal for experimental 'civil disobedience' in a single district of Bardoli in Bombay Presidency. He appointed Sardar Patel as in-charge of the campaign to undo the twenty-two percent increase in taxation for

11. I think that Gandhi would have been Gandhi even without Thoreau or Tolstoy." — Albert Einstein.

the peasants of Bardoli. The eighty-seven thousand peasants of Bardoli refused to pay the tax. While the campaign was totally non-violent, the Government resorted to large scale arrests, confiscation of property[12], cattle, land, etc. But the peasant stuck to their resolve and did not succumb to official pressure. The agitation lasted from 28th February to 6th August 1928 during which period money kept pouring in from the rest of India so that peasants did not have to starve. Gandhi called for a general hartal all over India on 12th June in sympathy with the peasants. Once again the entire country was totally paralyzed. However, there was no violence at all and the entire population maintained discipline and restraint in the face of provocations by the administration. Finally, on 6th August the Government gave in and repealed the twenty-two per cent tax, released all prisoners, returned confiscated property and promised to compensate the peasants for their losses. It was at this stage that the whole country wanted to know: "What next?" Complete independence became talk of the towns. The young hot heads in the Congress and outside wanted immediate declaration of "*Poorna Swarajya*" — complete independence. Gandhi asked them to wait for one year. If Swarajya did not come till then, he too would join them to support the declaration of complete independence.

'Frontier Gandhi' in the Fray

Khan Abdul Ghaffar Khan noted that to gain independence, two types of movements were launched in the Frontier province: violent and non-violent. The British crushed the violent movement in no time; but the non-violent movement launched in 1929 flourished in spite of intense repression. The former generated fear and cowardice while the latter made the Pathans brave and raised their morale. This is precisely what happened a couple of decades later to the movement led by Dr. Martin Luther King Jr. in the United States. The British considered a non-violent Pathan more dangerous than a violent Pathan. Launching of non-cooperation movement in the Frontier area had one sinister aspect that only the British could appreciate —- it would encourage a fresh Afghan invasion of India. Some local leaders like Khan Abdul Ghaffar Khan were therefore arrested. Afghan spies and Bolshevik agents would also have a field day if non-cooperation movement spread in the Frontier areas, which it was very much likely to. The British prestige would suffer a setback in a sensitive area.

12. "I own no property and yet I feel that I am perhaps the richest man in the world". — M.K. Gandhi. (*Autobiography*)

Ghaffar called himself "Khudai Khidmatgar" — a servant of God. Since God does not require any service from his creatures, the Khan immersed himself totally in serving the people of India in general and North West Frontier Province (NWFP) in particular of the then undivided India.[13] The essence of this organization was the element of saintliness which the Khan imbibed from Gandhi. It was this attribute together with non-violence as a politico-social creed that gave him the nickname of "Frontier Gandhi", which stuck to him all his life and thereafter. Above all, it was the Khan's educational background that made a vast difference, in that practically every single Pathan of those days was illiterate. But "My education had created in me that spirit of dedicated service to my community and country. I made up my mind to serve the creatures of God and particularly my people who, at that time, due to their stupidity and backwardness, were heading towards disaster and chaos".[14] The British Administration made sure that the Pathans were kept shrouded in total illiteracy. While laying emphasis on educating the masses, Abdul Ghaffar Khan came to the sad realization that there was extreme shortage of suitably qualified teachers. He remembered his childhood days in a mosque-school. It was at that early age in life when Ghaffar had come to the sad conclusion that his teachers, the Mullahs, could not even write. Their total education was comprised of remembering the holy Quran by heart, with the standard accents and *surahs*. They neither understood a word of what they were repeating, again and again, like a parrot, nor could they write it at all. The teachers knew no writing! This had come as a great shock to Ghaffar. Indeed, the Pathans were living in their own world of make-believe in total blissful ignorance. Ghaffar's father too noticed this monumental deficiency and shifted his son to the Municipal Board High School in Peshawar. For Ghaffar, this was also the beginning of close contact with the so called untouchables —— children of sweepers, dry or wet. Ghaffar spent more time playing with these tabooed children belonging to oppressed classes, than with those of his own. Hereafter, he was to espouse the cause of the weak and downtrodden as a matter of routine. The corollary of this social enigma was that the evil of untouchability was not restricted to the Hindus alone; untouchability and oppression of depressed classes was

13. Over a period of time, the NWFP came to have two boundaries: the international boundary represented by the Durand Line which separated British India from Afghanistan, and the administrative boundary, demarcating the zone actually held by the British. The Tract between these two was known as the Tribal Belt, and that constituted a no man's land.

14. Frontier Gandhi: op. cit. p.1.

an all India phenomenon: Agreed, its prevalence amongst the Muslims and Sikhs was at much lesser a scale.

Accompanied by Devadas Gandhi, Khan Abdul Ghaffar Khan ('Badshah Khan' for short) toured the Bardoli villages on June 6, 1931. It was with great difficulty that Kasturba Gandhi managed to persuade the Khan to speak to a joint gathering of Hindus and Muslims presided over by her: "I am greatly surprised that the very name of the Congress scares away some of my Muslim brethren. They think that the Congress is a Hindu organization and that I really do not understand how Muslims can remain aloof from the Congress. Surely there is nothing surprising in a Musalman or a Pathan like me, subscribing to the creed (of non-violence). It is not a new creed. It was followed fourteen hundred years ago by the Prophet, all the time he was in Mecca ... But we had forgotten it ..." The credit for being the first amongst us to revive a forgotten creed and to place it before the nation for redressing of collective grievances belongs to Mahatma Gandhi; by no stretch of imagination did he invent the creed. Moreover, "Remember this also that the Musalmans alone are not the creatures of God. The Hindus, Sikhs, Musalmans, Jews, Christians and Parsis, in short, all the creatures who live in this world, are the creatures of God. ... And to serve the creatures of God is to serve God. The Prophet has said that the most pious and God-fearing youth is he who brings comfort to the creatures of God. ..."[15]

Mahatma Gandhi issued a statement: "... Civil Disobedience cannot be withdrawn so long as so many civil resisters are imprisoned ... no settlement can be arrived at so long as ... Khan Sahib, Abdul Ghaffar Khan ... and others are buried alive." As a last resort, Gandhi undertook a fast in jail. Ghaffar also went on seven days' fast from 17th August 1934 in sympathy with Gandhi. That could perhaps be considered a most important milestone in the life of Khan Abdul Ghaffar Khan since it marked the emergence of Ghaffar rising up on his way to his new avatar as "Frontier Gandhi". Soon India had two Gandhis — Mahatma Gandhi and Frontier Gandhi. Furthermore, even though NWFP was a Muslim majority province, in the scheme of Partition of India, the Pathans were for unity with India. That was all because of immense influence of the Frontier Gandhi who was revered by his people for his non-violent leadership. Khan Abdul Ghaffar Khan proved to be an outstanding soldier who fought for liberation of India from foreign domination and exploitation. He was arrested and imprisoned time

15. Tendulkar: op. cit. pp. 94 and 128.

and again, first by the British and then by the Government of Pakistan. In the process, he spent thirty years in various jails out of his life span of seventy-seven years, a world record of sorts that was nearly equaled by the South African black leader, Dr. Nelson Rolihlahla Mandela who started a campaign in 1952 against South African "pass laws" saying he owed "no duty to obey the laws of white Parliament in which he was not represented". During the 1950's dread of communist ideology had overtaken the western democracies. So it did in South Africa too. The white racial regime found it convenient to convict Mandela for contravening the Suppression of Communism Act. Under the brutal apartheid laws, he along with his some colleagues was ordered to move their legal practice out of the urban areas to some remote countryside. Mandela and party refused. In 1955 the 'Congress of the People' under the aegis of African National Congress adopted "Freedom Charter". After the subsequent 'Treason Trial' and Sharpeville Massacre in 1960, the ANC was outlawed. Mandela was sentenced to life imprisonment which he started in the notorious maximum security prison in Robben Island, seven km off the coast near Cape Town. However, in December 1988 he was moved to Victor Verster Prison near Paarl from where he was eventually released on February 11, 1990, to be elected as the President at the national conference of African National Congress held in 1991.

Ghaffar and his brother, Dr. Khan Sahib were released from the Hazari Bagh Central Jail on 27th August 1934. Their entry to Punjab and NWFP was banned. This became a God-sent opportunity for the Khan Brothers to spend time with Mahatma Gandhi in his Wardha Ashram, which became Ghaffar's second home. Soon his daughter Mehar Taj and three sons, Ghani, Wali and Ali, joined their Father to live with him after a lapse of three years. Mehar was entrusted to the care of Mirabehn. All four children and, of course their father took part in every activity of the Ashram as full members. Ghaffar used to attend the evening prayers meetings also, and recite the holy Koran at these meetings. Thus he became the embodiment of universality of teachings of Islam, Hinduism and Christianity.

Before ending his tour of Bengal and returning to Wardha, Abdul Ghaffar paid a quick visit to Shantiniketan (Ghaffar's son, Ghani, was then studying in Shantiniketan) where he made a tremendous impression on one and all. The reciprocal love and respect for each other is best expressed in the farewell address read out by Rabindranath Tagore in Urdu:

"Dear Friend — You are with us only for a while, but even that is a rare good fortune for us all. Your presence has created a new strength and vigor in our hearts. Love is never taught by the word of mouth; the soul of a true lover is love's own touch-stone. When we come into contact with it, the value of whatever sentiment there is in our own hearts gets magnified manifold. Those are really great, whose hearts are for all, who belong to all the lands of the world, transcend also the bounds of moments; they are for all time. Truth is the very foundation of your life, and I am sure you radiate its influence all around you. We have realized this too that all our efforts are every day being frustrated for lack of this devotion to Truth. You have come to this land whose unhappy being is shattered into fragments, in order to fulfill the purpose of Providence to save her from the poison of fratricidal hatred with which she is drugging herself to self-destruction. I have not the slightest doubt that you have been able to stimulate the heart of our folk here with some of that great force of character which is your own."[16]

Salt Satyagraha

Meanwhile, there was a change of government in London. After the elections, a coalition government with Ramsay MacDonald as Prime Minister and Wedgwood at the India Office came to power. The Viceroy, Lord Irwin after a visit to London made a statement suggesting a "Round Table Conference" of British and Indian representatives to examine the question of a constitution for India with 'Dominion Status' as the basis. The British Parliament reacted very strongly to the proposal, particularly with reference to the Dominion Status. The Round Table Conference turned out to be Irwin's still-born baby. Gandhi thereafter retired to his Ashram to draft the Declaration of Independence of India which was proclaimed on 26th January 1930. Gandhi's first step in that direction was to break the British monopoly over common man's absolute necessity, the common salt, and God's gift to man, over which the government had established total monopoly. The 'Salt Laws' imposed by the Government of India prohibited any person from making or selling salt except by and through the Government agency. This was gross exploitation of indigenous resources of the country amounting to tyranny. Gandhi planned to make the 'Salt Laws' the target of his Satyagraha which commenced on 12th March 1930. After the usual morning prayers, Gandhi with his seventy-eight disciples started the 'Salt March' with ever

16. Summarized from the English version by Tendulkar: op. cit. p. 181.

changing crowds for company. "We are marching in the name of God", said Gandhi.

The march lasted twenty-four days during which the frail old man in loincloth became the centre of world's attention. India was excited as never before. He marched for about twelve miles a day. The villagers sprinkled water on the track to keep down the dust. At each village en-route, Gandhi exhorted the people to lead a pure life:

- Always speak the Truth;
- No drugs or alcohol;
- Wash regularly;
- Wear *khadi*;
- Integrate with 'Untouchables' — They are 'Harijans', children of God.[17]
- Shed the negative aspects of Hindu religion.

"The procession went on and on, involving immense number of people, while the government sat back, bewildered and already aghast at the power of this strange new movement." It was a perfect example of how Satyagraha should be conducted. The signal for contravening the Salt Laws was given at Dandi, a small hamlet at the western seashore of India. Everybody started making salt wherever they could. The authorities started arresting people all over the place, but Gandhi was not touched; he remained in camp for weeks along with seventy eight of his followers.[18] Boycott of foreign goods, particularly textiles was made an additional item of protest. In a single month the authorities jailed over sixty thousand persons. Leaders of the Congress including Nehru and 'C.R.' were put in jail. Strict censorship was imposed. The Congress papers were not permitted to publish at all. Gandhi too was arrested at forty-five minutes past midnight on the night of 4/5 May. The peculiar thing about Gandhi's arrest was that he was taken into custody under an old regulation of 1827 which had been in disuse for a long time. The warrant merely stated that M.K. Gandhi was to be "placed under restraint and imprisoned at the pleasure of the Government". No chargesheet. No trial. He was

---

17. Some American authors and intellectuals have wrongly assumed that 'untouchables' or 'outcastes' are the dark skinned descendants of original inhabitants of India, the Dravidians. They were, and to some extent still are, a part of the social environment of all parts of India, and even of Pakistan too.
18. The lump of salt that Gandhi had picked up at Dandi seashore fetched 1,600 rupees.

taken to Yervada Central Jail where, of course, he was mighty happy[19] with his books, letter writing and the spinning-wheel. May be, the Alabama Government borrowed a leaf from the British when they took recourse to a similar archaic regulation to place Martin King under detention, without charge sheet or trial, but sans the magnanimity of books and writing material. Meanwhile the Salt Satyagraha continued. Dharasana Salt Works were raided under the leadership of Sarojini Naidu. She was arrested and put safely out of the harm's way. But the rank and file of the marchers was hit by the police with steel-shod *lathis* breaking skulls and bones *ad lib, ad infinitum.* This inhumane treatment of the Satyagrahis went on for a few days. The authorities were in a quandary, not knowing what to do with these volunteers who did not even raise their arms to ward of the lathi-blows from their skulls. They were totally non-violent, non-retaliatory. The British brutality in putting down the disturbances was no less severe than what white-America had meted out to their Blacks using snarling dogs and bull-headed steel shod thick sticks and whips. The British also revived their antiquated Emergency Whipping Act, which was put to liberal use, particularly in the Bombay area. Since an American press correspondent, Webb Miller was present; he described the events of the day(s) most vividly and the world at large came to know of the treatment being meted out to peaceful agitators who were merely asking for such a simple basic commodity: salt.

After all, a Round Table Conference on India did take place in London in November 1930, but it proved to be a damp squib. No leader of any consequence attended. The sole exception was Mohammed Ali Jinnah, and that was as good as nobody. Gandhi and other leaders of the Congress Party were released starting from the Indian Independence Day, 30th January 1931, leading to a series of historic meetings between Gandhi and Irwin. These talks and the resultant Gandhi-Irwin Pact signed on 5th March 1931 laid the foundations of ultimate complete independence for India which took another sixteen years to materialize. However, the immediate outcome of this Pact was restoration of peace in the country, suspension of civil disobedience campaign, release of political prisoners, and above all, salt was made free all along the seacoasts. The essential point to note is that this pact was signed as if between equals, tacitly acknowledging Independence. Gandhi was now at the apex of his political career. He was elected as the sole representative of Indian National Congress for the forthcoming London Round Table

19. Happiness, the goal to which we all are striving is reached by endeavoring to make the lives of others happy ...M.K. Gandhi.

Conference.[20] This Conference had an exceptionally large number of representatives. Amongst the Indians present in the Conference were twenty-three princes or their representatives and sixty-four representatives from British India. The Viceroy had sent a collection of hand-picked reactionaries and factional representatives whose sole aim was to wreck the Conference by demanding identities and voting rights. Thus the RTC ended in complete failure more by design than by accident.

World War II

India was dragged into the Second World War by the British without even the minimal courtesy of a consultation with its political leaders. The Congress leaders did not want to obstruct the war-effort, but at the same time they could not accept the way the British treated Indian opinion on the subject. On one hand the Pathans from Peshawar district had contributed 12,000 recruits for the Army to fight in the First World War, on the other, the British did not deem it fit to let them even run their own schools. The people were very much disenchanted with this attitude. The Pathans at large resented being treated in this manner. When the nationalist leaders of the liberation movement gave a call for All India total hartal on 6th April 1919, the Pathans from the NWFP whole heartedly joined their compatriots in the rest of India. The point to note is that the people of the Frontier under the leadership of Ghaffar Khan had thrown their lot with Gandhi and other Indian nationalist leaders of the time for the liberation movement of their homeland. So Gandhi started a small scale campaign of civil disobedience restricted to leading members of the Congress Party only. However, it was unanimously decided that Gandhi would not offer himself for prison. He therefore asked Vinoba Bhave to go to jail first, then Patel who was detained under the Defence of India Rules. The Congress President, Maulana Azad was the next. He was arrested and sentenced to eighteen months imprisonment; and so on till all the top leaders of the Congress were behind bars. But it was Subhash Chandra Bose's disappearance from his house arrest on 27th January 1941 that took the cake. It was indeed the most sensational news and development, quite embarrassing to the British authorities. "In something like a year, 23,223 persons were jailed for speaking against the war effort or the war itself." The German invasion of Soviet Russia in mid June 1941 caused a sea-change in the international politico-military situation. By the end of the year, the writing was on the wall: something had to be done, and done pretty quickly, to improve the Indian political situation. While German advance into

20. Gandhi sailed for England on 29 August 1931.

Russia continued steadily, Japan had consolidated her military position in Indo-China. While more than 25,000 Satyagrahis were jailed in a short span of four months, general release of political prisoners commenced on 4th December 1941 throughout India. In all fairness it must be recorded that the American public opinion was always pro-Indian and they were not happy over the treatment meted out to India by the British Government under Sir Winston Churchill. President Roosevelt often dwelt on the subject of India in his correspondence with the British Prime Minister. The fall of Rangoon on 7th March 1942 opened the gates for the Japanese to Bengal and Madras. Four days later Sir Winston Churchill conceded that something had to be done to enlist Indian political support for the Anglo-American war-effort. The Cripps Mission was the result of much prodding by Roosevelt and the American media, as well as of the wheel of fate turning in favor of the Japanese. Its failure was, in a way, a matter of satisfaction for Churchill since he did not want to be a party to the dissolution of the British Empire. It is a matter of conjecture if immediate independence to India in the wake of Cripps Mission in 1942 could have saved India the ordeal of Partition that came five years later.[21] Be that as it may, the emotional reaction to Rajagopalachari's proposal for acceptance of Pakistan in principle as a basis of settlement was so intense that he had to resign from the All India Congress Committee. It was only after that that the "Quit India"-demand started taking shape. Gandhi was equally emotional in elaborating his demand and wrote in May 1942: "When slavery was abolished in America many slaves protested, some even wept. ... the abolition was the result of a bloody war between the South and the North; and so though the Negro's lot is considerably better than before, he still remains the outcaste of high society. ... I ask for a bloodless end of an unnatural domination and for a new era, even though there may be protests and wailing from some of us." The 'Quit India' demand soon turned into a powerful movement, a sort of rebellion against the British Indian Government requiring immediate end of British rule in India leading to establishment of a genuinely democratic non-violent polity. Unfortunately, there was an inherent contradiction in Gandhi's stand on the question of 'two nation' theory and a separate homeland

---

21. Louis Fischer is of the opinion that the transfer of power to an Indian government could have taken place in 1942 in an orderly manner because of the presence of British and Allied troops, and that 'real power' would have remained in British hands for the duration of war. But in the same breath, he adds that the Muslim separatist elements under Jinnah were already powerful enough and would have obstructed any settlement in 1942 the same way as they did five years later. ... The 'ifs' and 'buts' of history!

for Muslims — the carving of Pakistan as a separate state. On the one hand he vehemently opposed any such move, on the other he emphasized: "I know no non-violent method of compelling the obedience of eight crores of Muslims to the will of the rest of India, however powerful the rest may represent. The Muslims must have the same right of self-determination that the rest of India has. We are at present a joint family. Any member may claim a division. ... As a man of non-violence, I cannot forcibly resist the proposed partition if the Muslims of India really insist upon it. But I can never be a willing party to the vivisection. ..." Thus, willy-nilly, Gandhi accepted the principle of Partition as early as 1940, but failed to take a firm stand either way. And in the end India had to pay a heavy price.

The prerequisite for Indian active cooperation in the wareffort was immediate independence for India. The Wardha Committee resolved on 14 July 1942 that if this was refused, they would be 'reluctantly compelled' to resort to a campaign of 'civil disobedience'. The All India Committee meeting held at Bombay on 7-8 August 1942 decided to launch a civil disobedience campaign — the 'Quit India' Movement. Gandhi was arrested at very late hours during the night of 8/9 August and taken to his last prison, the Agha Khan Palace in Poona. Concurrently, most of the other Congress leaders were also arrested. This action by the Government ended all hopes of a peaceful civil disobedience campaign. No agitation could be peaceful without Gandhi. And Gandhi was not even given newspapers for the early part of his imprisonment. As it happened, the large scale arrests worked up the Indians to frenzy. The campaign took a violent turn. Telephone/telegraph wires were cut; rail track damaged at numerous places; policemen were attacked. Sporadic acts of violence took place all over the country. The Governments in Delhi and London put the blame squarely on Gandhi and the Congress Party for violent acts of vandalism. This was complete distortion and misrepresentation of truth. This was typical example of war-propaganda. The blame lay squarely on the Government's peremptory arrest of Gandhi. In fact, Gandhi wrote to Linlithgow that he was pained over his arrest ordered by such an old friend without even the courtesy of a hearing. Perhaps, the Viceroy had his orders from London.

While Gandhi deplored the disruptive activities in the country, he laid the blame at the door of the Government. He emphasized that he could neither influence nor control the violence, which in any case, he always abhorred. However, Linlithgow replied that Gandhi and the Congress must bear the blame for whatever was happening. Gandhi responded by announcing a twenty-one day fast beginning 9th February

1942. The Viceroy took strong exception to the use of fast as a weapon of "political blackmail' for which there is no moral justification. In turn, Gandhi replied: "Despite your description of it as a form of political blackmail, it is on my part an appeal to the Highest Tribunal for justice, which I have failed to secure from you. If I do not survive the ordeal I shall go to the Judgment Seat with the fullest faith in my innocence. Posterity will judge between you as a representative of an all-powerful government and me a humble man who has tried to serve his country and humanity through it."

This fast lasted from 10th February to 2nd March 1943. It was a terrible experience for everyone in India. The Government too was under intense pressure from all quarters. Gandhi was sinking slowly. The fear of his death gripped the country. The Government was compelled to allow crowds of people to visit the Palace-prison to have '*darshan*' of Gandhi before the inevitable could happen.

Memphis: Garbage Strike

When Charles Blackburn, Director of Public Works in the City of Memphis, Tennessee, drove up to the Scott Street installation at 7:00 a.m. he immediately knew that there was a work-stoppage in the sanitation department. Nine hundred and thirty workers out of 1,100 handling 2,500 tons of garbage daily had walked off their jobs. In the asphalt and sewers-drainage sections, 214 men out of a work force of 230 were on strike. The garbage workers who were mostly blacks were observing what was to become a long drawn strike in Memphis. During that period a severe tornado struck the town, blowing away the garbage all over the town and its numerous streets. A heavy shower that invariably follows a tornado did the rest. The strike and its after effects assumed racial overtones. National staff members of the American Federation of State, County and Municipal Employees began pouring into Memphis that night. The leader of the Local 1733, T.O. Jones, met P.J. Ciampa at the airport and took him to meet some of the men.

The short chunky T.O. Jones had joined as a garbage worker in 1959. He was unhappy with the working conditions and the meagre compensation package. The workers were non-classified, hourly labourers. There was no job security. Jones started taking active interest in the small struggling Local union and soon rose to be its president. In January 1964 he set up a formal Independent Workers Association complete with rules and bylaws. He organized some minor agitations asking for improved conditions and pay packets. The then Public Works

Commissioner, Pete Sisson, affected some changes. He standardized pay scales and starting wage was increased from $1.27 to $1.60, and $1.80 to some categories. Measures were initiated to bring the employees under Social Security, Civil Service standards on vacations and sick leave. Nevertheless, the men were afraid; they knew how the City felt about their Union and they did not want the new boss, Charles Blackburn, to know they were supporting the Union.

Memphis, then twenty-second largest city in the nation, was almost 40 percent black. It never snowed in Memphis but frequent showers causing ice on the asphalt was common occurrence during winter. One fine morning there was light rain for about half an hour. Twenty-one black workers were sent home to cut costs. However, the whites worked; they stayed on the job with full pay irrespective of weather. Next morning Jones called the men to Union meeting and did not allow the men to go out on the trucks to work. After Blackburn arrived on the scene, Jones agreed to let the men go and discuss the matter with the Commissioner. In the process, several hours of work were lost. Jones wanted full pay for the twenty-one workers for the previous day, but the Commissioner would stick to the rules and pay for only two hours of show-up pay. Racial discrimination was written on the wall. After some discussions between the Commissioner, Ciampa and Jones, it was agreed to continue the negotiations. Soon after Ciampa took off, two men were killed in a freak accident; at least one of the men was eaten up by the grinder, a horrible sight if there was any.

There was no Workmen's Compensation, no life insurance. The City paid the families back pay, one month additional salary and $500 towards burial expenses. That is how far Mayor Henry Loeb and Blackburn could go, more on moral rather than legal grounds. Jones was unhappy over the whole affair of rainy-day pay, wages and compensation. A meeting was held in the Director's office at 8:00 p.m. Sunday, February 11, between the Commissioner and his two assistants, Maynard Stiles and Charles Woodall on the one side, and Jones and several union stewards who came with him. The Union put forward their demands:

- $2.35 per hour wage for labourers against existing scale of $1.65-$1.85.
- $3 an hour for truck drivers; scale $2.10.
- Time and a half for overtime over eight hours.
- Deductions of Union dues.

- Participation in the safety program.
- Sanitation trucks to drive more slowly.
- A Union newsletter.

Since no agreement could be reached on substantive issues, the meeting dispersed. A meeting with the Mayor proved to be a worse failure. This followed by a mass meeting of about 1,300 members of the Union held in the Firestone auditorium. The meeting approved the proposal to march to the City Hall to prove their strength. Mayor Loeb decided to address the gathering, but to no avail. The labour decided to go on strike. The City went in for hiring new hands. By the end of the first week 111 new hands were hired and 23 trucks out of 180 were on the roads.

NAACP in the Fray

The civic leaders, who were otherwise proud of racial progress and law and order situation in their City, were taken aback by the turn the events had taken. The strikers enjoyed full moral, legal and financial support of the NAACP, which decided to broaden the base of the protests to include tougher problems involving economics of black Memphis, unemployment, underemployment, lack of access to white collar and higher paying jobs, job-discrimination, and such other issues as housing, health-care, *et al.* A community coalition came into being to undertake this broad-based agenda. It was named COME — Community On the Move for Equality. Its strategy committee wanted to bring in outside speakers to provide fresh blood and impetus to the Memphis Movement. Three names were in prominence — Bayard Rustin to come through the Union, Roy Wilkins on behalf of NAACP and Dr. King being the nation leader of practically all the black organizations. Rev. Lawson was already in touch with King. His invitation supported by other COME leaders was indeed urgent. King could not ignore it, notwithstanding the pressures of PPC scheduled for April 28. After all, the issues in Memphis had taken on economic colors, and that is what the PPC was all about.

Tempers on both sides were already frayed. An explosion of violence was just waiting for a spark. King had no option but to visit Memphis to douse the impending flames of a violent confrontation. However, his emphasis on non-violence was like adding fuel to the fire since the Blacks were quite fed up with the White Power and its cruelties. The trouble was that the Whites were far more vindictive on the non-violent peaceloving Blacks than over the 'militant blacks'. It was like a replay of the treatment meted out to Nehru in India, the white troops getting upset with Nehru's non-violent behavior when he just did not react to their beatings and ill-treatment. On the other hand the overwhelming majority of white citizens of Memphis, as elsewhere, followed their cherished moral principles more in defiance than in their observance. They preached peace and goodness, but often indulged in violence against the poor so much so that visitors to the 1968-Funeral at Atlanta were openly insulted by the whites of the town.

Since the Garbage Strike at Memphis had undergone a transformation having undertones of a civil rights movement with economic issues as dominating factors, it was felt that the techniques of the old movement could be usefully applied to current economic demands. After all, that is what 'Poor Peoples' Campaign' was all about. It was finally decided to defer the PPC march so that King could come to Memphis for atleast one rally in the first place. And it was a massive rally, held in Mason Temple on the night of March 18. The crowd was beyond managing, overflowing the main hall, sitting on steps, standing in aisles and doorways, spilling outside, virtually barring the chief speaker of the evening from reaching the podium. King had to be sneaked into the hall through a side entrance by forming a wedge. As soon as the crowd saw Martin, they were on their feet; the applause reached a crescendo. They were cheering, shouting, arms raised in clenched fist salute. The labourers were thus giving vent to thirty-six days of fruitless negotiations, inaction, frustrations, workless-payless period of depression and poverty. King informed the gathering that he was in the midst of planning for the forthcoming 'Poor People's March' to Washington for improvement of economic conditions of the Negroes through better employment opportunities. He was carried away by the spirit of the moment and announced that if they wanted, he could make a march to Memphis City Hall as the starting point of the PPC. The crowd was hilarious beyond description. It was like getting the moon without asking for it! Some wanted him to start the march there and then, at that very moment itself. However, the date was set for four days later — March 28, 1968. Martin promised to return that day to lead the march. And he did.

While there was every justification for special provisions to be made for betterment of the poor and economically depressed classes, would it not infringe the rights of the rest of the populace? Would it not be morally and ethically incorrect to deprive one set of people for the benefit of the other, more competent and better qualified? This certainly gnawed at King's conscience and intellect, as well as that of the white liberals who were being called upon to sacrifice their rights and privileges in favour of those who were much less qualified to receive those, and not competent enough to make best use of those opportunities. Indian Prime Minister Nehru came to King's, as well as the white American's rescue. — Martin King recalled his discussion with Nehru on this vexing issue. When King asked Nehru how he could justify the special program of jobs and education preference for the "untouchables" and other low castes, Nehru replied: "Well, that may be, but it is our way of atoning for the centuries of injustices we have inflicted upon these people." Recalling this anecdote, King had no hesitation in introducing a similar proposal of 'national redress for the cumulative effects of American slavery and segregation'. Thus the 'Negro Bill of Rights' became the "Bill of Rights for the Disadvantaged."

Clayborn Temple was the starting point. The people started collecting there from early morning. By 9:00 a.m. quite a crowd had collected. Reverends Blackburn and Jackson walked around the Temple. The excitement was mounting. But it appeared peaceful and the two leaders were confident that the march would be non-violent as directed by Dr. King. But the police were not so confident. They apprehended trouble and were suitably deployed without making themselves overly conspicuous. Since King's plane was late, and the crowd was becoming restless, the leaders decided to start the march, Dr. King joining in later. Jesse Epps drove King in a white Continental found it difficult to maneuver to the head of the march. By then it was about 11:00 a.m. The estimates of the number of the marchers varied between ten and fifteen thousand. Pandemonium broke loose as soon as King reached the head of the marching column. Suddenly there was a resounding crack, smashing of glass. Soon a few more windows were targeted by young lads who were out for fun, and possibly some looting too. However, there was no real looting as such. The sound of smashing-cracking glass was enough to satisfy the violent streak of the youngsters.

The march was a solid phalanx stretching from curb to curb, led by King, Abernathy and local leaders with arms interlocked. Lawson and other marshals were in front and all along the side to keep a semblance of order. Soon the march swung around onto the Main Street. Suddenly a large group of kids sneaked from a side corner and started smashing store windows. Looting started. Black Power concept had taken over. Non-violence was down the drain. By this time the march had come about seven blocks and lasted barely twenty-five minutes. At this point, Reverend Lawson stopped the march and ordered all to turn about, back to the Church. Dr. King was then escorted by three motorcycle policemen dispatched by Police Chief MacDonald with orders to stay with him and to protect him. A few seconds later, 11:18 a.m. to be precise,[22] the Police Chief ordered the march dispersed. After holding a meeting with the militants, King returned to Atlanta, restless, confused, bewildered — like the rest of the SCLC leadership. His entire concept of non-violence was under attack, threatened to be consigned to oblivion so that Black Power could fill the vacuum. He could not possibly reconcile to such an ignominious end to an otherwise highly successful campaign for emancipation of the Negro. And of course he could not abandon Memphis. That had to be accommodated in the PPC schedule, which could be deferred by about two weeks. Another march in Memphis was thus again on the cards since King felt that his whole future and that of the Movement depended on a successful non-violent march in Memphis. Further, Martin Luther King himself would lead it. He was back in Memphis on Wednesday, April 3, and that night spoke to an enthusiastic rally of about 2,000 people at Mason Temple Church. Once again late since his flight was delayed due to a bomb-hoax. Hoax, or no hoax; the threat perception in the police was pretty high. They had reports of a number of threats to King's life if he returned to Memphis. Commissioner Holloman had made specific enquiries from the black leadership about King's proposed schedule. The police were extremely edgy and uneasy about King's security. 'The tempo and volume of threats against him were increasing' while cooperation by the SCLC had declined to almost nil inasmuch as his whereabouts, schedules, Motel room numbers, local engagements and travel plans, *et al*, were all open secrets. He had often stayed at the Loraine. During the current trip he had room 306 on the second floor, clearly marked on the doorway while entering from the balcony, which in turn overlooked a combination parking lot and courtyard, a small empty swimming pool and a few shabby buildings beyond.

End of Garbage Strike

An injunction had been issued against the proposed march. The court hearings were keeping the staff and attorneys busy as ever. Judge Brown had ruled that the proposed march be allowed to go on, subject to certain restrictions. Reverend Andy Young and Chauncey Eskridge returned to the Loraine to report to Dr. King on the court hearings. Reverend Kyles joined King and Abernathy in their room around 5:30 p.m. A large white Cadillac loaned by R.S. Lewis and Sons Funeral Home[23] for King's visit and the driver Solomon Jones stood in the courtyard below. So did many others including a number of youngsters who had gathered there to have

22. Garrow David J: op. cit. p. 225.

23. What an unfortunate coincidence!

a glimpse of their beloved leader. The time was just about 6:00 p.m., about half an hour before sunset. All of a sudden, there was a sharp cracking sound, like a fire-cracker or something like that. The sound appeared to have come from the direction of the courtyard. Dr. Martin Luther King Jr. had been shot. He fell down, severely wounded in the neck and face. Abernathy rushed from the room and knelt beside King. Patrolman Richmond saw King fall. His shouts brought out other police officers rushing towards the Lorraine. The first call at police dispatch came in at 6:03 p.m. Calls went out for ambulance. A terse order came from the Police Chief MacDonald: "Verify that report". The area of the motel and the brick building west of the Lorraine from which direction the shot was reported to have come was immediately sealed by TAC units. The police seized a rifle having a telescopic sight along with a box of shells covered by a bedspread. The suspect was described as a young white male who had hurriedly left the area in a white Mustang. Meanwhile, King was lifted onto a stretcher and carefully carried down the main stairs to an ambulance. The "loop lights", red lights to halt all cross traffic downtown in an emergency were thrown on while the police escort screamed through the streets to St. Joseph Hospital. At 6:19 p.m. police at the hospital radioed the Emergency Room report to headquarters: "Condition critical". As the news spread, Memphis was stunned. Unbelieving. Meanwhile Lawson kept up repeated advice to the people to stay calm, and not to panic. The Hospital had been sealed off as a precautionary measure. A mass of reporters had collected in the Emergency Room lobby.

The doctors worked feverishly. It was all hopeless. The autopsy later showed that a high velocity bullet had pierced through the chin and neck at a downward angle, severing the spinal chord in both the lower neck and upper chest regions. The heart beat stopped. Brain activity also ceased soon thereafter.

Dr. Martin Luther King Jr. was declared dead.

Atlanta's Mayor Ivan Allen, Jr. was the best known white civil rights advocates in the South. As soon as he heard of the shooting, he called Mrs. Coretta King and arranged a flight to Memphis. She was all set in Atlanta to board a plane when she was told that her husband was dead. She returned to the family's modest home on the edge of Atlanta's Vine City, a middle-class Negro neighborhood, and to her four children. At home the phone was already ringing with calls from across the country. Mrs. Eugene McCarthy, wife of the Minnesota Senator was on hand to answer the calls. Soon after the autopsy, the body was secured in a bronze casket, loaded into the hearse, and the long procession of cars escorted by police made its way to Memphis Metropolitan Airport. Flags flew at half mast at the Airport. Mrs. Coretta Scott King was already there with her children to escort her husband's body to Atlanta. She did not come out of her Electra prop jet sent by Robert Kennedy that brought her from Atlanta. However, the Attorney General spent some time with her in the plane. That Palm Sunday, April 7, was observed as a day of national mourning when flags all over the country flew at half mast.

In Memphis, Lawson went on the TV. His message:

> "It would be a compounding of his death if now Negro people or white people around our country should despair and decide that now is the time to let loose an orgy of violence. It would not be a tribute to Dr. King but a denial of his life and work."

A heavy curfew from 7:00 p.m. to 5:00 a.m. was in force in Memphis. Similar curfew restrictions were also declared in adjoining parts of Arkansas and Mississippi. The evening meeting planned earlier was cancelled. Rock throwing incidents, sniping, arson and looting were rampant. By 10:00 p.m. the biggest fire of the night was raging at a building materials supplies company north of downtown. The first contingent of 4,000 national guardsmen were being deployed to support the local police, Sheriff's deputies, highway patrol, and fifty Arkansas highway patrol who had come over to help restore some semblance of order. On hearing the news of shooting of Dr. King, Mrs. Loree Bailey, co-owners of Lorraine, suffered a stroke. She died the following Tuesday as the funeral for Dr. King got underway. By 10:00 p.m. that Sunday night a semblance of peace had returned to Memphis. Violence had almost ended. The final toll: three civilian deaths, forty-seven seriously wounded, 275 stores looted-burnt, and property-damage to the tune of \$900,000[24] — Considering the extreme seriousness of the situation, the casualties and damage was indeed minimal.

The next day a Memorial March was held in Memphis, led by Coretta King herself, and her three children. She had come since it was a matter of honour that the march scheduled by her husband be completed as he would have liked to. She informed the crowd that 'she had come because when it was impossible for her husband to be where he was needed, he would sometimes send her'. Police Commissioner Holloman was deeply concerned about her safety in the open march

24. Garrow David J.: op. cit. p. 339.

and stayed beside her throughout, along with a few others so as to make it virtually impossible for a sniper to take a pot shot at her. A new slogan was added to the Memorial March: "HONOUR KING — END RACISM". It was a large crowd, may be around 40,000, stretched along nine blocks from City Hall down Main to Linden. At the City Hall Plaza, Coretta spoke first in tribute to her husband, his courage and his achievements. Many others followed. The funeral in Atlanta the next day was the final rite of passage for Dr. Martin Luther King Jr.

Strike Finally Ends

Mayor Loeb continued to be intransigent as heretofore. The negotiations to end the strike were frustratingly long and tortuous; more so in the light of Dr. King's assassination was being directly connected with the strike. The bargaining continued *ad infinitum*. A hunger strike and sit-in had to be resorted to, to bring Mayor Loeb to agree to some sort of mutually acceptable agreement. The City did not have the financial resources for pay hikes. The multi-million dollar pharmaceutical firm of Plough Inc. offered $50,000 to cover the cost of wage-raises for two months. He had to add an additional $10,000 when the estimated expenditure was found to exceed the original estimate. The City accepted the generous offer. It was a most remarkable gesture on the part of a citizen to bail out his City. The final memorandum on the contentious issue of recognition and status of the Union to end the strike read as follows:

> The City of Memphis recognizes the American Federation of State, County and Municipal Employees, AFL-CIO, Local 1773, as the designated representative for certain employees in the Division of Public Works, for the purposes of negotiations on wages, hours and conditions of employment to the full extent and authority provided by the Charter of the City of Memphis and the laws of State of Tennessee. The term "certain employees" as used herein places no limitations or restrictions on the right of any employee to belong and be represented by the union.

The compromise on other matters like fringe benefits, insurance, vacations, sick leave, overtime, pensions, etc. was easy enough and need not be gone into here. The agreement was adopted by the City Council on Tuesday, April 16, 1968. The Garbage Strike came to an end early next morning when the workers went back to work after sixty-five days.

12

Means and Ends

Violent means will give violent Freedom that would be a menace to the world. We are merely the instruments of the Almighty's will and therefore ignorant of what helps us forward and what acts as impediment. We must rest satisfied with the knowledge of the means and if these are pure, we can fearlessly leave the end to take care of itself.

Dr. Martin Luther King Jr. used non-violent struggle as a form of social protest to achieve legal reforms for the Black minority. Though the ends towards which Gandhi and King strove were different, the means were the same — universal principles of non-violent behaviour towards creating peaceful transition of power. Both of them cherished non-violence as a creed for living. Like Gandhi, for King too the 'means must be as pure as the end'... the end represents the means in process and the ideal in the making'. Thus King's own ethical framework coincided with that of Gandhi even though the two lived in almost different ages and culturally oceans apart.[1] King went on to add that even though man has achieved mastery over science and technology thereby creating a highly complex civilization and society, yet 'there is an appalling lack of mastery over those primitive forces which result in wars and conflicts between races, nations and religious groups'. In his historic address at Riverside Church in New York City, exactly a year before his assassination, King said: "One of the great philosophical debates of history has been over the whole question of means and ends. .... But we will never have peace in the world until men everywhere recognize that ends are not cut off from the means, because the means represent the ideal in the making, and the end in process, and ultimately you can't reach good ends through evil means, because the

1. King, Martin Luther, Jr.: *Love, Law, and Civil Disobedience; A Testament of Hope*: op. cit., p. 45.

means represent the seed and the end represents the tree." In this address, Dr. Martin Luther King Jr. directly attacked the Johnson administration's policy on the war in Vietnam, and linked the struggle for civil rights with the anti-war movement. The question of Vietnam War was uppermost in the minds of the public and colored every aspect of the day to day actions of the Administration. It is indeed ironic that all great military geniuses and dictators talk(ed) about peace. "Every time we drop our bombs in North Vietnam, President Johnson talks eloquently about peace." The problem was not the intention or the ultimate end: It was the means adopted to achieve that end that was at the bottom line. "Destructive means cannot bring about constructive ends."[2]

The war in Vietnam had taken on the dimensions of a national issue penetrating every facet of political activity all over the United States. Like every leader that mattered, Martin Luther King was also drawn into this controversy. In 1967 he came out openly against the unjust and evil war in Vietnam, loud and clear. He made no bones about the horrible acts of cruelty, death and destruction being wrought on the hapless Asians in the name of democracy and equality, while at home the same principles of humanitarianism and justice were being openly flouted by white racists against their own black countrymen. It is noteworthy that, during his goodwill visit to India in December 1959, President Dwight D. Eisenhower said in his reply to the Civic Reception:

> Between the first largest democracy on earth, India, and the second largest, America, lie ten thousand miles of land and ocean. But in our fundamental ideas and convictions about democracy we are close neighbours.

However, following the murder of Dr. King, the emphasis shifted from Vietnam as the central point of electioneering to black rioting and law and order problems. The school desegregation question became one of the most emotional and divisive issues within the early Nixon Administration. It was generally believed that Nixon would manage the imbroglio in his usual crafty manner by currying favour with the whites in the South, at the expense of the Blacks and the Civil Rights. Unfortunately, some members of the Administration including the C.I.A. Chief Hoover, stooped down so low as to take undue advantage of unsubstantiated craftily created eavesdrop reports on the alleged sexual indiscretions of the late Dr. King. Hoover's vendetta against Dr. King was much too deeprooted to care for any moral qualms.

2. Ibid. *A Time tò Break Silence*; New York, 4 April 1967. *A Testament of Hope*; op. cit., p. 231.

Nehru Adapts Gandhian Non-violence

Gandhi hailed Gopal Gokhle (died in 1915) as his 'political Guru'. During World War I Gandhi personally went from village to village in Kheda district of Gujarat in India on a recruitment drive for the British-Indian Army. His friends and the public were indeed puzzled by his role of a recruiting agent for the (British) Indian Army. He met 'cold incomprehension and even hostility'. People asked him how he reconciled this fighting with his motto of non-violence. His explanation was simple: Loyalty to the British Empire.[3] In the process he worked himself sick and had a nervous breakdown. He had followed this policy even in his much younger days in South Africa. In 1906 there was an uprising by the Zulus in Natal. The British Army was deployed to put down the revolt. Gandhi believed that if Indians could agitate for citizenship, they were under moral obligation to perform civic duty and render help to the British when they were faced with some problem(s). He raised a party of twenty-four volunteers to work as stretcher-bearers. They were put in uniform and Gandhi was given the rank of sergeant-major. Most of the work of Gandhi's corps was nursing the wounded Zulus. The whites merely watched the Indians and jeered at them for looking after the 'niggers'. This work kept Gandhi busy for a month or so during which time his family moved over to Phoenix. It would be of interest to note that the first president of African National Congress, John Dube, and M.K. Gandhi were neighbours in Inanda in South Africa. Each of them established one monumental institution for human development — Ohlange Institute by John Dube and Phoenix Settlement by Gandhi. Both the institutions were within a stone throw of each other, one for the Blacks and the other primarily for the Indians settled in South Africa.

Around the same time, young Ghaffar Khan had revealed the mettle he was made of. Abdul Ghaffar was in the sixth class when, in 1906, his elder brother moved to Bombay to pursue his medical studies. The impressionable young mind of Abdul Ghaffar was impressed by the smart turnout of British officers with an attractive sword hanging in the shining scabbard on the side. The glamour of army uniform and the power that went with it was enough to persuade young Ghaffar to apply for a commission in the Indian army. Since he came from a rich and influential Khan family, he was cleared for grant of a direct commission without the formality of at least passing his Matriculation examination. He joined the Guides at Mardan. As luck would have it, a young Englishman passed a

3. Gandhi had exhibited similar sense of loyalty to the British during the Boer and Zulu Wars in South Africa.

humiliating personal remark against Ghaffar and he resolved, there and then, not to serve in the army. Good for him and the country.

Nehru went to his first meeting of Indian National Congress (INC) along with his father, Motilal, to Bankipore in remote Bihar. Notwithstanding the rustic surroundings, these English-educated upper class Indians were dressed in "morning coats and well pressed trousers". Nehru did not appreciate the "timid moderate loyalist insistence that the only way to reach that goal was by peaceful methods"[4] So Gandhi wrote to Nehru: "Our progress towards the goal will be in exact proportion to the purity of our means. If we can give an ocular demonstration of our uttermost truthfulness and non-violence, I am convinced that our statement of the national goal cannot long offend the interests" of those whose livelihood depends upon exploitation of the masses. Nehru was much younger and flamboyant. At that point of time, he found it difficult to imbibe Gandhi's matured philosophy that was the bottom line for his freedom struggle. Differences between Nehru and Gandhi thus grew deeper and wider — ideologically, as well as regarding tactics and strategy, means and ends, goals, and methods of achieving the same. Nehru was a product of modern revolutionary ideas of 'Marxist-Leninist in theory and Fabian or Trotskyite in practice.'[5] Conversely, Gandhi was a product of Hinduism with ideas of '*satya*' (Truth) and '*ahimsa*' (Non-violence) based on the Vedas. For Gandhi: "Truth was God". His ideas of development of rural economy through weaving and use of '*khadi*' (*khaddar* — homespun cloth) with *Charkha* (the spinning wheel) as the mechanical contrivance were the corner stones of his concept of generating full rural-employment, thereby making the villages economically self-sufficient. "Even as each home cooks its own food without difficulty, so may each home weave its own yarn. And just as, in spite of every home having its own kitchen, restaurants continue to flourish, so will mills continue to supply our additional wants."

These notions of rural industrialization were archaic to Nehru, who wrote in his autobiography: Gandhi is a "curious phenomenon — a person of the type of a medieval Catholic saint ... and at the same time a practical leader ..."[6] The cap-stone was the typical style 'Gandhi-topee' (cap) stitched out of *khadi* cloth as symbolic wear of a congressman. However, in public Nehru always maintained that there were no differences between him and Gandhi. Be that as it may, Gandhi explicitly rejected

4. Akbar M.J.: *Nehru — The Making of India*; Harmondsworth, Penguin, 1988, p. 30.
5. Wolpert S.: *Nehru*; New York, p.156.
6. Nehru, Jawaharlal: *An Autobiography*, London, John Lane, 1936.

Nehru's view that one's methods can be separated from the results achieved. Gandhi argued that a good objective does not justify morally bankrupt or violent means. To Gandhi, 'means are after all everything'. In many respects, Martin Luther King Jr. was a Xerox copy of Gandhi and an antithesis of Nehru, except the western style dress of course (!).

In those days Socialism was a fashionable cult in the Third world. Perhaps it still is. Nehru was its ardent advocate. And communism was on an ascending curve by virtue of Russian power of the gun, and its nuclear arsenal. Chinese brand of the ideology was not far behind either. These were comparatively easy means to the ends sought by Gandhi, and later by King. But neither of them faltered for the simple reason that Communism was based on 'ethical relativism' where the ends justified the means. But Gandhi always considered means and ends as one closely linked entity in which means were as important as the ends, if not more so. And King followed this line implicitly, even though he imparted a religious shade to his precept: "Christianity sets forth a system of absolute moral values and affirms that God has placed within the very structure of this universe certain moral principles that are fixed and immutable."[7] Since communism hardly had any political power base in America, except perhaps as a lion-syndrome-ploy in the minds of FBI, King made very little reference to this as a means to achieve his social and political ends. While Gandhi would not touch Communism even with a barge pole, Nehru continued to be "neutral' on the side of Russia (Read Communism).

Gandhi sought his own Hermitage or Ashram and founded it on 25th May 1915 across the river Sabramati from Ahmedabad in Gujarat, India. In 1916 the Ashram had three country looms and three fly-shuttles; in 1917 four more fly-shuttles were added. Gandhi learnt to weave himself and spent nearly three hours on the job everyday. His austere life-style cut off from worldly temptations was an example in 'simple-living high-thinking' to his followers. He would wake up at 4:00 a.m. for prayers, followed by sweeping-cleansing of living quarters, washing clothes in the river, and cleaning the latrines. Every ashramite was equal and nobody performed any personal service for someone else except on a collective basis. There were no servants.

The landmark political events of the year 1920, which need not be gone into here, led to mass upheaval and confrontation with the British. The Congress session held in Dec 1920 declared its intention to acquire Swaraj within one year. Gandhiji announced the following guiding principles towards that end:

7. King M.L.K.: *Strength to Love*; Harper, New York, 1963, pp. 96-98.

1. Acquire greater mastery over our own selves. Remain perfectly calm, peaceful, have with goodwill. Seek forgiveness for any unkind words or actions.
2. Hindu-Muslim unity without suspecting each other.
3. Completely give up untouchability.
4. Complete abstinence from alcohol.
5. Spinning wheel in every home. Give up foreign cloth; only khadi to be used.

Gandhi further elaborated: chastity in work is as essential as chastity in life. Loyalty without subordination. No boycott of opponents. No coercion. Conversion by gentle persuasion. Be ever courteous and patient. That is why Gandhi believed that self-rule depended on how good India was, not how bad the British were. "I live for India's freedom and would die for it because it is a part of Truth. Only a free India can worship the true God. Man does not live by bread alone. Many prefer self respect to food...." The golden rule of conduct is mutual toleration. We should pray that a Hindu should be a better Hindu, a Moslem a better Moslem, and Christian a better Christian. "I broaden my Hinduism by loving other religions as my own."[8] *In Ethical Religion*, Gandhi says, "True morality consists not in following the beaten track but in finding out the true path for ourselves and fearlessly following it."[9]

Jawaharlal was in the forefront of this mass movement called Satyagraha. Motilal was dead against this concept of Satyagraha and going to jail. When Jawaharlal fell for this new idea head over shoulders, Motilal was appalled. He distrusted Satyagraha thoroughly and called it 'stupid idiocy' and 'futile waste of time and energy.' Nevertheless, by May 1922 he too was soon converted to this mass movement. The emphasis was on rural economy and development at the village level. Liberation through khadi became the key to Independence — non-violent resistance in another form to expel the British from India by boycotting English mill-made imported cloth to stifle the British economy at home. King's Montgomery Bus Boycott was like a leaf out of khadi movement (!) and it almost suffocated the franchise bus-line into bankruptcy.

The Indian Muslim League was in the opposite camp, on the side of the British, to perpetuate the foreign rule. They were voluntary victims of British 'Divide and Rule' strategy. Their basic theme of propaganda:

8. Fischer Louis: *Young India*; op. cit. pp. 191, 197 and 212.
9. Gandhi M.K.: *Ethical Religion*; p. 38

Real Muslims were those who were in the Muslim League. Any Muslim who opted for Gandhi and secularism of the Congress Party was a paid agent of the Hindus, and hence despicable. The nationalist Congress had no right to seek the support of any Muslims since Muslims were the sole preserve of the Muslim League, or its allied organizations. Should there be any deviation from these three fundamentals, it would lead to a catastrophe. The Muslim League had injected so much poison that their Chief, M.A. Jinnah refused to shake hands with Maulana Azad or Khan Abdul Ghaffar Khan when the League and the Congress delegations met at the Viceregal Lodge at 10 a.m. on Sunday 5th May 1946, (which happened to be Lord Wavel's sixty-third birthday) for a second meeting for discussions with the Cabinet Mission. Jinnah shook hands only with Nehru and Patel. When the Frontier Gandhi merged his Khudai Khidmatgars (Servants of God) into the Indian National Congress, he had to face similar charges from the cronies of the League along with the usual identical propaganda. Khan Abdul Ghaffar Khan defended himself publicly in November 1931 and took the stand that:

> The Congress is a national and not a Hindu body. It is a *Jirga* (assembly of representatives Pathan tribes) composed of Hindus, Jews, Sikhs, Parsis and Muslims. The Congress as a body is working against the British. The British nation is the enemy of the nationalist Congress and of the Pathans. I have therefore joined it and made common cause with the Congress to get rid of the British.

In order to find a solution to the Indian imbroglio, Gandhi had to deal with Jinnah on a regular basis. And Jinnah was such a man that if Gandhi had a solution to every problem, Jinnah had a problem for every solution.[10]

Chauri Chaura and Chicago West Side Episodes

While the experimental Civil Disobedience Movement was in progress in the small district of Bardoli in the Bombay Presidency, Gandhi received a report on 8th February 1922 of a macabre incident of horrendous proportions from Chauri Chaura in United Provinces. A peaceful legal procession was taken out there without any police interference. But after it was all over, a few stragglers were manhandled by the police. The mob thereupon returned. The constables opened fire and the few rounds of ammunition they had were soon exhausted. The police then took shelter in the *Thaana* for safety. The mob then set fire to the Thaana. "The self-imprisoned constables had to come out for dear life and as they did so, they were hacked to pieces and the mangled

10. Anonymous Quote.

remains were thrown into the raging flames."[11] The dreadful atrocity took Gandhi completely by surprise, and he was terribly depressed by the ferocity of this incident. He suspended the civil disobedience campaign in Bardoli and cancelled non-cooperation in the rest of India. As a penance for the Chauri Chaura crime, he fasted for five days.

When Gandhi called off the Bardoli experiment, Indian nationalist and revolutionary leaders protested against Gandhi's action, more so since the Movement had already gone that far. But Gandhi was adamant. He accepted that it might be politically unwise to call off the aggressive program at that stage, but it was morally and religiously a sound decision. It was in accord with the fundamental principles of Satyagraha and there was no going back on that. Gandhi was arrested, after all. The Viceroy issued the order on 1st March 1922, and it was executed on March 10 at half past ten at night. Calm and peace once again prevailed all over the country, not because of the brutal power of the Raj, but through the actions and edicts of one man whom India obeyed implicitly. Notwithstanding Gandhi and the obedience he commanded from one and all, violent incidents were bound to occur in a mass movement some time or the other, somewhere or the other. Dr. King too had to face similar depressing situations. For instance: the riots in Watts perpetrated by the black protesters resulted in more than thirty fatalities, of which all but two were Negroes themselves besides loss of property worth many millions. The worst part of the Watts episode was that there was "joy among the rioters of Watts, not shame"[12]. The same holds good for the 'social eruption' of July 1966, the riots in Chicago West Side, the Los Angeles riots, and violent disorders in many other northern slums. Howsoever influential the leader of a mass movement might be, the frustrations and hopelessness generated by decades of living in revolting conditions, injustice and cruelties silently faced, the oppression let loose by the powers that be — all this and a lot more — is bound to burst into open some day, somewhere or the other. Gandhi and King were no exception to the laws of society.

"I am unable to subscribe to the methods of bribery and deceit even for gaining entrance into heaven, much less for gaining India's freedom. For heaven will not be heaven and freedom will not be freedom if either is gained through such methods. ... I remain loyal to an institution so long that institution conduces to my growth, to the growth of the nation.

---

11. Extract from Gandhi's own account from his weekly paper *Young India,* dated 16 February 1922.
12. King M.L.: *Autobiography,* op. cit. p. 293.

Immediately I find that the institution, instead of conducing to this growth, impedes it, I hold it my bounden duty to be disloyal to it. ... There is only one sovereign remedy, namely, non-violent non-cooperation."[13]

"No organization can run smoothly when it is divided into camps, each growling at the other and each determined to have its own way by hook or by crook. ... To prepare for home rule individuals must cultivate the spirit of service, renunciation, truth, non-violence, self-restraint, patience ... they must engage in constructive work — Removal of untouchability, Hindu-Moslem Unity, and universal spinning. ... A true Congressman is a true servant. He ever gives, ever wants service. He is easily satisfied so long as his own comfort is concerned. He is always content to take a back seat. He is never communal or provincial. His country is his paramount consideration. He is brave to a fault because he has shed all earthly ambition, fear of Death himself. And he is generous because he is brave, forgiving because he is humble and conscious of his own failings and limitations. ... I cannot picture to myself a time when no man shall be richer than another. But I do picture to myself a time when the rich will spurn to enrich themselves at the expense of the poor and the poor will cease to envy the rich. ... Why should men arrogate to themselves the right to regulate female purity? ..." The British rule has impoverished India by a system of progressive exploitation and by a ruinous expensive military and civil administration which the country can never afford. "How can one be compelled to accept slavery?"

India was at the crossroads of destiny. While Gandhi made all possible efforts to save India from 'vivisection', the militant Muslim League under Jinnah was prepared to accept nothing short of a separate State, the creation of a new nation. Jinnah had come to hold the "two nation" theory as a fundamental principle of his political creed. It may be recalled that while delivering his Presidential address to the Lahore session of Muslim League in March 1940, Jinnah categorically stated that "the present unity of India was artificial, dating from the British period and maintained by British bayonet. ... The Muslims are a nation and they must have their homelands, their territory and their state." Gandhi told Jinnah: "You can cut me in two if you wish but don't cut India in two." Jinnah was adamant and extremely intransigent. In any case he had full support of the British Government to achieve his nefarious objective. His jealousy of Gandhi's unique position on the world scene and his immense dislike of Nehru were the added factors for his vain attitude and sense of personal superiority. Be that as it may, the Cabinet Mission published

---

13. *Young India* (Louis Fischer; op. cit.); pp. 217-18.

their decisions on 16 May 1946 and, in the aftermath of the terrible communal riots of Calcutta as the consequence of Direct Action Day ordered by Jinnah[14] the month before, Lord Wavell, on the advice of His Majesty's Government, invited Nehru to form an Interim Government which came into being on 2nd September 1946. British policy of 'Divide and Rule' was having a heyday and communal frenzy knew no bounds. In Delhi, the capital of the new nation in the making, murder was rife. No street was safe. Gandhi undertook his last fast on 13th January 1948 for restoring peace in Delhi itself. In his words: "If Delhi goes, India goes, and with that the last hope of world peace." It was again a fast unto death, or until peace returns to Delhi, which fortunately it did. Leaders of both the communities pledged to keep the peace and the fast ended on 18th January 1948 when a glass of orange juice was accepted by Gandhi from his old friend, Maulana Azad.

In the aftermath of communal strife prevailing in the country, nationalist Congress members in the Interim Government were considerably agitated over intrigues of British officials who were in *de facto* control of the administration, as well as the obstructionist posture adopted by the League on every single issue. In February 1947 Nehru confessed to Gandhi: "We are drifting everywhere, and sometimes I doubt if we are drifting in the right direction. We live in a state of perpetual crisis and have no real grip of the situation." Very brave of Nehru, as the Prime Minister, to admit his helplessness in so many words in so candid a manner.

And that holds good for King too. Martin had a strong unbendable and formidable sense of conscience. It kept him throughout on the path that he thought was right. And if he did slip up sometime, he made it a point to apologize and seek forgiveness. No wonder therefore that Martin did feel that many an honour heaped on him in later life did not belong to him alone; his colleagues and the organizations he represented deserved an equal, if not larger share of those honours. Indeed, Martin was a humble man by nature. For him: "Constructive ends can never give absolute moral justification to destructive means, because in the final analysis the end is pre-existent in the means. ... Man is not made for the State; the State is made for the man. To deprive man of freedom is to relegate him to the status of a thing, rather than elevate him to the status of a person. Man must never be treated as a means to the end of the state, but always as an end within himself."[15]

---

14. At least five thousand were killed and fifteen thousand wounded in those riots which claimed many more lives in other parts of India.
15. King Martin Luther: op. cit. (*Autobiography*) p. 20.

13

Struggle for Freedom

Indeed, segregation and discrimination are strange paradoxes in a nation founded on the principle that 'All Men are Created Equal'.

The initial modus operandi to gain freedom and justice was non-cooperation. It was soon transformed into non-violence, and then the basic doctrine of Satyagraha. The latter is a means to an end, to secure the rights of the oppressed; those who are made to suffer by the authority of the State. Satyagraha believes that the authority of the State is not unlimited. The tyranny of the majority is not necessarily to be tolerated merely because it is imposed by the majority. In fact, the State invariably tends to trample on the rights and privileges of the people, the minorities in particular. According to Raghavan N. Iyer: "In essence, Satyagraha emphasizes that social and political conflicts can be handled best in an atmosphere in which the contestants respect the moral worth of each other, distinguish between measures and persons, conduct their battles in a spirit of self-criticism, and abstain from the cruder forms of coercion."[1]

Desegregation through legal provisions assists in merely bringing the people physically closer. It is symbolic and is enforced through fear of punishment for breaking the law. And that certainly is not enough. In a vibrant society intermingling of people of different races and creeds should come from the heart, and not through fear of the law. No doubt, the law gives a helping hand; but it is the heart and soul that bring about true unity. For this reason, Dr. King's ultimate goal was "genuine inter-group and inter-personal living. Only through non-violence can this goal be attained, for the aftermath of non-violence is reconciliation and the creation of the beloved community." But this is easier said than

1. Williams A. John: op. cit. p. 174.

done. Every legal victory of the Negro in federal courts brought in its wake angry passions and deep prejudices from the white race. The exceptions were indeed microscopic. City ordinances and State laws were enacted to counter the positive outfall from the Federal Courts. Negro leaders were continuously harassed and arrested under these local laws and their houses were bombed. Dr. Martin Luther King's own house was bombed at about nine-thirty in the late evening of Monday, 30th January 1956. It was a thunderous blast causing considerable damage to the house, but fortunately no injuries to Coretta or the children. At that time, Martin was addressing a big gathering when he noticed that something was fishy. On his persistent queries, he was told what had happened. He interrupted his speech to tell the people what had happened and urged them all to go straight home. "Don't get panicky and lose your heads. Let us keep moving with the faith that what we are doing is right, and with the even greater faith that God is with us in this struggle." There was great tension in and around Kings' bombed out house. The white reporters were even afraid to leave to go and file their stories. The Commissioner Sellers and Mayor Gayle apologized to Martin for what had happened in their city. But the people were furious, angry and excited. Martin appreciated the gravity of the situation in that a slight slip could trigger the most awful riot in U.S. history. In a confident calm voice he said: "My wife and my baby are all right. I want you to go home and put down your weapons. We cannot solve this problem through retaliatory violence. We must meet violence with nonviolence. Remember the words of Jesus: 'He who lives by the sword will perish by the sword.' We must love our white brothers, no matter what they do to us. ... We must meet hate with love."[2] It is as if Mahatma Gandhi was personified at that point of time, and inspired Martin to say what Gandhi too would himself have said. As the crowd started thinning out, a white policeman said: "If it hadn't been for that nigger preacher, we'd all be dead."

One of his noteworthy speeches in his preaching career was at New York on 17 May 1956, the second anniversary of the Supreme Court ruling on desegregation in schools, when on the invitation of James A. Pike (later Bishop), he preached at the Cathedral of St. John the Divine. The subject was based on Exodus 14:30 (And Israel saw the Egyptians dead on the seashore) "The Death of Evil Upon the Seashore" in which Martin compared the Negro struggle to the Hebrews' escape from Egyptian bondage — the inevitability of victory of good over evil — like

2. King Scott Coretta: op. cit. pp. 140-44.

Mahatma Gandhi had faith in Indians' struggle for independence from the British Raj. In July Martin spoke in the same vein at the Democratic National Convention about the 'civil rights as one of the supreme moral issues of our time', again taking a cue from Mahatma Gandhi's struggle for the rights of Indians to run their country in their own way. The treatment of Indian freedom fighters by the British-Indian police, the atrocities inflicted by them on the hapless citizenry, was comparable to that of the Blacks by the Montgomery police.

The next target of whites' ire was the house of E.D. Nixon which was bombed soon after the King's house. However, things cooled down thereafter. Coretta and the baby left for the safety of her parents' and in-laws' house while Martin went out on a lecture tour. It was then that a Montgomery attorney dug out some ancient regulation prohibiting 'boycotts'. The grand jury was summoned and indictments were issued against Martin and about ninety other leaders of the Movement. The police swung into action and started filling in the jails. Martin rushed to Atlanta to pick up Coretta and the baby. Daddy King protested. Martin protested. "I must go back to Montgomery. I would be a coward to stay away. ... while my brothers and sisters were being arrested ... I have reached the point of no return." Coretta stood by her husband's decision irrespective of the dangers inherent in that decision. So Daddy King too decided to return to Montgomery. Martin went down to the courthouse, booked, fingerprinted, photographed as a criminal with a number hung on his chest, and then released on bail to stand trial on March 19th before Judge Eugene Carter. Verdict: Guilty. Meanwhile, the case regarding constitutionality or otherwise of bus-segregation was taken up by the Federal Supreme Court which turned down the State law.

The Negro leaders took all this in their stride. They made a virtue of their suffering. "To suffer in a righteous cause is to grow to our humanity's full stature. ... If he has to go to jail for the cause of freedom, let him enter it in the fashion Gandhi urged his countrymen, 'as the bridegroom enters the bride's chamber' — that is, with a little trepidation but with a great expectation." Thus, Dr. Martin Luther King Jr. became a national figure at the young age of twenty-seven. A number of people, both Blacks and Whites, came from all over America to merely see him, to have his '*darshan*'. "Some came all the way from India, touched by the Gandhian aspects of our nonviolent protest."[3] A white librarian and member of the local Human Relations Council, Juliette Morgan wrote a letter to the print-media praising, and comparing

3. Ibid. p. 151.

the Montgomery Movement to that in India against the British regime. The white community completely ostracized her. She went into a depression and committed suicide. A tragic end to laudable personal conviction of high moral standing ... And of course there was no end to the long list of Negro leaders who made a beeline to the King's house.

Dr. King charted out the following program for his people's emancipation:

- Non-violent resistance to all forms of racial injustice, including local laws and practices;
- Imaginative, bold, constructive action to end the demoralization caused by the legacy of slavery and segregation including schools — Black schools were very different and extremely unequal from white schools. The latter had fine buildings, issued free textbooks, had well stocked libraries and ran for nine months in a year while the black ones did not have any of these facilities and had only seven months sessions — slums and second-class citizenship;
- Continue the struggle with dignity and courage to end demoralization;
- A new frontal assault on poverty, disease and ignorance.

The Corresponding Indian and American Scenes

Initially, there was general consensus amongst the Indian political parties regarding distribution of seats on the new Executive Council under the Viceroy. But it was a short-lived consensus. While the number of seats to be allotted to the Muslims was to be the same as to the Caste Hindus, some seats were to be earmarked for the Scheduled Castes, Sikhs and other minorities. The points at dispute were:

- Who those Muslims members would be;
- Jinnah objected to liberal allocation of seats to the other minorities, as he feared that they would vote with the Congress.

Since Maulana Azad representing the Congress and Jinnah on behalf of the League failed to come to an understanding as to the strength and composition of the proposed Executive Council, the Conference was adjourned till 14th July to enable the parties to submit lists of their nominees. All the parties except Jinnah complied by 7th July 1945. The Nationalist Congress list included Maulana Azad himself and Asaf Ali since it was a matter of principle for the Congress as a national and not a communal organization like the Muslim League of Jinnah. Jinnah continued to be adamant that all Muslim members of the Council shall be nominees of the League alone, and therefore did not submit his list. That was the end of the Simla Conference. At this failure, Maulana Azad observed: "If the Conference had not broken down because of Jinnah's opposition, the result would have been that the Muslims, who constituted only about twenty-five per cent of the total population of India, would have had seven representatives in a Council of fourteen. ..." The Congress had indeed been generous and gone as far as it possibly could, while the League remained stupid in its obduracy. The claim by the League that it alone represented all the Muslims of India in spite of the fact that the predominantly Muslim Frontier Province had a Congress Ministry and did not elect even a single candidate on behalf of the League. In fact, a large block of Muslim population of India had nothing to do with the League. But Jinnah's apprehension was domination of Muslim minority by the Hindu majority.

The Negroes in the South were also fearful of the white majority. It was not merely in the mind of the Negro; it was a physical entity in the form of Ku Klux Klan and racial hatred. The administrative machinery of the Southern States gave unflinching support to these disruptive elements and treated the Negroes as sub-human species whose life had no value or sanctity. One of the sermons Martin gave was on the subject of 'Fear' in its totality; its title: "Antidotes for Fear" for which he took as his text I John 4:18 — "There is no fear in love; but perfect love casteth out fear; because fear hath torment. He that feareth is not made perfect in love." A person can overcome fear by facing it squarely; secondly, through courage of mind since 'courage is the power of the mind to overcome fear'; and thirdly, fear is mastered by true love; and finally, faith is the sure antidote to fear — faith in God, faith in one's cause and faith in the self.

The international situation was in a flux. The Labour assumed power in London on 26th July 1945, barely two weeks after the Simla Conference. The Japanese surrender on 14th August 1945 brought the Second World War to an end. The end of British Empire was in sight. Khan Abdul Ghaffar Khan was Gandhi's constant companion, more so after Gandhi's devoted Secretary Mahadev Desai and Kasturba Gandhi were no more. Ghaffar Khan kept reminding the people of India that "to serve humanity was to serve God, and this could be done only through non-violent means. ... that the Musalmans were the brethren of the Hindus. They had to join their hands in the task of driving away the British who cunningly sowed the seeds of dissension to an extent that even children were taught to talk in terms of Hindus and Muslims."

Initially, Khan Abdul Ghaffar Khan was against his personal participation in the election campaign in the Frontier Province. But when he saw English men and women actively participating in the election work in favour of the League, he changed his mind, and plunged headlong in the campaign barely one month before the voting. Unfortunately, the election was fought on a totally sectarian basis insofar as the League was concerned. For Jinnah, the question was Hindustan or Pakistan, Hindu or Musalman, Islam or Kafir, mosque or temple? The British authorities worked ceaselessly on the side of the League and against the Khudai Khidmatgars. In the end, truth and non-violence triumphed. The League was decisively defeated.

The Birmingham demonstrations goaded President Kennedy to submit fresh legislation for a 'new and broadened civil rights program'. He told the Congress in no uncertain terms that racial discrimination was not only economically costly: "Above all, it is wrong". The President did not push the reforms as hard as he should have done. Perhaps, "Vote Bank" politics made the President drag his feet. One of the devices to keep the Blacks off the voter's list was the high poll tax. In Alabama it cost two dollars to vote! And if a black went to vote for the first time at, say age thirty, he had to pay all the back taxes since he reached the age of twenty-one! He wanted the votes of both sides with the result that he, or the Administration for that matter, was "paralyzed by the conflicting needs of each." Around the same time National Guards were deployed to secure the admission of two Negroes to the University of Alabama. Concurrently, the President declared: "We face a moral crisis as a country and as a people. It cannot be met by repressive police action. It cannot be left to increased demonstrations in the streets. ..." The President put forward a new civil rights bill before the Congress. There was bitter opposition to many of the liberal provisions of the proposed legislation.

The mutiny by the Ratings of the Royal Indian Navy, and the emotional upsurge amongst the public at large due to the trials of members of the Indian National Army who fought under the leadership of Netaji Subhas Chandra Bose against the British-Indian army, *et al*, brought sense to His Majesty's Government in London as to the dire consequences that might result if the situation was allowed to drift any further. The result: the three member Cabinet Mission comprising of Lord Pethick-Lawrence, Sir Stafford Cripps and Lord Alexander arrived in India on 23rd March 1946. After prolonged discussions and series of meetings, and in the absence of a mutually acceptable solution, the Mission recommended a federal type of government for the whole of India including the princely states. The

Federal Government would deal with Foreign Affairs, Defence and Communications while the other powers of governance would be vested in the Provincial and State governments. British India was proposed to be divided into three groups of provinces: one comprising the Punjab, North West Frontier Province, Sind and Baluchistan; second comprising Bengal and Assam; and the third the rest. A Constituent Assembly composed of 296 members elected on the basis of communal franchise was to frame the Constitution. Each unit had the right to opt out of the Union after the first election was held under the new Constitution. By reconstituting the Viceroy's Executive Council, an Interim Government was formally installed at the Centre on 2nd September 1946 with Jawaharlal Nehru as the leader. The entire scheme was highly complicated and ambiguous in many respects leaving loopholes for misinterpretation. The fact was that the British did not want the Muslims and Hindus to join hands; they were bent upon dividing India for their own strategic reasons. At the very outset Nehru asked whether the British were now prepared to give freedom to India and withdraw their army. When the Viceroy replied that they were prepared to leave India, but give it to whom was the question. The Congress and the League must first come to a settlement. Nehru responded: "Give India to Muslims, but you must quit."

Notwithstanding the various palliative measures, the progress in equal rights for the Negroes was much too slow. Massive demonstrations were therefore organized, the most critical one being in Birmingham on 3rd April 1963. It was held under the leadership of Martin Luther King Jr. and the Southern Christian Leadership Conference, "demanding fair employment opportunities, desegregation of public facilities, creation of a committee to plan desegregation, and dropping of charges against King and the other 2,500 persons who were arrested in the course of the demonstrations."[4] It was a matter of deep anguish for American democracy. There were loud cries of human rights violations when, on 3rd May, the Birmingham police-dogs and high pressure water hoses were let loose against the demonstrators, who retaliated by using stones and bottles. Many liberals in the country were deeply pained and shocked over the police behavior. School children also joined their elders. They too endured police dogs and fire hoses, were arrested and taken to jail in school buses (!) singing 'freedom songs', and shouting "We want Freedom". Sympathetic demonstrations were held in a number of Northern cities and some in the Southern cities too. The tempo of demonstrations increased after Medgar Evers, the leader of the Mississippi

---

4. Franklin John Hope: op. cit. pp. 630-31.

NAACP was shot outside his home in Jackson. It is the police dogs and pressure hoses that went a long way in galvanizing the nation's collective conscience, aroused to a crescendo by extraordinary television coverage depicting snarling dogs and small children in the same shot. Peace was finally restored in July after the National Guards were called out, when agreement was reached to desegregate schools and public accommodations, to enlarge employment opportunities and building of low-rent houses for Negroes. The Black leaders were insisting on *de facto* de-segregation in housing and education; mere cosmetic legal measures were spurned. Before the 35th President of the United States was assassinated, passions in the Black Movement had reached a high point of no return. Birmingham was indeed the flash point. King warned the Administration that the Country was at a "historical crossroads". The nation's moral commitment and political fortunes were at stake. The Blacks talked of freedom in every slogan: freedom songs, freedom rides, freedom movement, freedom schools. Nothing but freedom only. In this respect they were following in the footsteps of Ella Baker: "You must let the oppressed themselves define their own freedom."[5]

Thus the Cabinet Mission too failed to resolve the matter. They announced their own Plan, as briefly summarized above, and the Mission left India on 29th June 1946, all to its own fate.

'Servants of God'

Khan Abdul Ghaffar Khan continued to keep company with Gandhi. In one of the prayer meetings Badshah Khan's theme was meaning the significance of prayer. "The object of prayer, *prarthana* or *namaz*, was the same — to purge ourselves of all dross and baseness, so as to enable us to realize the bond of unity with the entire human family. ... Prayer should fit one for service not of a particular section or community but of God's entire creation, for which He has sent us into this world." While elaborating on the concept of freedom and unity of India, Badshah Khan stressed: "I am a Khudai Khidmatgar, and service of God for me is service of humanity. Islam teaches me that and I have endeavored to follow that noble teaching by trying to serve all people. ... Freedom of India is essential for me and that means the freedom and well-being of all who live in this country ..." irrespective of caste or creed. "Freedom can only flourish in India on a basis of amity and cooperation of all the different communities. ..."[6]

5. Burns M. James: op. cit. p. 375.
6. Tendulkar: op. cit. p. 373.

In view of the communal upheaval all over the country, as well as some disaffection in some elements of the Defence Services, the Labour Government in London was keen on earliest possible transfer of power in India. For the first time a date was set: "not later than June 1948." The British Prime Minister, Mr. Atlee, made an excellent choice in Admiral Lord Louis Mountbatten as the last Viceroy of India. He arrived in Delhi on 22nd March 1947 and immediately sent word inviting Gandhi to Delhi. Gandhi accompanied by Badshah Khan reached the Capital on 31st March while the Asian Relations Conference was being held there. It was a unique gathering of its kind. Almost all the countries of Asia including the Arab countries, Tibet, Mongolia, South-East Asian countries including the Asian Republics of the Soviet Union were represented. Of course the Muslim League was disgruntled and sulky, and hence kept itself out. Gandhi candidly admitted before the delegates to the Conference: "... We do not know how to keep peace among ourselves. We think we must resort to law of the jungle. It is not the experience I would like you to carry to your respective countries. ... It will be a sorry thing if we go away from this Conference without a fixed determination that Asia shall live, and live as free as any other western nation. ... If India falls, Asia dies."[7]

Gandhi and Abdul Ghaffar had a series of meetings with Mountbatten. Both were totally against the very logic of Partition, and were strongly opposed to any partition of India under the aegis of the British. Gandhi went so very far to accommodate Jinnah that he suggested to the new Viceroy to give Jinnah the option of forming the Government at the Centre, that the selection of members of the new Government be left entirely to Jinnah — be they all Muslims, or all non-Muslims, or they be representative of all classes and creeds. The Nationalist Congress on its part would extend full cooperation to Jinnah to govern the country in a manner that he liked. The sole judge of right or wrong would be Lord Mountbatten only. The issue of Pakistan should be decided by the Constituent Assembly and no province, or part of a province, should be forced to join Pakistan against its wishes. Should Jinnah decline to accept so generous and unconditional an offer, the same offer, *mutatis mutandis*, should then be extended to the Indian National Congress.

The Muslims were killing Hindus and the Hindus were killing the Muslims. The scale of massacre was horrendous. It is estimated that seven to eight millions lost their lives in this man made carnage, and about fifteen million people were uprooted from their homes and hearths

---

7. Ibid. pp. 409-10.

to seek safety — a mass transmigration of populations unknown in the annals of history. An appeal signed by Gandhi and Jinnah for communal harmony and peace was issued under the Viceroy's aegis. But peace eluded and violence continued unabated. The Frontier Province was engulfed in massive unrest and violence. The Muslim League was all out to grab power in the Province and evict the Congress Ministry headed by Dr. Khan Sahib, by hook or by crook. The Viceroy conferred with the Governor, Sir Olaf Caroe, Dr. Khan Sahib and Pandit Nehru. Lord Mountbatten decided to visit the Province to see things for himself. He arrived at Peshawar on 28th April and was confronted by a dangerous situation bordering on panic. A large crowd of nearly seventy thousand Muslim Leaguers with green flags and armed with all sorts of local armament had gathered about a mile or so from the Government House and were threatening to march on to the Governor's House where the Viceroy was staying to present their case to him personally. Mountbatten consulted with the Governor and Dr. Khan Sahib. The latter advised him to march towards the demonstrators and show his face to them, which by itself would calm down the agitators. So he did. Lady Mountbatten showed great courage and insisted on accompanying her husband. Soon after the Viceregal party was observed by the demonstrators, the seething tension mellowed down. Their mood changed from "Pakistan *Zindabad*" to "Mountbatten *Zindabad*". (Long Live Mountbatten) The crisis was averted through the power of non-violence. While the Muslim League and agent *provocateurs* had organized a hostile demonstration in favour of Pakistan, Dr. Khan Sahib ensured that the Khudai Khidmatgars and the Red Shirts did not do so to ensure peaceful atmosphere.

The Viceroy held meetings with Dr. Khan Sahib and his cabinet colleagues, deputations of Hindus and Muslim League, political party leaders, and others. He emphasized that he had come to India to transfer power to Indians and not to rule over them. When Dr. Khan Sahib raised the question of the long standing demand of all Pathans for Pathanistan or Pakhtunistan, the tension mounted. Throughout the discussions, Governor Caroe's attitude was pro-Pakistan and palpably anti the popular ministry ruling the Province after free and fair elections in which the Muslim League was decisively defeated. The verdict of the Pathans was crystal clear against Pakistan. But that did not suit Caroe or the British Government. While Caroe insisted that the communal situation as well law and order were well under control with the exception of Hazara district, murder, violence and forcible conversions were rampant in the entire Province through kind courtesy of Jinnah and his League.

However, it was the Governor's word that eventually carried weight with the Viceroy. The League deputation included the fanatical young Pir of Manki Sharif and Abdul Qaiyum, amongst others. They represented their case at length for Pakistan with considerable heat and vehemence. In their demand for promulgation of Section 93 to enforce Governor's Rule in the Province, Caroe went all out to support the League to trample the democratic norms, and to order fresh elections.

By the end of April, Mountbatten had formulated his outline Plan of action towards immediate transfer of power. There was a new sense of urgency after what he had observed in Peshawar. The Congress High Command too was afraid that if the matters were allowed to drift further, complete chaos and disruption might engulf the entire process of transfer of power. Serious violent riots, death and destruction, arson and loot, were the order of the day all over the country, as communalism reigned supreme. Obstructionist tactics adopted by the League in running the Interim Government were painfully frustrating. There was no option but to accept Jinnah's demand for carving out a sovereign independent Pakistan. By the evening of 1st May, the political leaders of nationalist India accepted the principle of Partition based on 'self-determination applied to definitely ascertained areas' as the only viable solution to the prevailing Indian imbroglio. Partition of Bengal, Punjab and partial dismembering of Assam were inherent in the proposed scheme of Partition, besides the various complications born out of the future status of the Princely States numbering nearly 560. Without naming the Frontier Province as such, Nehru specifically mentioned: "Any proposal to put an end to a duly constituted provincial government having a large majority must not be considered ..." Obviously, Badshah Khan and his Khudai Khidmatgars were lost in the wilderness. They had cast their lot with the Congress, but now that the Congress had discarded them and the League would have nothing to do with them, "We shall be outcasts in the eyes of both. ... Before long we shall become aliens in Hindustan. The end of our long fight will be to pass under the domination of Pakistan ...While Independence will come to India, the brave Pathan will lose his. They are faced with a grim prospect."

In the 1946-elections, the Pathans had already given a clear verdict insofar as Pakistan was concerned. The proposal to hold fresh elections in NWFP was not to elicit public opinion, but to install the Muslim League ministry in the Province through means fair or foul. Moreover, the Muslim League agitation in NWFP was largely confined to urban areas only. The British Governor was willingly and knowingly playing in the hands of the League. He was taking decisions and actions which were legitimately in the sphere of the popular ministry of Dr. Khan Sahib, but without even the knowledge of the minister concerned, let alone his concurrence. For instance, the League leaders were released from jail on parole without prior knowledge of the Minister for Jails. While emphasizing that the Zalme Pakhtun party recently founded by his son Ghani was a separate body with no connection whatsoever with the Red Shirts, Badshah Khan categorically stated: "I still believe in non-violence, as it is my firm conviction that the country in general and the Frontier Province in particular should stick to non-violence. Violence spreads hatred, while non-violence spreads love." The Zalme Pakhtun was the direct result of violence and terrorist activities heaped on the Pathans by the Muslim League. The Pathans had been provoked beyond tolerance and hence their violent reaction through the aegis of the new Party. Those who believed in non-violence were drifting to violence as a direct consequence of Jinnah's tactics of grabbing ministerial power in the Frontier through the connivance of British administrators. It was totally illegal and unethical. "The object of Zalme Pakhtun is to defend and not to offend. Their volunteers believe in violence. They wear deep red uniforms and carry fire-arms." The pettiness of power politics repelled Badshah Khan. He gave serious thought to retirement from active politics; but then changed his mind since doing so at that point of time would tantamount to deserting the Pathans in the hour of their need. "The Englishmen and their henchmen are worried over the prospect of losing power. ... We are passing through critical times", warned Abdul Ghaffar.

The Governor had the audacity to say that "the violent demonstrations in the province indicated lack of confidence in the ministry." This was a complete travesty of truth inasmuch as the Governor was conniving with the criminal elements of the League to cause disturbances. If he had done his duty honestly, the communal riots and consequent loss of life could have been easily prevented. It may be recalled that in 1930 a Pathan had fired on a British officer. The culprit was arrested, condemned and executed within forty-eight hours. Or take the case of Miss Mollie Ellis who was abducted and rescued since all the resources of the Empire were mobilized to retrieve the honour of a British woman. Again, during the entire period of the Great War when the British themselves were in trouble, there was complete peace in the entire tribal territory. Since the British wanted peace, there was peace. However, with the approaching Partition and Independence, the British were no longer interested in maintaining peace and tranquility. During the current developments, hundreds had been killed in cold blood and thousands had been orphaned but the British Empire turned its face the other way.

"Caroe must feel ashamed that four hundred innocent citizens have been killed in the Province and not a single culprit is arrested. What sort of administration it is!"

Meanwhile, the proposal for dismissal of Dr. Khan Sahib's ministry as a prelude to holding fresh elections in the Province leaked out. The reaction by the Congress leaders was so prompt and strong that the British Government was warned of dangerous consequences of such an ill-conceived plan. The Congress might even resort to overturning the entire apple-cart of Partition and Independence. Similarly, the proposal to give an option to the Provinces to opt out of either Dominion was scuttled because of extremely strong reaction by the Congress. Yet another modification of the original Plan of Partition was proposed by Jinnah — He wanted the whole of Punjab and Bengal to be part of Pakistan besides claiming a corridor to connect the two Wings of Pakistan. All this kite-flying came to a stop after the Congress attitude hardened against the League.

Lord Mountbatten returned to Delhi from London on 31st May 1947 with the final Plan as approved by His Majesty's Government. Badshah Khan said to Gandhi: "Mahatmaji, so you will now regard us as Pakistanis. A terrible situation faces the Frontier Province and Baluchistan. We do not know what to do." June 2, 1947 was an ominons day in the life of the Frontier Gandhi. His fate along with that of his people who were proud to be Indians was sealed. The Congress Working Committee meeting on 3rd June 1947 accepted the Partition Plan and referendum in the Frontier Province as a prelude to Independence. The Frontier Gandhi told Mahatma Gandhi and the Working Committee: "We Pakhtuns stood by you and had undergone great sacrifices for attaining freedom, but you have now deserted us and thrown us to the wolves. ... Mahatmaji, you have thrown us to the wolves."

The Final American Scene

Dr Martin Luther King Jr. had already taught the Blacks and the Whites how to be both militant and non-violent—a contradiction of concepts and terminology in itself. His political skills and intellectual qualities contributed in large measure in reconciliation of this inherent contradiction. It was now left to Lyndon Baines Johnson to create history, to write the last chapter of the Freedom Movement. Just five days after the assassination of John Fitzgerald Kennedy, he told the Congress in a brief address: "We have talked long enough in this country about equal rights. We have talked for one hundred years or more. It is time now to write the next chapter, and to write it in the books of law."[8]

Montgomery had given a new meaning to Mahatma Gandhi's non-violence. It had defined and removed the inherent contradiction between non-violence and 'militant non-violence'. In its new avatar militancy acquired a fresh concept. It avoided violence but achieved 'dramatic confrontation' besides 'electrifying and educating the entire nation'. A new 'era of social change' had opened up new vistas for the Negro community not only of the South but of the entire United States. Montgomery gave rise and courage to other similar movements of liberation in other parts of the country — Florida, Birmingham, Tallahassee, Alabama, Mobile, *et al.* This is how the freedom movement under the inspiring leadership of Mahatma Gandhi had spread its roots all over the vast hinterland of India. Martin and other leaders in the South decided to expand, organize and coordinate the activities in the Southern States. A meeting attended by about one hundred southern leaders was convened at Atlanta for January 10 and 11, 1957. Reverend Fred Lee Shuttlesworth was the president of the Alabama Christian Movement which soon engulfed the Southern Region and Shuttlesworth became the Secretary of the south-wide movement to be known as the Southern Leadership Conference, later Southern Christian Leadership Conference. He was a fearless man, sent his children to public schools to desegregate them. Consequently, he was beaten up, his church and home were bombed. His wife was jailed and beaten. The entire family had suffered terribly in the cause of social justice, freedom and desegregation. The Atlanta meeting invited President Eisenhower and the Attorney General to visit the South to learn about the situation at first hand, and to initiate suitable steps to curb the white-violence. Of course there was no response from Washington. It was also decided to convene a much larger meeting in New Orleans on 14th February to give the expanded Movement a permanent shape. Meanwhile, Washington was informed that unless some effective remedial steps were undertaken immediately, "we shall be compelled to initiate a mighty Prayer Pilgrimage to Washington."[9]

Concurrently in Montgomery, the house and church of Ralph Abernathy were bombed and almost completely destroyed, all in one night only. Two other church buildings were also destroyed by bombing — the Bell Street and Mount Olive Baptist Churches. As a result of this

8. Burns M. James: op. cit. p. 375.
9. King Scott Coretta: op. cit. p. 166.

wave of white violence, the Montgomery City Commission ordered all buses off the roads. The black community was afraid that the City Fathers might use the reign of terror as an excuse to cancel the Bus Company's franchise. The general morale was low. It seemed all "our gains were lost". Martin went to the evening mass meeting in a depressed mood, and said:

> "Lord, I hope no one will have to die as a result of our struggle for freedom in Montgomery. Certainly I don't want to die. But if some one has to die, let it be me."

The audience roared back "no, no..." The emotional reaction was so intense that King broke down. The episode was welcome inasmuch as it released the pent up emotions and feelings of depression, and brought relief to King. After that the city was quiet for a few days. Bus service was resumed, albeit on a day time schedule only. Unfortunately, another wave of bombing and white terror soon followed. On 28th January early in the morning, the Peoples' Service Station and Cab Stand was bombed. Another bomb fell at the house of a Negro hospital worker followed by yet another crudely assembled unexploded, but smoldering, bomb at King's own house. King's reaction to this spate of bombing of homes of Negro leaders, their churches and public places was typical of the man: "Remember, if I am stopped, this movement will not be stopped, because God is with this movement." Fortunately, there were no casualties in all these bombings, though damage to property and Negro-psyche was extensive. At long last, the City started investigating in earnest the perpetrators of these criminal acts, and seven white men were arrested. In spite of their signed confessions, the jury returned the verdict of 'Not Guilty'!

With the decline in agricultural activity and corresponding rise in industrial development, the Negro came out of his isolation in the plantation to the urban centre, thereby resulting in improvement of his economic status as well as his own image of himself. Gone was the inferiority complex born out of centuries of repression. On the question of race relations, America had suffered from a 'schizophrenic personality' ever since the Declaration of Independence was issued!

14

Gandhian Philosophy

No religion which is narrow and which cannot satisfy the test of reason, will survive the coming reconstruction of society in which the values would have changed and character, not possession of wealth, title, or birth, will be the test of merit.

During the early years of the twentieth century, there was a lot of common ground between the situation of Negroes in the United States and the Indians in India. Both were suffering under white domination. While the Indians were like 'slaves' under the English occupying power, the Negroes were slaves in the country of their adoption — very few voluntarily, but otherwise most were brought in as a commodity in slave ships and were traded as a commodity in slave markets. Both the people were non-whites, and were subjected to oppression and injustice by their white masters. Racial and social discrimination, inequality before the law, segregation and color bar, *et al,* were the common characteristics imposed on the two people who were geographically oceans apart. However, Gandhi trusted equality amongst all human beings as a fundamental principle. So did King. It was all the more important for King since the Negroes were the descendents of slaves, which fact alone made them inferior to the other races. For both 'all men are borne equal' was part of their creed. Equality of human beings was an antidote to exploitation of the poor and the deprived. There were notable exceptions too; and these were predominant amongst the Indians by virtue of the liberal and merciful attitude of the British. As long as the Indians did not interfere with the English Empire and its security and prosperity, the English left them alone. Thus the Indians were comparatively better off, educationally, economically and professionally. The Black community of America was unlucky in this respect, even though there were notable exceptions amongst them too. As long as the Negroes did not demand equal rights with the whites, as long as the Blacks continued to serve their white masters and did their bidding, the whites left them to themselves. In both cases this *status-quo* could not be maintained *ad infinitum.* Change had to come. And it did. That is when the problems arose.

Indians were the first to demand independence, initially partial, but later complete: *Purna Swarajya.* This demand was the crux of nationalist movement in India. Gandhi was the towering figure in Indian politics. He introduced concepts of non-violent resistance, Satyagraha and Ahimsa as the means to achieve total independence from British rule. Indians did not have the power or the means to fight the British to attain their goal. Therefore, of necessity, they had to find a workable via media. The Negroes too were in a similar state and there was no possibility of a violent upheaval, a revolution, which could put the Blacks at par with the whites. So they too had to find a via media. Since Indians had a headstart in this direction, it was but natural for the Negroes to look towards the Indian technique of non-violent revolution as the panacea for all their ills. And so they did. Martin Luther King Jr. became their 'Gandhi', and the Indians had theirs already besides the person who came to be known as the 'Frontier Gandhi'— Khan Abdul Ghaffar Khan, a Pathan belonging to one of the martial tribes of North West Frontier Province (N.W.F.P.) who underwent a complete metamorphosis and took to non-violence as if it was part of his ancestral heritage.

The situation faced by the American Blacks was such as to bring about a swell of Gandhian thinking amongst them, more so since the Indian experiment was on the verge of total success. Indians suffered from the evil of untouchability while the Negro in America had to face the bitter consequences of segregation on grounds of race and colour of the skin. Gandhi's fight against untouchability brought the Negroes closer to 'that little man with big ideas'. This one aspect of segregation born out of accident of birth was the most common denominator in the unfortunate situation of the two people. The Indian National Congress under Gandhi's leadership aimed at ameliorating the lot of 'untouchables' amongst one of its objectives; it had its counterpart in America where the organization was known as National Association for the Advancement of Colored People (NAACP). The Negro organization was established through the help of, and led by, W.E.B. Du Bois, the great black philosopher and social thinker who was a contemporary of Gandhi. Du Bois learnt of Gandhi after the First World War. He met Gandhi through the good offices of some Indian leaders like Lala Lajpat Rai and Sarojini

Naidu. He invited Gandhi to visit the United States but soon came to the conclusion that 'America was not civilized enough to receive a coloured man as an honoured guest'. In 1929 he published a letter from Gandhi in a special anniversary edition of *The Crisis*, the regular publication of the NAACP. There was such a great demand for this issue of the magazine that Gandhi's letter was reprinted many times over. It was then that Du Bois predicted that "real human equality and brotherhood in the United States will come only under the leadership of another Gandhi." How prophetic!

A number of black leaders visited India to study Gandhian way of non-violent social revolution with the ultimate objective of attaining independence from the British. Dr. Dodd who was in charge of a girls' college in the United States had a long interview with Gandhi on 14th September 1934. It was recorded and published. Mrs. and Dr. Howard Thurman, Professor of Comparative Religion and Philosophy, met Gandhi on 21st February 1936.[1] They too had a long recorded discussion with Gandhi about the problems faced by the black community in the U.S. They requested Gandhi to visit the United States, "not for White America but for the Negroes. We have many problems that cry for solution, and we need you badly." Gandhi politely declined the invitation with the remarks that "I must make good the message here before I bring it to you." They parted with Gandhi's prophetic words: "It may be through the Negroes that the unadulterated message of non-violence will be delivered to the world." Martin was a seven years old lad at that time.

Dr. Channing Tobias, Director of the Phelps-Stokes Fund and Dr. Benjamin E. Mays, President of the prestigious Morehouse College, met Gandhi on January 10, 1937. They had a long discussion regarding non-violent resistance and its implications for the black community back home. On return to the States, Mays described his meeting with Gandhi in a long essay published in the University Journal in which he emphasized that the cardinal principles of non-violence were love and fearlessness. Martin was then a student at Morehouse and he was greatly impressed by the Gandhian philosophy of non-violent mass movement as elucidated by Mays. Other prominent black visitors to meet Gandhi were: A. Philip Randolph, E.D. Nixon, Adam Clayton Powell, Bayard Rustin, and a host of others. They sought meetings with Gandhi to discuss the problem of Negroes, and Gandhi was particularly qualified to advise in this direction by virtue of his experience in South Africa, besides the current trends

---

1. Dr. Thurman was Dean of Rankin Chapel at Howard University in Washington D.C.

in the Indian struggle against the British. It will thus be seen that there was a continuing process of dialogue between leaders of the Indian freedom struggle and the Negro leadership in the United States well before Martin came on the scene. Moreover, Gandhi's concept of non-violence did not imply cowardice. On the contrary, Gandhi emphasized that if cowardice was the only other option, it would be better to resort to violence, and to fight it out.

Black-Muslim Fundamentalism

Martin King was terribly upset by the mob violence, more so when the Albany Blacks retaliated by going on a rampage. Martin had studied Gandhi's philosophy and technique and had learnt how India had won independence without firing a gun. He had imbibed the lesson: "Hate cannot drive out hate; only love can". He "cancelled a scheduled march, and in the spirit of Gandhi, declared a day of penance."[2] However, the climax was yet to come.

Like Gandhi, Martin too followed a strict grueling daily schedule. He used to be up and about by 6:30 a.m. and devoted the first forty-five minutes of the day to serious reading. Some fruit juice and coffee for breakfast and at 9 a.m. he drove to his office in one of his two cars — a 1960 Ford and a 1960 Rambler. His office was a 16 feet square room filled with about 200 volumes on religious and Negro subjects. It was like having a private library on one's favourite topics. A voluminous heap of mail awaited his attention, about seventy letters per day. Writing his speeches and his sermons used to take the major portion of his working time, interspersed with tele-conferences with other civil rights leaders spread all over the country, as well as his aides. A quick light lunch on the working table was followed by more work till about 2 or 3 a.m. the next morning. He hardly had time to sleep! As his stature as a national leader climbed upwards, he had to travel a lot more spending time in airplanes. During these outings he preached, or gave speeches to huge crowds. In 1963 alone he traveled about 275,000 miles and gave more than 350 speeches — and that was an otherwise difficult and extremely busy period, besides spending time in jails.

Martin had called 1961 "a year of the victory of the non-violent method: though blood flowed, not one drop was drawn by a Negro from his adversary." Indeed, Gandhi's philosophy had permeated from the Negro's original home in Africa to America by a circuitous route via India. Professor Kenneth Clark, a Negro psychologist at the City College

---

2. Burns M. James: op. cit. p. 364.

of New York. "... anticipated a total rejection of the American pattern being incorrigibly hypocritical and corrupt and therefore unworkable in terms of a meaningful change in the status of the Negro." The rise of Muslim fundamentalism in the steaming black ghettoes of the North, where "Elijah Muhammad and Malcolm X preached the ineradicable evil of the white man, contained chilling portents for the future." Malcolm X was a leading figure in 'The Nation of Islam', and head of his 'Black Pride' movement of the Northern Ghettos. He sought to inculcate an 'upright, puritanical, moralistic, disciplined and deeply religious approach to life' wherein the followers were expected to forsake liquor, drugs and tobacco.[3] To cap it all, Robert F. Williams' book, *Negroes with Guns* advocated armed force in self-defense as the only viable solution to racial injustice. Indeed, but for Dr. Martin Luther King Jr. imbibing the non-violence creed of Gandhi, the American Negro was on the verge of 'quasi-Maoist belief in the virtues of violence'. When Martin's younger brother's house and church were bombed, he simply said, "Father, forgive them for they know not what they do." This was in the true style of Gandhi! In April 1963 in Birmingham, Alabama, the situation took a turn for the worse. Much as the Attorney-General tried to persuade the Negro leaders to postpone their dharnas (sit-ins) in shops and restaurants, by now the Movement had a momentum of its own. Nobody could dam the flood of protests, more so after the Mayor of Birmingham issued a statement with reference to Martin King castigating the Attorney-General: "This nigger has got the blessing of the Attorney-General and the White House."[4]

Martin King was arrested four times in Albany. During his last arrest, two thousand demonstrators went to jail with him. This time he vowed that he would stay in jail until the demands of the Blacks were met. This statement went a long way in resolving the differences between various Black organizations like SNCC, NAACP and SCLC. The Black people came closer together and were anxious about King's safety in that Georgia countryside jail. King referred to this as "creative tension". Some black GI's at the nearby Base were reported to be ready with hidden arms. Then the whole thing burst like a bubble. Louis Lomax who was there recorded: "Then Martin King changed his mind. He had promised that he would stay in jail until a change came; he invited others to come and spend Christmas in jail with him. Had he stuck to this, as Gandhi would have done, Albany would have been desegregated. But Martin came out on

3. Malcolm X was shot dead on 21st February 1965 while addressing a meeting in Harlem.
4. Schelsinger M. Arthur: op. cit. pp. 815-17

bond." .... "Sellout" ... "Uncle Tom Nigger"... "Jive Cat" ... "Martin Loser" ... With these charges sticking, the image was badly tarnished. Most whites believe that Albany was a disaster for King. Most Blacks agree. Martin was sad and disheartened over these self-defeating internal rivalries. This is one side of the coin. The other side of the same story is — Martin, Ralph and many others were tried on 27th February 1962. The sentences were handed out on 10th June: $178 as fine or forty-five days at hard labour. In accordance with their earlier resolve, they refused to pay the fine and elected to do time in jail. But following the precedence set by Commissioner Clyde Sellers, some one arranged to pay the fine and the two leaders were 'ejected out of jail'. The criticism leveled against Martin certainly caused him anguish, but he was not at all embittered by the criticism, more so since personal integrity, honesty, and truthfulness acted as a shield for Dr. King. Like Mahatma Gandhi, total honesty and absolute truth, the 'Truth-Force' was his primary weapon. "Martin did not have a one-dimensional negative view of black nationalism."[5] It was more a question of black self-respect than mere nationalism. While on this aspect of Dr. King's character, one might as well also say that Martin never compromised with hate or violence. The approach to solution of black problems had to be via the non-violence route. In any case, the weak and the poor have no other way, more so since violence will lead to their own destruction because of their inherent weakness. And above all, Martin was always open to correction and acceptance of his mistake if he had erred at all. Be that as it may, in the wake of internal dissentions Martin offered to resign. And that had an electrifying effect on the MIA Board members; unity once again prevailed in the Movement. And it was no longer a local Movement, not even a nationwide Movement. Indeed, it was an international phenomenon, a worldwide revolution in which the downtrodden oppressed segments of humanity were seeking freedom, self-respect and asserting the rights of the individual. An international bill of rights, so to say. The efficacy of non-violent method was not restricted to conflicts between individuals or groups of people; it had much wider application in that conflicts between nations, territorial and economic international disputes could be resolved through mutual respect and non-violent approach. After all, Mahatma Gandhi had successfully challenged the might of the British Empire and freed India from centuries of political domination and economic exploitation besides oppression and servitude. His sole weapons were Truth, Soul-Force, nonviolent mass movement steeped with plenty of courage and fortitude. If India could do that, why not the rest of the world?

---

5. King Scott Coretta: op. cit. p. 286.

Violence Displaces Non-violence

Since the City Commissioners of Albany refused to integrate any more than the little that they had done, the struggle in Albany continued unabated throughout the summer of 1962. The Commissioners preferred to close the public library and the parks, rather than integrate, or desegregate. That turned out to be a classic case of cutting the nose to spite the face! Dr. King described the year 1962 as "the year that civil rights was displaced as the dominant issue in domestic politics. ... The issue no longer commanded the conscience of the nation."

Unfortunately, there was a violent outburst in July. This time it was by the Black community when nearly two thousand youngsters resorted to throwing rocks, stones and bottles at the police, damaging property and injuring passersby. Martin was quite upset. His fundamental basis of agitation had been violated by his own people. And he reacted like Gandhi would have, in fact had done so many times during India's struggle for freedom. Martin decided to observe a day of penance: he called it a "Day of Penitence". The active part of the agitation was suspended in the Gandhian style for one week during which period direct action was restricted to prayer vigils only. Ralph, Anderson and Martin led the first of these vigils on 27th July. Although these were merely prayer vigils, the police still went out of their way and arrested the three of them, as if even praying by Blacks had also become a criminal act. It was during this period that Yoki and Marty, the two eldest of Kings' children, were taken to jail to visit their father. Again, it was during this period that the idea of wives of the leaders of the Movement should lead a demonstration was mooted — the Female Contingent of the Albany Movement. The women were disappointed in not getting an opportunity to do what they so ardently wished to do. During the same period when the Albany Movement was at its peak, in late March 1962, Coretta was invited by the 'Women's Strike for Peace' to go as a delegate to Geneva for an international conference on atomic test ban. Fifty women from the United States, four of them Black, took part in the proceedings. The irony of the situation was that Arthur Dean, the United States representative considered female participation on a subject like test ban as feminine intrusion by "hysterical females" into the man's world.

"Non-violence as the salvation of a world in peril" — This was the crux of Gandhian philosophy as imbibed by Martin as a panacea for world peace. He was particularly impressed by Gandhi's 'Salt Satyagraha' and his use of fasting as a political weapon. Hereafter, Martin's political approach was based on Mahatma Gandhi's unshakable cult of total nonviolence. Thoreau's *Essay on Civil Disobedience* acted as the catalyst. Soon Martin put the basic idea into practice: "Christ furnished the spirit; Gandhi showed how it will work." Martin went a step ahead and introduced the concept 'Non-violent Militancy'. Leaving *Erõs*[6] and *Philia*[7] (reciprocal love) aside, Martin adopted *Agape*, the disinterested love, as his basic approach in dealing with inter-racial matters. It was this kind of love that Martin aspired to give to his enemies. "For Gandhi, love was a potent instrument for social and collective transformation. It was in this Gandhian emphasis on love and non-violence that I discovered the method for social reform that I had been seeking for so many months."[8] Indeed, Gandhi was compellingly provocative to King in ways more than one, more so since Gandhi was a highly religious man, and as for King, faith was integral to all his thinking, and influenced all his actions.

It was more or less a coincidence that two descendents of two of the most notable personalities of the twentieth century shared the dais in San Francisco to celebrate the 50th anniversary of the United Nations Declaration of Human Rights — Martin Luther King III and Arun Gandhi, grandson of M.K. Gandhi. They shared their childhood memories of a father and a grandfather — Gandhi and Dr. King were the "two brown men, small in stature, who peacefully defeated the tyranny of two mighty empires. Two men of immeasurable character who influenced others with the dimension of their belief. Two men of spiritual conviction — Eastern and Western — who demonstrated the universal power of love. Two men who lived in peace, yet died violently at the hands of assassins, Gandhi and King. As a youngster King III had only vague memories of Mahatma Gandhi's influence on his Father. However, later in life King III came to fully appreciate the impact Gandhian non-violent technique had on "my father and, ultimately, on my nation."[9]

When the announcement of award of Nobel Peace Prize to Martin Luther King was made, press reporters made a bee-line to his house. One of them told Coretta: "This year (1964) the total prize is worth

---

6. Erõs is known to be one of the oldest and most powerful of all the mythological gods in the Greek pantheon. It is the god of love, uncontrollable desire, both dangerous and incomprehensible. It represents passionate love that combines with fertility, Hermes. Cupid is Its Roman equivalent.
7. Philia represents abnormal fondness or love. The word is derived from Greek *Philos* which means loving.
8. King M.K., Jr.: *Stride Towards Freedom*; op. cit. pp. 92-95. Also Coretta: op. cit. p. 72.
9. *Time* dated 23-30 August, 1999, p.54.

fifty-four thousand dollars. What do you suppose Dr King will do with all that money?"

"Knowing him", she answered, "I'm sure he will give it all to the Freedom Movement."

Exactly as Gandhi did when he was presented fabulous farewell-gifts on his final departure from South Africa. Of course he protested vehemently. But his compatriots for whom he had made so many personal sacrifices and undergone such hardships, besides many months in jails, insisted. Gandhi accepted the gifts but he put them in a trust in South Africa itself for the benefit of the Indian community, much against the wishes of his wife who wanted to use at least part of those wonderful things.

15

Montgomery Bus Boycott

It is one of the ironies of our day that Montgomery, the Cradle of the Confederacy, is being transformed into Montgomery, the Cradle of Freedom and Justice.

It may be recalled that on 17th May 1954, the US Supreme Court under Chief Justice Warren had issued what came to be described as a historic ruling against segregated schools.[1] The President of the United State, General Dwight D. Eisenhower was rather upset over the Warren-Court's decision, and the Southern States were totally distressed. They had no intention of implementing the decision of the Court, taking shelter behind a couple of centuries old vague doctrine of "interposition" that conferred on individual States the right to oppose any federal action that infringes on the powers of the States. That doctrine, or interpretation thereof, was the *casus belli* for the Civil War which the South undertook, all because they felt that the North 'meddled' in their affairs. The courts could hand out favourable decisions on civil rights, but it was virtually impossible to have the same implemented, more so if the white majority found them inconvenient. Since the executive and legislative branches of the state machinery were reluctant to intervene on behalf of the black minority, particularly in the Southern States, Gandhi's technique of nonviolent civil disobedience added a new dimension to the struggle for freedom and equal rights, thereby compelling the federal machinery of the government to move forward towards racial equality and integration.

1. In the school textbooks the children were taught: Slavery was the earliest form of social security. The Ku Klux Klan was a law enforcement agency; and so on and so forth — Burns M. James: op. cit. p. 353.

The Lady who triggered the movement in the first place:
Mrs. Rosa Parks

Courageous Stand by Rosa Parks

Montgomery, the capital of Alabama State, is situated in the middle of rich and fertile farmland and enjoys the distinction of being one of the oldest cities in the United States. Montgomery was the first capital of the Confederacy, and was also a centre of slave auction. The State Capitol is an imposing white building of exceptional beauty — one of the finest examples of classical Georgian architecture in America. It was here on January 7, 1861, that Alabama voted to secede from the Union and on February 18, on the steps of the portico, Jefferson Davis was sworn in as President of the Confederate States. The first Confederate flag was made and unfurled in Montgomery, known over the years as the 'Cradle of Confederacy'.

The rules framed by the Montgomery City Bus Lines required the Blacks to pay the fare at the front of the bus, get down and run to the rear to board the bus. This procedure had to be followed irrespective of the weather conditions, age or disability of the passenger, and was made into a big joke by the drivers if a pregnant black woman happened to be involved. Sometimes the drivers would just move off with the black passenger stranded on the roadside and the fare in the box of the bus, as a cruel joke on the poor black people. As for seating — Section 10, Chapter 6 of the Montgomery City Code stated: "Every person operating a bus line shall provide equal accommodations ... in such a manner as to separate the white people from the Negroes." The bus-segregation system further stipulated that black passengers could occupy a row between the 'whites only' section, and the rear seats if the latter were filled up.

Rosa Parks, a forty-three years old seamstress worked as a tailoring assistant in Montgomery. After the day's work she was returning home. She took a seat in the middle section. However, when a white man boarded the bus, the driver ordered Rosa L. Parks and three other black passengers to the rear so that the white man could sit down. While the other three complied, Rosa refused to surrender her seat to the white passenger. It may be recalled that almost similar colour-prejudice and segregationist attitude met M.K. Gandhi in South Africa. He had a first class rail travel ticket; but the color of his skin was brown. The train conductor would not therefore permit Gandhi to travel first class. He was ordered to go to third class which, of course, Gandhi refused to do, quoting rail rules and regulations. He was therefore pulled down from the first class coach, bag and baggage, and thrown at the platform where he had to pass a sleepless night, shivering in the cold. Now back to Rosa: The police was summoned. Rosa was arrested, tried, convicted and sent to jail.

That was on 1st December 1955. She said, "I had decided that I would have to know once and for all what rights I had as a human being and a citizen." This incident was not her first brush with the segregation laws; she had been ejected from a bus by the very same driver a decade earlier for refusing to enter through the back door.[2] Now it was a heroic act of defiance. Further, she had been taking active part in desegregating the system and allied political activities. So the news of her arrest and detention quickly spread through the black community with black leaders like Martin Luther King Jr., Ralph Abernathy, E.D. Nixon — Nixon was a fiery Pullman porter who had been active in Brotherhood of Sleeping Car Porters as well as in other civil-rights activities — jumping into the fray. Initially, only E.D. Nixon who signed Mrs. Parks's bail-bond and a couple of other persons knew of her arrest early Thursday evening. Her trial was set for Monday, December 5. Rosa Parks support group quickly mobilized. E.D. Nixon had been a militant leader of the local NAACP and Brotherhood of Sleeping Car Porters for a long time. He was waiting for exactly such a situation to challenge the constitutionality of bus-segregation laws. He rushed to the jail to bail out Rosa Parks. Meanwhile, the Women's Political Council, a Civil Rights group of black professional women, convinced E.D. Nixon that the Community should resort to a boycott of the bus service. However, Nixon appreciated that they would require wholehearted voluntary support of the entire community to make the boycott a success. And that required mobilizing the Negroes through the black ministers who were the most influential leaders. He called them one by one, starting with Ralph Abernathy who was quite enthusiastic. In fact, King used to call Abernathy his "dearest friend and cellmate". Next on his list was the twenty-six years old young pastor, Martin Luther King Jr., minister of the Dexter Street Baptist Church.[3]

The series of events following the arrest and detention of Mrs. Rosa Parks is the chronicle of fifty thousand Negroes who took to heart the principles of non-violence. It is the story of the Black minority fighting for their rights with the weapon of love. Rosa Parks had been tracked down by the *Zeitgeist*[4] — the spirit of the time. In the process, the Negroes overcame their inferiority complex and obliterated the psychological scars resulting from centuries of slavery, servitude and

2. Burns Macgregor James: *Striding Towards Freedom*; Asia Books, New Delhi, 1990; p. 349.
3. Burns M. James: op. cit. p. 349.
4. King believed that the universe was under the control of a loving purpose, and that in the struggle for righteousness we have cosmic companionship. He used the German phrase *Zeiteist* to describe this belief — Cones James: op. cit. p.134.

cruel oppression inflicted by the so-called civilized freedom-loving democratic white majority. E.D. Nixon called the first meeting of Black ministers, community leaders and the Women's Political Council members at Martin's church. The die was cast. Monday morning was the first day of the boycott. The course of action thereafter was left to the public to decide at a mass meeting — all in true democratic style. Martin explained to the gathering that what they were soon to launch was not a war between the Negro and the white; there was no enmity between them as such. What was at stake was 'justice', and it was a conflict between justice and injustice, between right and wrong, between truth and falsehood.

While Rosa Parks incident triggered what later turned out to be the nation-wide movement for desegregation and racial equality, it certainly was not the first such incident. In fact, a number of such incidents involving black bus-passengers had taken place well before Rosa Parks or Martin Luther King, Jr. came on the scene. The best-known involved Claudette Colvin, a fifteen-year high school student who refused to give her seat to a white male passenger. She was pulled off the bus, handcuffed and taken to jail. The incident nearly led to a boycott. Instead, a citizens committee came into being to discuss the matter with the bus-company and City Commission[5] so that better courtesy was shown to black passengers. However, nothing changed after many meetings. Thus stage was being set for Rosa Parks to create history and catapult Martin to the height of leadership which he hardly desired or aspired for.

'Daddy' King seldom rode in buses because Negroes were forced to ride in the back seats. But well before he could afford this luxury, he used to say: "Even though the law may force me to ride in the back, my mind is always up front." This attitude of mind was the product of Daddy King's political affiliations and achievements. He was a leading figure in the local chapter of NAACP — National Association for the Advancement of Colored People[6] — and Atlanta Negro Voters League, besides having the honour of having successfully fought for equalizing salaries for black teachers. In yet another instance witnessed by Martin with pride was when, instead of moving to the back of the shoe-store

---

5. Malcolm X: *Autobiography*, pp. 40-43.
6. National Association for Advancement of Colored People was borne out of race-riots in Springfield, Illinois, in 1910. At that point of time it was a misnomer in as much as it was a white dominated organization; its first and only black official was W.E.B. Dubois, the well known Negro philosopher-intellectual, and also the first editor of its periodical, *The Crisis*.

as requested by a sales person, he told that him: "You will wait on us here or we won't buy any shoes." Even before the Rosa Parks incident, Joe Ann Robinson, a leader of the Women's Political Council and E.D. Nixon joined by a local businessman, Rufus Lewis, had met with the City bus company officials four times between 1953 and 1955 to protest against discriminatory policies.[7] But all in vain. Discrimination and segregation had continued.

Bus Desegregation Movement

Montgomery was the beginning. However, the bus boycott movement did not begin with a personal commitment to non-violence by King; that came much later when he shifted the primary focus of his socio-political thought from mere 'justice' alone to 'love and justice'. In fact, following the bombing of his house (January 30, 1956), he had armed guards around his house and had even applied for a permit to carry a gun in his car. All this changed drastically soon after non-violence became a total personal commitment, a way of life. He urged his fellow blacks to follow his example and to practice non-violence as a way of life. Instead of being the 'Cradle of Confederacy', Montgomery was transformed into the 'Cradle for Mass Non-cooperation Movement' for the entire nation, even though the process of change was long drawn. It set the trend for the vast protest movement that was to sweep the South for the next ten years — emotional church meetings, Christian hymns adapted for the protest demonstrations in progress, commitment to non-violence, segregation and racial injustice, Civil Rights, implementation of constitutional provisions, *et al.* Now they unanimously decided to boycott the city bus service, effective Monday 5th December. The message of boycott was spread to Montgomery's 50,000 Blacks through mimeographed flyers prepared overnight by Robinson. The circular announced:[8]

> Don't ride the bus to work, to town, to school, to any place, Monday, 5th December. Another Negro woman has been arrested and put in jail because she refused to give up her seat. Come to a mass meeting at 7 p.m. at the Holt Street Baptist Church for further instructions.

Meetings of community leaders were held in various Baptist churches to organize alternative transportation. However, it was for the mass meeting to decide whether to continue the boycott or not. Meanwhile, thousands were

7. Fairclough Adam: *To Redeem the Soul of America; The Southern Christian Leadership Conference and Martin Luther King Jr.*; University of Georgia, Athens, 1987; p. 12.op. cit.; p. 16.
8. Ibid. p. 46.

driven to work in black cabs at specially cut rates. Many hitch-hiked in Black private cars while some rode mules, or just walked. It was estimated that approximately ninety per cent of the fifty thousand Black populace refused to ride the buses that day. The buses ran empty, up and down. Eighteen of the City's black pastors established the Montgomery Improvement Association (MIA) to coordinate the effort, and unanimously elected Dr. Martin Luther King Jr. to head the new born organization, and to address the mass meeting. He rose to the occasion and his speech proved to be the most important one of his political career, blending militancy with moderation to fire the imagination of the people. Martin spoke extempore, no notes at all, in which he told the story of Rosa Parks 'simply but passionately'. It seems as if Martin and Gandhi were cast in the same mould insofar as speech capability was concerned. In spite of Gandhi's general demeanour and dress, when Gandhi talked, the impression was different. "He is direct, and expresses himself well in excellent English with a fine appreciation of value of the words he uses. There is no hesitation about him and there is a ring of sincerity in all that he utters ..."

Martin clarified that the protest was not merely over the buses; it was over all those things that 'go deep down into the archives of history.' He advised persuasion and not coercion to keep the flock together. "If you will protest courageously, and yet with dignity and Christian love, when the history books are written in future generations, the historians will have to pause and say, 'There lived a great people — a Black people — who injected new meaning and dignity into the veins of civilization.' This is our challenge and our overwhelming responsibility."[9] Martin went on to add:[10]

> "We have known humiliation, we have known abusive language, and we have been plunged into the abyss of oppression. And we decided to rise up only with the weapon of protest. It is one of the greatest glories of America that we have the right of protest.
>
> If we are arrested every day, if we are exploited every day, if we are trampled over every day, don't ever let anyone pull you so low as to hate them. We are seeking to improve not the Negro of Montgomery but the whole of Montgomery. We must use the weapon of love. We must have compassion and understanding for those who hate us. We must realize so many people are taught to hate us that they are not totally responsible for their hate. But when we stand in life at midnight, we are always at the threshold of a new dawn...."

9. Burns, Macregor James: *The Cross Winds of Freedom*; p. 351.
10. Zinn Howard: op. cit. p. 443.

A Black man, a Ph.D, whose movement is covered by *Time* magazine as a cover story in February 1957, is arrested in Montgomery in September 1958 on charge of "loitering"!

The Montgomery Bus Strike
"My feet is tired but my soul is rested."

There were waves of applause which rose again when Miss Rosa Parks came on the dais. This was the first great meeting of the freedom movement. They decided to continue the boycott till their demands were met. Forty-eight dispatch-stations were established to pick up passengers and carry them to work, with dispatchers to match passengers and destinations. A pool of volunteer drivers was organized, with over three hundred cars participating. When it was discovered that the car pool was unable to cope up with the load, MIA helped ten of the Negro churches to buy station wagons to supplement the car pool. Many literally walked miles to reach their work stations. Mother Pollard vowed to King that she would walk until it was over.

"But aren't your feet tired?" King asked her.

"Yes", she said, "my feet is tired, but my soul is rested."[11]

Martin had read Gandhi's Autobiography but it was only now that he got the true lesson of *Satyagraha,* or 'Truth-Force', turning the church meetings into schools of "Christianity in action", non-violent resistance, and direct action techniques. Martin justified the action of his Church on the grounds that "Religion deals with both heaven and earth. Any religion that professes to be concerned with the souls of men and is not concerned with the slums that doom them, the economic conditions that strangle them, and the social conditions that cripple them, is a dry-as-dust religion."[12] But somehow Martin did not like the negative implications of the word 'boycott'. Hereafter he called it as an act of 'massive non-cooperation'. The City bus boycott lasted almost one year and established beyond any doubt that the black people could stand united to follow Gandhi's non-violent technique in order to attain their social objectives. King's stress on love and non-violence earned the Black community the sympathy and understanding of the entire liberal America. Martin was fortunate in getting expert advice on Gandhian technique from Glenn Smiley of Fellowship of Reconciliation and Bayard Rustin. But there were many in the audience as well as in the rest of the country who thought all this talk about love and non-violence as naïve. For instance, two years after the Montgomery boycott, Robert William, an ex-marine and President of the local NAACP in Monroe, North Carolina, successfully took up arms against a raid by KKK. The Red-Indian community also successfully repulsed a Klan raid on their settlement, firing their weapons.

11. Burns M. James: op. cit. p. 351.
12. King Scott Coretta: op. cit. p. 127.

This was an interesting year in ways more than one. In order to break the boycott movement, the Mayor issued a proclamation that all black domestic workers be fired from their jobs. In turn, many white women declared that the Mayor could, instead, come and clean their houses! The Ladies drove the black workers to their place of work in the morning, and then drove them back home in the evenings, thereby helping the boycott to succeed. The media provided free coverage to the Movement and educated the black community in the philosophy of Gandhi's nonviolent resistance by comparing the bus-boycott with Gandhi's 'Salt Satyagraha'. The *Montgomery Advertiser* was in the forefront. Night after night the black people gathered at the churches to sing and pray to re-learn lessons from the Bible and Jesus' life. Skits and dramatizations portrayed Gandhi and his techniques for non-violent resistance with special emphasis on non-retaliation and love instead of hatred for the powerful oppressors.

Another mass meeting of the MIA was held on 30 January 1956 at the Rev. Ralph D. Abernathy's First Baptist Church in which 2,000 persons participated. Martin was the main speaker. He declared:

> We don't advocate violence. WE WILL STAY WITHIN THE LAW. When we are RIGHT, WE DON'T MIND GOING TO JAIL! If all I have to pay is going to jail a few times and getting about twenty threatening calls a day, I think that is a very small price to pay for what we are fighting for.[13]

Cruelty and savagery against Blacks touched the bottom of human degradation in the same year as the Rosa Parks incident. A fourteen-years old Chicago-lad, Emmett Till, while visiting relatives in Mississippi was dragged out of the house on account of an alleged misdemeanor in that he had whistled at a white woman. He was beaten blue and black. His testicles were cut off and his body was dumped into the Tallahatchie River with a cotton-gin fan chained around his neck. To cap it all, the confessed perpetrators of this unimaginable atrocity were tried according to American standards of jurisprudence, and acquitted.[14] A couple of years later, while talking to white audience in western Alabama, Buford Boone castigated the whites for 'white violence', the audience reacted with shouts of "Kill him" and "Hang him". Another example of

---

13. King Mary: op. cit., p. 278.

14. Burns M. James: op. cit. p. 352. The day on which this atrocious verdict was announced was proclaimed as "September 23, 1955 —— BLACK FRIDAY!" — Sanford Wexler: pp. 56-59.

"Christian Love" for the brotherhood of man which soon accusingly linked civil rights leaders to Communism through Moscow![15]

On Sunday, 4th November 1956 Martin preached one of his most beautiful sermons at Dexter. It was based on an imaginary letter from Saint Paul to American Christians exhorting them to guard against the pitfalls of materialism over spiritualism, like Mahatma Gandhi had done time and again during India's freedom struggle in the early 1940's. "The greatest of all virtues is love." All said and done, Martin had practically no experience in handling a delicate subject like non-violent resistance movement. A white Georgian lady, Lillian Smith, author of the acclaimed anti-lynching novel *Strange Fruits* that created a stir in the 1940's, was impressed by the dedicated selfless service of MIA leadership. In February 1956, she decided to provide a helping hand through Bayard Rustin, a black socialist and conscientious objector during the Second World War. Rustin had spent six months in India studying Gandhi's techniques of non-violence, and was well versed in Gandhian thought and philosophy. Rustin was deputed to go to Montgomery as advisor to young Martin. Lillian also wrote to Martin recommending Rustin as one of the few Northerner outsiders she would trust to help the nascent movement.[16] During the same period when one hundred leaders of the bus-protest were indicted, they did not wait for the police to come and take them. Instead, they walked over to the police station and voluntarily surrendered. E.D. Nixon was the first to do so, with his head held high. It was a lesson in how Gandhian self-suffering works.

Martin had refused offers to pastor churches in the North. Instead, since Coretta felt they were under some 'moral obligation to return — at least for a few years' to the South. So they did. His intellectual inclination leaned heavily towards 'systematic theology' rather than straightforward preaching. His doctoral dissertation: *A Comparison of God in the Thinking of Paul Tillich and Henry Nelson Wieman* certainly points in that direction.[17] His conclusions in his dissertation were fairly Niebuhrian. Martin's own concept of God as an active personal entity. In his first speech to the Group as its president, Martin declared:

---

15. Bufford Boone of the Tuscaloosa News described himself as "I am a Jew, a Yankee and a radical" and proposed the 'Golden Vertical Negro Plan' which would integrate the races in the schools by providing desks without seats! — Burns M. James: op. cit. p.353.
16. Jervis Anderson: *Bayard Rustin, Troubles I've Seen*; New York, 1997; p. 185.
17. Williams A. John: *The King God Didn't Save*; p. 26.

"We have no alternative but to protest. For many years we have shown an amazing patience. We have sometimes given our white brothers the feeling that we liked the way we were being treated. But we come here to night to be saved from that patience that makes us patient with anything less than freedom and justice."[18]

The above speech imparted fresh voice, a skillful rhetoric, an inspiring personality, and in course of time a dynamic new doctrine of civil struggle.

Martin found that the years 1954 and 1955 were the years of the Race(s). "Montgomery Boycott" made headlines in the print and electronic media. So did Dr Martin Luther King Jr. Contributions in support of the Boycott started pouring in from all over the world. The world at large was openly sympathetic to the Black Cause, more so since Martin's technique was based on non-violence. In fact, the Blacks had no other option. They could not possibly fight the White Power physically. Of sheer necessity therefore, the Blacks had to fight for their survival through non-violent means only. The Montgomery Boycott thus followed in the footsteps of Philip Randolph's *Brotherhood of Sleeping Car Porters* as well as E.D. Nixon's role-model in keeping the agitation strictly non-violent in accordance with the principles of Gandhian philosophy of *Satyagraha.* The Montgomery of 1955 was the beginning of adoption in the United States of techniques of Mahatma Gandhi of South African fame, and later of Indian independence movement. Martin's fondness for explaining his philosophy and technique in terms of *agape*[19] was merely another name for what had already been firmly established as the Gandhian philosophy of Satyagraha, which ultimately succeeded in gaining freedom for India through non-violent means. While Gandhi demanded complete freedom for India, the Montgomery Blacks were asking for much less, very little indeed, in that all that the Blacks were asking for was justice within the framework of segregation laws. However, the Bus Boycott movement launched by Martin was not first bus-boycott in the United States: Reverend Theodore Jemison had led a bus-boycott in Baton Rouge, Louisiana, sometime back.

When Dr. King assumed the leadership of Montgomery Bus Boycott, he had every reason to expect white clergymen to come forward to support the blacks in their struggle for justice. Since most of the ministers had studied in reputed seminaries, he had no doubt that they would, in keeping with the gospel of Jesus, demand justice for the poor and the

---

18. King Martin Luther: op. cit. p. 472.
19. Greek word for Brotherly Love.

oppressed people. To his great dismay, King found that only one white clergyman, Robert Graetz, openly came forward in support of the Boycott, and he was the pastor of a black congregation. No other white clergyman came out in support of the black agitation. Instead, a number of ministers accused Martin of mixing religion with politics while others openly supported segregation in bus-seating. Still others advised Martin that the job of a clergy man was to 'lead the soul of men to God', and not to create confusion by getting involved in transitory social problems. Martin was indeed very disappointed with the white-clergy's attitude.

In the early stages of the movement for de-segregation of city buses, Negro taxi companies came to the rescue. They agreed to transport the people at the same ten- cent fare that they paid on the buses. However, in the course of 'negotiation meeting' held with Police Commissioner Sellers on 8th December, it transpired that there was a law that enjoined the taxis to a minimum fare. Martin took the hint that Sellers might use that law to prevent the taxis companies from helping in the protest movement. Martin therefore requested the people in the mass meeting held that very evening if they would offer their cars. The response was tremendous. More than a hundred and fifty volunteered their services for limited periods of time every day, while those who were not working, offered to join the car pool for the whole day. Soon the number of volunteers swelled to three hundred for which forty-eight dispatch and forty-two pick-up stations were organized. With all these arrangements in place, there were some in the community who preferred to follow the example of Gandhi's Salt March, and walked. While declining to take a lift, one old lady commented: "I am not walking for myself. ... I am walking for my children and grandchildren."

Another grand old lady, this one of the white race, Miss Juliette Morgan, who understood and sympathized with the Negro's movement for freedom and desegregation, wrote a letter to *Montgomery Advertiser* comparing the bus boycott with the Gandhian movement in India for total independence. The local white community condemned the old lady for her views and sympathy for the Black cause. She could not stand the rejection by her own people and died in the summer of 1957. However, before she died, the name of India's saint, Mahatma Gandhi had become familiar in the entire community. "In other words, Christ furnished the spirit and motivation while Gandhi furnished the method."[20] Martin also pointed out that arrest of Mrs. Park was not the cause of the protest; it was merely a precipitating factor. The action taken by the

---

20. King M.L.: op. cit. (*Autobiography*), p. 67.

MIA was the 'culmination of a series of injustices and indignities' that had been perpetuated over the years. Meanwhile, when Martin was driving a few persons from downtown, he was arrested for allegedly driving 30 M.P.H. in a 25-mile zone. Since Martin knew that he was being trailed by the police on motor cycles, he was extra careful to drive meticulously within the rules. The allegation was totally false, but Martin was sent to Montgomery City Jail and shoved into an overcrowded cell where he found the conditions so appalling that he forgot about his own predicament. Men were lying on bare wooden slats. Mattresses were torn, filthy or non-existent. The toilet was in a corner of the cell, stinking filthy with a semblance of an enclosure. It was a shocking state of affairs.

As usual, Ralph Abernathy was soon at the jail, trying to arrange bail-bond. He was told to get a certified statement from the court that he owned sufficient property to sign a bond. But the courts were already closed for the day. He was not even allowed to see Martin. Finally, Abernathy offered a cash-bond which the jailer could not refuse. As he was making arrangements to get the cash, a large crowd of Negroes had collected at jail gate. The jailer sensed trouble brewing up. He therefore let Martin out on his own bond!

When all the cajoling by the City Government did not bear any fruits, they took a leaf out of the British policy of 'Divide and Rule' in India. The City Commissioners announced in the local paper on Sunday, 22nd January that they had come to an agreement with a group of prominent Negro ministers, and a settlement had been reached. The move was calculated to get a fair number of Negroes to ride the buses on Sunday morning. Once buses started running with some Negroes as passengers, the others would follow leading to breaking down of the Boycott.

About eleven o'clock on Saturday night the MIA got the information that indeed the Commissioners had met three ministers, but they were neither prominent nor were members of the MIA. All the black ministers were contacted late at night and asked to inform the Sunday-morning congregations there had been no such meeting, nor a settlement, and that the bus-boycott continues. Concurrently, Martin with a group of leaders went around various bars, taverns and night clubs to inform the people of the correct position. In the bargain, Martin and his colleagues had the taste of Blacks' night-life of Montgomery! The MIA was thus successful in putting an end to the insidious attempt by the City Commissioners to break the protest. The buses still ran empty on Sunday morning, as usual.

The Bombing

On 30th January, Martin left home for the evening mass meeting at the First Baptist Church. A member of the congregation had come to the parsonage to keep Coretta Company. About nine-thirty they heard a loud explosion. A bomb had gone off on the porch. The news soon reached the mass meeting, but not to Martin who noticed some unusual suspicious movements going on. Finally, he interrupted his speech to enquire if anything was wrong when he was told: "Your house has been bombed".[21] He dispersed the meeting calmly and urged the people not to panic, go straight home and follow the path of non-violence whatever be the provocation.

Martin was driven home. Several hundred angry looking Blacks had collected near the bombed house. The crowd was livid and the situation volatile. The Mayor and Police Commissioner and several white reporters had also reached the spot. They expressed their regret when some one retorted that this was the result of their get-tough policies. The police was having trouble in controlling the situation, more so since many people were armed. All the whites appeared scared since violence could erupt any moment, and they had no way of escaping the menacing crowd. In this tense moment, Martin walked out to the porch, asked the motley crowd to come to order. There was complete silence within a few seconds when Martin addressed his people:[22]

> "We believe in law and order. Don't get panicky. Don't get your weapons. He who lives by the sword shall perish by the sword. Remember that is what God said. We want to love our enemies. I want you to love our enemies. I did not start this boycott. I was asked by you to serve as your spokesman. I want it known the length and breadth of this land that if I am stopped this movement will not stop. For what we are doing is right just. And God is with us."

The crowd responded: "Amen'. God bless you. ... We are with you all the way, Reverend." And they dispersed peacefully. The whites heaved a sigh of relief.

Just two nights later, a stick of dynamite was thrown on the lawn of E.D. Nixon. Fortunately, no one was hurt. The proposal to hire armed bodyguards and watchmen was of course turned down.

---

21. It happened on 30th January 1956, the anniversary of M.K. Gandhi's death.
22. King M.L.: op. cit. (*Autobiography*), p. 80.

"When I decided that, as a teacher of the philosophy of non-violence, I couldn't keep a gun, I came face to face with the question of death and I dealt with it. And from that pint on, I no longer needed a gun nor have I been afraid. Ultimately, one's sense of manhood must come from within."

However, Martin and Coretta agreed to have floodlights mounted around the house, while they got rid of the only weapon they possessed.

Boycotting is a Crime

The Bus Line Company was going bankrupt. The authorities were now desperate, more so since violence could not subdue the protests. A local attorney brought to light an old state-law making boycott a crime. A grand jury endorsed this version and indicted more than one hundred persons, including Martin of course. During this period Martin was on a lecture tour in Fisk University Nashville. Ralph Abernathy informed Martin of the indictments on 21st February. The arrests were scheduled for the next day. Martin was anxious, more so since the people had undergone harassments, humiliations, cruelties, police brutalities, besides having had to walk or hitch-hike for more than thirteen weeks. And now, to cap it all, these mass arrests. As it happened in a number of instances in India, particularly in the Frontier Gandhi's Province, the authorities found it difficult to accommodate all the prisoners who offered themselves for arrest.[23] Martin was afraid that 'battle-fatigue' might lead to failure of the Movement. Subsequent developments showed that his apprehensions were misplaced.

Martin returned to Montgomery despite protests from 'Daddy' King and other family members at Atlanta. Daddy King also came with him. Ralph Abernathy was arrested and released on bail the next day. It was now Martin's turn. Accompanied by Ralph and Daddy King, Martin set out for the county jail. Several church members followed him to the jail where it was like a holiday atmosphere with people rushing in to get arrested. They were no longer afraid of jail. None attempted to evade arrest. People were proud to go to jail for the cause of freedom. A Negro was now a transformed man, since he was armed with the weapon of non-violence, sharpened by non-retaliation. Martin was photographed, finger-printed released on bond paid by one of the members of his church. The trial was set for March 19, and lasted four days at the end of which Judge Eugene Carter announced his verdict:

---

23. Zutshi G.L.: op. cit. p. 87.

"I declare the defendant guilty of violating the State's anti-boycott law." The penalty: $500 fine plus court costs, or 386 days at hard labour. Martin was released on bond pending disposal of the final appeal. The black crowd outside the jail was proud of themselves and of their smiling leader; they began to sing: "We ain't gonna ride the buses no more." Meanwhile, the insurance company notified that all the motor-vehicle insurance policies would be cancelled, effective September 15, since the risk was too high. However, Lloyds of London took up the insurance. The oppressor again failed in his nefarious methods to smother the movement for equality and freedom.

Finally, God Almighty spoke from Washington on November 13th 1956 when "the United States Supreme Court today affirmed a decision of a special three-judge U.S. District Court in declaring Alabama's state and local laws requiring segregation on buses unconstitutional. The Supreme Court acted without listening to any argument; it simply said 'the motion to affirm is granted and the judgment is affirmed'. Thus it was the U.S. Supreme Court that came to the rescue of the Blacks when the Montgomery Improvement Association received a favourable ruling in the case regarding racial segregation in matters of public accommodation. In fact, the Supreme Court held the Alabama State and local laws embodying racial segregation throughout public accommodations as unconstitutional. The corollary was an intellectual irony by itself: "The Segregationists helped to create Martin King, the public man."[24] Montgomery was a great personal success for Martin. He came to stand on his own pedestal of success. Gandhian political philosophy of non-violent non-cooperation as a political weapon of the weak and depressed sections of society against oppression and exploitation found universal application. Needless to say that this metamorphosis created an aura of success, self-sacrifice and saintly virtues as a way of life. Martin felt that non-violent non-cooperation could be applied to the prevailing political imbroglio in the U.S., particularly towards implementation of de-segregation in the school system. In the process, Gandhi was 'resurrected' in the American South. Gandhian philosophy did not imply whole sale submission of the weak to the power of majority's tyranny. On the contrary, it meant courage of conviction to face unjust and unequal confrontation through the medium of love and non-violent non-cooperation with, or against, the powers that be. On the other side of the coin, some detractors of Martin King, Lomax for example, say that "Martin King left Montgomery, his work undone; the

24. Williams A. John: op. cit. p. 30.

buses are integrated but the schools are not; neither are the parks, playgrounds or other public facilities ... one of the questions now plaguing the social scientists is why such a deep-rooted movement as the Montgomery boycott resulted in nothing more than the integration of buses."[25] While the Gandhi of India fought for, and won, independence from foreign rule, the Negroes of America were fighting for integration, social justice and *de facto* equal rights. Obviously, the Negroes' task was far more complicated than what Gandhi had at his hands.

The above hypercritical comment is totally misplaced inasmuch as it ignores the fact that immediately after the successful conclusion of the Bus Boycott movement, King immersed himself in the related fields of school integration, civil rights, voting rights, equality and justice, *et al.* Secondly: every movement or individual has a set aim. Any deviation from that results in frittering away of limited resources. When success has come one's way, the primary requirement at that point of time is consolidation of the gains, before putting one's finger in another pie.

At the end of another mass meeting held late in the evening on 5th December 1955, it was decided that the Negroes would ride the buses again only after the following moderate demands put forward by the MIA were met by the Administration:

- Courteous treatment by the bus operatives must be guaranteed.
- Passengers to be seated on a first-come first-served basis — Negroes sitting from the back forward, whites from front to back.
- Negro bus-drivers to be employed on predominantly Negro routes.

The above was followed by another high level meeting the next day. It is beyond comprehension of an average rational person that even these simple demands were turned down by the Administration, more so when they were aware that bus-integration was just a few days away. — The Supreme Court order on bus-integration reached Montgomery on 20th December 1956. "Four days before Christmas 8,000 souls voted to end the boycott, the largest and longest protest by black people in the nation's history to that date." A mass meeting was scheduled for that evening to prepare the people for riding the integrated service. King ended his message to the over flowing crowd at the St. John A.M.E. Church with the following words:

---

25. Extract from *Negro Revolt*; and Coretta Scott King: op. cit. p. 133.

With this dedication we will be able to emerge from the bleak and desolate midnight of man's inhumanity to man to the bright and glittering daybreak of freedom and justice.

Glenn Smiley of the Fellowship of Reconciliation (FOR) was one of chief aides to King in this boycott movement. King accompanied by Ralph Abernathy, E.D. Nixon and Glenn Smiley rode the first integrated bus at 5:55 a.m. next morning in the glare of TV cameras. Thus ended the largest and longest protest by the Blacks in the history of the United States till date, when desegregated buses started plying on the Montgomery roads. However, Martin told his people not to boast of victory since it was not a victory for the Blacks alone, but for all Montgomery and the South. He advised the Negro community to continue to show courtesy to the Whites and not to sit near a white man if another seat was available. Nonetheless, White fundamentalism could not accept bus-desegregation gracefully. They instigated violence against the Blacks to a level as never before. Buses were stoned. Shots were fired on the buses. A bullet was fired through the King's house while Ralph Albernathy's house became a target of a sneak guerrilla attack. His church was dynamited along with three more Negro churches. The King-house was bombed again on the night of January 28th. At this stage, white ministers intervened and appealed for peaceful acceptance of desegregation. Leading white citizens too joined their ministers. The violence ended, after all.

The protest boycott lasted for 381 days. According to a *Jet* magazine article "Man on the Go", during this period Martin delivered two hundred and eight speeches and travelled 780,000 miles besides writing his first book, *Stride Towards Freedom,* in which he told the story of the Montgomery protest. This was Martin's first book, published on 17th September 1958. While he was autographing the Book in a department store, Martin was seriously wounded when a deranged black woman, Mrs. Izola Ware Curry stabbed him. A delicate and dangerous operation was performed by Dr. Aubre Maynard in Harlem Hospital to remove the sharp-edged knife. The procedure was all the more dangerous since the razor tip of the knife was just touching King's aorta. "If you had sneezed during all those hours of waiting, your aorta would have been punctured and you would have drowned in your own blood." Indeed, Martin had a dangerous brush with death. Martin's weeks of recuperation[26] were the time for quiet contemplation such as Gandhi

26. After release from hospital on October 3, 1958, Martin started convalescing at the home of Reverend Sandy F. Ray.

and Nehru had in their prison cells. It was ironic that 'one of our own people' used violence against Martin. "We could not help remembering that Gandhi had been assassinated by one of his own people".[27] And one could not afford to forget that Atlanta was by far the most forward looking city in the South. It was Martin's home base and was blessed with a university, Morehouse College, Spellman College, Morris Brown College and Clark College. These institutions produced the cream of black middle class. There was so much black potential in this Southern city that it was a matter of considerable surprise and regret that Atlanta had not been desegregated.

Consequential Developments

An Umbrella Organization: While Martin was away to Africa and Europe, Ela Baker played a leading role in giving shape to a new organization of which he was elected in absentia as the President — Southern Christian Leadership Conference. Ela was appointed the first Executive Director with Bayard Rustin and Stanley Levinson as members of the Executive Committee, amongst others. SCLC was a cumbersome coalition of about one hundred church or church-oriented organizations. It was virtually impossible to achieve consensus in such a conglomeration. But Martin had a big advantage since, besides becoming the President of SCLC; he was already president of the Montgomery Improvement Association. And, of course, he was the Pastor of Dexter Avenue Baptist Church. All these responsibilities weighed heavily on his time and body when one takes into consideration his large number of public-speaking assignments.

12th February 1958 was Lincoln's birthday. Twenty-one mass meetings were held in key southern cities. The year was observed as the year of "Crusade for Citizenship". Rightly so, outside India Gandhi was taken as a symbol of 'struggle against European imperialism and white racism', which reinforces validity of King's message for these meetings:

> "Let us make our intentions crystal clear. We must and will be free. We want freedom — NOW. We do not want freedom fed to us in teaspoons over another hundred and fifty year!"

As a fall-out of the Montgomery Bus Boycott, the basic tenets for the civil rights movement of the 1960's were established. The strategic parameters, whose primary source was Gandhian philosophy, were set. Martin had no hesitation in saying: "India's Gandhi was the guiding light

27. Coretta: op. cit. p. 185.

of our technique of our non-violent social change."[28] Martin's Montgomery crusade transformed the Negro psyche. What Gandhi had done to the Indian collective psyche to wipe out the stains of subservience, King did the same for the Negroes by following in the footsteps of Gandhi. Both made a great impact on their respective people and instilled in them an element of self respect and dignity which they had lacked for centuries. By this time Rev Martin Luther King had made his way up to the cover of the *Time* Magazine, 3rd January 1964. Notwithstanding all this and a lot more, the Federal Government maintained silence. They did not react lest the Southern States get infuriated. Martin and his top-team were not even invited for a meeting with the President despite their repeated efforts in that direction. President Eisenhower merely responded with a statement "you can't legislate men's hearts" adding a provocative remark about the white South's concern for the "mongrelization of the races."[29] It may be recalled that in the Battle of the Bulge when German offensive almost succeeded in shattering the Allied defenses, Eisenhower, the Supreme Commander, specifically asked for Black troops as reinforcements. But when it came to race relations at home during his Presidency, he "was consistent; he did little."[30] However, Eisenhower was right in that Legislating is one thing; its implementation is altogether a different matter. A number of laws abolishing segregation in inter-state travel had been passed over many years, including the U.S. Supreme Court ruling of December 1960. But they remained mere paper rulings, all because the transportation companies, the train and buses, did not comply for fear of losing their business in the Southern states even though President Harry Truman had desegregated the armed forces as far back as 1948.

Bayard Rustin referred to Martin as a "spiritual intellectual". The right to ride in a bus in a seat of one's choosing was a small matter indeed. It was the principle behind it that mattered. Martin established the sanctity of that principle. He made the Negro proud and fearless, confident of his ability to establish his rights, and above all, devoid of

---

28. King Martin Luther: *My Trip to the Land of Gandhi*; *Ebony*, July 1959; *A Testament of Hope: The Essential Writings of Martin Luther King Jr.*, San Francisco, 1986, p. 23.
29. Wexler Sanford: op. cit. p. 90.
30. Williams A. John: op. cit. p. 46. In fairness to Eisenhower it should be recorded that he did order troops to Little Rock, albeit reluctantly, to enforce the Federal Court orders for gradual integration in schools. However, the fact still remained that neither the Executive nor the Legislative Branches of the Federal Government took any worthwhile initiative in civil rights at home.

centuries old inferiority complex. The black man imbibed the feeling that he could stand up on his own, be strong and courageous, bigger and better, and successfully fight for his economic and racial rights on equal terms. These abstract qualitative changes were far more important than the right to eat at a 'whites only' lunch counter, or use the exclusive restroom, or drink from the 'whites only' fountain — a total negation of 'Jim Crow' culture.

In order to coordinate bus-desegregation throughout the Southern States, Martin called a meeting of Negro leaders from all over the South. The conference was scheduled for 10-11 January 1957, just three weeks after the Montgomery boycott. Unfortunately, in the wake of spate of bombings of black churches and houses, both King and his constant companion Abernathy had to rush to Montgomery lest the situation there get out of control. Coretta Scott King and Shuttlesworth therefore presided over the session. Sixty Negro leaders from ten Southern States came for this first session of Negro Leaders Conference on Nonviolent Integration. Economic issues were predominant. Economic boycott and reprisals in South Carolina were matters of concern for delegates from that State while underground night work in Mississippi Delta was a disturbing issue for the others. And the first person who took the floor was the one who had been shot because he had dared to vote.[31] Before adjourning, the meeting voted to form the Southern Leaders Conference, which later became the Southern Christian Leadership Conference or SCLC for short. It met formally for the first time on February 14, 1957 in New Orleans. Dr. Martin Luther King Jr. who had proven himself a charismatic leader fresh from his success in Montgomery was chosen as the first president of this umbrella organization. Tree months later on May 17, 1957, he delivered his famous "Give us the Ballot" speech that catapulted him to the national platform.

31. Rustin Bayard: *Even in the Face of Death;* New York, 1971, p. 101.

16

Visits Abroad

The oppressor never voluntarily gives freedom to the oppressed. You have to work for it, like the Indians and Ghanaians did for themselves. Freedom is never given to anybody. Privileged classes never give up their privileges without strong resistance.

Ghana: African Heritage

The Kingdom of Ghana was a flourishing conglomeration of chiefdoms around the 8th century A.D. It commanded the gold sources near the Senegal River, hence the name Gold Coast. Islamic forces captured Ghana in 1076 A.D. when it broke up into its constituent units. In 1821, British possessions in Sierra Leone, the Gold Coast and Gambia were joined as the British West Africa Settlements. The British also wrested control of Dutch possessions in the Gold Coast on April 6, 1872 thereby establishing a full-fledged British colony on the African West Coast as part of the Great Empire. The French controlled vast tracts of the West Africa. When they tried to recruit soldiers to fight for them during the First World War, many Africans fled to neighboring countries including the British Colony of Gold Coast. The export of coffee, cocoa and peanuts was the major source of income, besides whatever gold was still left. By 1925, Gold Coast was supplying almost half of world's demand for cocoa making the Colony the wealthiest country in tropical Africa. While the indigenous Africans produced the cash crop, the expatriates controlled the export trade. The same year a new constitution based on the Clifford model was implemented in the Colony. About ten years later, I.T.A. Johnson, a Marxist trade unionist established the West African Youth League in the Gold Coast. However, the British deported him to Sierra Leone in 1938.

University College of Gold Coast was established in 1947, the year of Indian Independence, giving rise to an educated middle class, howsoever small, providing a source of young educated leadership. Ever since India achieved her independence through non-violent mass civil disobedience movement, the people of Gold Coast under the leadership of Kwame Nkrumah began their struggle to attain freedom from British yoke. Nkrumah returned from Britain to Gold Coast in 1947 and started a campaign on the Indian pattern for self-government for his country. A mass demonstration by ex-servicemen against poor living conditions led to severe rioting resulting in death of twenty-nine people. In early next year, in the footsteps of Gandhi, he organized a boycott of European imports. In 1949, Nkrumah established the Convention People's Party (CPP) and adopted the slogan of "Self-Government NOW". The British authorities jailed Nkrumah and other leaders of the CPP. But in the elections held in 1951 gave overwhelming majority to CPP. Nkrumah and others were released. The CPP performed equally well in the 1956-General Elections leading to negotiations for immediate independence.

Ghana became independent in 1957 with Kwame Nkrumah as its first Prime Minister. The decolonization era had already set in and Ghana was the first to achieve complete independence. By this time Dr. Martin Luther King Jr. had gained sufficient importance as an American leader, not merely of the Blacks but of the entire U.S. It was his success in Montgomery that took his reputation sky high, enough to merit him an invitation to the Independence celebrations of Ghana. Martin travelled real high — on board the same flight were the Vice President, Richard M. Nixon, Adam Clayton Powell, Ralph Bunche, Philip Randolph, *et al.* They arrived in Accra, capital of Ghana, on 4th March 1957. The ceremonial declaration of Freedom of Ghana by Nkrumah as an independent country on the midnight of 6th March was an emotionally high point for Martin and Coretta, more so when Nkrumah talked non-violence as the effective weapon against powerful oppressors. We felt so 'proud of our African heritage.' But the bubble of pride burst when they witnessed the 'appalling poverty of the people' of Ghana in Central Nigeria. The vestiges of colonialism were evident in every facet of Ghanian social and private life. Every body that was some body in Ghana had a train of servants whose servitude was most distressing to Martin and other Black leaders from the United States. "In Kano we saw people living under conditions of filth and squalor that exceeded even the worst state of Negroes in America."[1]

We did not fly in high company on the way back. Instead, Martin took the opportunity to visit Europe — Rome, Paris, London and Geneva.

---

1. King Scott Coretta: op. cit. pp. 170-71.

While in Paris he met the expatriate Black novelist, Richard Wright. The triumphal trip was soon over. "The attention lavished on King in Europe tended to reinforce the illusion of his power". On return to America, Martin was awarded the NAACP's Spingarn Medal for the person making the biggest contribution in the field of race relations. Yet there was plenty of work back home awaiting King.

One Way Traffic to Meet M.K. Gandhi

In so far non-violent struggle was concerned, the visitors from the United States, mostly black leaders, constituted the one way traffic to meet with Gandhi, observe his work and performance at first hand, study his philosophy and technique. The first major contact in this direction occurred during 1935 when a small group of educators visited India, Ceylon and Burma. They included Dean Howard Thurman of Howard University, Sue Bailey Thurman, Rev. Edward G. Carroll and Phenola Carroll. They spent about six months in various universities of the three eastern countries all of which constituted single politico-geographical mass in the then British Empire. When Benjamin May was dean of School of Religions of Howard University, he had met with Gandhi for about ninety minutes in his Sevagram Ashram in Wardha. However, it was only about ten years later in 1936 that Benjamin May, now President of Morehouse College, in his Tuesday Chapel lectures, spoke in some detail about Gandhi and his philosophy. It had a dramatic effect on the young Martin Luther King Jr. who imbibed Gandhi's teachings in full, and decided that Gandhi's technique was the most suited line of action for liberation of Negroes in America. That is what May had in mind when on returning to the U.S. after his meeting with Gandhi, he spread the idea that 'the black community needed to assimilate Gandhi's wealth of knowledge':

> The Negro people have much to learn from the Indian. The Indians have learned what we have not learned. They have learned how to sacrifice for a principle. They have learned how to sacrifice position, prestige, economic security, and even life itself for what they consider a righteous and respectable cause. Thousands of them in recent times have gone to jail for their cause. Thousands of them have died for their cause.[2]

In the same vein, Mordecai Johnson who had visited India and met with Gandhi in 1950 said that Gandhi was a great man on five counts:

---

2. Kapur op. cit.: *Raising up a Prophet*, pp. 96-97.

1. He had liberated India.
2. He had done so without firing a shot. He embraced the 'untouchables' as the children of God, and assimilated them in a society which had excluded them, segregated them. Gandhi's campaigns against untouchability and his personal examples in this regard drew instant recognition by Afro-Americans, as the Blacks of America came to be called in course of time. — 'Integration' means elimination of racial segregation; and that is more complicated than mere independence. While Gandhi had to tackle both, King had the difficult task of integration only.
3. For his exemplary and saintly personal life alone, he was a great man.
4. He had shown how to harness the redemptive power of love to social issues.
5. Like Jesus, he also died a redemptive death which abated the fearful carnage of communal riots that had raged after Independence.[3]

'Pilgrimage' to India

Martin's release from hospital after that stabbing incident appeared a good time to fulfill his long standing desire to visit India since the doctors had advised a period of rest and recuperation. An invitation from Gandhi Peace Foundation to make a speaking tour of India and to meet its leaders including Prime Minister Jawaharlal Nehru was long outstanding. It was now made possible to undertake the tour through a grant of five thousand dollars from a devoted friend, Libby Holman Reynolds. The Kings and their friend Professor Lawrence D. Reddick, a black professor of history at Montgomery's Alabama State University, undertook the trip that Martin wanted to for so long. While Coretta was interested in the empowerment of women of India, Dr. L.D. Reddick who had written a biography of Dr. King, *Crusader Without Violence*, was particularly interested in the 'history and the government of that great country'. They landed at Bombay on the night of March 9, 1959 instead of Delhi, since the flight was diverted due to bad weather. "But as we drove in from the airport through narrow, odorous streets, we saw thousands of people dressed in rags sleeping on the sidewalks or huddled in doorways, lying wherever they could find space. We were appalled. ... They had no homes. They carried everything they owned with them, wrapped up in a rag or a newspaper. ... The sight of

3. Mays Benjamin E.: *The Relevance of Mordecai Wyatt Johnson for Our Times*, 27 January 1978, pp. 2, 4. Also; Bayard Rustin: *The Negro and Non-violence*, Chicago, 1971; pp. 10-11.

emaciated human beings wearing only a dirty loincloth, picking through garbage cans ... Colonialism was responsible. Never, even in Africa, such abject, despairing poverty."[4]

On arrival at Delhi the next day, Martin told the reporters: "To other countries, I may go as a tourist, but to India I come as a pilgrim. ... I have read so much about Gandhi and the success of the non-violent movement here that I wanted to come and see for myself." Martin King was particularly impressed by the amazing results of Gandhi's campaigns for Indian Independence. He did not perceive any hatred against the British in the hearts of Indians; instead, he witnessed friendship and mutual respect between the two. Indians had used non-violence and brotherly love to challenge the might of British Empire and succeeded in achieving their independence, instead of bequeathing a legacy of bitterness that violence would have engendered. However, Gandhi never saw non-violence as a retreat from confrontation, as an avoidance of risk. Gandhi stressed that nonviolence was not passive; instead it was active resistance. "I do believe that when there is only a choice between cowardice and violence, I would advise violence. ... I would rather have India resort to arms in order to defend her honour than that she should in a cowardly manner become or remain a helpless victim to her own dishonour. But I believe that non-violence is infinitely superior to violence, forgiveness is manlier than punishment."

And Martin took it to its logical conclusion of 'militant non-violence'. For Gandhi, and thereafter for Martin King, it was a matter of principle, a moral obligation, to resist evil. In both cases, non-violent protests were directed against the forces of evil, but not against the perpetrators of evil. They were fighting the unjust system, but not the persons operating that system; the latter were merely cog in the wheel, doing what was deemed to be their official duty. It was repetition of St. Augustine's plea: "Hate the sin, but not the sinner". The redemptive power of unearned suffering was a recurrent theme in the philosophy of both Gandhi and King — to meet hate with love, to confront physical force with soul-force.

---

4. It is easy to find colonialism as the scapegoat. The picture today remains almost the same, with marginal improvements only. The fault, Dear Brutus, lies not in colonialism but in our own mismanagement of our affairs over the past more than four decades. Misplaced socialism and rhetorical narrow political sloganeering, rather than positive steps to effect material improvement. Again it is corruption in high places that has kept India's poor in the bondage of poverty. But the Kings could not possibly have known this inner truth — The Author.

Dr. Martin Luther King Jr. And Mrs. Coretta Scott King, on a month's visit to India at the invitation of Gandhi Peace Foundation with Prime Minister Jawaharlal Nehru: February 10, 1959.

Dr. Martin Luther King Jr.and Mrs. Coretta Scott King, at Mahatma Gandhi's Samadhi at Rajghat, New Delhi: February 8, 1959.

Gandhi had rejected the materialism of the western civilization.[5] He had vowed poverty. Many of the Gandhian types still dressed in the Gandhian style of simplicity and rough handwoven cloth; but paradoxically enough, they still lived in the luxurious houses and style of their former masters, the British.[6] Of course, still there were some notable exceptions, like the saintly Vinoba Bhave, a true Gandhian disciple still preaching the idealistic doctrine of *Sarvodaya* = spiritual decentralized socialism. Vinoba Bhave strongly believed that people would be better of if they had no government, because government corrupts. The more organizations the society has, the more corrupt people become. The Kings literally walked the dusty track with Vinoba Bhave and enjoyed talking to him en route. However, Martin was of the opinion that, although Vinoba's ideas were idealistic, they were impractical of implementation. Nonetheless, Martin was impressed by Vinoba's idea of total unilateral disarmament by a country like India would have a profound moral effect on the rest of the world. Be that as it may, wherever the visitors went, they met 'crowded humanity' eager to listen to his speech, and her Negro spirituals. In all his speeches in India, Martin expressed his deep gratitude, indeed indebtedness, for the Gandhian thought that had guided him in his non-violent struggle in his own country. His speeches were invariably spiced with Coretta's songs of Negro spirituals; the Indians loved to listen to Negro spirituals.

Jayaprakash Narayan had his higher education in the United States. He too was a man of great intellect and sensitive nature. He and Vinoba Bhave combined well to launch a land reform movement the like of which had not been tried anywhere else in the world, and particularly so in America. It was known as 'Bhoodan' whose objective was to reduce the gap between the rich land-owning class and the poor cultivators, to usher in economic and social change by common consent rather than by force of law or otherwise, thereby making the villages economically self-sufficient. The proposed reforms envisaged persuading owners of large tracts of agricultural-forest lands to voluntarily forsake a part of their holdings for the benefit of the poor, creating a land-bank leading to formation of agricultural cooperatives. Concurrently, the farmers were encouraged to follow Gandhi's 'Charkha' (spinning wheel) movement in their spare time

5. Gandhi believed: "There is nothing to prevent us from profiting by the light that may come from the West. Only we must take care that we are not overpowered by the glamour of the West. We must not mistake glamour for true light."
6. A number of renowned congressmen still follow that practice of outward simplicity, but luxury in their life style including their privately built houses actually costing a few hundred millions, but on paper for taxation purposes, they are reflected as worth peanuts — The Author.

to spin and weave cloth for their own clothes. Thus the villagers' basic needs of food, clothing and employment would be met. In turn, the villages would not only become self-sufficient but would also not fall a prey to urban slums. However, somehow such ideas and propositions were not a practical proposition for the American economic and social system.

Notwithstanding the terrible contrasts of rich and poor, materialism and spiritualism, philosophers and self-seekers, the Indian visit and the experience that it imparted — all this had a profound effect on Martin's mind. Above all, it taught him a lesson in patience. He came to appreciate that it had taken Indians nearly half a century of struggle, through thick and thin, to gain freedom from a powerful Empire in which the sun never set. Moreover, freedom for India brought freedom to a number of other oppressed countries and territories all over the world. Martin returned home from India "more devoted than ever to Gandhian ideals of nonviolence and simplicity of living. ... His great problem was the enormous difference between the mechanical complexity of our way of living and theirs" and how to reconcile the two.[7] Hereafter, Martin strove more and more to be like Gandhi, spiritually of course. Gandhi was literally worshipped by a multitude of Indians. Shrines were built in his honor. The black masses of America did the same for their hero, Dr. Martin Luther King Jr. His people treated him as if he was the President of the Negroes! Very close to Gandhi indeed. "We were looked upon as brothers with the colour of skins ... an asset."[8] It came as a pleasant surprise to Martin that the Montgomery protests with all their gory tales were well known to the educated Indians. King was equally impressed by the news media in India, particularly for their astonishing grasp of developments at the global level generally, and in the United States in particular. Above all, King was carried away by complete absence of bitterness or animosity towards the Colonial rulers, all because the campaign for independence was totally non-violent with 'Love-Force' and 'Truth-Force' as the primary ingredients. For instance: Lady Mountbatten, wife of Lord Mountbatten, the last British Viceroy and Governor General of India, was a guest with us when we had dinner with Prime Minister Nehru. There was lasting friendship between the peoples of the two countries all because Gandhi followed the path of love and non-violence in his struggle to free India from the British shackles; and violence would have left nothing but bitterness in its wake.

---

7. Coretta: p. 192.
8. King, Martin Luther Jr.: *My Trip to the Land of Gandhi*; p.24.

"As we travelled through the land, we were greatly impressed by the part women played in the political life of India, far more than in our own country. We knew that Gandhi had involved the women of India in the struggle for independence and that many of them had gone to jail like the men. Gandhi also worked to liberate women from the bondage of Hindu and Muslim traditions."[9] In the course of their travels in India, the Kings made the usual round of tourist spots in passing. What impressed them most was not the Taj or the likes of it; it was the southern tip of the great land mass of India, the Cape Comorin — "it is one of the most beautiful parts of the entire world. Three great bodies of water meet together in their entire majestic splendour: the Bay of Bengal, the Arabian Sea, and the Indian Ocean." This is perhaps one of the few, if not the only spot in the world, where one can watch the setting of the sun and rising of the moon simultaneously.

The Kings' most interesting meetings were with the philosopher-politician Vice-President of India, Sarvepalli Radhakrishnan. Indeed, they enjoyed listening to him. He talked about his philosophy of life and reminded Coretta of Mordecai Johnson, who had first inspired Martin's interest in Gandhian ideals. In fact, Martin said that "our first twenty-four hours in India had been like meeting George Washington, Thomas Jefferson, and James Madison in a single day."

Martin had called 1961 "a year of the victory of the non-violent method: though blood flowed, not one drop was drawn by a Negro from his adversary." Indeed, Gandhi's philosophy had permeated from the Negro's original home in Africa to America by the circuitous route via India. Professor Kenneth Clark, a Negro psychologist at the City College of New York: "... anticipated a total rejection of the American pattern being incorrigibly hypocritical and corrupt and therefore unworkable in terms of a meaningful change in the status of the Negro." The rise of Muslim fundamentalism in the steaming black ghettoes of the North, where "Elijah Muhammad and Malcolm X preached the ineradicable evil of the white man, contained chilling portents for the future."

Untouchability was — and perhaps still is to some extent — an internal social problem of India. But somehow King had a good insight and understanding of this social stigma. That is evident from his sermon at Ebenezer Baptist Church on July 4, 1965 when he said: "Yes, I am an untouchable, and every Negro is in the United States of America is an untouchable." King was indirectly alluding to an incident that occurred at Trivendrum in the Indian State of Kerala during his visit to India. In

9. King Scott Coretta: op. cit. pp.189-90.

fact, King was also aware of the domestic disharmony that resulted from Gandhi's insistence on adopting an untouchable young girl as his daughter and ensuring that she stayed in the Ashram without any discrimination from any quarter, including his wife who had vehemently objected to this unimaginable act of abnormal behaviour. In his discussions with Nehru, the latter enlightened King about the provisions in the Indian Constitution which made discrimination of any sort against the 'untouchables' an offence, punishable by imprisonment. In fact, calling a person an untouchable was itself a crime. That is what made King to remark: "India appeared to be integrating its untouchables faster than the United States was integrating its Negro minority."

Some of the personal opinions King cherished, and the statements he made thereon, go to show that Dr. Martin Luther King Jr. was well on his way to creating a niche for himself as a world statesman. For instance: at the time of his departure from India on March 10, 1959, he made a fervent plea for unilateral disarmament by the people and the Government of India. In this connection he referred to the Gandhi's and Vinoba Bhave's views on the subject of unilateral disarmament in the overall interest of world peace. His departing message to India was: "It may be that just as India had to take the lead and show the world that national independence could be achieved non-violently, so India may have to take the lead and call for universal disarmament, and if no other nation will join her immediately, India should declare itself for disarmament unilaterally. ...".[10]

To Europe

The frustration and disappointments with the authorities had been much too much. A change was required. So King accepted the invitation of Mayor Willy Brandt of West Berlin and flew to Germany in September 1964. Rome and Madrid were the next destinations. The euphoria of Presidential elections was in the air. King was of the opinion that a white Southern would make a better President than a white Northern. The former will do more good for the Blacks than the latter. King's subtle tilt towards Johnson and Goldwater's thinly veiled apprehensions against the Blacks brought the Blacks out into the hustings in exceptionally large numbers in favour of Johnson that resulted in his landslide victory. Most Negroes were quite happy about this outcome. However, through private sources, it was well known that "Nigger is a household word in Johnson's White House...."[11]

10. Statement made on 9th March 1959 on Leaving India.

11. Williams A. John: op. cit. p. 73.

17

Apartheid and Desegregation

All prejudice is evil, but the prejudice that rejects a man because of the color of his skin is the most despicable expression of man's inhumanity to man. Desegregation will breakdown the legal barriers and bring men together physically, but something must touch the hearts and souls of men so that they will come together spiritually because it is natural and right.

Racial Segregation in the United States was legally institutionalized for the first time in 1896 when the Supreme Court rendered the infamous doctrine of "Separate but Equal" facilities in the Plessy v. Ferguson decision. The genesis of the case was arrest of Homer Plessy, a 'black man' who was otherwise seven-eighths white, for riding on a Louisiana train in a section reserved for "whites only". Desegregation through legal provisions assists in merely bringing the people physically closer. It is symbolic and enforced through fear of punishment for breaking the law. And that certainly is not enough. In a vibrant society intermingling of people of different races and creeds should come from the heart, and not through fear of the law. No doubt, the law gives a helping hand; but it is the heart and soul that bring about true unity. For this reason, Dr. King's ultimate goal was "genuine inter-group and inter-personal living. Only through non-violence can this goal be attained, for the aftermath of non-violence is reconciliation and the creation of the beloved community." But this is easier said than done. Every legal victory of the Negro in federal courts brought in its wake angry passions and deep prejudices from the white race. The exceptions are indeed microscopic. City ordinances and State laws were enacted to counter the positive outfall from the Federal Courts. Negro leaders were continuously harassed and arrested under these local laws and their houses were bombed. Dr. Martin Luther King's own house was bombed in the late evening of

Monday, 30th January 1956. It was a thunderous blast causing considerable damage to the house, but fortunately no injuries to Coretta or the children.

The practice of segregation by the whites against the blacks was an ironic paradox, an absurdity in stupidity. Employment of domestic help by whites inside their homes, for their own comfort and privileged life-style, was accepted as routine. A black maid could move around a white household, bathe the babies, look after the children, dress them up for school, cook food for the family, wash and iron their clothes, look after them when they fell ill, so on and so forth. That held good for the Japanese, Chinese and Mexican domestic help too. The whites had no qualms for such close contacts with the Afro-Americans and other racial minorities. But when it came to sitting in a bus next to each other, or common accommodation, lunch counter, or even restrooms, it was as if the planet earth would be reduced to smithereens. The intrinsic contradiction in whites' attitude towards racial minorities was totally irrational, besides being intellectually bankrupt. A more or less similar situation prevailed in South Africa too when M.K. Gandhi came on the scene to bring home the absurdity of colour-bar as practised by the white minority ruling elite.

Integration v. Black Nationalism

Slavery and consequential segregation had created a deep void in the collective psyche of the Negroes. It was a dilemma which they found extremely difficult to resolve. Martin considered segregation as a product of "adultery of an illicit intercourse between injustice and immorality" which cannot be cured by the 'vaseline of gradualism'. The Negro intellectual-author-philosopher, W.E.B. Du Bois put it most succinctly when he referred to the classic problem as a "peculiar sensation", "a double consciousness", "two souls, two thoughts, two un-reconciled strivings; two warring ideals in one dark body, whose dogged strength alone keeps it from being torn asunder." — An African in America: that was the crux of the problem of races in the brave new world. Is the American Black an American or a Negro? Can he be both at the same time and place? The Declaration of Independence and the Constitution, the American creed of freedom and democratic tradition, Christian and Jewish scriptures, *et al*, were reasons enough to be optimistic about the future of integrated society at peace with itself and the world around. But that was all on paper. The reality on the ground was entirely to the contrary. The 'black nationalists' believed what they saw; what they perceived as the American white reality. The two could not possibly be reconciled. These were two 'separate but inter-dependent' streams of black thought, which represented Martin Luther King Jr. and Malcolm X and their respective perspectives on America.

Integrationism as a viable proposition was on the cards well before Martin King turned it into a doctrine for racial groups to live in harmony with each other. Frederick Douglas was an ardent advocate, so were the NAACP, CORE, National Urban League and a host of black Baptist preachers. The constitution of America read: "We the people" and not as 'we the white people'; the Negroes were therefore entitled to the benefits of the Constitution as much as the whites were. The Independence Day speech in Rochester, New York, by Douglas in which he told White America that "Your celebration is a sham" to the slave(s). "Your denunciation of tyrants, brass fronted impudence; your shouts of liberty and equality , hollow mockery ... There is not a nation on the earth guilty of practices more shocking and bloody than are the people of the United States.'[1]

The black preachers were the backbone of integration movement. To them, "Christianity is the gospel of justice and love. God, the Creator is no respecter of persons. Out of one blood God has created all people. Jesus Christ died on the Cross for all people, blacks and whites alike. No Christian can condone slavery or segregation in churches or society..." and so on and so forth. A mix of religion, politics and socio-economic rhetoric imparted to Martin that rare capacity for empathy which is the hall mark of leadership, notwithstanding his known deficiencies in some fields. After all, no one is perfect, nor can one possess all the attributes that go to make a top leader. Of necessity, it has to be a collective affair, more so in a democracy. King's ideal objective was in the minds of black preachers; it was not necessarily the view of the white community or their preachers. Moreover, Jesus was not a white man, but he was not a black either, and certainly not a Negro. To the whites at large, slaves were slaves and masters were the masters. And that's all that really mattered. Whether Jesus was white or black did not matter to white ministers, the representatives of God on earth. Segregation in their churches was an established practice, a fact of life no black could defy, or deny. King thus managed to inculcate amongst his people a degree of Christian forbearance that created a sense of hope, and extinguish the scars of injustice heaped on them. However, as far back as 1816 Richard Allen, an ex-slave and a Methodist minister, founded the African Methodist Episcopal (AME) Church. He

1. Philips S. Foner (ed.): *Frederick Douglas: Selections from His Writings*, New York, 1964, pp. 52-53.

did this because he and his followers refused to accept segregation in the 'Lord's House'.

It would be totally wrong to assume that Afro-Americans were the only victims of segregation and racial discrimination. It was not so in South Africa where M.K. Gandhi suffered for the cause of racial equality and civil rights of the non-white population. And it was not so in America either. The American-born Mexicans were in the forefront to assert their rights and privileges with the rest of the Americans. While in Montgomery Ms. Rosa Parks was the ignition-spark, in the South-West, it was the Texas-Mexicans returning from military service in the First World War who took the initiative to form civic organizations in various cities of Texas to gain civil rights and collective respect for their community. They named their organizations to lay emphasis on their American identity and its intrinsic Americanism, such as *La Orden Hijos de America* (The Order of the Sons of America) and *La Orden Caballeros de America* (The Order of the Knights of America).[2] The Japanese-Americans and Chinese-Americans followed more or less similar path, although the same cannot be said for the initial waves of Indian immigrant workers to the United States, or even to South Africa for that matter. However, the Afro-Americans were predominantly integrationist rather than segregationists and they too laid emphasis on their American identity, barring odd exceptions. They could not possibly think of any other country as their home except America!

It was strange, indeed a paradox, that the white church and its ministers could not understand the concept "All men are Created Equal" in its true perspective. Of course they understood; but they refused to accept its implications. They did not wish to implement the scriptures, which were meant for preaching only, and not for putting into practice. "American Christianity" was indeed a peculiar phenomenon. Both Martin and Malcolm were highly critical of what had come to be known as the American Christianity, as if Christianity, its doctrines and beliefs differed from region to region, country to country, in conformity with the geo-political conditions and convenience of the white race. Martin and Malcolm both were highly critical of the so-called American Christianity. Both focused on racism — "one making a powerful internal critique and the other a devastating external one."[3] King emphasized: "Racial segregation is a blatant denial of the unity we have in Christ. Segregation

---

2. Gutierrez G. David: *Walls and Mirrors: Mexican Americans, Mexican Immigrants, and the Politics of Ethnicity*, Austin, 1987; p. 75.

3. Cones James H.: op. cit. p. 295

is a tragic evil which is utterly un-Christian." Over a period of centuries, racism developed into a form of idolatry, a sort of idolatry. Perhaps, it was a 'justificatory device' to meet the socio-economic needs of the time. Nevertheless, as affirmed by King:

> Racism is a philosophy based on contempt for life. It is an arrogant assertion that one race is the centre of value and object of devotion before which other races must kneel in submission.

In this context, the definition of 'racism' by Ruth Benedict, which in part is endorsement of the Nazi interpretation, is perhaps more relevant:

> The dogma that one ethnic group is condemned by Nature to hereditary inferiority and another group is destined to ethnic superiority, is the dogma that the hope of civilization depends upon eliminating some races, and keeping others pure. It is the dogma that one race has carried progress throughout human history and can alone ensure future progress.

King was especially critical of conservative Negro preachers. He told them:

> I'm sick and tired of seeing Negro preachers riding around in big cars and living in big houses and not concerned about the problems of the people who made it possible for them to get these things. ... you are doing nothing (for these people) but being concerned about yourself. ... The church that overlooks this is a dangerously irrelevant church.

Exposing Racism

Malcolm X propagated similar ideas, albeit in a different way. The white man had built his heaven on this earth. So must the black man do by providing food, clothing, jobs and shelter for themselves rather than depending on the white man for these basic material necessities of life. Malcolm went a step further. He objected to the Negro Christian clergymen preaching love of whites. They taught the poor blacks to be patient, loving and forgiving, 'turn the other cheek' to the "cruel white Christian slave-master who was holding a Bible in one hand and the Lyncher's Rope in the other." Malcolm told the blacks: "Don't love your enemy, love yourself." He was critical of Martin King for advocating non-violence because he wanted the Negro to defend himself against the cruelties and atrocities committed by the whites. He advocated the God-given right of self-defence as much to the Negro as it was to the white man.

While King was trying to expose the evil of racism through non-violent means, the white privileged oppressors felt threatened and they reacted in a manner that was to rebound in violence on one part or the other. There were three prerequisites for the anti-racist protests to remain non-violent:

- The non-violent demonstrators march through the streets to register their protest against the injustices inflicted by racism, thereby exposing the evil system.
- The law enforcement authorities who were essentially racist in character and composition allow peaceful marchers to go ahead unmolested by the police or the white thugs.
- Americans of conscience not only demand federal intervention and legislation but also restrain their compatriots from interfering and resorting to violence.

Since in most instances one or the other essential ingredient was found lacking, a certain degree of violence did occur. But King and his team of leadership was certainly not to blame, except possibly in some odd rare instance. The responsibility for the resultant counter-violence, as and when it did occur, rested squarely on the shoulders of white racists who had no hesitation in brutalizing the members of the otherwise non-violent Black Movement. Furthermore, it is a matter for consideration: Did Dr. King has an option? Some one had to expose, to resist racism. It was fortunate for white America that the Movement was under the control of Dr. Martin Luther King, Jr. Just imagine the bloodbath that would have occurred if leaders like Elijah Muhammad, Malcolm X, *et al*, were at the helm of affairs. Above all, King's directives and intentions were totally pure and non-violent in all respects. In January 1965, Dr. King explained the need for exposing, and thereby perhaps precipitating a crisis-situation in order to achieve social transformation:

> Our non-violent direct action program has its objective not the creation of tensions, but the surfacing of tensions already present. ... I am not afraid of the words 'crisis' and 'tension'. I deeply oppose violence, but constructive crisis and tensions are necessary for growth. ... To cure injustices, you must expose them before the light of human conscience and the bar of public opinion. ...

In the process if violence occurred, well it had to. Why blame the Gandhian concept and technique for that, or even King for that matter. King was always in favor of seeking the middle course. His flock would march to a point where they faced troopers. If the latter showed any inclination to use force King, having made the point, would order withdrawal to avoid violent confrontation. In the process the Movement clearly established who were the oppressors, and who the oppressed and the victims of brutal injustice inherent in the evil system.

Court Ordered Integration

On 17 May 1954 the U.S. Supreme Court under the leadership of Chief Justice Earl Warren handed down the first of its five landmark decisions in Brown v. Board of Education of Topeka outlawing segregation in public schools.[4] The doctrine of "Separate but Equal" that remained in force for nearly sixty years thus got a final burial. The decision of the Court was unanimous, and so was its order that integration be followed 'with all deliberate speed'. Voluntary compliance led to public school integration in a number of sates and cities; but in the Deep South there was "massive resistance". 'White Citizens Councils' were formed in a number of cities against alleged 'federal encroachment on the sovereignty of the states'. In Elloree, South Carolina, twenty-five Negro teachers were dismissed when they refused to sign disclaimer statements. In the face of this general resistance to implement the law, John F. Kennedy remarked: "We might alienate southern support, but the Supreme Court decision is the law of the land". President Kennedy and Martin both had faith in the rule of law, and ultimate destiny of the United States: like Mahatma Gandhi — who was called by Churchill a "nauseating" and a "half-naked fakir" — had faith in Indians' struggle for independence from the British Raj. One of the great themes of the 20th Century was the success of those who resisted authority in order to seek civil rights, decolonization and end to repression and oppression on grounds of race, colour or creed. In July Martin spoke in the same vein at the Democratic National Convention about the 'civil rights as one of the supreme moral issues of our time', again taking a cue from Mahatma Gandhi's struggle for the rights of Indians to run their country in their own way. The treatment of Indian freedom fighters by the British-Indian police, the atrocities inflicted on the freedom-fighters and the hapless citizenry, were comparable to that of the Blacks by the Montgomery police.

> We have no alternative but to protest. For many years we have shown an amazing patience. We have sometimes given our white

4. In 1952 Thurgood Marshall, counsel for the NAACP Legal Defence and Education Fund presented five cases to the Supreme Court. In his judgment, Chief Justice Earl Warren said: "In the field of public education, the doctrine of 'separate but equal' has no place. ..." thereby granting the Blacks equal protection of the laws guaranteed by the Fourteenth Amendment. Earlier on in 1881, Booker T. Washington, educator and author, had made a substantial contribution in this direction concentrating on economic improvement of the Blacks.

brothers the feeling that we liked the way we were being treated. But we come here tonight to be saved from that patience that makes us patient with anything less than freedom and justice.

The above speech imparted fresh voice, a skillful rhetoric, an inspiring personality, and in course of time a dynamic new doctrine of civil struggle.

Back in the South, Martin found that the years 1954 and 1955 were the years of the Race(s). "Montgomery Boycott" made headlines in the print and electronic media. So did Dr Martin Luther King, Jr. Contributions in support of the Boycott started pouring in from all over the world. The world at large was openly sympathetic to the Black Cause, more so since Martin's technique was based on non-violence. The Montgomery Boycott thus followed in the footsteps of Philip Randolph's *Brotherhood of Sleeping Car Porters* as well as E.D.. Nixon's role-model in keeping the agitation strictly non-violent in accordance with the principles of Gandhian philosophy of *Śatyagraha.* The Montgomery of 1955 was the beginning of adoption in the United States of techniques of Mahatma Gandhi of South African fame, and later of Indian independence movement. Martin's fondness for explaining his philosophy and technique in terms of *agape* (Greek: Brotherly Love; otherwise Redemptive Goodwill) was merely another name for what had already been firmly established as the Gandhian philosophy of Satyagraha, which ultimately succeeded in gaining freedom for India through non-violent means. Agape, Satyagraha and the Christian idea of redemption accomplished in Jesus Christ, therefore, respresented the same basic philosophical thought process.

The regulating ideal of King's non-violent movement was LOVE. But the question was what form that love should take? — Greek New Testament has three words for 'Love': Eros, Philia and Agape. Eros is aesthetic or romantic love which Plato[5] presented in his dialogues as the yearning of the soul for the realm of the divine. That is the philosophical definition; but for all practical purposes, Eros implies romantic love. Philia is intimate affection between close friends, a sort of reciprocal love. We love because we are loved, totally mutual. If one of the parties does not respond, there is no Philia. Agape is overflowing, spontaneous, unmotivated, groundless and creative love. It is completely disinterested, redemptive goodwill towards all men. This is true love in action, seeking to create and preserve the community. It is not motivated by any attractive or particular quality in the object. It enables us to love every person because God loves every person, every human being. It is the

5. Plato's doctrines of Eros and Philia are not relevant to the present discussion; hence have been omitted.

love of God operating in every human heart. King further elaborated that Agape does not require a sentimental or affectionate emotion. That is why Jesus said: "Love your enemies"; He did not say, "Like your enemies." King was convinced that Agape could serve as the life-force of creative non-violence because 'it does not distinguish between worthy and unworthy persons', nor does it make any distinction between friend and enemy.[6]

While Gandhi demanded complete freedom for India, the Montgomery Blacks were asking for much less, very little indeed, in that all that the Blacks were asking for was justice within the framework of segregation laws.[7]

"The Segregationists helped to create Martin King, the public man."[8] Montgomery was a great personal success for Martin. He came to stand on his own pedestal of success. Gandhian political philosophy of non-violent non-cooperation as a political weapon of the weak and depressed sections of society against oppression and exploitation found universal application. Needless to say that this metamorphosis created an aura of success, self-sacrifice and saintly virtues as a way of life. Martin felt that non-violent non-cooperation could be applied to the prevailing political imbroglio in the U.S., particularly towards implementation of desegregation in the school system. In the process, Gandhi was 'resurrected' in the American South. Gandhian philosophy did not imply wholesale submission of the weak to the power of majority's tyranny. On the contrary, it meant courage of conviction to face unjust and unequal confrontation through the medium of love and non-violent non-cooperation with, or against, the powers that be. On the other side of the coin, some detractors of Martin King, Lomax for example, say that "Martin King left Montgomery, his work undone; the buses are integrated but the schools are not; neither are the parks, playgrounds or other public facilities ... one of the questions now plaguing the social scientists is why such a deep-rooted movement as the Montgomery boycott resulted in nothing more than the integration of buses."[9]

Negroes were not the only victims of practice of segregation. Anybody who was not white was an anathema to the racist American, particularly of the Southern variety, so much so that even Indian students doing

---

6. Ansbro John J: *Martin Luther King, Jr. : The Making of a Mind*; New York, 1982, p. 9.
7. King M.L.: *Stride Towards Freedom* published on 17th September 1958.
8. Williams A. John: op. cit. p. 30.
9. Extract from *Negro Revolt.*

higher studies in the United States were not spared. In an interesting incident at integration, during the prelude to an evening service on 22 March 1964 twenty-four young boys and girls were seated in front pews of 'Cathedral of Mississippi Methodism' for ceremonies connected with enrolment of new members of the Methodist Church in Jackson, Mississippi. All of a sudden as if out of the blues, a group of five integrationists slipped into the Church through a side entrance causing considerable commotion. The alarmed ushers wanting to avoid a scene quietly went down the aisle and took the unwelcome visitors by the arms to pull them silently out of the Church. "I am from India" cried out Madabusi Savithri, a diminutive new Ph.D. from Syracuse University and an interim Professor at Tougaloo. She asked them in disgust and protest what they would think if their women or their missionaries were manhandled like that on a visit to India.[10] The new pastor, Rev. W.J. Cunningham was totally upset over the unpleasant incident and that too on a Palm Sunday. In a similar incident involving Cunningham's predecessor the previous year, the official board had resolved by a vote of 184-13: "It is not unchristian that we prefer to remain an all-white congregation ..." Ultimately, it was Johnson who challenged the South's leading white ministers to stand up to the principles of religious liberty in keeping with Baptists' struggle for religious freedom. Nevertheless, the reverberations of that Easter Sunday led to formation of independent Methodist churches in conformity with the integrationist doctrine when some five hundred members withdrew from the mainstream church.

Desegregation in the Armed Forces

The Second World War came as a god-sent boon to boost the American economy which had suffered the pangs of depression over a period of ten long years. An unprecedented military build up took place across the nation, resulting in millions of new jobs, skilled as well as unskilled. A. Philip Randolph was a labour leader in his own right, having founded in 1925 the Brotherhood of Sleeping Cars Porters. In 1941 he along with other prominent black leaders approached the federal officials to open the doors of defence industries to blacks. But their appeals to end discrimination in employment were ignored. Randolph therefore planned a massive protest-march on Washington right up to the White House by about fifty thousand blacks. When all was set for the march that was to become the precursor of the Civil Rights Movement of the 1960s, President Franklin Roosevelt held a meeting with Randolph after which he issued an Executive Order 8802: "the policy of the

10. Branch Taylor: op. cit. p. 261.

United States is to encourage full participation in the national defence program by all citizens of the United States, regardless of race, creed, colour, or national origins." This turned out to be the first Presidential Order for civil rights since Reconstruction ended in 1877. Consequentially, the Fair Employment Practices Committee was established to enforce the Directive, and about two million blacks got employment in defence related industries, albeit in lower paid positions. Nonetheless, it went a long way to improve the economic position of the Negroes. In return, Randolph called off the proposed March on Washington.

Insofar as recruitment in the armed forces was concerned, the blacks were accepted with open arms. About half a million black soldiers served in the European and Pacific theatres. But they were placed in segregated units under white commanders, just like what their fathers had gone through in the First World War. They proved excellent fighting material, so much so that when General Eisenhower was in a tight corner and required immediate reinforcements to avoid a disaster, he specifically requested for black soldiers. Notwithstanding such outstanding reputation and performance, racial segregation continued in the services even well after the Second War came to a successful conclusion. Once again, Randolph and other black leaders started making plans for a mass civil disobedience campaign unless their demands for racial integration of units at all levels were accepted. It was only after that that President Harry S. Truman issued an Executive Order in July 1948 declaring racial segregation in the armed forces as illegal. Of necessity, this had to be a slow process; but full integration in all branches was achieved in about ten years. The armed forces thus became completely desegregated.

In this connection it is of interest to note that President Johnson signed into law the $947 million Economic Opportunity Act for 'War on Poverty' while at the same session he appropriated more than fifty times that amount as Securities Reforms Bill!

Now back to Gandhian non-violence. When someone was admitted as full member of Gandhi's Ashram, that person had to take fourteen vows:

- Truth;
- Ahimsa;
- Chastity;
- Control of the Palate;
- Non-Thieving;
- Non-Attachment;

- Poverty,
- Swadeshi;
- Fearlessness;
- Rejection of Untouchability;
- Use of Vernaculars;
- Manual Labour;
- Khadi; and
- Study of Politics in the light of Religion.

Following the murder of Martin Luther King Jr. the emphasis shifted from Vietnam as the central point of electioneering to black rioting and law and order problems. "The school desegregation question became one of the most emotional and divisive issues within the early Nixon Administration." It was generally believed that Nixon would manage the imbroglio in his usual crafty manner by currying favour with the whites in the South, at the expense of the Blacks and civil rights. Some members of the Administration including Hoover stooped down to take undue advantage of unsubstantiated eavesdrop reports on the sexual indiscretions of the late Martin Luther King Jr. Hoover's vendetta against Martin Luther King Jr. was much too deep rooted to care for any moral qualms.

The Conference on Race and Religion held at Chicago in January 1963 was a landmark event in the history of race-relations in the United States. It drew an unprecedented ecumenical gathering of nearly one thousand delegates, including some of the world renowned theologians. Since the Protestant churches deeply involved in disputes over racial segregation in the South, they were on the defensive. On the other hand, the minority Roman Catholic and Jewish clergy considered the race relations disputes as an opportunity to make membership inroads in the new territories so as to increase their numbers, as well as to overcome the stigma of orthodoxy. That perhaps explained the voluntary presence of twenty-four Catholic bishops, a historic record for a non-Catholic assembly. As for the Jewish clergy, they emphasized that they all died in Auschwitz but survived the holocaust because of their continued faith in God. However, the segregationists remained strong and unaffected as ever before. There was no change in the attitude of white clergymen of the South who continued to describe King's Birmingham campaign as "unwise and untimely" without making any alternate recommendation as to what would in their opinion constitute 'wise and timely'.

18

Love, Law and Liberation

Along the way of life, someone must have sense enough and morality enough to cut off the chain of hate and evil. The greatest way to do that is through love. I firmly believe that love is a transforming power that can lift a whole community to new horizons of fair play, good will and justice.

After his return from India, Martin's life was in constant danger. King came to the conclusion that new and more radical methods were now required to carry on the struggle in a meaningful manner. Meanwhile, on 1st February 1960 four well dressed freshmen from North Carolina Shaw University Agriculture & Technical (A&T) College in Greensboro bought some school-supplies and groceries from Woolworth's five-and-dime store. Then they sat down at the lunch counter and ordered coffee and some doughnuts. The waitress declined to serve them, the coloured people. "I beg to disagree with you," Ezell Blair Jr. politely replied. "We've in fact already been served; you have already served us at a (store) counter only two feet from here." The waitress then dashed off ignoring the young black customers — Ezell Blair Jr., Franklin McCain, Joseph McNeil and David Richmond remained seated until the store closed at 5:30 p.m. The manager tried to reason with the young students, but in vain. The protest technique of "sit-in" — Gandhi's non-violent 'dharna' — had thus begun.

The next day the four students returned to the lunch counter accompanied by another twenty fellow students, including four black women from Bennett College. They sat through the day without being served. As more and more students joined the sit-in, the store was closed for the day. On the third day of the sit-in, they were joined by three white students from the Women's College and scores of supporters from A&T and Bennett. They occupied 63 of the 66 seats at the lunch counter. This was the beginning of the sit-in movement in earnest. Soon they overflowed Woolworth's and spilled over into the lunch counter of the S.H. Kress store down the street, thereby spreading the sit-in movement to other stores in the Campus. And Greensboro grabbed the national headlines, inspiring similar protest sit-ins in Virginia and South Carolina. Within two weeks the Movement had spread to 54 cities in the nine Southern states, besides in some Northern cities too. What had precipitated the spontaneous action was the 'courage each of us instilled within each other'. By April, this protest spilled over to the entire South. One of the student leaders of this lunch-counter sit-in movement was Reverend James M. Lawson Jr., a young divinity student in Nashville. He was a Methodist missionary in India for three years during which period he became a devotee of the Gandhian tradition. It was Lawson who led the Memphis 'Garbage Strike'. Another student leader, Ezell Blair Jr., was primarily responsible for following the path of non-violence in pursuing the students' sit-in movement. By the end of 1960 their numbers had swelled to 70,000 including many whites, while some 4,000 had been arrested. They were picketing or sitting-in at the segregated eating places. Soon the lunch-counter sit-ins had spread to Winston-Salem, Durham, and a number of other communities in the South. The whites retaliated by sticking chewing gum into the hair of protesters; by pouring tomato ketchup and mustard into their eyes; by grounding burning cigarettes onto their arms. But the protesters took all this smilingly and did not retaliate, which in turn put the white segregationists to more shame. Many students carried placards that said: "Remember the teachings of Gandhi and Martin Luther King."

Miss Ella Baker Picks up the Guantlet

When Miss Ella Baker, a black activist in her mid-fifties and an Executive Director in the SCLC, heard of the lunch-counters agitation, she too jumped into the fray. Her family background reflected defiance of slavery and oppression by the Whites. Her grandmother was flogged for refusing to marry the person the slave-master had chosen for her. But the old woman did not relent. The strong genes Ella imbibed imparted her courage and extraordinary ability to lead young people and give them a deeper understanding of social change. Ella was not happy with the autocratic manner in which SCLC and MIA were being run by the top leadership. As she grew more and more critical, she found her presence was a pin-prick to the rest of the SCLC executives. So she resigned her job as Executive Director in the summer of 1960.

Let us leave that digression aside. Soon, Ella Baker called her contacts at Southern colleges and asked them what *they* were going to do. She realized that the nascent student movement had no chance of survival unless effective matured leadership was inducted for coordination, and adequate funds infused. She borrowed some funds from the SCLC and organized a south-wide conference of student representatives from some fifty colleges and schools. The meeting took place at Shaw University during the Easter weekend. Her opening address was "More Than a Hamburger". She spoke fervently to some two hundred student-activists who felt that they needed an autonomous organization to conduct their affairs. Thus it became rather easy for Ella to fight off some insidious attempts by the SCLC to take the student-body under its wings as their youth wing. Martin Luther King was also in attendance. One student declared: "The greatest progress of the American Negro in the future will not be made in Congress or in the Supreme Court; it will come in the jails." Both Ella and the students desired to be somewhat more militant in their non-violence than what the SCLC was prepared to concede. The young men pledged themselves to work for complete racial integration through absolute non-violence, while SCLC agreed to finance the infant organization — Students Non-violent Coordinating Committee, SNCC, popularly pronounced as the 'Snick'— till it found its feet. Ella and the students believed that it was dangerous to have one powerful charismatic person who might start believing that 'he is the movement', and hence the need for a separate autonomous organization at the college-school level. They liked Ella's ideas of 'group-centred leadership' and wished to develop the values of a redemptive society. "This seeming anti-leadership ethos was actually an affirmation of an alternative kind of leadership — decentralized, participatory, comradely."[1]

It was at these 'dharnas' that "We Shall Overcome" became the anthem of the Freedom Movement. The Blacks talked of freedom in every slogan: freedom songs, freedom rides, freedom movement, freedom schools. Nothing but freedom only. In this respect they were following in the footsteps of Ella Baker: "You must let the oppressed themselves define their own freedom." It may be recalled that the 'Red Shirts" of 'Frontier Gandhi had composed a similar 'Freedom Song":

We are the army of God,
By death or wealth unmoved.
We march, our leader and we,
Ready to die.

---

1. Burns M. James: op.cit. p. 358.

We serve and we love
Our people and our cause,
Freedom is our goal,
Our lives the price we pay.

'Love is the key to the problems of this world'; it is one of the principal parts of the Christian faith. Justice is the other aspect which is equally important.

Soon the 'dharnas' were adopted as the SOP (Standard Operating Procedure) through which buses had already been desegregated in Atlanta by a boycott organized by Love, Law and Liberation Movement under the leadership of Rev. William Holmes Borders. King Sr. was one of the organizers of this Movement. On that occasion Borders said: "Thank you, Montgomery! Thank you Martin Luther King."

One seventeen-years-old sophomore at Spellman College in Atlanta, Ruby Doris Smith heard about the Greensboro sit-ins. She volunteered to have her name listed for a sit-in. When six students were selected for the first such demonstration, she went through the food line in the restaurant at the State Capitol. "But when we got to the cashier, she wouldn't take our money. ... The Lieutenant-Governor came down and told us to leave. We didn't and went to the county jail." There was violence against some sit-inners, but the protests continued unabated, without retaliation by the Blacks. In the next twelve months more than fifty thousand young persons, mostly blacks, but some whites too, resorted to sit-ins at lunch counters in more than one hundred cities in the Southern States. Over 3,600 youngsters went to jail. "Jail Over Bail" was the new slogan. By the end of 1960, some 70,000 supporters had taken part in sit-ins, picketing, marching and rallies. They carried signs: "We do not picket just because we want to eat. We can eat at home or walking down the street. We picket to protest the lack of dignity and respect shown us as human beings." Ultimately, lunch counters in Greensboro and many other cities were open to blacks.[2]

The above sit-ins gave rise to inter-racial "Freedom Rides", a parallel movement against segregation in inter-state transportation.

Reading Karl Marx convinced Martin that neither Marxism nor 'traditional capitalism' embraced the whole truth; each held a partial truth. "I could never be a communist. ... I think a society based on

2. Zinn Howard: op.cit. p. 444.

making all the money you can and ignoring people's needs is wrong. ..." In fact, a talk on Gandhi given at Friendship Hall in Philadelphia by Dr. Mordecai Johnson of Howard University proved to be a turning point in Martin's political thinking. His political philosophy took concrete shape after he had devoured every book on Gandhi that he could lay his hands on: "Non-violence as the salvation of a world in peril". Hereafter, Martin's political approach was based on Mahatma Gandhi's unshakable cult of total non-violence. Thoreau's *Essay on Civil Disobedience* acted as the catalyst. Soon Martin put the basic idea into practice: "Christ furnished the spirit; Gandhi showed how it will work." Martin introduced the concept 'Non-violent Militancy'. But Malcolm X rejected Martin's idea that the Negroes should love the whites and 'show the other cheek'-syndrome so as to integrate with the whites. Instead, he advocated "Separation" from the whites. In Malcolm's theology "God was Black". After all, Jesus was not a Caucasian. May be, this was 'reverse racism'. In a society where whites have enslaved, segregated and oppressed the blacks for nearly four centuries all because of the colour of their skin, where in religious and cultural values 'evil' has been portrayed as black and 'good' as white, "the idea that 'GOD IS BLACK' is not only theologically defencible, but is a necessary corrective against the powers of domination." It is all a matter of attitudes, and makes no substantive difference either way since Hinduism attributes all types of shades and shapes to a variety of gods. However, there is but one God who has no colour or shape; HE is formless. What Martin believed was the product of his exposure to Western Christianity; while Malcolm's concept was influenced by Islam as followed in Africa, Middle East and Asia. Malcolm advised his followers that they could not bank on the whites to transform their wretched condition since the same white men were instrumental in creating those very conditions; the blacks therefore had to rely on themselves to shake off the shackles of slavery and oppression.

The roots of non-violence as a means of achieving socio-political ends were getting stronger day by day. The Southern Christian Leadership Conference held on Columbus Day in 1960 was attended by delegates from all the thirteen southern states. They decided to escalate non-violent Direct Action by defying segregation in transportation, waiting rooms schools, voter's registration besides resorting to boycott throughout the South. Accordingly, about seventy-five black college students went en mass to Rich's and Davidson's department stores and requested for service in the restaurant. Although previous similar attempts had been easily thwarted, this time, the presence of King made a difference and the sit-in received considerable publicity. King and the students were arrested on charge of illegal trespassing. Martin and thirty-six others refused to put up bail. He was produced before DeKalb Country Judge Oscar Mitchell in handcuffs and leg chains and sentenced to four months hard labour, closest thing possible to Georgia chain gangs where prisoners die from beatings, malnourishment, and of course murder too — an atrocious example of terrible 'crackers' swift justice" for the blacks. This is how White America sent one of its great sons to jail On the other hand, Gandhian philosophy of non-violent non-retaliation had won him so much regard and courtesy that, more often than not, the Indian Government sent Gandhi to jail reluctantly, and generally with profuse apologies. The credit for such humane treatment goes as much to Gandhi as to the British sense of morality, may be a little more to the latter. Justice is a vital ingredient of good governance. While Martin and Malcolm generally disagreed on the methodology to be adopted for restoring the Blacks to their rightful place in the polity, 'justice' was one singular exception on which they generally agreed.

Fortunately for Martin, the Presidential candidate Kennedy brought his influence to bear on Judge Mitchell, and kept up the pressure until the Judge agreed to release King on $2,000/- bond. The Kennedys almost saved Martin's life. In return John F. Kennedy won the very close election on the strength of Black vote bank who acknowledged Kennedy's timely help to King by voting for him.

Gandhi's 'dharna' had successfully crossed the oceans, giving rise to Theodore Roosevelt's 'Square Deal', FDR's 'New Deal' and Truman's 'Fair Deal', thereby providing a degree of economic support to the non-violent movement. Martin was very enthusiastic. SCLC proposed to sponsor a meeting of student leaders to set seal on non-violence. The three-day meeting at Shaw University in Raleigh, North Carolina, commenced on Good Friday, 15th April 1960, giving birth to Students Non-violent Coordinating Committee (SNCC or Snick). However, King did not join the sit-ins or participate in the Freedom Rides, giving an impression that he was avoiding going to jail, unlike Gandhi who took the first opportunity to plead guilty of whatever the charge and go to jail, besides undertaking a fast as part of self-suffering. King was criticized for his reluctance to face the odds, and his reputation did suffer damage. Finally when King did go to jail for his one sit-in at Rich's department store in Atlanta, he vowed to serve full time and not to seek bail. He also started to fast. But when fifty-one of King's fellow protesters were released, he was hauled before a jail-judge for a prior offence in that he drove his car in Georgia with Alabama automobile license tags. He was given a suspended sentence and placed on probation for one year.

This was too insignificant an event, and the punishment of no consequence, that Martin soon completely forgot about it. However, down the road Mass Movement and frequent protest marches leading to arrests and trials, the white vengeance were to extract its pound of flesh by putting Martin's life in severe danger of a mortal nature. Nevertheless, King's faith in duality-mutuality of the two races remained unshaken: "The Negro needs the white man to free him from his fears. The white man needs the Negro to free him from his guilt. A doctrine of black supremacy is as evil as a doctrine of white supremacy."

19

A Night of Horror

"Freedom Rides"

The oceans of history are made turbulent by the ever-rising tide of hate. History is cluttered with the wreckage of nations and individuals that pursued that self-defeating path of hate. Somehow we must be able to stand up before our most bitter opponents and say: "We shall match your capacity to inflict suffering by our capacity to endure suffering. We will meet your physical force with our soul-force. ..."

The roots of non-violence as a means of achieving socio-political ends were getting stronger day by day. The Southern Christian Leadership Conference held on Columbus Day in 1960 was attended by delegates from all the thirteen southern states. They decided to escalate non-violent Direct Action by defying segregation in transportation, waiting rooms, public accommodations and schools; by launching a revamped voters' registration program, besides resorting to boycott throughout the South.

It may be recalled that in the Battle of the Bulge when German offensive almost succeeded in shattering the Allied defences, General Dwight D. Eisenhower, the Supreme Commander, specifically asked for Black troops as reinforcements. But when it came to race relations at home during his Presidency, he "was consistent; he did little."[1]

Legislating is one thing; its implementation is altogether a different matter. A number of laws abolishing segregation in inter-state travel had been passed over many years, including the U.S. Supreme Court ruling of December 1960. But they remained mere paper rulings, all because

1. William A. John: op.cit. pp. 46, 48

the transportation companies, the train and buses, did not comply for fear of losing their business in the Southern states. It was so not in the Southern states only; even the North too was not much of an exception either. The railroad conductors even in Northern cities like Chicago, Washington and Los Angeles seated the blacks in the 'Jim Crow' car sections. The railroad and bus stations all over America had two water fountains and two bathrooms, one for the Whites and one for the Blacks. The entire environment was so degrading and distasteful. "Nothing is quite so humiliating, so murderously angering as to know that because you are black you may have to walk a half mile farther than whites just to urinate; that because you are black you have to receive your food through a window in the back of a restaurant, or sit in a garbage littered yard to eat." The Blacks of America were the counterparts of 'untouchables' in India — the latter could not even cast their 'evil' shadow on a caste Hindu. However, an infringement by an Indian untouchable did not lead to severe lynching as it often did for the Blacks in America.

Freedom Rides

The above dismal state of affairs was the background that led to 'Freedom Rides' under the aegis of CORE. Its founder and new national director, James Farmer, issued a call in March 1961 for volunteers to participate in inter-racial "Freedom Rides" through the Southern states to test racial discrimination in bus stations and terminals. On 4th May 1961 twelve intelligent educated persons, blacks and whites, boarded Trailways and Greyhound buses at Washington D.C. as Freedom Riders. These buses had interstate points of call so the black riders would test white facilities and white riders would test black lunch-counters and restrooms. The Freedom Riders had a hard time at the hands of hundreds of 'crackers', men and women, but the Freedom Riders remained non-violent, true to the dictum of Reverend Martin Luther King Jr. They did not react to the violence, abuse and beatings they were subjected to; they just accepted all the atrocities without demur. "Fill up the jails as Gandhi did in India; fill them to bursting if we have to." James Farmer envisioned the Freedom Rides as a logical continuation of the sit-ins. Fresh batches of Riders continued to offer themselves. On Mother's Day, May 14, the Riders divided themselves into two batches to travel from Atlanta to Birmingham. When the Greyhound carrying the first batch reached Anniston, it was surrounded by an angry vicious mob of about two hundred whites. They were armed with iron bars, clubs and tyre chains. Windows were smashed. Tyres slashed. The bus could move forward only after the police arrived. However, six miles out of Anniston the Riders were attacked again. A fire bomb was thrown in. The bus soon burst into flames, but the passengers and the driver managed to escape unhurt. However, when the Trailways bus carrying the second batch reached Birmingham, a mob of about thirty youngsters armed with cycle chains, baseball bats, and lead pipes fell upon them. The Commissioner for Public Safety, Theophilus Eugene (Bull) Connor had promised fifteen minutes to KKK to beat up the riders. He had also arranged for the police to be absent from the scene of attack. The attack was most violent and vicious; Jim Peck required thirty-five stitches to his head. The drivers thereafter refused to take the buses on the road. The Riders per force had to fly to New Orleans to continue on their mission.

After two weeks of travels, beatings and humiliations and several incidents of violence and harassment, the action scene reached Montgomery, Alabama. Over there were Freedom Riders, Martin Luther King and a mob of crackers besides the four hundred U.S. marshals sent by Robert Kennedy. King addressed the Riders and about 1,200 other supporters in the First Baptist Church. The white mob outside threw stones smashing the church windows. Governor John Patterson called out the Guards but at the same time informed Robert Kennedy that Major General Henry Graham, the commander of the Guards, was unable to see to the safety of Martin King. Robert Kennedy told the Governor: "Have the General call me. I want him to say it to me. I want to hear a general of the U.S. Army say he can't protect Martin Luther King Jr." It was a night of horror. But for the strong stand taken by Robert Kennedy, there might well have occurred a massacre of horrendous proportions, of more than 1,200 black and white men and women in Montgomery on that fateful night, reminiscent of the middle ages, a sad and disgraceful reflection on the so-called white civilization and American brand of democracy as practiced at home.

King, the Riders and the people were saved. Freedom Rides continued. The next bus leaving the following morning was escorted by twenty-two highway patrol squad cars, three planes, two helicopters and two battalions of national guardsmen!

The President put personal pressure on Governor Patterson to declare martial law in Montgomery. The latter complied, most reluctantly of course, and 800 national guardsmen were deployed. The first batch, heavily protected by the guardsmen, left for Mississippi on May 24, 1961. Mississippi National Guards took over protection duties at the State line. When the Riders arrived at Jackson, all twelve were arrested as they attempted to use 'whites only' restrooms. They were tried, convicted, fined $200 besides 60 days suspended sentence. Since they refused to pay the fine and preferred to go to jail, they were sent to Parchman Penitentiary. King visited Lawson and other Freedom Riders in the Penitentiary in 1961 and smuggled books on Gandhi concealed within Billy Graham jacket covers.

The Indian Scene

While the Black Freedom Movement in the United States had one, or perhaps a couple more 'nights of horror', unfortunately, the Indian Freedom Movement suffered months, if not years, of horror involving orgy of savage killings on a scale unparalleled in the world history. As a consequence of Calcutta killings, Noakhali district of East Bengal with a Muslim majority of eighty-five per cent was marked by an orgy of killing, abduction, rape, arson, loot, forced marriages and conversions by the Muslims. There was a complete breakdown of civil law and order in which the district administration under British control freely connived. Thousands of refugees poured out into the border districts of Bengal and Bihar. Their harrowing tales of atrocities sent shock waves all over the country. India was thus plunged into civil strife of colossal proportions unheard of in the annals of civilization. Men turned into savage beasts in the name of God and religion. Bihar avenged Bengal. Gandhi followed Abdul Ghaffar to Bihar. Badshah Khan wrote to Gandhi: "... When I see the politicians surrounding us wrongly using the name of God and religion to propagate hatred, I begin to hate politics. Muslim with a big majority over the Hindus in Hazara district of Frontier Province took revenge to even the score of Bihar. The disturbances spread to Punjab, Sind, United Provinces and many parts of south India too, thus enveloping the entire country in the communal conflagration, all at *ad lib.* Gandhi and Ghaffar were both completely shaken by the scale and intensity of the disturbances. Gandhi resorted to his favourite weapon, the fast, and managed to bring some order and sense. Abdul Ghaffar emulated Gandhi in trying to preserve peace in the Frontier Province. But Abdul Qaiyum retorted: "The Frontier Muslim League will take necessary steps to defeat his sinister move."[2]

The Frontier Gandhi became emotional and expressed his sentiments thus: "Insanity prevails in Bihar. Today, India is an inferno. My heart weeps to see our homes set on fire by ourselves. I find today darkness reigning over India and my eyes vainly turn from one direction to

2. Tendukar: *Frontier Gandhi;* op.cit. p. 397.

another to see light. ... India is one single nation inhabited by Hindus and Muslims." Some areas may be Muslim majority, and others Hindu majority. Whatever has been happening in Naokhali and Bihar is a shameful blot on the good name of the country. If the same is repeated elsewhere too, the fate of our Nation will surely be sealed. He was quite candid in admitting that while other communities were tolerant of other religions, Islam — which is otherwise a most tolerant religion in the world — is no longer so insofar as the communal situation in India is concerned. "We should rectify this fault to become true Muslims."[3]

Gandhi often gave the example of conversion of Badshah Khan to non-violence. The Khan came from a tribe whose tradition was eye for an eye, blow for a blow. There were numerous cases in which blood feuds were handed down from one generation to the next. That is what the Pathan culture was all about. After Badshah Khan came under Gandhi's influence and founded the Khudai Khidmatgar movement, a sort of transformation came over the Pathans. Not that all Pathans accepted non-violence as a creed overnight; but there was a definite perceptible change for the good. Since 16th Match was Gandhi's weekly day of silence, Badshah Khan conducted the prayer meeting. The Khan was indeed in deep anguish. He confessed that he was surrounded by darkness all round. India was on fire. It was for all the communities to realize that if India was burnt down, so would they all be. The common man would be the real loser irrespective of his religious affiliation. The British policy of 'Divide and Rule' had succeeded beyond all expectations. The Muslim League's wish and prayer to grab power without making any sacrifices for the same had come about so easily that the British bureaucracy were immensely pleased over their own performance in conniving at the savagery of communal riots so that they could 'paint the Indians as the beasts, thirsting for each other's blood', totally unfit to be entrusted with the administration of the country. And they almost succeeded in proving their point to the Americans who were all the time coaxing them to hand over power to the people of India. Sir Winston Churchill had every reason to gloat over the events as they took shape. He could easily say, "I told you so!" The vandalism and anarchy that prevailed in India during those crucial months just before and after Independence had no parallel in history of civilizations over the millenniums. — Perhaps, Gandhi too would have given a similar sermon if he was to conduct that prayer meeting, since both of them held identical views on most problems of the day. They were emotionally

3. Tendulkar: op.cit. p. 403.

very close, and were intensely attracted to each other. Common thoughts and beliefs were the bonding factors cemented by the power of Truth and Non-violence.

The proposed division of Bengal and Punjab, and partial division of Assam, besides the disputes about accession of princely states to one or the other Dominion — all these added fuel to the flames already enveloping the countryside. Punjab, Sind and the Frontier Province were soon afire. Dr. Khan Sahib was abused, even attacked, by the Muslim League hooligans. They wanted him to resign and make way for the League to take over administration of the Province before Pakistan formally came into being. *Agents provocateurs* from other provinces were active in the Frontier, particularly so in Peshawar. Their constant refrain was invocation of the Governor's rule in NWFP. Badshah Khan's response: "I hope and trust that God will help us in the sacred mission and people will recognize that the essence of love, truth and non-violence is the hall-mark of every good, free and prosperous society."

"Brute force has been the ruling factor in the world for thousands of years, and mankind has been reaping its bitter harvest all along. There is little hope of anything good coming out of it in the future. If light can come out of darkness, then alone can love emerge from hatred."[4]

---

4. Gandhi M.K.: *Satyagraha in South Africa*, p. 89.

20

Albany Movement

Non-violent direct action seeks to create such a crisis and foster such a tension that a community which has constantly refused to negotiate is forced to confront the issue. It is not violent tension, but a constructive non-violent tension — indeed a Creative Tension.

Albany, Georgia, was the hub of segregationists, a thoroughly segregated farming community of 56,000 people, forty per cent of them black. Before the Civil War, it was a trading centre for the surrounding slaveholding plantations. By the end of the 19th century, blacks outnumbered the whites, and segregation got still more deeply entrenched. Conflicts and tensions were galore, straining the social life of the countryside. While the segregationists were adamant on discrimination in all spheres — schools, restaurants, hotels, parks, libraries, buses and what have you. The Negroes "lived in segregation; they ate in segregation; they learned in segregation; they prayed and rode and worked and died in segregation".[1] But all the same, the Blacks were putting up demonstrations and protest marches, all peaceful and non-violent. During the Thanksgiving week in 1961, rallies and protest marches were held at Albany to end segregation in transportation. Dr. William G. Anderson held meetings with Mayor Kelley, but without any results. In response to urgent call from Anderson, King accompanied by his constant companion, Ralph Abernathy, came over to Albany and joined the Rally. This gesture boosted the morale of the youngsters and the rally was a great success.

Just as Rosa Parks had provided the spark for the Montgomery Bus Boycott, the arrival, and violent reception the eleven 'Freedom Riders'

1. King Martin Luther Jr.: op. cit. *Autobiography*, pp. 152-53.

received at the hands of white anarchists, triggered the historic non-violent movement in Albany. Hereafter, the 'Freedom Rides' — interstate travel in the South by Black passengers in large numbers as never before came to be the main protest activity since the whites were violently against this idea of 'Freedom Rides' by the Blacks. The rides were joined by all age groups — men, women, youngsters and children. And the whites maliciously mal-treated them, one and all, whenever they could lay their hands on them. They resorted to burning some buses too. Meanwhile, the Interstate Commerce Commission ordered all busterminals to be integrated, which by itself was a great achievement. Again, it was merely a paper-integration. In order to test the implementation of the new law, nine students led by activists Sherrod and Cordell Reagon sat down in the whites-only waiting room. They were asked to leave failing which they would be arrested. The students left the waiting room as planned, having made the point to the black residents of the town that they did not have equal access to those facilities, notwithstanding the legal position.

A few weeks after the above episode, an umbrella organization comprising of the NAACP, its Youth Council, the Ministerial Alliance, the Federation of Women's Clubs, the Negro Voters League, and the Criterion Club was formed on November 17, 1961. Five days later, five black students were arrested for their sit-in at the lunch counter of Trailways bus terminal. SNCC notified the Department of Justice of these illegal detentions, but the Justice Department failed to enforce the ICC ruling. Therefore, the Albany Movement under the presidentship of Dr. William Anderson held its first mass meeting three days later at Mount Zion Baptist Church. When the five students were put on trial on November 27, a protest march was held at the end of which a petition signed by about 400 persons was submitted. However, the federal government's intention to ensure compliance with the law was beyond doubt. That became evident on December 10 when an integrated group of Freedom Riders, five blacks and five whites, were greeted by a large crowd at Albany's Central Rail Terminal. The five blacks entered the white section and the whites in the black section. The differences in approach to integration by the federal and state authorities became crystal clear when the integrated group were ordered out and arrested for trespassing by Laurie Pritchett, the Albany Police Chief. Once again, Justice Department failed to act. These arrests sparked the Albany Movement into full gallop. A number of protest meetings and marches were held, and on December 13, over 200 protesters were arrested for marching on the City Hall without a permit. During the next two days another

300 were jailed. The stage was now set for King to step in. And Dr. Anderson invited him to come over to address a mass rally.

King told an audience of over one thousand: "Don't stop now. Keep moving. Don't get weary. We will wear them down with our capacity to suffer." The next day King led a march of over 250 hymn-singing men, women and children to the City Hall. All the three leaders and about seven hundred Albany protesters from every quarter of the City willingly went to jail on 16 December 1961. However, there was one powerful black leader, Dr. Joseph H. Jackson of the National Baptist Convention, who opposed Martin and Anderson at every step. He was anti-civil disobedience. Unfortunately, Jackson did not appreciate that Martin's civil disobedience did not call for disobedience of all laws *en mass*; the proposed resistance was against 'unjust laws' only. But the Blacks were not mere 'passive resisters'. They were militant in as much as their weapon was non-violence in the face of all provocation by the authorities. While the Albany agitation was in full swing, "Prayer Pilgrims", clergymen and laymen, took trains or planes to reach Albany to demonstrate their support for the agitation against segregation. But Dr. Jackson, himself a black, went out of his way to deny support to Albany. Inter-organizational jealousy as well as intra-organizational differences created further complications. The Student Non-violent coordinating Committee (SNCC) felt that while they did all the work, the credit went to Martin's Southern Christian Leadership Conference (SCLC). The mutual distrust and friction became so serious that King tried to oust Dr. Jackson from his office of President of NBC while Dr. Jackson in turn replaced King as the Negro Preacher in residence at the White House. However, Martin King's prestige and reputation was so high as it was that Jackson's bitter rivalry did not in any way harm King. In fact, his association with the Albany movement only added luster to King's position as the outstanding leader of the Negro desegregation and freedom movement.

Meanwhile, the Police Chief had been studying King's methodology. Laurie Pritchett concluded that his methods were indeed non-violent: "To fill the jails, same as Gandhi in India. And once they filled the jails we'd have no capacity to arrest and then we'd have to give in to his demands. ...". Pritchett then got in touch with all the jails within thirty mile radius and was assured that he could use all their jails. In the mean time Pritchett took a leaf out of British policy of "Divide and Rule" in India. He played a dirty trick on the blacks by asking them to take charge of their own movement, and not to permit outsiders like King to hijack their movement. In return he promised to meet with them and implement full integration besides releasing all detainees. Since King had not been a party to this nefarious agreement, he left Albany for Atlanta. In the end, the hoax exploded in the face of local blacks. King and Abernathy returned to Albany on February 27, 1962. Both were tried for their December arrests, found guilty of 'disorderly conduct' and of parading without a permit. The sentences were handed out later on July 10. They were ordered to pay $78 in fines, or serve 45 days in prison. They naturally chose jail. But since President got rather anxious about the whole Albany affair, a 'mysterious stranger' paid the fines and the duo was released. Abernathy reacted: "I've been thrown out of lot of places in my day, but never have I been thrown out of jail."

The Albany Movement continued unabated. However, there was one major change. In Albany the leaders 'attacked' on a broad front in that they took in their stride discrimination in public places, denial of free speech and voting rights, school segregation[2], housing, employment opportunities, and what have you. This broad front called for a variety of nonviolent tools — direct action through mass demonstrations; jail-ins; sit-ins; wade-ins; kneel-ins; boycotts; legal action; political action; *et al.* "In no other city of the deep South had all those weapons of non-violence been simultaneously exercised."[3] But it was one-sided non-violence only. On 24th July the authorities resorted to excessive force to disperse the protesters. A pregnant woman was brutally beaten up while one of the lawyers for the Movement was mercilessly caned, besides a general cane-charge by the police. Some of the Negro onlookers, who were not part of the protest-march, resented this uncalled for violence against their brethren and started throwing bottles and stones etc. on the police. The police in turn reacted still more strongly resulting in more injuries and damage to property. This is one side of the story. Another version by James Macregor Burns says that the City's astute police chief, Laurie Pritchett, "systematically and non-violently herded protesters into city and nearby county jails, determined to avoid incidents that could cause an explosion of national outrage. Nonetheless, disturbances did take place, and so was racial violence on both sides.

Martin King was terribly upset when the Albany Blacks retaliated by going on a rampage. He "cancelled a scheduled march, and in the spirit

---

2. Enforcement of Mexican segregation was done quite ingeniously. The authorities located Mexican schools in Anglo and Mexican neighborhoods so that the Mexican children from white residential areas had to be bussed to Mexican areas. Eventually, some families did move out from white residential districts to Mexican residential areas!
3. Ibid.; p. 154.

of Gandhi, declared a day of penance."[4] Once again Martin proved his commitment to non-violence and 25th July was observed as a day of prayer and penance. The Negro leadership preached and taught the lesson of non-violence to its people that day. This action by Martin would naturally enhance the moral status and righteousness of the Negro cause, before the rest of America as well as the world at large. Lest the authorities get bad publicity in the bargain, Sheriff Pritchett declared to the Press that he too was an advocate of non-violence. "An equilibrium, in which the external use of force was excluded, settled over the troubled city."[5] By the end of 1962 the Albany Movement, for all practical purposes, had petered out. It was a 'staggering defeat' for Martin Luther King. King's lack of imagination as to how to steer the Albany Movement and to what objective were primarily responsible for its failure. He was bitterly criticized for the collapse of Albany Movement. His prestige in the Negro movement went down to its lowest ebb. In fact, King himself later admitted: "Our protest was so vague that we got nothing and the people were left depressed and in despair." Out of the ashes came the precious lesson for King: "We attacked the political power structure instead of the economic power structure. You don't win against a political power structure where you don't have the votes. But you can win against an economic structure when you have the economic power to make the difference between a merchant's profit and loss." In turn, King decided to stick to the 'ground floor' and not "to be a fireman."[6]

Mayor Kelley resumed negotiations that followed in the wake of mass arrests, and day of prayer and penance. The City Commission agreed to desegregate the rail and bus terminals, and also hire at least one Negro bus driver. For all practical purposes: Peanuts!

---

4. Burns M. James: op.cit. p. 364.
5. King Martin Luther Jr.: *Autobiography*, op.cit. p. 160.
6. Wexler Sanford: op.cit. p. 143.

21

Suffer the Jails

Birmingham

Mahatma Gandhi, an English educated Barrister, first went to jail in South Africa in October 1908 for the cause of indentured Indian labour. He was released from his last imprisonment on 6th May 1944. By then he had spent 249 days in South African jails and 2089 days in Indian prisons. In his view, a jailor is as much a prisoner as his prisoners; may be he is worse off! During his life time, Gandhi fasted forty-four times for 216 days, besides many one-day weekly fasts. Self suffering was the philosophy behind these frequent fasts while going to jail for the cause of FREEDOM was an honour. Dr. King imbibed this philosophy in his struggle for freedom for his oppressed people. Real suffering, bravely borne, melts even a heart of stone. Such is the potency of suffering. And there lies the key to Satyagraha.

Montgomery had given a new meaning to Mahatma Gandhi's non-violence. It had defined and removed the inherent contradiction between non-violence and 'militant non-violence'. In its new avatar, militancy acquired a fresh concept. It avoided violence but achieved 'dramatic confrontation' besides 'electrifying and educating the entire nation'. A new 'era of social change' had opened up new vistas for the Negro community not only of the South but of the entire United States. In fact, it was Montgomery that gave rise and courage to other similar movements of liberation in other parts of the country — Florida, Birmingham, Tallahassee, Alabama, Mobile, *et al.* This is how the freedom movement under the inspiring leadership of Mahatma Gandhi had spread its roots all over the vast hinterland of India. Martin and other leaders in the South decided to expand, organize and coordinate the activities in the Southern States. The post-Albany eclipse period was to be put to maximum advantage to plan the most audacious assault on the citadel of extreme segregation. Suffering in the total failure of Albany brought forth the new strategy. 'Crisis' was the crux of that strategy. If you don't create a crisis, you won't have a worthwhile objective to fight for. Crisis will hereafter be the *raison de etre* for conduct of future operations against segregation and injustice. But the methodology shall remain rooted to non-violence. For the forthcoming Birmingham operation, numerous workshops on non-violence were conducted to train the people not to deviate from the path of non-violence, howsoever severe may the provocation be.

A meeting attended by about one hundred southern leaders was convened at Atlanta for January 10 and 11, 1957. However, on the night of 9th January, at about 2:00 a.m., information regarding the bombings and terror let loose in Montgomery was received. Lest retaliatory violence by the Blacks upset the apple cart, Martin and Ralph left for Montgomery immediately to take charge of the situation there. Reverend Fred Lee Shuttlesworth was the president of the Alabama Christian Movement which soon engulfed the Southern Region and Shuttlesworth became the Secretary of the south-wide movement to be temporarily known as the Southern Conference on Transportation and Nonviolent Integration.

King was in a mood of aggressive humility when he addressed more than a thousand delegates from thirty-five states at the 47th Annual Session of the NAACP held at San Francisco on 27th June 1956, in which he declared:

> Wherever segregation exists we must be willing to stand up in mass and courageously and non-violently protest against it. And I might say that I must admit that this means sacrifice and suffering. Yes, it might even mean going to jail. We must be willing to fill up the jail houses of the South. Yes, it might even mean physical death. But if physical death is the price that some must pay to free our children from a permanent life of psychological death, then nothing could be more honorable. This is really the meaning of passive[1] resistance. It confronts physical force with an even greater force viz., Soul-Force.

12th February 1958 was Lincoln's birthday. Twenty-one mass meetings were held in key southern cities. The year was observed as the year of "Crusade for Citizenship". Martin's message for these meetings:

---

1. In earlier times, Gandhi had also used the term 'passive resistance', but later dropped it in favour of 'non-violent resistance', because of negative connotations of the former. King too stopped using this phrase.

> Let us make our intentions crystal clear. We must and will be free. We want freedom — NOW. We do not want freedom fed to us in teaspoons over another hundred and fifty years!

Martin had a strong unbendable formidable sense of conscience. It kept him throughout on the path that he thought was right. And if he did slip up sometime, he made it a point to apologize and seek forgiveness. No wonder therefore that Martin did feel that many an honor heaped on him in later life did not belong to him alone; his colleagues and the organizations he represented deserved an equal, if not larger share of those honours.

Martin Arrested

On 3rd September 1958 Martin was badly roughed up by two policemen for no rhyme or reason, just because of the colour of his skin. Two policemen grabbed Martin, twisted his arms behind him, and pushed him down the stairs towards the city hall. It was then that he resolved: "The time has come when I should no longer accept bail. If I commit a crime in the name of the Civil Rights, I will go to jail and serve time." This is exactly how Mahatma Gandhi repeatedly reacted to a number of such situations, and Martin was now following that saintly example, the non-violent technique of non-cooperation. Martin was now convinced that the Black people must suffer as Mahatma Gandhi had done. The new motto was "Suffer the Jails", the terror of southern jails. Martin realized that his imprisonment would arouse sympathy for the Black Movement He felt that if he expected other people to suffer for the cause of freedom, he as the leader had to suffer equally, if not more. When Martin was convicted for the episode created by those two policemen who had beaten him up, and pushed him down the stairs, the Judge Eugene Loc permitted Martin to make a statement before the Court. This historic statement made on Friday, 5th September 1958 in Montgomery, Alabama, is summarized below:

> Your Honour, you have no doubt rendered a decision which you believe to be just and right. Yet, I must reiterate that I am innocent. I was simply attempting to enter the court-hearing of a beloved friend, and at no time was I loitering. I have been a victim of police brutality for no reason. I was snatched from the steps of the courthouse, pushed through the street while my arms were twisted, choked and even kicked. In spite of this, I hold no animosity or bitterness in my heart towards the arresting officers. I have compassion for them as brothers, and as fellow human beings made in the image of God. ... our white brothers are the victims of their environment — blighted with more than 300 years of man's inhumanity to man as expressed in slavery and segregation.

Dr. King arrested at Lunch Counter: October, 1960

Dr. King arrested in Albany, Georgia, July 1962

Police dogs and horses in action to break up peaceful Negroes protesting against racial discrimination : Birmingham

> Your Honour, you have found me guilty. Last night my wife and I talked and prayed over the course of action that I should take in the event that this should happen. It was our conclusion that I should not in all good conscience pay a fine for an act that I did not commit and, above all, for the brutal treatment that I did not deserve. With all due respect to you and your court, I am inwardly compelled to take this stand. ... My action is motivated by the impelling voice of conscience and a desire to follow Truth and the will of God ...
>
> I also make this decision because of my deep concern for the injustices and indignities that my people continue to experience. ... Last month, in Mississippi, a sheriff who was pointed out by four eyewitnesses as the man who beat a Negro to death with a blackjack, was freed in twenty-three minutes. At this very moment in this state James Wilson sits in the death house condemned to die for stealing less than two dollars. Can anyone at this court believe that a white man could be condemned to death in Alabama for stealing this small amount? ... I am sure there are thousands of white persons of goodwill throughout the South who in their hearts condemn mob violence and inhuman treatment of Negroes. I call upon these persons to gird their courage and speak out for law and order.
>
> I also make this decision because of my love of America and the sublime principles of liberty and equality ... I have come to see that America is in danger of losing her soul and can so easily drift into tragic anarchy and crippling Fascism. ... The time has come when perhaps only the willing and non-violent acts of suffering by the innocent can arouse this nation to wipe out the scourge of brutality and violence inflicted upon Negroes who seek only to walk with dignity before God and man.

The Judge was surprised and startled by the course this trial had taken, and he recessed the court. It may be recalled that Gandhi also faced a similar situation while he was looking into grievances of labourers in indigo plantations owned by the British masters in Bihar, India. The civil authorities ordered Gandhi out of the district, which, of course, he refused pointblank. He was therefore summoned to stand trial the next day. The magistrate was completely flabbergasted by Gandhi's attitude. Gandhi simply declared that he was guilty as charged, and requested for legal punishment. The magistrate was at his wits' ends. The judgment was postponed. Meanwhile, the Government at Delhi was rather disturbed by the adverse publicity, and Sir Edward Gait, the Lieutenant-Governor of Bihar ordered the case as withdrawn. Gandhi's act of defiance had succeeded, not through retaliation, but through the power of Ahimsa, civil resistance without resorting to offensive conduct or language. In yet another similar case, but in South Africa, Gandhi delivered an impassioned speech calling on all to take a vow to defy a proposed draconian law. Gandhi was the first to be produced before a magistrate for defying the law that became effective on 31 July 1907. He pleaded guilty and requested the magistrate to impose on him the heaviest sentence since he had deliberately acted against the law. The magistrate imposed the lightest punishment — two months simple imprisonment, specifying that it shall be without hard labor. Thus M.K. Gandhi landed himself in a South African jail in October 1908. This was the beginning of Satyagraha — non-violent 'passive resistance' and 'civil disobedience'.

Martin's reaction and statement to the court was exactly in conformity with what Gandhi had gone through way back on 18th March 1922 at Ahmedabad.

Gandhi was charged with writing three seditious articles — "Tempering with Loyalty" (September 19, 1921); "A Puzzle and its Solution (December 15, 1921); "Shaking the Manes" (February 23, 1922). Gandhi's printer, S.G. Banker, was charged with printing and publishing the said three seditious articles in *Young India*. No doubt the articles were seditious, but the first in the series was published more than six months ago. Then why this delayed reaction! A great show of military strength was made that day. The attention of the entire country, perhaps the whole world, was riveted at Ahmedabad that day. Gandhi did not defend himself. He pleaded guilty as charged. He therefore asked the Judge, Mr. C.N. Broomfield, that if he believed in that law, he should inflict the maximum sentence on him. When Gandhi sat down, Mr. Justice Broomfield bowed to the prisoner.[2] The Judge was obviously embarrassed. He appeared regretful for doing this unpleasant duty. He remarked: "The determination of a just sentence is perhaps as difficult a proposition as a judge in this country could have to face. The law is no respecter of persons. Nevertheless, it would be impossible to ignore the fact that you are in a different category from any person I have ever tried or am likely to have to try." He further remarked that Gandhi was a "great patriot and a great leader. Even those who differ from you in politics look upon you as a man of high ideals and of noble and even saintly life." He then pronounced the sentence: six years simple imprisonment. "If the course of events in India should make it possible for the Government to reduce the period and release you, no one will be better pleased than I."[3]

---

2. That was like a good Englishman, unlike the American racist white of the mid twentieth century.

Gandhi replied that it was a mild sentence. He was then led away to prison between kneeling and weeping spectators. Gandhi was lodged in solitary confines in Yervada Jail from 20 March 1922 to 12 January 1924.This solitary life style suited him fine, giving him lots of time for contemplation and prayer. Gita, Koran and the Bible kept him mentally absorbed. The British were very courteous to him and knowing that he was particular to spin every day, they provided him with a spinning-wheel even though their Jails rules did not permit such a concession. After he was operated upon for appendicitis, the British decided that enough was enough and released him on 5th February 1924. His term in Jail had undone most of the good work. The boycott movement was completely dead and there was no civil disobedience since Gandhi himself had cancelled it. Worst of all, the Hindu-Muslim unity had been completely shattered. There were numerous communal riots in which arson, violence and murders were galore.

As expected, Martin was found guilty and sentenced to pay a fine of ten dollars, or fourteen days in jail. When Judge Eugene Loe advised Martin to pay the fine, he replied, "No, your honour, I do not wish to pay the fine." However, the authorities did not want bad publicity, and did not want Dr. Martin Luther King Jr. in their jail. They did not permit Martin to enter the wagon(s) meant to take the prisoners to Jail. Police Commissioner Clyde Sellers surreptitiously paid the fine out of his own pocket and Martin was told to go home. His explanation: He wanted to save the taxpayers the expense of feeding King for fourteen days!

The Virtue of Suffering

The Negro leaders took all this in their stride. They made a virtue of their suffering. "To suffer in a righteous cause is to grow to our humanity's full stature. ... If he has to go to jail for the cause of freedom, let him enter it in the fashion Gandhi urged his countrymen, 'as the bridegroom enters the bride's chamber' — that is, with a little trepidation but with a great expectation." Centuries of oppression 'had drained African-Americans of self respect'. Martin wrote: "Blacks were smothering in cages of poverty while affluence surrounded them." Giving a methodical analysis of 'Civil Disobedience', Dr. King went on to write: "Freedom is never voluntarily given by the oppressor. It must be demanded by the oppressed." The letter went on to say that Blacks had waited for 340 years for Constitutional and 'God given rights'. As for the laws, Martin wrote:

---

3. Louis Fischer: *The Life of*, Part II; pp. 201-204.

> There are two types of laws: there are just laws and there are unjust laws. ... What is the difference between the two? ... A just law is a man-made code that squares with the moral law or the law of God. An unjust law is a code that is out of harmony with the moral law. ... Isn't segregation an existential expression of man's tragic separation, an expression of his awful estrangement, his terrible sinfulness? ... Obey the 1954 decision of the Supreme Court because it is morally right ... disobey segregation ordinances because they are morally wrong.
>
> Reverting to the Biblical tradition, King wrote on: Everything that Hitler did was legal and everything that Hungarian freedom fighters did in Hungary was illegal. It was illegal to aid and comfort a Jew in Hitler's Germany. ... I would advocate disobeying anti-religious laws.

Dr. Martin Luther King Jr. became a national figure at the young age of twenty-seven. A number of people, both Blacks and Whites, came from all over America to merely see him, to have his 'darshan'. "Some came all the way from India, touched by the Gandhian aspects of our non-violent protest."[4] A white librarian and member of the local Human Relations Council, Juliette Morgan wrote a letter to the print-media praising, and comparing the Montgomery Movement to that in India against the British regime. The white community completely ostracized her. She went into a depression and committed suicide. A tragic end to laudable personal conviction of high moral standing ... And of course there was no end to the long list of Negro leaders who made a beeline to the King's house. "As long as injustice, racism and oppression of minorities persist, King's 'Letter from a Birmingham Jail' will be read."[5]

Operation 'C' in American "Johannesburg"

The Reverend Fred Shuttlesworth was the most outspoken hot-headed leader of SCLC in Birmingham — a loose alliance of 100 or so church-oriented groups. He was one of the nation's most courageous freedom fighters. In 1956 he had organized the Alabama Christian Movement for Human Rights (ACMHR) to change the pattern of race relations in Birmingham and to end the racist regime of 'Bull' Connor and George Wallace for ever. It did not take the 'Bull' long to perceive the indomitable character of Fred Shuttlesworth. He was a fearless man, sent his children to public schools to desegregate them. Consequently, that very year his

4. King Scott Coretta: op. cit. p. 151.
5. King Mary: op. cit. p. 6.

home was bombed and completely demolished, so was his Bethel Baptist Church. During early 1957 he and his wife were 'mobbed, beaten and stabbed'. They were jailed eight times, four times during the 'Freedom Rides'. The entire family suffered terribly for the cause of desegregation, freedom and social change The Negro leaders took all this in their stride. They made a virtue of their suffering.

In the aftermath of 'Ole Miss' and the Albany episodes where violence had erupted, Martin, in consultation with SCLC leadership, decided to accord the highest priority to desegregation in Birmingham — the American Johannesburg — a great manufacturing centre, the richest city in Alabama, the "most segregated metropolis in the country, the 'tragic city', was chosen as the primary target. The campaign slogan of Governor of Alabama, George Wallace, was "Segregation Forever". In his inaugural, George Wallace pledged: "Segregation now, segregation tomorrow, segregation for ever." He was the king-pin of white power structure which was constituted by three mutually reinforcing elements: the business and industrial elite who wielded the economic power of the City, the political and administrative elite personified by the Governor and the Police Commissioner, 'Bull' Connor — a man who was soon to earn the notoriety of being the symbol of police brutality in the United States — and last but not the least, the white supremacists, the KKK. The city officials were arch segregationists like their boss. Acts of violence in the City were as common as 'chitlings and ham hocks'. The Blacks constituted forty percent of the population of Birmingham, but only ten thousand were registered voters out of eighty thousand. They were the producer of wealth of Birmingham. But they were also the most ill-treated community in the whole of the United States. In January 1962 the students of Miles College joined the SCLC to begin a boycott of segregated stores in Birmingham. It was generally believed that if the campaign in Birmingham was successful, it would, perhaps, 'break the back of segregation all over the nation'.

It so happened that 'Bull' Connor was running for Mayor of Birmingham against a relative moderate, Albert Boutwell. In order not to give fuel to Connor for his election campaign, the Negro leadership decided to give the scheme a break till after the April 2, 1963 elections. During the intervening period, King went out on a whirlwind speaking tour and made twenty-eight speeches in sixteen cities all over the United States. In order to guard against bugging of their telephones, the leadership decided to refer to the project as 'C' — C for 'Confrontation'. They adopted code names to hide their identities. King became 'JFK', Abernathy 'Dean Rusk', Fred Shuttlesworth 'Bull', John Dew as 'Pope John'. The demonstrators were given the code name 'baptismal candidates'.

Soon it was time for the leaders of the Movement to show their hand. They chose 12th April, Good Friday, to offer themselves for arrest. The 'symbolic significance' of the day was much too obvious. Martin King, Abernathy, and fifty other activists were arrested on Good Friday while they marched downtown in a glare of publicity. For the first time Martin and Ralph were separated and both were put in solitary confinement[6], totally incommunicado, in bare cells with no mattress or blanket even, where the living conditions were akin to animal kingdom rather than for a human being. They were held totally incommunicado in a dark cell. No one was allowed to visit Martin, not even his lawyer. This was in sharp contrast to the treatment meted out by the British authorities to Gandhi and other senior leaders of the Freedom Movement in India — Gandhi and some others were detained in a palace-prison. Be that as it may, Coretta and their well wishers were terribly anxious about Martin's safety. Any thing was possible in Birmingham under Connor — who was out for vengeance after having lost the election — - and Wallace. On the advice of her friends, and remembering the Georgia episode of 1960, Coretta made a call to the White House pleading, not for the release of her husband, but only requested to ensure Martin's safety. Within minutes the Attorney General Robert Kennedy called back. A few hours later the President himself phoned Coretta. Meanwhile, the jailer put Martin through to Coretta, and the conditions improved considerably thereafter.

Notwithstanding some of the palliative measures implemented by the Federal Government and the courts, the progress on equal rights for the Negroes was much too slow. Massive demonstrations were therefore organized, the most critical one being in Birmingham on 7th May 1963. It was held under the leadership of Martin Luther King Jr. and the Southern Christian Leadership Conference, "demanding fair employment opportunities, desegregation of public facilities, creation of a committee to plan desegregation, and dropping of charges against King and the other 2,500 persons who were arrested in the course of the demonstrations."[7] It was a matter of deep anguish for American democracy and loud cries of human rights when, on 7th May the Birmingham police dogs and high pressure water hoses were let loose against the demonstrators, who retaliated by using stones and bottles. Many liberals in the country were deeply pained and shocked over the

---

6. For Martin, it was not really solitary confinement. "God's companionship does not stop at the door of a jail cell".

7. Franklin John Hope: op. cit. pp. 630-3.

police behaviour. School children also joined their elders. They too endured snarling police dogs, its 'lashing fire hoses that washed human beings along slippery avenues without washing away their dignity', were arrested and taken to jail in school buses, singing 'freedom songs', and shouting "We want Freedom". Men and women were pinned to the ground by officers of the law. Sympathetic demonstrations were held in a number of Northern cities and some in the Southern too. The tempo of demonstrations increased after Medgar Evers, the leader of the Mississippi NAACP was shot and killed outside his home in Jackson by a white man. Robert Kennedy attended Medgar's funeral in Arlington Cemetery and gave Charles Evers his office and home telephone numbers to call him any time day or night if Negroes were being harassed or intimidated. A week later, the President invited his wife, children and brother-in-law to the White House. It is the police dogs and pressure hoses that went a long way in galvanizing the nation's collective conscience, aroused to a crescendo by extraordinary television coverage depicting snarling dogs and small children in the same shot. Peace was finally restored in July after the National Guard was called out, when agreement was reached to desegregate schools and public accommodations, to enlarge employment opportunities and building of low-rent houses for Negroes. The Black leaders were insisting on *de facto* segregation in housing and education; mere cosmetic legal measures were being spurned. Before the 35th President of the United States was assassinated, passions in the Black Movement had reached a high point of no return.

The 'Crisis Strategy' had worked beautifully. 'Bull' Connor had made it a complete success. While King preached non-violence, violence spread.

Dr. King charted out the following program for his people's emancipation:

- Non-violent resistance to all forms of racial injustice, including local laws and practices;
- Imaginative, bold and constructive action to end the demoralization caused by the legacy of slavery and segregation including schools (Black schools were very different and extremely unequal from white schools. The latter had fine buildings, issued free textbooks, had well stocked libraries and ran for nine months in a year while the black ones did not have any of these facilities and had only seven months sessions) slums and second-class citizenship;

- Continue the struggle with dignity and courage to end the demoralization;
- A new frontal assault on poverty, disease and ignorance;

King added:

"We know through painful experience that freedom is never voluntarily given by the oppressor; it must be demanded by the oppressed. ... We have waited for more than 340 years for our constitutional and God-given rights. The nations of Asia and Africa are moving with jet-like speed towards gaining political independence, but we still creep at horse-and-buggy pace toward gaining a cup of coffee at a lunch counter. ... I have almost reached the regrettable conclusion that the Negro's great stumbling block in his stride toward freedom is not the White Citizens' Councilor or the Ku Klux Klanner, but the white moderate who is more devoted to 'order' than to justice. ... If our white brothers dismiss us as 'rabble-rousers' and 'outside agitators' those of us who employ non-violent direct action and refuse to support our non-violent efforts, millions of Negroes will, out of frustration and despair, seek solace and security in black-nationalist ideologies — a development that would inevitably lead to a frightening racial nightmare."

Those who would be prepared to go to jail in furtherance of the cause were required to sign a commitment card as follows:

I hereby pledge myself — my person and my body — to the non-violent movement. Therefore, I will keep the following ten commandants:

1. Meditate daily on the teachings and life of Jesus.
2. Remember always that the non-violent movement in Birmingham seeks justice and reconciliation — not victory.
3. Walk and talk in the manner of love; for God is love.
4. Pray daily to be used by God in order that all might be free.
5. Sacrifice personal wishes that all men might be free.
6. Observe with both friend and foe for ordinary rules of courtesy.
7. Seek to perform regular service for others and for the world.
8. Refrain from the violence of fist, tongue and heart.
9. Strive to be in good spiritual and bodily health.
10. Follow the directions of the movement and of the captains on a demonstration.

A rather poorly drafted set of commandments (!) but certainly good enough for the black masses However, one cannot overlook the similarity in methodology and system set by Mahatma Gandhi in respect of his Sabramati Ashram near Ahmedabad, India, where every entrant had to take fourteen vows before that person could be admitted. Frontier Gandhi had also laid down similar rules for those joining his Khudai Khidmatgar movement. Thus all three "Gandhis" followed the same pattern of instilling a sense of discipline and dedication amongst their trusted followers. The brutal reaction by the City Police gave rise to a sympathy wave that led to a number of sympathetic demonstrations in several cities in the North. A number of peaceful demonstrations were held in the border town of Cambridge, Maryland, over a period of weeks. However, violence broke out in July when the National Guard had to be deployed. The violence came to an end only after an agreement embodying desegregation of schools, public places and accommodation, greater employment opportunities and building of low-rent housing was arrived at.

The SCLC leadership decided to throw all their resources in eradicating segregation from Birmingham. "Project C" was launched around Easter season, the second biggest shopping period of the year, with a view to hurt the economic interests of the powerful elite. Following in the footsteps of Gandhi, the leaders had decided to make one last ditch effort to apprise the President that they could not wait indefinitely for full restoration of Negroes' civil rights in all their facets. In January 1963 Ralph Abernathy, Fred Shuttlesworth and Martin had a meeting with President Kennedy and the Attorney-general Robert Kennedy at the White House to urge the Federal Government to initiate necessary legislation to ensure equal civil rights for all citizens irrespective of the colour of their skin. But Kennedy brothers did not go beyond lip-sympathy. The Black leaders were left with no option but to resort to sit-ins at lunch counters, which commenced on 3rd April 1963. This was the most critical demonstration that was to change the course of Black Movement. About 250 persons had volunteered to participate in the demonstrations and were prepared to go to jail for at least five days. Since it was expected to be a long drawn struggle, the leaders rightly decided to make a modest beginning with a small number offering themselves for arrest each day. A number of demonstrators were arrested every day, 'politely escorted to paddy wagon' and taken to jail. Thousands of Negroes cheered them from the sidewalks. An important part of the demonstrations and marches was the 'freedom songs', adaptation of old 'slave songs' — "We shall overcome, Black and White together. We shall overcome some day." The Blacks did not carry any weapons of any kind whatsoever: their most potent weapon was non-violence and the conviction that they were fighting for the right cause. "We did not hesitate to call our movement an 'army'. It was special army, with no supplies but its sincerity, no uniform but its determination, no arsenal except its faith, no currency but its conscience. It was an army that would move but not maul. It was an army that would sing but not slay."[8]

An Unjust Law is No Law

He was a fearless man, sent his children to public schools to desegregate them. Consequently, he was beaten up, his church and home were bombed. His wife was jailed and beaten. The entire family had suffered terribly in the cause of social justice, freedom and desegregation. In January 1962 the students of Miles College joined the SCLC to begin a boycott of segregated stores in Birmingham. It was generally believed that if the campaign in Birmingham was successful, it would, perhaps, 'break the back of segregation all over the nation'. Those who would be prepared to go to jail in furtherance of the cause were required to sign a commitment card and abide by a set of ten commandents described in the preceding paras.

However, one cannot overlook the similarity in methodology and system set by 'Frontier Gandhi' who also laid down the following rules to be observed by his 'Red Shirts':

> "I am a Khudai Khidmatgar, and as God needs no service I shall serve Him by serving His creation selflessly. I promise to serve humanity in the name of God.
>
> I shall never use violence. — In the words of Gandhi: "People laugh at me at the idea of Khudai Khidmatgars becoming full-fledged non-violent soldiers of Swaraj. But their mockery does not affect me. Non-violence is a quality not of the body, but for the soul." I shall not retaliate or take revenge; and I shall forgive any one who indulges in oppression and excesses against me.
>
> I shall not be a party to any intrigue, family feuds and enmity, and I shall treat every Pathan as my brother and comrade.
>
> I shall give up evil customs and practices. I shall develop good character and cultivate good habits. I shall not lead an idle life.

---

8. King Martin Luther Jr.: op. cit. (Autobiography); p. 179.

I shall expect no reward for my services. I shall be fearless and be prepared for any sacrifice. I promise to refrain from anti-social customs and practices.

I promise to live a simple life, to practice virtue and to refrain from evil."[9]

Well before Abernathy and Martin had adopted the policy of defying unjust laws, African National Congress under the leadership of Dr. Nelson Mandela had set a good example in that direction. In 1952, they had launched a 'Campaign for the Defiance of Urban Laws' in order to resist discriminatory legislation. Mandela and his colleagues were arrested and tried. However, the court found that "Mandela and his co-accused had consistently advised their followers to adopt a peaceful course of action and to avoid all violence". The organization continued to follow the Gandhian philosophy of non-violence till frustration became so widespread that in June 1961 ANC switched over to armed struggle to achieve their long cherished dream of freedom from racial discrimination.

In January 1963 Ralph Abernathy, Fred Shuttlesworth and Martin had a meeting with President Kennedy and the Attorney General Robert Kennedy at the White House to urge the Federal Government to initiate necessary legislation to ensure equal civil-rights for all citizens irrespective of the colour of their skin. But Kennedy brothers did not go beyond lip-sympathy. The Black leaders were left with no option but to resort to sit-ins at lunch counters, which commenced on 3rd April 1963 by which time Martin was back in Birmingham after his whirlwind speaking tour in major cities of the nation. Freedom comes at a price. It is not given gratis. And it must be demanded by the oppressed, otherwise it will not come. In his letter from Birmingham City Jail dated 16 April 1963, King wrote:

"We know through painful experience that freedom is never voluntarily given by the oppressor; it must be demanded by the oppressed. Frankly, I have never yet engaged in a direct action movement that was 'well timed', according to the timetable of those who have not suffered unduly from the disease of segregation. For years now I have heard the words 'Wait!' It rings in the ear of every Negro with a piercing familiarity. This 'Wait' has almost always meant 'Never'."[10]

---

9. Frontier Gandhi: p. 51 and Tendulkar: op. cit. p. 59.
10. King Martin Luther Jr.: *A Testament of Hope*; op. cit. p. 292.

The protests began in earnestness. Negro men, women and children in their Sunday best cheerfully paraded in the downtown. A number of demonstrators were arrested every day, 'politely escorted to paddy wagons' and taken to jail. Thousands of Negroes cheered them from the sidewalks. Bull Connor was ecstatic over his triumph of putting so many 'niggers' behind bars, with so little. On Tuesday 7th May 1963 about 2,500 Negroes poured out of church, broke through the police barricades and swarmed the downtown. Connor was furious. He ordered police into action. Fire hoses were turned on. The policemen armed with clubs thrashed the hell out of any and everybody that happened to be in their way. An armored car bulldozed its way through the milling crowd. Soon it was time for the leaders of the Movement to show their hand. Martin and Ralph were sent to jail along with twenty-odd other leading members. For the first time Martin and Ralph were separated and both were put in solitary confinement, totally incommunicado. More than 3,300 Negroes were thrown into jail for resorting to peaceful nonviolent demonstrations.

Coretta and many others were anxious about the safety of Dr. King. On the advice of well wishers, Coretta called the President and told him that she was not asking for Martin to be released; far from it. But she was terribly anxious about his safety and that is what she wanted the President to ensure. Within fifteen minutes of this conversation with the President, Coretta got a call from Martin. The news of President Kennedy's intervention was all over the country. It gave a big boost to the momentum of Birmingham Movement. While he was in jail, eight white clergymen of Alabama issued a public statement on April 12, 1963, calling the protest marches and demonstrations as 'unwise and untimely'. They accused Martin, an outsider, of being a seeker after publicity. Even *Time* magazine and *New York Times* blamed King for creating 'inflamed tensions' and 'tensions that have grown alarmingly' in Birmingham. Martin then replied those white clergymen through his famous open letter dated April 16, 1963, written on odd bits and pieces of paper, toilet paper, margins of newspapers, anything that he could lay his hand on, and had it smuggled out to an aide, in bits and pieces. His "Letter from a Birmingham Jail" was addressed to "My Dear Fellow Clergymen", telling them that like one should obey just laws, it was a moral duty to disobey unjust laws. Martin quoted Saint Augustine: "An unjust law is no law" at all. "We should never forget that everything that Adolph Hitler did in Germany was legal and everything the Hungarian freedom fighters did was illegal. "We have waited for more than 340 years for our constitutional and God-given rights". Those who have never been on the receiving end of stinging poisonous barbs of segregation can easily advise: "Wait: But we cannot wait any more.

"When you have seen vicious mobs lynch your mothers and fathers at will and drown your sisters and brothers at whim; when you have seen hate filled police-men curse, kick, brutalize and even kill your black brothers and sisters; when you suddenly find your tongue twisted and your speech stammering as you seek to explain to your six-year-old daughter why she can't go the public amusement park that has just been advertised on TV, and see tears welling up in her little eyes when she is told that "Fun-town" is closed to coloured children, and see the depressing clouds of inferiority begin to form in her little mental sky, and see her begin to distort her little personality by unconsciously developing a bitterness toward white people; when you are humiliated day in and day out by nagging signs reading "white" and "colored"; when you are harried by day and haunted by night by the fact that you are a Negro, living constantly at tip-toe stance, never quite knowing what to expect next, and plagued by inner fears and outer resentment; when you are forever fighting a degenerating sense of 'nobodiness' — then you will understand why we find it difficult to wait. There comes a time when the cup of endurance runs over ... I hope, sirs, you can understand our legitimate and unavoidable impatience.

> "In your statement you assert that our actions, even though peaceful, must be condemned because they precipitate violence. This seems like condemning a robbed man because his possession of money precipitated the evil act of robbery. Isn't this like condemning Socrates for his unswerving commitment to truth and his philosophical inquiries precipitated the act by the misguided populace in which they made him drink hemlock? Isn't this like condemning Jesus because his unique God-consciousness and never ceasing devotion to God's will precipitated the evil act of crucifixion? You warmly commended the Birmingham police force for keeping "order" and "preventing violence." I doubt that you would have so warmly commended if you had seen its dogs sinking their teeth into unarmed, non-violent Negroes. If you were to watch the policemen push and curse old Negro women and young Negro girls; if you were to see them slap and kick old Negro men and young boys; if you were to observe them refuse to give us food because we wanted to sing our grace together ..."[11]

"As long as injustice, racism and oppression of minorities persist, King's 'Letter from a Birmingham Jail' will be read."[12]

---

11. King Martin Luther, Jr.: *Autobiography*, op. cit. Excerpts from King's letter from Jail; pp. 188-202.
12. King Mary: op. cit. p. 6.

This letter constitutes one of the most important documents[13] in the international literature on the subject of non-violent resistance. Martin wrote this in 1963 when the basic industries like coal and steel represented the worst of the industrial culture of the South. Reverend Fred L. Shuttlesworth had almost single handedly kept alive resistance to police brutality and industrial suppression. The SCLC had a good base in the region and their idea was to desegregate the restaurants in downtown department stores by resorting to demonstrations and boycotts, which would hurt the chain-stores financially thereby bringing the management to the negotiating table. Well before Shuttlesworth and Martin had to resolve the problem of industrial suppression, Gandhi too faced a similar situation in Ahmedabad, the industrial city of his native Gujarat. Here Gandhi was in a delicate situation. He had good personal relations with the mill-owners many of whom had made generous contributions to his Sabramati Ashram. And the Lady who had invited Gandhi to resolve the labour dispute was the sister of the head of mill-owners combine! But the grievances of the labour were genuine. Wages were low and working conditions still worse. The labour had been agitating for a long time for increased compensation. Gandhi requested the mill-owners to refer the dispute to arbitration, which the management refused pointblank.

Gandhi had no option but to advise the labour to go on strike. He explained to the labour-leaders the essential conditions for success of the proposed strike:

- Never to resort to violence.
- Never to molest the black sheep.
- Never to depend upon charity or alms.
- Remain firm, no matter how long the strike continued. During the strike, to earn a living through honest labour.

The labourers held a mass meeting and pledged that they will not return to work till their demands were met, or the mill-owners referred the dispute to arbitration. For the first two weeks the labour morale was high. But after that signs of weakness and dithering were perceptible, more so since prospects of a settlement appeared dim. Gandhi took recourse to the last weapon in his armory. He announced that unless

---

13. The long letter dated 16 April 1963 addressed to the white clergymen of Birmingham runs into almost fourteen pages. It has been reprinted so many times in so many books, and as a pamphlet too, that the Author thinks no useful purpose will be served by repeating the same as an appendix to this Chapter; it would only add to the bulk of the book.

strikers continued the strike till a settlement is reached, or they left the mills altogether, "I will not touch any food." The labourers were infused with a new strength. The mill-owners hearts were touched. An arbitrator was appointed and the strike was called off. Gandhi had fasted for three days only while the strike had lasted for twenty-one days.

Now back from' A' to 'B'. The whites also reacted in their own special way by spreading violence to counter the black nonviolence. "Freedom Walker" William Moore was shot and killed in Alabama. Medgar Evers, a leading figure in Mississippi's NAACP was assassinated outside his home. Violence erupted in a number of cities prominent amongst which was Jackson, Miss., Cambridge, Md., Danville, Va., and of course in Birmingham itself too, where in a church-bombing four Negro Sunday-school children were killed, besides two other youth who were shot and killed in another separate incident.

Birmingham had provided the spark. In the subsequent months, protests, demonstrations, marches and sit-ins continued in about eight hundred cities and towns all over the country. Many whites also joined the demonstrations. The whites and the Administration came to the realization that the Negro was not as dumb as they used to believe. He was literate enough to understand the fundamental provisions of the Constitution and demanded equal rights. There was no time to lose, lest the inferno of Birmingham is repeated in other places. So far, President Kennedy was taking his own time in proceeding with the Civil Rights Bill but now he made the Justice Department to draw up a 'tight and tough' bill, particularly insofar as desegregation of public facilities, voting rights and employment opportunities were concerned.

The Children's Crusade

Even small children wanted to join the marches and go to jail. But Andy Young told them: "You are too young to go to jail. Go to the library. You will learn something there." Six little children followed his advice. And in the bargain the library got desegregated since no one dare touch those small kids! But the high school youth were certainly a fertile ground for the freedom movement. There should be no moral objection to letting our budding youth to participate in the freedom struggle. James Bevel, a leader of the Movement in his own right learnt from Lawson, a colleague in the Movement, that Gandhi's 1930 Salt-March had 60,000 Indians imprisoned after the procession to the sea. Bevel fashioned his own 'Battle Cry': "Gandhi said to fill the jails! We're gonna fill the jails!" It may be recalled that during his twenty-one years in South Africa, Gandhi was sentenced to jail four times — 10 January 1908 for two months; October 7, 1908 for three months; 25 February 1913 for three months and on November 11, 1913 for nine months — but he was prematurely released each time to avoid bad publicity, and thereby he actually spent only seven months and ten days in South African prisons. He was lodged in the Fort in Johannesburg for his first prison term; so was Mandela in 1962 for five years after his first conviction. However, Gandhi was subjected to great personal humiliation when, while being moved from Pretoria to Volksrust and thence to Johannesburg, he, a Bar-at Law from London, "was marched from goal to station in prison garb, handcuffed, with his prison kit on his head ...For Gandhi it was part of his suffering, part of the struggle against inhumanity ... Suffering in the path of justice and freedom was part of his creed." While in South African prisons where living conditions were deplorable, to say the least, Gandhi always declined any favors offered to him exclusively. However, he accepted improvements when these were "shared with his fellow political prisoners". On Robben Island Mandela was proud to follow the same principle. Gandhi learnt Tamil while he was in South African prisons. And Mandela learnt Afrikaans in his time.

Hearing the above rallying cry for freedom, on 2nd May 1963, thousands of black children left their classrooms. They made their way to Sixteenth Street Baptist Church. The school children were formed into batches of fifty each. Batch by batch, they marched, singing freedom songs, clapping, laughing. They voluntarily went to the waiting police contingents. That day about one thousand persons were arrested, 319 of them were children, some of whom were, ironically, transported to the jail in the school buses. This process continued for about a week. It made Bull Connor furious. When the marchers, including the children, made their way from the Church to the police barricades, Connor ordered his six German shepherd police dogs set on the marchers, adults and children alike. The snarling dogs created havoc in their own peculiar way, yelling, chasing and biting any and everybody that was around. Now the marchers retaliated with stones, bricks, bottles and sticks to get the police-dogs off them. The news media went wild, giving graphic details of police brutalities inflicted on small children. The TV pictures added fuel to the fire. The whole of America, and the world, was aghast at the manner in which peaceful non-violent children were treated by the City Administration. The TV pictures and radio broadcasts united the black populace as nothing else would have done so.

The White House was terribly upset and felt embarrassed. On June 11, President John F. Kennedy gave a televised speech on the immorality of segregation. He made it abundantly clear that segregation will not be allowed as law of the land. Birmingham was indeed the flash point. King warned the Administration that the Country was at a "historical crossroads". The Nation's moral commitment and political fortunes were at stake. The Blacks talked of freedom in every slogan: freedom songs, freedom rides, freedom movement, freedom schools. Nothing but freedom only. In this respect they were following in the footsteps of Ella Baker: "You must let the oppressed themselves define their own freedom."

The Birmingham demonstrations spurred President Kennedy to submit fresh civil rights bill to the Hill, embodying a 'new and broadened civil rights program'. He told the Congress in no uncertain terms that racial discrimination was not only economically costly: "Above all, it is wrong". Yet the President did not push the reforms as hard as he should have done. Perhaps, "Vote Bank" politics made the President drag his feet. One of the devices to keep the Blacks off the voter's list was the high poll tax. In Alabama it cost two dollars to vote! And if a black went to vote for the first time at, say age thirty, he had to pay all the back taxes since he reached the age of twenty-one! The President wanted the votes of both sides with the result that he, or the Administration for that matter; was "paralyzed by the conflicting needs of each."

Concurrently, the President declared: "We face a moral crisis as a country and as a people. It cannot be met by repressive police action. It cannot be left to increased demonstrations in the streets. ..." The President put forward a new civil rights bill before the Congress. There was bitter opposition to many of the liberal provisions of the proposed legislation. During the same period a "March on Washington for Jobs and Freedom" was organized. The objectives of the March received broad support from most sections of the people, particularly in the North. It turned out to be a gigantic demonstration supported by a host of religious and social organizations of the country. The list was long and impressive resulting in mobilization of more than 200,000 Blacks and Whites from all over the United States. It was the largest demonstration in the history of the National Capital held on 28th August 1963. Nothing like that had ever been witnessed before. The meticulously organized "orderly procession moved from the Washington Monument to the Lincoln Memorial where A. Phillip Randolph, Martin Luther King, Roy Wilkins, Walter Reuther, *et al*, addressed" the mammoth gathering.[14] More about this in a later chapter.

---

14. A notable absentee was W.E.B. DuBois, an old timer Black leader of repute. After joining the Communist Party he renounced his U.S. citizenship in protest and moved to Ghana in 1961. He died in Accra in his 96th year on the eve of the Great March.

Dr Martin Luther King Jr. had already taught the Blacks and the Whites how to be both militant and non-violent, a contradiction of concepts and terminology in itself. His political skills and intellectual qualities contributed in large measure in reconciliation of the inherent contradiction. It was now left to Lyndon Baines Johnson to create history, to write the last chapter of Freedom Movement. Just five days after the assassination of John Fitzgerald Kennedy, he told the Congress in a brief address: "We have talked long enough in this country about equal rights. We have talked for one hundred years or more. It is time now to write the next chapter, and to write it in the books of law."[15] In all fairness to Johnson, it should be recorded that before the 35th President of the United States was assassinated, passions in the Black Movement had reached a high point of no return. However, by then, the number of Negroes holding jobs in the middle grades of the civil service increased 36.6 per cent from June 1961 to June 1963; in the top grades, 88.2 per cent.[16] The Equal Employment Opportunity under Vice President Johnson had certainly been doing the job seriously. Earlier on, Johnson had consistently voted against civil rights bills till 1957. It may be recalled that in 1948 he had described Truman's civil rights program as a 'farce and a sham'. But under the changed circumstances he was a man transformed: He summoned the heads of various firms doing business with the Government and urged them to join Plans and Progress providing for training and employment of Negroes.

---

15. Burns M. James: op. cit. p. 375.
16. Schlesinger M. Arthur Jr.: *A Thousand Days, John F. Kennedy in the White House*, London, 1965; p. 796.

22

Washington March

'I Have a Dream'

Washington is a city of spectacles. But in its entire glittering history, Washington had never seen such a spectacle of the size and grandeur that assembled there on August 28, 1963. As television beamed the images of this extraordinary gathering across the borders of oceans, everyone who believed in man's capacity to better himself had a moment of inspiration and confidence in the future of the human race. Millions of Americans, for the first time, had a clear long look at the Negroes and listened to the informed and thoughtful words of Negro spokesmen. The stereotype of the Negro suffered a heavy blow.

Martin King was terribly upset by the mob-violence, more so when the Albany Blacks retaliated by going on a rampage. He "cancelled a scheduled march, and in the spirit of Gandhi, declared a day of penance."[1] However, the climax was yet to come.

William Robert Miller compiled a list of all that went on during the year 1963: Nine hundred and thirty eight demonstrations occurred in atleast 115 Southern cities in eleven Southern States in which 20,083 arrests were made, one of which was Martin King. On the positive side of the balance sheet, 'some progress towards integration' in 186 localities had been made and negotiations in 102 bi-racial communities were in progress.

The King-children were deprived of the company of their father. So were those of M.K. Gandhi's family. Both suffered similar scars even though they reacted differently. The respective family lives of Mahatma Gandhi and Dr. Martin Luther King Jr. are an interesting study by themselves. While Gandhi hardly had any family life, Martin was certainly

---

1. Burns M. James: op. cit. p. 364.

much better off in this respect. He was in and out a family-man. But insofar as togetherness of the Family is concerned, Martin was only slightly better off. However, it needs to be borne in mind that the two couples had more than a generation gap, besides their cultures were oceans apart.

Slow Small Steps up the Ladder

After all, Negroes started getting their due, albeit at a very slow frustrating pace. But there was atleast some progress. For the first time in the twentieth century, there were three Negroes in the Congress, and one more was due to come in 1964 by which time there were six of them in the Lower House. Similarly, appointments of Negroes to high posts in the national government were showing an upward trend as mentioned in the preceding chapter. However, the whites could not easily reconcile to this upward movement by the blacks. Nevertheless, the trend did continue but often it was retarded due to resistance by white groups, as it happened in the case of fire department of Washington D.C. "The road to revolution had been paved by Supreme Court decisions on voting and school desegregation, by the Montgomery bus boycott and the emergence of Martin Luther King Jr., the passage of the Civil Rights Act of 1957, and the rise of national states in Africa."[2]

Since the Negro voters were being denied the right to vote through various administrative obstacles put forth by white registrars, concurrently, the Commission on Civil Rights held hearings in many cities and instituted suits in Alabama, Georgia and Louisiana. The white registrars were accordingly charge-sheeted. In some cases the white registrars resigned after cases were instituted. To overcome this legal lacuna, in 1960, the Congress passed another civil rights bill providing for cases to be filed against the states concerned in such cases. But the same year also witnessed one of the largest mass migrations when almost one a half million Blacks left their homes and hearths in the South to seek peace and shelter in the already overcrowded ghettos of the North. By the end of 1950 the Blacks constituted nearly half the population of Washington D.C., over a quarter of Philadelphia, Detroit, Cleveland, Chicago, Houston and St. Louis. The sociology and pathology of the black poor was vividly etched by Kenneth Clark in his *Dark Ghetto*. It was perhaps the cumulative effect of the preceding events, and President Kennedy's own voice of conscience, that were responsible for the message sent by the President to the Congress on 28th February 1963 "setting forth in moving detail the national shame of inequality not only in voting and education but

---

2. Franklin Hope John: *From Slavery to Freedom*, p. 624.

in employment and public accommodations. Racial discrimination hampered our economic growth and our world leadership; it increased the costs of public welfare, crime, delinquency and disorder; it marred the atmosphere of a united and classless society. Above all, it is wrong." The defiance of the Constitution of the United States of America in Mississippi forced the hands of the Civil Rights Commission, who took the unusual step of issuing an Interim Report:

> Citizens of the United States have been shot, set upon by vicious dogs, beaten, and otherwise terrorized because they sought to vote. Since October, students have been fired upon, ministers have been assaulted ... children, at the brink of starvation, have been deprived of assistance by the callous and discriminatory acts of Mississippi officials administering Federal Funds.

The irony of fate is that the same whites of so called western civilization had the audacity to call us Asians, particularly the Indians and Chinese, as uneducated uncivilized savages! Perhaps, this sad state of affairs prompted King to say: "I have a dream that my four little children will one day live in a nation where they will not be judged by the color of their skin but by the content of their merit." Notwithstanding the aforesaid palliative measures, the progress in equal rights for the Negroes was much too slow. Massive demonstrations were therefore organized, the most critical one being in Birmingham on 3rd April 1963.

The Unprecedented March

On 28th August 1963 the Nation was profoundly impressed by a mammoth, but peaceful, march undertaken by a quarter of a million people, mostly blacks but many whites too, about 10-15 per cent, in Washington D.C, under the leadership of Martin Luther King Jr. It was undertaken in support of the civil rights bill sent to the Congress by President Kennedy. Martin was the star performer of the show, in fact the only performer, the *raison d'?tre*, whose speech "I Have a Dream" has become history. It came to be known as the "March on Washington for Jobs and Freedom", whose 'battle cry' was "NOW". There were leaders of all hues, representing the entire gamut of the civil rights movement — Whitney Young Jr. of National Urban League, John Lewis of SNCC whose slogan was "We want our Freedom — and we want it NOW", Rabbi Joachim Prinz of American Jewish Congress, Rev. Dr. Eugene Carson Blake of United Presbyterian Church, A. Philip Randolph of Negro America Labor Council, Walter P. Reuther of United Auto Workers, Roy Wilkins of NAACP, Mathew Ahmann of National Conference of Catholic for Interracial Justice, the National Council of

Churches, Industrial Union Department, *et al*, were among the strong supporters of the March — the largest demonstration in the history of the nation's capital.[3]

The objectives of the March received broad support from most sections of the people, particularly in the North although "NOW! remained a long way off". The leaders of the March knew this before the march even got underway, when they called on the powerful elite of the Capitol — Senate Democrat leader Mike Mansfield, House Speaker John McCormack, Senate and House Republican Leaders Everett Dirksen and Charles Halleck. President Kennedy and Vice President Lyndon B. Johnson reinforced this position when the leaders called on them in the evening at the White House. Their demands for immediate passage of the President's entire civil rights package with additional provisions for setting up of Federal Fair Employment Practices Commission as well as grant of additional powers to the Justice Department were politely refused. So what did the March achieve? King said: "We subpoenaed the conscience of the Nation." Philip Randolph felt that the March had developed a new unity amongst the various civil rights leaders while Roy Wilkins of the NAACP was pleased over voluntary participation of the whites in an un-condescending manner, and a "coalition of conscience." All very well, as far as empty rhetoric goes! As far as the Negro community as a whole was concerned, their impeccable conduct on that memorable day had proved that they were ready to "accept the responsibilities of first-class citizenship."[4]

The Black Muslim leader, Elijah Muhammad was strongly opposed to this March, or any other march or demonstration by the Negro community. He instructed his followers to shun politics completely. They were told 'not to vote, march, petition, or otherwise implicate themselves in a system doomed to certain apocalypse'. Malcolm X faithfully parroted the 'sermon' and the invectives. The Administration was quite apprehensive about the proposed proportions of the demonstration. They could not accept the hypothesis that even about one hundred thousand 'militant Negroes' could be brought to the Capital without serious incidents, possibly accompanied by large scale rioting, let alone more than twice that number. *Life* magazine declared that the capital was suffering "its worst case of invasion jitters since the First Battle of Bull Run." Besides the usual precautionary steps to control such demonstrations and maintain law and order, President Kennedy's advance man, Jerry Bruno, had made preparations to cut off power

3. Franklin Hope John: op. cit. p. 632.

4. *Time* September 6, 1963, p. 14.

to the public address system should the rally speeches become too volatile. Sale of alcoholic beverages was banned. Hospitals made room for riot-related casualties and routine operations scheduled for the day were postponed. Similarly, some major baseball games were cancelled. The Pentagon alerted troops and some nineteen thousand were made stand-by in the suburbs to meet any eventualities, while 4,000 soldiers and marines were ready to cross the Potomac by helicopters. The District of Columbia Police Chief, Robert V. Murray deployed a force of 5,900 men, including 300 club-carrying firemen, 1,700 National Guardsmen including 300 newly recruited police-reservists. The security-precautionary measures were indeed gigantic in scope and reflected the apprehensions in the minds of the Administration.

As it was, Washington had a large press corps and yet another 1,700 additional special correspondents landed in the City. Thus the media assembly for the march was bigger than that was to cover Kennedy inauguration two years earlier. And all apprehension was not racial in nature; it was part of the on-going process, characteristic of a capital of a powerful nation. Although the Senate did not have any special or urgent business to dispose off, it remained in session throughout that day to put on an unperturbed face.

Notwithstanding the above, the Washington March turned out to be a gigantic demonstration supported by a host of religious and social organizations of the country. The people came from everywhere and nowhere. They came by buses, cars and trains, all jam packed. The "Freedom Special" from Jacksonville carrying 785 marchers, mostly youngsters who had been to jail for the Negro cause and bore the scars of police brutality, deserves a special mention. The marchers were all over the place in the nation's capital. Many were milling around the green-and-white circular tent pitched on the Monument ground that served as the headquarters for the March. The marchers were busy eating peanut butter and jelly sandwiches. When they got ready to get a move on, there were nearly two hundred and fifty thousand heads in that teeming sea of humanity, perhaps more, well disciplined and totally non-violent. There were black legs, brown legs and white legs all over. Surprisingly, about one-fourth of that multitude of humanity was white! The meticulously organized great mass of people, in an orderly procession, moved from the Washington Monument to the Lincoln Memorial. Most marched on their two tired legs, some were in wheel chairs while others were carried. They were so tightly packed, like sardines in a can; one just could not pass through their ranks. The TV cameras were everywhere, so were the correspondents from all over the U.S. and the world. The most important feature of the march was that it was totally peaceful, and orderly, belying the 'dread' of the many. There were only four march-related arrests, a record by itself for any large scale demonstration. And they were all whites; one Nazi, two violent hecklers and one insurance-computing man. Not one black out of the quarter million created any untoward incident. The finale turned out to be an embarrassment for the elaborate safety preparations made for the occasion. The credit for the organizing so large a gathering in such an orderly manner went to Bayard Rustin who gained the reputation of a 'wizard of social engineering'. His command of scheduling and portable toilets impressed one and all, where total racial harmony prevailed. Above all, Martin Luther King emerged as the undisputed leader of the Negro people. And Bayard Rustin became a house-hold name, his past blemishes, if at all any, were completely forgotten, if not forgiven. A sense of relief pervaded the air, raising the goodwill of the march into heights of inspiration for the millions of TV viewers.

The March covering a distance of about one kilometer from Washington Monument to Lincoln Memorial was scheduled to start at 11:30 a.m. The American Nazi Party led by George Lincoln Rockwell appeared all set to create violence. A scruffy-looking bunch of about fifty white nit-wits stood across 15th Street from the Monument Grounds. But the police force prevented them from crossing over to the Monument side, thereby nipping the white-inspired violence in the bud. The crowd started moving about twenty minutes ahead of schedule and soon the Constitution and Independence Avenues were transformed into an 'ocean of bobbing placards'. Some wept with joy; others were happy to be participating in the momentous event. It was a quiet affair. No bands. No singing. No shouting. No slogans — just the shuffling of feet, slowly, steadily, absorbed in silent thoughts, they marched ahead, to the make-shift temple erected in the name of Abraham Lincoln.

Finale

At the Memorial a short program of entertainment was the first item on the agenda. Folk songs and hymns by Joan Baez, Josh White, Odetta, Bob Dylan, Peter-Paul-Mary, all in the professional style. Famous names from the film industry made appearance — Actors Burt Lancaster, Paul Newman, Marion Brando, Charlton Heston, *et al*, followed by a series of short lectures by some top-notch leaders. John Lewis had scripted an aggressive speech in keeping with his personality, and that could have caused problems. However, he was prevailed upon to tone it down. After Mahalia Jackson's fascinating voice had rendered "I've Been 'Buked and I've Been Scorned", A. Philip Randolph introduced Martin, calling him the "moral leader of the nation". Martin's stirring speech echoed Lincoln: "I still have a dream. ... deep rooted in the American dream. ... one day this nation will rise up, live up to the true meaning of its creed ... that all men are created equal. ... I still have a dream that one day ... the sons of former slaves and the sons of former slave owners will be able to sit down together at the table of brotherhood. ... that one day even the State of Mississippi ... will be transformed into an oasis of freedom and justice. ... I have a dream that my four little children ... will not be judged by the color of their skin, but by the content of their character. ..." Martin departed from the original script and switched over to extempore oratory at which he was a master of the art of public speaking — dramatic, impromptu and inspirational. He carried on and on in the same vein, rather he was carried away by his own words and emotions and the faith that was generated in him and the people listening to him with rapt attention. Millions were watching him on TV all over the country as if it had come to a standstill for the day, so did a large part of the world. And they heard him all through. Even the President, his family and staff heard King for the full duration for the first and the last time that day. The President remarked: "He's damn good." A short time later when King and other leaders of the March filed into the Cabinet Room, the President greeted King with a smile and a quip: "I have a Dream."[5] According to King's biographer Taylor Branch, Kennedy was especially impressed with King's departure from his prepared text to sound the electrifying refrain that became the oratorical high point of Black's freedom struggle. "With this faith we will be able to work together, to pray together, to struggle together, to go to jail together, to stand up for freedom together, knowing we will be free one day. ... we will be able to speed up that day when all of God's children, black men and white men, Jews and Gentiles, Protestants and Catholics, will be able to join hands and sing ... we are free at last!"

The listeners and viewers could perceive King's disappointment with failure of democratic justice in the country. Despair was writ large in his voice. There was a distinct streak of orator's passion, calling on the American heritage to rise above petty racial distinctions and severe injustices of the past centuries. He stressed on a common political ideal and partnership of all peoples known as Americans. As Martin finished, there was a stunning silence broken by a 'thunderous crash of sound' as if, for that "brief moment the Kingdom of God seemed to have come down to earth."[6]

---

5. *Time* dateline Aug. 28, 1963.
6. King Scott Coretta: op. cit. p. 254.

As soon as the function was officially over, and in compliance with the specific instructions of their leader, the crowd quietly made their way back to their buses, trains, planes and cars. Once again the movement was without any fuss, and totally orderly. The splendidly successful march that went off without a blemish did not create even a minor dent on the attitude at the Hill. For the Negro revolution to be successful, a lot more was still required in concrete terms. "In April 1963 the unemployment rate for the non-whites was 12.1 per cent, for the whites 4.8 per cent. Poverty afflicted half the non-white population, less than one-fifth the white population. Three out of five non-white families lived in dilapidated buildings, or without plumbing. The racial and social problems were inextricably intermingled."[7]

Life's review issue on the march put Bayard Rustin on the cover. The text evoked "beatific calm" instead of Bull Run. However, *Newsweek* magazine had published a special issue before the Washington March, entitled "The Negro in America". The editors asked: "Who are these revolutionaries? What do they want?" They went on to say that the "answers lie in a world as remote and as unfamiliar to most white Americans as the far side of the moon — the dark side." The *Newsweek* poll showed that Martin Luther King had a national rating of 88 per cent amongst the Negroes against 68 per cent for Roy Wilkins and 51 percent for Adam Clayton Powell and a mere 15 percent for Elijah Muhammad. More than 40 percent said they did not know or recognize Malcolm X, or the Muslim Americans. It should be noted that this poll was conducted *before* the March while Bayard Rustin came on Life's cover *after* the March. A large majority of Negroes swore by non-violence. They were looking forward to acquiring consumer durables at par with the whites, and to integrate with White America, to become active partners of the nation they thought they really belonged to. The magazine concluded: "The Negroes are playing to win. They think they can."[8]

While there was not a single unpleasant incident despite the vast multitude of humanity that had gathered together for the 'Washington March', tragedy struck when the Sixteenth Street Baptist Church was bombed on 15th September killing four little innocent girls. Resolutions of sympathy, expressions of grief, poured in from all over the country,

---

7. Schlesinger M. Arthur, Jr.: op. cit. p. 830.
8. Branch Taylor: op. cit. pp. 135-136. There was a second special issue of the *Newsweek* covering the whites' reaction and connected matters. The constraints of space do not permit to go into those elaborate statistics and details. In fact, connected stories occupied the print and electronic media for quite a while after the March was long over.

including some from the Southern white clergymen. President Kennedy went on record: "I know I speak on behalf of all Americans in expressing a deep sense of outrage and grief." But even JFK held back; he pledged the full power of the federal government to the "detection" of those responsible but did not go far enough to say, 'trial or conviction' of the perpetrators of the ghastly crime. The City was on the verge of 'open racial warfare'. The President deputed Burke Marshall of Justice Department to the City. The funerals produced the largest collections of inter-racial clergy in the history of Birmingham. But none of the City officials showed the courtesy of attending any of the funerals. The poison, the bitterness of racial hatred, had percolated much too deep. Birmingham had acquired the notoriety of "Bombingham". A local reporter had compiled a list of twenty bombings in Birmingham, starting with Fred Shuttlesworth home in December 1956. None of these crimes had been solved, and all of them were against the members of the Freedom Movement.

The president deputed two retired Army officers, General Kenneth Royall and Colonel Earl 'Red' Blaik as non-binding mediators. This proved to be an exercise in futility in which King suffered great loss of face and prestige so much so that many Blacks turned hostile to King's philosophy and technique of nonviolence. In desperation, King admitted that "his leadership was standing still, doing nothing, going nowhere."

Unfortunately, a bigger tragedy was waiting in the wings. That struck all Americans and the rest of the world too, when on 22nd November 1963 John Fitzgerald Kennedy was shot and killed. While alive, President Kennedy was facing tough opposition to his Civil Rights Bill, but his assassination moved all and sundry to see that that piece of legislation was passed as quickly as possible as a tribute to the departed President.

The march was an unqualified success, even though the National Council of AFL-CIO did not support the march, but the member unions independently did. Inter-racial couples with their children held placards proclaiming the oneness of all people. The most important feature of the march was that it was totally peaceful. And that made Martin King the undisputed leader of the Negro people. Indeed, the day belonged to Martin King. The high point of King's Dream was: "I have a dream that one day in Alabama little black boys and black girls will join hands with little white boys and white girls as sisters and brothers."

The world famous words, "I Have A Dream", have come to be closely associated with the name of Dr. King. The summarized text of that speech is given as an Appendix to this Chapter.

Appendix

'I Have a Dream'

When the architects of our republic wrote the magnificent words of the Constitution and the Declaration of Independence, they were signing a promissory note to which every American was to fall heir. This note was the promise that all men, yes, black men as well as white men, would be guaranteed the unalienable rights of life, liberty, and the pursuit of happiness....

But there is something that I must say to my people, who stand on the warm threshold which leads into the palace of justice. In the process of gaining our rightful place, we must not be guilty of wrongful deeds. Let us not seek to satisfy our thirst for freedom by drinking from the cup of bitterness and hatred. We must forever conduct our struggle on the high plain of dignity and discipline. We must not allow our creative protest to degenerate into physical violence. Again and again we must rise to the majestic heights of meeting physical force with soul force; and the marvelous new militancy, which has engulfed the Negro community, must not lead us to a distrust of all white people. For many of our white brothers, as evidenced by their presence here today, have come to realize that their destiny is tied up with our destiny. And they have come to realize that their freedom is inextricably bound to our freedom. We cannot walk alone. And as we talk, we must make the pledge that we shall always march ahead. We cannot turn back....

I say to you today, my friends, so even though we face the difficulties of today and tomorrow, I still have a dream. It is a dream deeply rooted in the American dream. I have a dream that one day this nation will rise up and live out the true meaning of its creed, "We hold these truths to be self evident, that all men are created equal." I have a dream that one day on the red hills of Georgia, sons of former slaves and the sons of former slave owners will be able to sit down together at the table of brotherhood. I have a dream that one day even the state of Mississippi, a state sweltering with the heat of injustice, sweltering with the heat of oppression, will be transformed into an oasis of freedom and justice. I have a dream that my four little children will one day live in a nation where they will not be judged by the colour of their skin, but by the content of their character....

When we allow freedom to ring, when we let it ring from every village and every hamlet, from every state and every city, we will be able to speed up that day when all God's children, black men and white men, Jews and Gentiles, Protestants and Catholics, will be able to join hands and sing in the words of the old Negro spiritual: "Free at last. Free at last. Thank God Almighty, we are free at last."

The Washington March: August 28, 1963

23

The Lion-Cloth Syndrome

The misery of the poor in Africa and Asia is shared misery, a fact of life for the vast majority; they are all poor together as a result of years of exploitation and under-development. In sad contrast, the poor in America know that they live in the richest nation in the world. The Negro today is not struggling for some abstract, vague rights, but for concrete improvement in his way of life. However, Gandhi's strength lay in the richness of his personality, not in the multitude of his possessions. His goal was To Be, not To Have.

The Trio in overall charge of the Black movement decided to observe the third anniversary of Supreme Court decision on desegregation in a befitting manner. Ella Baker was always readily available for the good cause. So was Rustin. About forty thousand people collected together at the Lincoln Memorial on 17th May 1957 to take part in the March designated as the "Prayer Pilgrimage for Freedom". Besides the march itself, the highlight of the occasion was Martin's "Give us the Ballot Speech" that coincided with the National Association for the Advancement of Coloured People (NAACP) voting rights drive:[1]

- Give us the ballot and we will no longer plead — we will write the proper laws on the books.
- Give us the ballot and we will fill up the legislatures with men of goodwill.

---

1. According to *Jet* magazine article "Man on the Go", during this period Martin delivered two hundred and eight speeches and traveled 780,000 miles besides writing his first book, *Stride Towards Freedom*, in which he told the story of the Montgomery protest.

- Give us the ballot and we will get people's judges who love mercy.
- Give us the ballot and we will quietly, lawfully implement the May 17th 1954 decision of the Supreme Court.
- Give us the ballot and we will transform the salient misdeeds of the bloodthirsty mobs into the calculated good deeds of orderly citizens.

"The Lion Cloth Syndrome of Mahatma Gandhi had captivated Martin Luther King Jr. also. He started believing strongly that he did not wish to own things. Money and material possessions meant very little to him. In fact, like Gandhi, he too wanted to take a vow of poverty as a way of life. Soon he felt that all these fancy clothes and suites were meaningless paraphernalia, and started boasting that he could travel around the world without a suitcase, with one suit and only a change of underwear. He always tried to eliminate all *things* one could do without, and he hoped to influence his followers to do the same. If the 'Naked Fakir' could attend international conferences and meet the King Emperor of British Empire, dressed merely in a 'lion cloth' with a shawl of sorts hung over his shoulders, surely, Martin could travel all over without a suitcase. "We've got to learn that a man's worth is not measured by his bank account or the size of the wheelbase of his car; it is measured by his commitment."[2] Indeed Gandhi was no longer mere M.K. Gandhi; he was Mahatma Gandhi who had permeated the life and work-style of the King family. "Generations to come will scarce believe that such a one as this ever in flesh and blood walked upon this earth." — Albert Einstein.[3] Gandhi's spirit and philosophy transformed the entire 20th century besides taking Dr. Martin Luther King, Jr., his most notable heir in its tide. "If humanity is to progress, Gandhi is inescapable", declared Gandhi's most ardent follower and heir, Dr. Martin Luther King, Jr.

"Give us the Ballot" was followed by "Crusade for Citizenship" launched on Lincoln's Birthday, 12th February 1958, when twenty-one simultaneous meetings were held in key southern towns, for which the key-note was:

> "We must and will be free. We want freedom — *now*. We do not want freedom fed to us in teaspoons over another hundred and fifty years!"

---

2. King Scott Coretta: op. cit. p. 174.
3. Ram Manohar Lohia, a Gandhian in his own right, once remarked: "Man has thought twice in this century, once with Einstein, then with Gandhi. Einstein's thought transformed understanding of physical world; Gandhi's thought transformed understanding of the political world." And for Einstein who was otherwise an unpromising student; "Politics is for the moment. An equation is for eternity."

Gandhi and Socialism

Although Gandhi did not say so in so many words, his writings and utterances, the principles he applied in running his Ashrams, leave a lingering impression that Gandhi had leftist leanings. He believed that every one in the Ashram should do physical work. His emphasis on observing poverty and austerity leaves little doubt about the principle: 'to each according to his needs'. It may not have been a streak of communism, but a degree of extreme socialism, certainly yes. A purely intellectual worker, a total professional, was categorized a parasite, to some degree at least. Be that as it may, Gandhi was considered a Mahatma, and mahatmas are not communists! He radically differed from socialists and communists over their belief in 'class struggle'. Any such struggle between various segments of society was bound to lead to mutual animosity bordering on hatred and violence. To Gandhi, this was counter-productive and that is the last thing he wanted to happen in the Indian society of his cherished dreams. Gandhi did not want to destroy capitalists; he sought to destroy capitalism. In his view, a capitalist was a trustee of the wealth of the society that was meant for the common good of one and all. Capital certainly represented power; but so did the work. If the workers did not produce, how would capital be generated? Of necessity, there had to be a certain stratification of society. Absolute equality was against the fundamental principle of natural selection. In other words, the rich would hold their assets in trust for the good of the society, and deploy their wealth for the benefit of those who worked for them. It was not a one way street; both parties were to derive the benefits accruing from the capital and its working by the workers. This concept of trusteeship might sound vain idealism; nonetheless, it represented a via media between extremes of communism and socialism thereby eliminating class struggle with all its violent consequences as had happened in parts of Europe.

While in London he refused to stay in a West End hotel. Instead, he stayed at Miss Muriel Lester's settlement house in the slums. He always preferred to stay amongst the poor. Since this place was far away from St. James Palace, as a compromise, an office was hired at 88 Knightsbridge. However, Gandhi still went to Kingsley Hall every night! His idiosyncrasies — loincloth dress with a shawl to cover the body, his simple food habits and frugal life style — attracted more attention than his ideas. Nonetheless, the travel to London and the Round Table Conference brought Gandhi to the world's centre stage. He had traveled to England as a deck passenger, taking along his goat which he milked for his two principal meals. The world at large was indeed curious about this 'Naked Fakir' whose achievements in South Africa and then in India had surpassed all expectations. His simplicity, transparent honesty and friendly attitude towards one and all won the peoples' hearts wherever he went. He spent almost three months in England, but his time was taken more for creating a sense of friendliness and sympathy in the minds of English people for India and its people, rather than on the RTC itself. Sir Winston Churchill and the Pope, Pius XI, were the only two amongst the VIPs who declined a meeting with Gandhi. Was Roman Catholicism so exclusive, and the Vatican so bigoted? Nevertheless, Gandhi was invited to Buckingham Palace for tea with King George V and Queen Mary. He went there in his usual loincloth, sandals, a shawl and his dangling watch. Later when Gandhi was asked if he had enough on, Gandhi replied: "The King had enough on for both of us".[4] This Conference too was doomed to failure right from the start because Gandhi demanded full independence for India, which the British were not prepared to concede. Gandhi therefore spent lot of time on lecture tours and informal talks to prepare the English people for eventual complete independence for India — a partnership and friendship of mutual love and respect on equal terms.

Work is Worship

The famous *Kumbh Mela* (a religious gathering of a large size) was held at Haridwar in April 1915. It is a sacred bathing ceremony where over one million pilgrims gather together. The Servants of India society sent volunteers to look after their welfare. Gandhi was one of them. By then he was on the verge of being venerated as a Mahatma. As was his wont, he accorded the first priority to hygiene and sanitation and tackled some of the latrine work himself. But his reputation from South Africa had made him an object of pilgrimage himself. He was therefore obliged to sit in a tent so that people could have his *darshan* — blessings, a sort of spiritual tonic.

Badshah Khan was invited by the Chief Commissioner of the Frontier Province to attend his durbar to be held on 22nd December 1931. The Khan declined. He also declined the summons, and finally, in desperation, the Chief Commissioner had to send a policeman to fetch him for the interview, which started on a sour note because of the opening remarks made by the Commissioner. The Chief Commissioner commented: "Look at those people there, the Khans and Khan Bahadurs. They wait for an interview with me for days together, but I don't meet them. And in spite

4. Fischer Louis: *Life of Gandhi, Part II*, p. 280.

of my repeated requests you don't want to oblige me." — Abdul Ghaffar laughingly replied: "Sir Ralph, these people are around you for personal gains. I have no desire to approach you for that. Why should I then tire myself out that way?"

Sir Ralph banged the table, saying: An unfortunate government from which the honest people keep away and which is surrounded by dishonest people, is destined to be doomed. May God help the British Government!"

Non-violence Not a One-Way Street

Martin King was conscious of the obvious contradiction in 'militant non-violence'. The two are more or less self-contradictory. Again, while the Whites were pleased with Martin's policy of non-violence, there was an obvious incongruity in their approach to domestic and foreign matters. On the one hand the Whites desired non-violence in their dealings with the Blacks and other non-white — one way non-violence only, since the Whites retained the option to use violence against the Blacks, Yellows and Browns — on the other they were fighting a full scale war in South-East Asia. In any case the white people had been making full use of white ethnic power from the day they landed on the shores of the 'New World'; but they called it immoral if the Blacks, the aborigines used their ethnic power in retaliation. This was the crux of white morality since the ages. "Heads I win; tails you lose"! Martin King was a man of morality, more or less pristine, and he spoke against the white morality. He was rather mild in his chastisement in the initial stages, but later came out strongly against this one way morality. Martin's views on the subject were moulded, at least partially, by Bayard Rustin. The latter generally remained in the background but still had a subtle influence on King's ideas regarding morality of violence and war. Rustin was a Quaker and believed: "... the law of violence is such that each side becomes equally vicious. To try to distinguish between which is more vicious is to fail to recognize the logic of war. It is war that is evil, not the Viet Cong, not the United States."[5]

Appearances can be deceptive. So they were in Vietnam. It came to be accepted that Blacks and Whites had found a "new brotherhood" while fighting the 'common enemy' shoulder to shoulder in Vietnam. This so called brotherhood was merely on the surface; it was only skin deep. Many observers on the battlefield came to the conclusion that more racism was exercised by the white soldiers even while on the

---

5. Williams A. John: op. cit. p. 101.

battlefield. But back home, Martin King had built up a tremendous reputation. He had agreed to serve as a co-chairman of "Clergy and Laymen Concerned About Vietnam". In fact, many whites saw King as the next Presidential candidate for 1968, more so since a large number of Americans were bored stiff with Democratic politics.

The Spring Mobilization Committee had scheduled a march for 15 April 1967 under the leadership of Reverend Dr. Martin Luther King Jr. and Dr. Benjamin Spock together with other religious and civil rights leaders. The march started from Central Park on a gray drizzling morning. Law and order was an important factor. However, insofar as the Whites were concerned, law and order simply meant repression of Blacks, poor people and political dissenters. By now the times had changed. It was not at all easy for the leaders, not even Martin King, to keep control on the mobs. There were four days of serious rioting in Newark from 12 to 16 July followed by similar severe riots in Detroit that too lasted for four days. In both riots the police was on the side of the whites, and carrying out major portion of their task of suppressing the downtrodden. The casualties at both places were high. In Newark, twenty-one blacks and two whites were killed while in Detroit thirty-three blacks and ten whites died. The number of wounded was so high that a count could not be kept.[6] In order to prevent such riots in future more and more draconian laws were enacted, which only made the matter go from bad to worse. It became a vicious circle. It may be recalled that Rustin's 'Poor People's March' came towards the end of 1967 followed by another march by America's poor — the poor Mexican-Americans, poor Puerto Rican-Americans, poor Black Americans, poor White Americans, and poor Red-Americans. This could well be the beginning of a grass-roots movement in the U.S. That is perhaps the reason why more Blacks re-enlist in the army than the whites because "they find more democracy in the Army than in civilian life."

---

6. Ibid. p.106.

24

The Florida March

St. Augustine

They tried to stop us by threats and fear, the tactics that had long worked so effectively. But non-violence had muzzled their guns and Negro defiance had shaken their confidence. When they finally reached for clubs, dogs and guns, they found the world was watching, and then the power of non-violence protest became manifest.

Montgomery was important in its own right in as much as it was the first serious attempt by the Black minority to assert their fundamental rights as citizens of the United States. But the significance of Tallahassee, Florida, lay in acceptance of boycott in 1956 as an effective weapon in the hands of the Negroes. The rise of national states in Africa carried the process of Black emancipation many strides forward. The morale of the Negroes was sky high after their splendid success in the Washington March. With Birmingham and Concord as positive backdrops, the two years period 1963 and 1964 could be considered as historical turning point for the Civil Rights movement in America, more so from the Black perspective. The Negro was no longer interested in compromising, nor was he prepared to scale down his objectives, and his methodology of non-violent direct action had already proved its efficacy. The acid test came about in Florida in the beautiful and the nation's oldest city, St. Augustine which had been developed by the Ku Klux Klan as a formidable stronghold of segregationist violence in coordination with John Birch Society. Perhaps, Mississippi was the only other State that could surpass the level of white violence practised in Florida in general, and St, Augustine in particular, while Birmingham was no patch on the other two.

President Kennedy had appointed a federal commission to make preparations for the forthcoming 1965-Quadricentennial of the nation's oldest 'city'. It fell on the broad shoulders of Vice President Lyndon B. Johnson to ceremoniously visit the small tourist town of fifteen thousand to set the ball rolling for the celebrations of founding of St Augustine in 1565 by the Spanish Catholics. Johnson was there to swear-in the members of the proposed Commission. He grabbed an opportune moment to make a quiet private visit to a shrine marking the first permanent outpost of European culture in North America. Johnson had the good fortune of viewing the small wooden casket of the Spanish explorer Don Pedro Menendez de Aviles who had named the new settlement as St. Augustine in honor of the feast-date marking Augustine's death on 28th August 430 A.D. He was observing the feast aboard his ship when the Florida coastline first came into view, and hence the name he chose. The fleet chaplain held an outdoor mass on September 8, 1565, thus establishing a permanent Christian presence on the American soil. Concurrently, King Phillip II of Spain gave Royal permission for Menendez to bring in five hundred African slaves to the new colony. The Spaniards continued to stay on in St. Augustine thereafter. It will thus be seen that, although 1619 is the historically accepted date of institutionalizing of African slavery in America, in point of fact, it came about at least fifty years earlier.[1]

While the Administration and the white population were making preparations for the celebrations, the leading lights of Negro movement petitioned Johnson not to accord approval for $350,000 earmarked for the purpose. They objected to federal assistance for the simple reason that the City still excluded the Negro citizens through legal segregation. Racial segregation, untold oppression and cruelties heaped on the Negroes were strong enough reasons for the Negroes to object to such celebrations. The Spanish Government was also a party to the 1965-Quadricentennial, both by their physical participation as well as financial contribution. The proposed lavish program and ceremonies made no mention of integration, Negro participation as if Lincolnville was not a part of the historic city.

"Hayling" Episode

Ku Klux Klan had planned a rally at the Slave Market Plaza in St. Augustine Florida, on Wednesday evening, the day of the Birmingham funeral. As it was, churches had been bombed and the racist authorities had brutally repressed a local rally by the blacks seeking racial harmony and democracy. Dr. Robert Hayling, a dental surgeon and an adviser on youth affairs with NAACP decided that the KKK rally must not be allowed

1. Branch Taylor: op. cit. p. 34.

to go unchallenged. He along with three other NAACP volunteers went out to scout the Klan rally just to prove to them that the Negroes were no longer afraid of them. They drove slowly, hesitantly, through a wooded field off the main highway when a car pulled up behind them. A white man with a shot-gun smashed their car-windows, pulled them out and marched them off to the rally-site, in prisoner like fashion. There were about three hundred persons at the rally being addressed by Klansman Rev. Connie Lynch of California who, after the ceremonial burning of twenty-foot cross, told the gathering that when some of you say that Jesus was a Jew, it just goes to show "how these cotton-picking, half witted preachers have fooled you. Jesus wasn't no Jew. He was a white man."[2] Talking about the Birmingham church bombings, Lynch went a step further saying that those four young girls were old enough to have "venereal diseases" and was no more human than rattlesnakes. "So I kill 'em all." Three cheers for Christian love and ethics as preached by the worthy reverends of that time! A chance gun-shot brought the law-officers to the scene; Hayling and his companions were evacuated to the hospital with broken teeth, bones and abrasions.

Just to prove the point, the KKK from various Southern States congregated at the Slave Market Plaza and established a strong base at St. Augustine. They abducted four Negroes and beat them up black and blue into unconsciousness using ture-chains, pistol butts, ax handles and clubs, and left them almost dead. On November 5, 1963, Assistant Attorney General Burke Marshall submitted a report to Robert Kennedy stating, *Inter alia,* that the situation in St Augustine has been quite bad. "There has been shooting, beatings and one killing." Joyriding whites speed through Lincolnville almost every night, shooting along and spreading terror. Sniper fire intensified so much that curfew had to be imposed on Halloween night to protect the children. Consequentially, Federal agents swarmed all over the small town, but without authority to investigate violent enforcement of segregation. On March 6 he led a small caravan from St. Augustine to Orlando and met with Rev. C.T. Vivian of SCLC, a pioneer of the Freedom Rides. Hayling sent out a letter requesting that the student community coming down south for spring vacation stop en-route to join the struggle for human rights in St. Augustine. His letter and numerous personal telephone calls highlighted the plight of St. Augustine. The violent police repression in Danville of the previous June was still fresh in the minds of many. Three weeks before Easter the staff and volunteers of Massachusetts SCLC recruited a second line of volunteers

2. Ibid., pp. 141-42.

for Hayling to end segregation in St. Augustine before its Quadricentennial. Professor Harvey Cox of Andover-Newton requested three Episcopal bishops to escort the students but they declined citing reasons of protocol. Wives of SCLC clergy then obtained consent of the wives of the bishops, the capstone of this development was wife of Bishop Malcolm Peabody, mother of Massachusetts Governor Endicott Peabody whose intention to be witness to nonviolence certainly raised some eyebrows. Meanwhile, King left St. Augustine with the intention of returning South later on. During his absence, Andrew Young was his designated spokesman; and that left Hosea Williams slighted, and sulking.

The people had collected for the next march. Williams informed the gathering that Rev. Andrew Young was going to lead the march. Meanwhile, information came in that about five hundred Klansmen armed with clubs and shot guns had collected at the Old Slave Market. Young was sure there would be a clash and some fatalities too. But march they had to. So it was agreed that it would be a totally silent march; no slogan shouting, none of those morale-building songs: The intention was to ensure there was no cause for provocation from the marchers, and the march started off through Lincolnville lined with single-storey homes. As the procession neared the King Street intersection, Police Chief Virgil Stuart halted the line to announce that serious trouble was lurking around the corner in darkness. He informed Rev. Andrew Young that his officers could not protect the marchers even a step further and therefore advised him to retreat. Young withdrew the marchers to a nearby park for a short speech: "And so tonight we have to decide whether to stand back and give in to fear, or whether we really mean the words we sing — Before I'd be a slave, I'd be buried in my grave, and go home to my Lord and be free." Then he called for volunteers to continue the march. Nearly everyone raised arms, clasping hands and singing hymns. It was a beautiful emotional moment. Tears were rolling Young's cheeks like shining pearls.

"May we march," is all that Young said. About three hundred and fifty people in long double rows silently crossed King Street and turned towards the old cathedral. As luck would have it, there was practically no violence from the Klansmen. Just a few epithets, shouts of 'niggers'; but that was about all. The marchers reached Lincolnville without much ado. Of course, the Police Chief had evacuated his officers after delivering his warning to Young, as if that was all that constituted the Police duties. Concurrently, King informed President Johnson on May 29 that the Negroes could not call off their protest marches merely because of large number of death threats. The KKK in St. Augustine was conducting regular roving patrols every night vowing to hang a Negro. There was an explicit threat against King. And to cap it all, there was a problem on the home front when Coretta King complained bitterly about his "constant and prolonged abandonments" after which the couple exploded over the phone line in mutual recrimination. The strain was indeed becoming unbearable. Washington knew about this private problem since the lines were bugged by Hoover.

On June 5, Robert Kennedy received reports from his personal emissary in St. Augustine that the town was too volatile for 'overt mediation let alone enforcement initiatives. King addressed a mass meeting in St. Augustine that night praising the manner in which the march was conducted under Andrew Young. Two days later King left for Connecticut taking Coretta along in deference to recent marital discord, and from there for New York to be the first gentile to receive an honorary degree from the Jewish Theological Seminary sponsored by Rabbi Herschel.

St. Augustine beach cottage was set on fire by arsonists for the second time on June 7 in retaliation for the on-going integration of the beach. Two days later the ban on marches in St. Augustine was withdrawn under orders of Judge Bryan Simpson. The various degrading and disgraceful forms of punishments like 'chicken coop', 'concrete sweatboxes', 'miniature padded cells' and thirty-fold bail increase for misdemeanor charges, *et al,* prescribed for civil rights workers were also declared illegal when the Judge wrote: "Here is exposed, in its raw ugliness, studied and cynical brutality, deliberately contrived to break men physically and mentally." The orders of the Judge were made instantly effective. Robert Hayling and Hosea Williams therefore decided to undertake a 'celebration march' that very night. It was part of William's character that he was always volatile for which some of his colleagues blamed the head-wounds he had received in Germany while serving with an all-Negro unit of the 41st Infantry. A counter-rally by the whites led by J.B. Stoner protesting against integration was held at the Plaza soon after the blacks had dispersed. Stoner was a police suspect in the 1958-bombing of the Atlanta Temple, Birmingham church bombing, and a number of other bombing-cum-murder charges. At the whites' rally Stoner waved a Confederate flag and gave a new twist to the Founding Fathers' declaration: "When they said that all men are created equal, they weren't talking about niggers. ..." In his pronouncements he stated that the "niggers want to integrate because they want our white women". The white rally escorted by police then started its march through the black neighborhood. The black residents responded by Andrew Young's favourite hymn "I Love Everybody, I Love Everybody in my Heart." And that nonviolent reaction completely put off the white procession which soon dispersed. Nevertheless, two churches summoned police to arrest a few Yale University black students who wanted to worship in the white churches. The irony of the incident was brought home with a bang when the Yale University President Kingman Brewster, while conferring the honorary degree of Doctor of Law, introduced King, saying: "The gratitude of the people everywhere and of generations of Americans yet unborn will echo our admiration."

With King already in jail and William on his way to jail, and in order that momentum of the movement is maintained, a bus load of temporary reinforcements were requisitioned from Birmingham. They reached St. Augustine on Friday, June 12.

Integrating Swimming Pool/Beaches

Jim Crow code prohibited the blacks from using the 'whites only' swimming pools and beachhead. King and Williams worked out a 'low-cost' integration exercise by getting some blacks in the swimming pool of downtown Monson Motor Lodge. Much against the entreaties and efforts of the owner James Brock, black and white wet bodies created a scene, and a new precedence. This episode and other considerations led the authorities to order a sort of conditional banishment of King from St. Augustine in that he would leave the town for thirty days, but only if a 'biracial committee' was established first as demanded by King.

An agreement had been reached in the biracial committee to desegregate the beach. An attempted wade-in in the forenoon did not succeed. At about 2:30 p.m. on Thursday, 25th June, a second attempt at wade-in was made. A day earlier the segregationist had broken the nose of the sole white woman who was in the line for wade-in along with the blacks. A newcomer, a white clergyman Rev. Elizabeth Miller was therefore quite apprehensive. She had come in answer to an appeal to her assembly, the American Baptist Convention of Valley Forge where she was head of the Division of Christian Social Concern.[3] Miller joined the double columns of forty marching down the broad low-tide beach. They were protected by an assorted group of state and local officers who formed a sort of corridor through which the marchers were funneled into the water. They halted in knee-deep water before an opposing segregationist white crowd of about one hundred stretched across the mouth of the funnel. The marchers were

---

3. The Valley Forge Convention had given Dr. King the Dahlberg Peace Award. Taylor Branch: *Pillar of Fire*, New York, 1998, p. 376.

abused, insulted and assaulted in some cases when an officer of the law with a bullhorn warned that anyone who interfered with the integrated swimmers would be arrested. This was a radical departure from the old policy under which the black victims used to be arrested. It came as a rude shock to the whites. They grew more rowdy. Several of them knocked down Shuttlesworth and a visiting Episcopal minister off their feet thereby exposing Miller to the segregationists. Three white women rushed at Miller, knocked her down then pummeled her with a rubber thong sandal. This set in motion a general assault on the marchers. The law-officers reacted strongly and moved to make arrests. Some segregationists resisted fiercely so much so that one had to be clubbed by the officers to subdue him. The sight of a bleeding white was most unexpected. When some officers started taking sides, a fist-fight erupted amongst the law-officers themselves!

The white population was outraged over these developments. About five hundred of them held a rally that night at the Old Slave Market. Confederate flags were fluttering at the site. When the state troopers arrived with their prisoners, the white-crowd gesticulated violently demanding release of the arrested segregationists. The law-officers cowed down before the crowd and released the white prisoners. A free for all followed. The blacks were severely assaulted. Many were seriously injured. A number of black women had their clothes torn off when they were being clawed and beaten by the white thugs. A few demonstrators fought back aggressively, sending three whites to the hospital. Law-officers promptly forgot the negotiated agreement and started arresting the blacks instead of the perpetrators of criminal acts. "White Justice" was on full display. Back at the St. Paul's King preached to the wounded and the rescued. He informed New York: "This is the worst night we've ever had."[4]

The Black citizens in St. Augustine numbered a mere 3,700. They could not possibly face the combined onslaught of KKK and John Birch Society without outside assistance. The level of violence and lawlessness perpetrated by the white hoodlums far exceeded that of even Birmingham. Not that the Negroes stopped demonstrating; far from it. They did so every day. But whenever they ventured out as a group, they were greeted by showers of bricks, bottles and abuses. They were humiliated day in and day out. When the situation became intolerable, the local civil rights leader, Robert Hayling requested the SCLC on February 9, 1964, to come to their aid, to join the struggle with the following objectives in mind:

4. Branch Taylor: *Pillar of Fire*; New York. 1998, pp. 376-379.

- Formation of a bi-racial committee to redress their grievances;
- Desegregation of public accommodations;
- Employment of Blacks in such jobs as policemen, firemen, odd jobs in the municipal departments;
- Withdraw charges framed on account of peaceful demonstrations protesting for their constitutional rights.

Hundreds of volunteers were arrested and jailed. So was Dr. King. He appealed for outside assistance on 28th May. Dr. King and other senior leaders of SCLC held frustratingly long parleys with the State and Federal officials concerned. Finally, the State Governor managed to persuade four distinguished citizens of St. Augustine to serve on a biracial committee to find ways and means to resolve the racial imbroglio. In return, the Negroes agreed to suspend their protest marches. Meanwhile, the Civil Rights Act was passed by Congress. It was signed into the statute books two days before the fourth of July. Dr. King and party were assured by the local business community and the officials that they would abide by the provisions of the act. It was certainly a significant achievement. However, there was an apprehension in the minds of many that the new Act would suffer the same fate as the Supreme Court ruling on school-desegregation. The issue of integration of public accommodation was particularly singled out for massive white defiance leading to more violence against the Blacks. However, Martin did not share this pessimism. He was of the view that the new legislation was not an act of 'charity by white America' bestowed on a 'supine Black America', nor was it the result of enlightened leadership by the judiciary ... This legislation was first written in the streets[5] through the sacrifices made and sufferings undergone by millions of Blacks all over the United States. Many had laid down their lives for the cause of this Legislation.

The new law also focused attention on economic needs of the Black minority, as well as job opportunities, equal health care, de-facto integration of schools besides provision of low cost low-rental housing for the Negro. It was a sort of omnibus Act that would, hopefully, ensure equal protection of the law and justice for all. The end of police brutalities and white-violence was nearer than ever before. However, immediately following the passage of this law some unfortunate incidents shook the nation. Some of these were:

---

5. King Martin Luther: op. cit. (Autobiography), p. 245.

- The Republican Convention held in San Francisco in which Barry Goldwater was nominated as the Party's candidate for Presidency.
- Kidnapping and hideous lynching of three civil rights workers in Mississippi, two of whom were whites.
- Outbreak of race-riots in several Northern cities, July 18-21, 1964. This racial violence was the expression of growing Black dissatisfaction with life in the urban North. The first major eruption occurred in Harlem after the police shot a black criminal suspect. Soon the riots spread to New Jersey, Chicago and Philadelphia.[6]

Both Dr. King and Mahatma Gandhi achieved their respective objectives, although the means varied considerably. Gandhi fasted as an act of penance, against the sins of others, against communal riots and injustice, for the benefit of depressed classes or untouchables, as a prayer, for self-discipline and self-purification, *et al.* King followed the Gandhian technique of non-violent mass movement without having to resort to self-inflicted pain and anguish of fasting as a weapon.

Malcolm X often indulged in lot of rhetoric about reciprocal bleeding; but he did not formulate or implement any program of action to do so. He talked a lot about organizing self-defence units in order to give the Ku Klux Klan a taste of their own medicine, but again he did nothing to put this threat into practice. In fact, he also sent a telegram to George Lincoln Rockwell to this effect but did not pursue the threat to its logical conclusion. Malcolm himself never even carried a gun. It came as a shock to many when Ronald Stokes, an unarmed Muslim Minister was shot dead in cold blood by the Los Angeles police, Malcolm and his cronies did not react at all, except to pray to Allah. All said and done, Malcolm certainly was not the type of man who believed in the Muslim tradition of "an eye for an eye".

---

6. Stearns N. Peter: op. cit. p. 920.

25

Ole Miss[1]

Racism is a philosophy based on contempt for life. It is the arrogant assertion that one race is the centre of value and object of devotion, before which other races must kneel in submission. Racism is total estrangement and is not a mere American phenomenon. Its vicious grasp knows no geographical boundaries.

James Howard Meredith was a native Mississippian from Kosciusko in Atlanta County in the central part of the State. On 20th January 1961 he, a veteran of nine years in the Air Force, requested the University of Mississippi for an application form for transfer from the all-black college to the all-white University. While returning the completed form, he explained: "I am an American-Mississippi-Negro citizen ... I certainly hope that this matter will be handled in a manner that will be complimentary to the University and to the State of Mississippi. Of course I am the one that will, no doubt, suffer the greatest consequences of this event." It was believed that 'Ole Miss' — as the University at Oxford was known throughout the State of Mississippi — had never admitted a Negro. Perhaps, it was conveniently forgotten that during 1945-46 Harry S. Murphy, a light-skinned Negro, had studied there as a Navy V-12 student. Since the University was established way back in 1848, possibility of a number of other Negro students having passed through its portals cannot be ruled out. Be that as it may, the University offered complicated academic reasons for rejecting Meredith's candidature.

James Meredith had applied for admission to the whites-only University because he felt a "Divine Responsibility" to break white

1. Main source for this chapter: Schlesinger M. Arthur, Jr.; pp 801-809; 822-24; and Sanford Wexler: op. cit pp. 143-147.

supremacy. Governor Ross Barnett was adamant and would not let "that boy" backed by "Communist" NAACP get into 'Ole Miss'. Meredith therefore filed a lawsuit in the United States District Court of Southern Mississippi citing 'race' as the grounds for being turned down. NAACP Legal Defence Fund represented him in Court. But the Federal District Judge dismissed Meredith's plea. Meredith appealed. In June 1962 the Fifth Circuit Court accepted his plea in that he had been turned down "solely because he was a Negro" and reversed Judge Mize's decision. Since the Governor continued to disregard the judicial process, Justice Hugo Black issued an enforcing order from the Supreme Court backed by federal marshals ordered to the Oxford area. The Governor promptly declared: "We will not surrender to the evil and illegal forces of tyranny." In his televised speech on September 13, 1962, he told Mississippi residents: "There is no case in history where the Caucasian race has survived racial integration. ... We must either submit to the unlawful dictates of the federal government or stand up like men and tell them, 'Never'". A week later the State Board of Trustees for the University gave Barnett "full power, authority, right, and discretion of this Board to act upon all matters pertaining to, or concerned with" Meredith's registration, admission and attendance. This resolution of the Board had, in effect, made Barnett registrar of the university. That same day, Barnett sped from Jackson to Oxford to personally deny Meredith's entry to Ole Miss. Thereupon the Attorney-general, Robert Kennedy telephoned the Governor and told him that, since he was proposing to defy a federal court order, they should preferably workout a solution together. But the Governor remained adamant. His response was the neo-Confederate rhetoric. The legislature, the public and print media were all behind the Governor's defiance of federal authority. However, in compliance with the federal court order, James Meredith, accompanied by federal marshals, presented himself at Oxford for registration. There was excitement all round. The students were marching around the Campus singing: "Glory, Glory, Segregation". The Governor "grandiloquently read aloud a long proclamation rejecting Meredith's application." After concluding reading of his proclamation, he thrust the document in the hands of Meredith, telling him: "Take it and abide by it."

Racial discrimination and segregationist policies of the South had given rise to a state of constitutional crisis. It was a question of federal versus the state, an open defiance of the federal authority of the President by the Governor of a state. "Constitutional scholarship had evidently languished in Jackson since 1832".[2] The irony of the situation was that just two days after Governor Ross Barnett's public defiance of the Federal Government, the country marked the first century of the Emancipation Proclamation. The President in his message emphasized: "The essential effort, the sustained struggle was borne by the Negro alone with steadfast dignity and faith. ... Abraham Lincoln emancipated the slaves, but in this century our Negro citizens have emancipated themselves." Meanwhile, the Attorney-General had already responded to Governor Barnett's open defiance of federal authority by citing the three top officers of the University of Mississippi for contempt of court. As soon as they appeared in the court, they readily agreed to enroll James Meredith. However, the Governor refused to change track. He told the Attorney-General: "I consider that the Mississippi courts as high as any other court and a lot more capable. ... I am going to obey the laws of Mississippi" to which the Attorney-General responded: "My job is to enforce the laws of the United States — I intend to fulfill it." The next day he obtained a restraining order from the Fifth Circuit Court enjoining the Governor and other state officials not to interfere with Meredith's registration. But when Meredith tried again to register, the Governor himself physically barred his way while the excited crowd of students shouted: "Communists ... Go home, nigger."

In those days when the cold war was raging at freezing point, the tag of communism was one easy way out to eliminate inconvenient political opposition. The white southerners lost no time or opportunity to put this technique into practice, collectively against NAACP, and individually against Martin and some of his colleagues. In fact this label was stuck on NAACP in Alabama and the organization was declared illegal even though there was not an iota of proof to bring home the allegations. NAACP was well known to be fanatically anti-communist and its allegiance to America was beyond any doubt. They were as far away from Moscow as the earth was from the Mars. But ... NAACP was branded communist and declared an illegal outfit. Similarly, Martin and other civil rights workers were labeled communist agitators. The racist Southerners were confident that if they could convince the American public that the civil rights movement had been infiltrated by agents of Moscow, they would be able to discredit them so much as to be able to cut off public moral and financial support to the Negro freedom struggle for equal rights. In this nefarious plot, the white Southerners could bank on the FBI and its bag of dirty tricks. The association of Stanley Levison, Jack O'Dell and possibly Bayard Rustin too

2. Schlesinger M. Arthur, Jr.: op. cit. p. 803.

with Martin and the NAACP provided some ground, howsoever slippery, for the attempt to stick the 'dirty label'. However, Martin was fully aware of the pitfalls and made doubly sure that he and his colleagues kept themselves miles away from anything that even remotely smelt of a communist connection. Hoover and his band of tricksters did not make much headway either. Moreover, Martin went a step further. In one of his sermons entitled "How Should a Christian View Communism?" Martin proclaimed that "Communism and Christianity are fundamentally incompatible". The crux of Communist ideology is "atheistic materialism' while the Christian doctrine is essentially "theistic idealism".[3]

The situation became highly critical at Meredith's third attempt to register. Robert Kennedy wanted to avoid bad blood. He instructed Meredith and the federal marshals to withdraw. The next day the Governor was found guilty of civil contempt and ordered to purge himself by the following Tuesday, or face arrest and a fine of ten thousand dollars a day. The President and the Attorney-General were resolute in their determination to ensure implementation of civil rights of their people irrespective of the colour of their skin. The Governor was equally resolute in continuing to defy the federal authority of the President. The constitutional crisis arising out of de-segregation and implementation of equal rights and opportunities had gone much beyond the point of no return. In a way, the philosophy of non-violence and Satyagraha as preached by Gandhi and imbibed by Dr. Martin Luther King Jr. was coming to full blossom. On Friday, 28th September, the Attorney-General met with General Maxwell Taylor to complete the formalities for troop-deployment to enforce the federal laws. Obviously, all this planning was being done in tight secrecy.

The next afternoon, Saturday 29th September, a secret meeting was held in the office of the President attended by the Attorney-General, Harvard Professor Arthur M. Schlesinger Jr., Burke Marshal and Kenneth O'Donnell. The Vice President was conspicuous by his absence. The omission was all the more glaring because of the highly volatile and complex situation that the Federal Government was faced with. In a final effort to bring this affair to a peaceful end, the President put in a personal call to Governor Barnett. While the meeting was awaiting the Governor's call, there was palpable tension in the air, made light by the fraternal banter and little jokes for which the two Brothers were well known. Finally, the silence of the room was shattered. "Governor, this is the President of the United States. ... I am concerned about this matter as I know you must be. ... Here's my problem, Governor. I

3. King M.L.K.: *Strength to Love*; Fortress, Philadelphia, 1963, pp. 96-98. Also, James H. Cone: op. cit. p. 281.

don't know Nr. Meredith, and I didn't put him in there. But under the Constitution I have to carry out the law. I want your help in doing it." The Governor proposed to send the Mississippi lawyer, Tom Watkins to meet with the Attorney-general in Washington to present a new plan. The President responded: "... We have two or three problems. Firstly, the Court's order gives you till Tuesday to permit the entry of Mr. Meredith. What is your position on that? ... The Attorney-General can talk to Watkins tomorrow. I want to work this out in an amicable way. I don't want a lot of people down there to be hurt or killed." Watkins came to Washington with the suggestion to sneak in Meredith to Jackson and register him there. This back-door solution was not acceptable to Washington. There was now no alternative to a collision between the national and the state governments. The situation was indeed explosive. After midnight the President issued orders federalizing the Mississippi National Guards[4] and, concurrently, the Army was ordered out to Memphis. In the face of these developments, Governor Barnett capitulated.

On Sunday night, September 30, Meredith was flown from Memphis, Tennessee, to Oxford in a federal plane. He was met at the University airport by U.S. Deputy Attorney-General Nicholas Katzenbach and driven to the Campus in a convoy of military trucks and automobiles. In a few hours Meredith, accompanied by federal marshals led by their Chief, James McShane arrived at the Campus and went off to a dormitory. The Deputy Attorney-General and other federal officials waited in the Lyceum which housed the University's administrative buildings. Before one knew whether he was coming or going, a hostile mob had surrounded the Lyceum, shouting slogans: "Kill the nigger-loving bastards". Stones and bottles were flying all over. A number of federal marshals were hurt, but they stood their ground. At last, a few tear gas shells were fired, but to no effect. Soon the menacing mob had swelled to nearly 2,500. Confederate slogans were in the air. Some shots came from that direction. Katzenbach concluded that the time had come to call in the Army. A federalized Nation Guard unit was summoned from Oxford, while the regular Army started moving in by helicopters for which the necessary formal orders were issued by the President in Washington. Meanwhile the battle-royal raged between the well armed mob and hapless National Guardsmen many of whom were injured till the regular army troops arrived at the scene from Memphis. Two men were killed in the mêlée, one of whom was a French reporter, Paul Guihard, a correspondent from Agence France-Presse. The other fatal casualty was Roy Gunter,

4. Later, President Johnson followed this as precedence to federalize the Alabama National Guards.

killed by a stray .38-caliber bullet. The federal troops joined the marshals around 5:00 a.m. and drove off the rioters. Chief United States Marshal James P. McShane escorted Meredith to the office of the University Registrar on October 1, 1962, and Meredith was enrolled at 8:30 a.m. That evening more than 5,000 soldiers and federalized national guards patrolled Oxford, a town of just 6,500.

The army troops stayed on the Campus for a few weeks while about 500 marshals accompanied Meredith to classes for many months thereafter. All the troops were withdrawn on June 5, 1963, while Meredith graduated on August 18, 1963 with a Bachelor of Arts degree in political science. At the graduation ceremony he wore a Ross Barnett campaign button on his graduation gown. The button was inscribed "Never, Never" and Meredith wore it upside down!

> The future of the United States of America may well be determined here, in Mississippi, for it is here that democracy faces its most serious challenge. Can we have government in Mississippi which represents all of the people? This is the question that must be answered in the affirmative if these United States are to continue to give moral leadership to the Free World.

President Kennedy had upheld the federal authority and established the principle. He had proved to his countrymen, and the world at large, as to what constitutes leadership at the national level. His action had a profound effect, particularly in Africa. The "Third World" was aghast at the happenings in the most powerful nation of the world. There was all round disappointment and depression over the developments in Oxford area. Even Martin King who had profound regard for President Kennedy remarked that the Blacks were being used as pawns while "voting registration strategy was merely a White House device to enlarge the black constituency for the next election."[5] This was indeed an uncharitable remark by a man of the caliber of Dr. Martin Luther King Jr. While commenting on the recent events, King said, "A sweeping revolutionary force was being pressed into a narrow tunnel." He therefore, in consultation with the SCLC leadership, decided to accord the highest priority to desegregation and Birmingham was chosen as the primary target.

Throughout the above period the United States was going through a life-and-death type crisis. But the white clergy remained totally silent; and if at all they reacted, it was only in support of the evil forces of segregation. That was White Christianity against Black Christianity, as if Jesus was born

---

5. Burns M. James: op. cit. p. 366.

a Caucasian. Indeed, religious fanaticism knows no bounds, moral or physical. The deafening silence of Montgomery, Alabama, continued to prevail in the lush green fertile countryside of Mississippi dotted with beautiful churches with tall spires and brick monuments dedicated to the glory of the Lord. "Where was the cry of the Lord's prophets?" In deep anguish, King wrote: "When I review the painful memory of the last week at oxford and cannot recall a single voice 'crying in the wilderness', the questions are still the same: 'What kind of people worship there? Who is their God?'" Unfortunately, white Christians in general and their clergy in particular were totally blind to the truth of the gospel: "All Men are Created Equal". Indeed, Christian identity of the whites was in jeopardy. No doubt the black clergy, by and large, supported the civil rights movements; but there were many who were either silent or luke-warm in their denunciation of segregation. How can a minister preach the glories of heaven when hellish social conditions prevail in his congregation on earth?

University of Alabama in Tuscaloosa

Two Negro students applied for admission to the University of Alabama in Tuscaloosa for the summer session commencing 1st June. Defying the law of the land, admission was denied. On 21st May a Federal District Judge ruled that the University of Alabama must admit the two Negro students. But Governor George Wallace replied: "and I will be present to bar the entrance of any Negro who attempts to enroll." On 12th June the President instructed the Governor not to try and stop integration of the University at Tuscaloosa. But on the next morning the Governor personally blocked the entry of the Negro students and federal marshals into the administrative building. The President was the last man to accept this open defiance of his legitimate federal authority. He promptly ordered federalization of the Alabama National Guards. When the Guardsmen arrived at the campus, better sense prevailed on the Governor. He withdrew quietly. The students were registered. In the evening the President addressed the Nation on television:

> "It ought to be possible for American students of any colour to attend any public institution without having to be backed up by troops. It ought to be possible for American consumers of any colour to receive equal service in places of public accommodation, such as hotels and restaurants, theatres and retail stores without being forced to resort to demonstrations in the street, and it ought to be possible for American citizens of any colour to register and to vote in a free election without interference or fear of reprisal.... But this is not the case.... This is a moral issue — as old as the scriptures and ... as clear as the American Constitution.

The university admissions apart, there was serious danger of democracy being derailed in the highly racist segregationist Mississippi.

> There is no human institution but has its dangers. The greater the institution, the greater the chances of abuse. Democracy is a great institution and therefore liable to be greatly abused. The remedy therefore is not avoidance of democracy but reduction of the possibility of abuse to a minimum. The spirit of democracy is not a mechanical thing to be adjusted by abolition of forms. It requires change of heart.

On 21 June 1964 the Black leadership had planned to launch the "Freedom Summer" campaign in the State. On the eve of this event, three civil rights workers — James Chaney, Andrew Goodman and Michael Schwerner — were found missing after their arrest in Philadelphia. This high handed treatment of arrested personnel caused considerable consternation amongst the Black community, all the more so since their mutilated bodies were discovered on August 4, 1964. Two of the victims of this hideous lynching were whites.[6] There was panic and the Blacks were seething with anger. Retaliation was in the air.

Meanwhile, the Republican Party nominated Barry Goldwater as its candidate for Presidency. In so far as Martin was concerned, the choice was unfortunate and disastrous for the simple reason that Goldwater advocated a 'narrow nationalism, a crippling isolationism' besides a trigger-happy attitude in foreign policy. On the home front, "Goldwater represented an unrealistic conservatism that was totally out of touch with the realities"[7] of social and economic issues facing the country. His elevation to the Presidency would have reversed the trend of Black emancipation from the shackles of segregation and racism. 'Freedom Democratic Party' was the answer to the impending developments which could well have proved disastrous. By this time Martin was in the thick of domestic politics!

Concurrently, a team of more than a thousand white students from the North, under the leadership of Bob Moses, in coordination with the Blacks of Mississippi, initiated a program of voter registration. It was one of the most creative attempts to radically change the Negro's life in the most segregationist State in the nation. The Blacks were on the move in the national political arena. It was the culmination of about one decade of Martin's nonviolent mass movement. What King was fighting for was not a war between whites and Negroes; it was a 'conflict between justice and injustice'.

---

6. Stearns N. Peter: op. cit. p. 920.
7. King Martin Luther Jr.: *Autobiography;* p. 247.

26

Martin Elects the President

There is no human institution but has its dangers. The greater the institution, the greater the chances of abuse. Democracy is a great institution and therefore it is liable to be greatly abused. The remedy therefore is not avoidance of democracy but reduction of the possibility of abuse to a minimum.

The Presidency of the United States is, by itself, a unique institution demanding the highest standard of personal leadership, devotion and integrity. From about the mid-1950's onwards, the civil rights issue was the most pressing and thorny problem for the Administration. The word Negro was an anathema to the Black community of America who were not prepared to accept segregation in public places, particularly segregation in schools, and the status of 'second class citizenship' to which they had been reduced by the white majority. Soon they were to be called Afro-Americans and segregation in schools was abolished. The acceptance speech was the last essential pre-election item of the nomination-campaign process. On Friday, 15th July 1960 John F. Kennedy addressed eighty thousand people in Los Angeles Coliseum:[1]

> We stand today at the edge of a New Frontier — the frontier of the 1960's — a frontier of unknown opportunities and perils, a frontier of unfulfilled hopes and threats. ... The New Frontier of which I speak is not a set of promises — it is a set of challenges. It sums up not what I intend to offer the American people but what I intend to ask of them. ..."

In the election campaign, Kennedy incorporated the plight of the Negroes with a tilt towards emotionalism and rational statistics. "The

1. *Triumph and Tragedy*, p. 144.

Negro baby has one-half, regardless of his talents, statistically has one-half as much chance of finishing high school as the white-baby, one-third as much chance of finishing college, one-fourth as much chance of becoming a professional man or woman, four time as much chance of being out of work. ... Only a President willing to use all the resources of his office can provide the leadership, determination and the direction ... to eliminate racial and religious discrimination from American society." John Kennedy also advocated more vigorous measures to win the Negro the right to vote, the right to employment, and the right to federal appointments, especially in the Foreign Service where there were only twenty-six Negro officers at that point of time. In 1960 when the Cold War was at its coldest and man's achievements in outer space exceeded all expectations, the Americans elected John Fitzgerald Kennedy, a Democratic Senator from Massachusetts, as their 35th President with Senate majority leader Lyndon B. Johnson of Texas as the Vice President. Although the Negroes overwhelmingly voted[2] for Kennedy, he won against the Republican candidate Richard M. Nixon by an extremely narrow margin of one half of one per cent. In other words, it was the Negro vote that placed JFK in the White House. However, that vote did not come merely by the emotional appeal incorporated by Senator Kennedy in his election campaign. When Martin had been sentenced by the Georgia judge to four months hard labour for a trifling traffic offence, and Martin had been shifted to a distant countryside jail, Coretta was mortally afraid: "they are going to kill him, I know they are going to kill him," she told Harris Wofford, the Civil Rights Coordinator for the Presidential candidate. Harris spoke to Morris Abram[3] in Atlanta who in turn spoke to the Mayor who informed the media that "in response to Senator Kennedy's personal intervention he has reached an agreement with Negro leaders for the release of King and other sit-in prisoners." But in fact, till that point in time, the Senator knew nothing about Harris's call to Morris and the latter's to the Mayor Bill Hartsfield! The Blacks were jubilant while the white Southern Democrats were livid with consternation. However, while all prisoners from the sit-in at Magnolia Room in Rich's famous store were released from the local jail, Martin was shifted to the distant prison in the 'cracker country'. A most dangerous situation indeed. Meanwhile, Sargent Shriver who held the Civil Rights appointment in the election-campaign prevailed upon the Senator to

2. Both the Gallup and Harris Poll assessed the Negro vote in favour of Kennedy to be around 68 to 70 percent.
3. Morris Abram was a leading lawyer and strong supporter of civil liberties movement. He was also close to the Mayor William Hartsfield.

call Coretta. The Senator talked to her warmly and reassuringly. King Sr. made the entire episode public. And that did it!

On October 28, 1960, the congregation in Ebenezer Baptist Church at Atlanta accorded a rousing welcome to Martin. He told the congregation:

> "I never intend to reject a man running for President of the United States just because he is a Catholic. Religious bigotry is as immoral, undemocratic, un-American and un-Christian as racial bigotry."

That call from JFK to Coretta and subsequent intervention by Robert Kennedy made all the difference to the outcome of the election — it put JFK in the White House.[4] On his part, John Kennedy categorically stated that the Civil Rights issue was of overwhelming moral significance to him; and if elected he would use the full weight of his office to completely eliminate second-class citizenship in America.

King met with the President in the White House for the first time in the spring of 1961. A clergyman, always a clergyman! His moral approach and tone completely put off the President. In turn, Martin was also completely cut up with the President on account of his plans to delay legislative action on Civil Rights. While the Black leadership expected the new President to move heaven and earth to get the Civil Rights legislation through, JFK had his own compulsions. The Southern power in the Congress was a racist Command Post in itself. They held chairmanship of key congressional committees and were past masters in parliamentary delaying tactics. Senate filibuster was their favourite weapon. Thus the Southerners could hold up not only the civil rights but the entire legislative program of the President. The President's hands were tied, and the only freedom that he could exercise to meet the Black wishes was through executive action. The appointment of his brother, Robert Kennedy as the Attorney General and in-charge of civil rights matters, was certainly a step in that direction. However, the Black leadership was not satisfied with this policy of 'WAIT'. Martin's response was: "Wait! For years I have heard the word 'Wait'. We have waited for more than three hundred and forty years for our rights."

---

4. More than two-thirds of the Blacks voted for Kennedy. The Negro turn-out was also substantially higher than in 1956. JFK won by a paper-thin margin of only 120,000 popular votes and a mere eighty-four electoral votes. While Kennedy had 49.7 percent of the voters behind him, Nixon had 49.6 percent. And it was the first Democratic victory since 1932. ... "The finest strategies are usually the result of accidents." — Harris Wofford on JFK.

Nixon had learnt a lesson of a lifetime from that electoral defeat. During the 1966-67, one major issue for Presidential Campaign was the Civil Rights'. And Nixon laid down the following position for the Republican Party:[5]

> 'Southern Republicans must not climb aboard the sinking ship of racial injustice. Any Republican victory that would come from courting racists, black or white, would be a defeat for our future in the South and Party in the nation.'

The use of the phrase 'Black or White' was a clever stratagem in asmuchas it did not wish to rub either of the two races on the wrong side. Crafty as usual!

President Kennedy was the youngest ever to be elected to this most powerful job in the world — he was barely forty-three years when he assumed the Presidency. Unfortunately he could serve for just two years and ten months when, on 22nd November 1963, he was shot and killed by a sniper in Dallas, Texas while riding in an open car — a fearless man who left behind memorable words: "Let us never fear to negotiate. But let us never negotiate out of fear".[6]

---

5. Wickers Tom: *One Of Us*, p. 281.
6. Kennedy was the fourth President of the United States to be assassinated while in office, the other three were Abraham Lincoln, James Garfield and William McKinley.

Time: Man of the Year 1963

27

Time's Man of the Year 1963

On Cover Page: February 18, 1957

The average man reaches the heights may be in his late forties or early fifties. But when you reach it so young, your life becomes a kind of decrescendo. You feel yourself fading from the screen at a time you should just be starting to work towards your goal. A man who hits the peak at twenty-seven has a tough job ahead. People will be expecting him to pull rabbits out of the hat for the rest of his life. And if he doesn't, or there are no rabbits to be pulled out, then they will say he is no good.

The Year 1963 was the centennial of the Emancipation Proclamation, and it was also significant inasmuch as it was the most decisive year in the Negro's fight for equality as a result of the terrible heart-rending brutal atrocities heaped on the black populace of Birmingham by Public Safety Commissioner Theophilus Eugene ("Bull") Connor. Indeed it was the year of Birmingham, when twenty million Negro citizens of the United States impressed the issue of Civil Rights on the Administration and the Congress through massive non-violent demonstrations, protest marches accompanied by psalm singing, sit-ins, and filling up the jails. The man who made this possible was the Black leader, Reverend Martin Luther King Jr. *Time* Magazine chose him as the "Man of the Year" and Martin was on the cover page of the Magazine issue dated 3rd January 1964 — a rare and sought after Honor. Until then, Emperor Haile Selassie was the only black person to have achieved this distinction in 1927; Martins was now the second while Dr. Nelson Mandela spearheading the South African Blacks' struggle got his turn much later in 1993. In the words of Andre Brink: "As the world's most famous prisoner, and now his country's leader, he exemplifies a moral integrity that shines far beyond South Africa". Mandela had spent twenty-seven years of his life in prison, a world record indeed. No doubt his first name, Rolihlahla, was prophetic inasmuch as it meant "trouble-maker"![1] But Mandela himself was modest enough to admit that "I was not a messiah, but an ordinary man who had become a leader because of extraordinary circumstances." Initially he believed in, and practised non-violence but later took up armed struggle against the white regime. Ultimately, he succeeded in transforming a brutal repressive racial system into an open democracy.

Martin was endowed with that rare quality that enabled him to claim full attention from his audience, their attention indeed arrested by the speaker. He stirred in his people a certain Christian forbearance that 'nourishes hope and smothers injustice'. Above all, Dr. King was a 'humble man, down to earth, honest' who sought to save the nation and its soul, and not the Negro only. He proved beyond any doubt that the misconception of Negro being sub-human was merely a myth. Dr. King was therefore quite aptly called the symbol of the Revolution.

Birmingham became a symbol of police brutality on a scale that none could imagine possible in the civilized democratic polity of the United States — Birmingham with its snarling dogs let loose on the peaceful demonstrators; with its bombing of churches and black residences; its shots in the night and deaths in the streets; its high pressure water hoses pinning men, women and children to the ground with the police using their batons *ad lib*; *et al.* The cap-stone was laid by the Federal Government turning its face away from reality, maintaining silence all the while. They did not react lest the Southern States get infuriated. Martin and his top-team were not even invited for a meeting with the President despite their repeated efforts in that direction. President Eisenhower merely responded with a statement: "you can't legislate men's hearts." Least expected words from a General who had commanded the greatest amphibian operation in history, who was the Supreme Commander of Supreme Headquarters of the Allied Expeditionary Force, SHAEF; who had specifically asked for Black troops as reinforcements when he was in real thick jam. Indeed, the Blacks had fought gallantly for their country, proved their worth and developed a new sense of self-confidence in their capabilities, replacing the age-old inferiority complex.

Martin Luther King had a family background of standing up for dignity, and jealously guarded their rights. His maternal grandfather, the

1. Mandela's primary school teacher took the liberty of adding Nelson before his first name to sound it great, rather than a mere 'trouble-maker'!

Rev. A.D. Williams was one of the first leaders of NAACP in Georgia. When one of the local newspapers made some disparaging remarks about Negro voters, he organized a boycott of that paper. Again, he was in the forefront for the struggle to get black teachers salaries at par with the whites, as well as abolition of 'Jim Crow' elevators in the Atlanta courthouse.

Notwithstanding his upbringing in a prosperous middle class family environment rich in love and warmth, Martin Luther King Jr. tried to commit suicide twice, before he was thirteen. He seemed to have a tendency towards self-destruction. Is that what led him to a severe confrontation with the white supremacy that had no hesitation in letting loose snarling dogs and high pressure water hoses on peaceful women and children protesters? Be that as it may, he was a bright student and finished his graduate-education by the age of fifteen by skipping a year. Although his bent of mind was towards medicine or law as a profession, his family wanted him to continue the tradition of serving the ministry. And he made up his mind to do so after he had read and re-read Thoreau's essay, '*Civil Disobedience*'. This route took him to Gandhian philosophy and technique of *Satyagraha* and *Ahimsa*. He said: "From my background I gained my regulating of Christian ideals. From Gandhi I learned my operational technique."

Montgomery Bus Boycott in 1955 was his first major battle, while December 1961 saw King in the midst of Albany mass protest. While the former earned him worldwide attention, the latter proved a fiasco whose ramifications, fortunately for Martin, were restricted to local environment only. However, Albany had a positive fall-out too. While it is virtually impossible to win against political power structure without the advantage of votes, economic power structure was certainly easier to tackle. The Supreme Court order forbidding 'Jim Crow' seating in the city buses proved a boon to uphold his public image.

Two years later, in 1963 Dr. King took the fight to Birmingham, the 'most thoroughly segregated big city in the US'. Since the brutal Bull Connor was then running for mayor, Martin undertook a whirlwind speaking tour of sixteen cities across the nation and made twenty-eight speeches during January 16 and March 29, thereby avoiding giving campaign fuel to the Bull. Martin was back to Birmingham in the first week of April to undertake "Project C" — C for Confrontation.

"The Negroes had created their crisis — and Connor had made it a success. President Kennedy told Dr. King: 'The Civil Rights Movement owes Bull Connor as much as it owes Abraham Lincoln'. That was at best an oversimplification; nevertheless, because of Eugene Connor, the riots smeared the front pages of the world press, outraged millions of people. ..."[2]. The more vicious the police brutality, the more the demonstrations followed by sit-ins in every major city in the North and a number of new places in the South. It was vicious circle, giving rise to more demands by the black population for better job opportunities, effective all round desegregation. At this stage a number of whites also joined in the protest marches since they were convinced of the moral basis of the agitations. The white clergy that was earlier against the Negroes' resistance was by now in the forefront of the whites' participation so much so that Rev. Dr. Eugene Carson Blake, executive head of the United Presbyterian Church in the United States was arrested when he too joined one of the protest marches. A series of protest marches, sit-ins, demonstrations and agitations culminated in the famous 'March on Washington'. "It was remarkable spectacle". The speech by Martin Luther King totally captivated the crowd. His articulation of grievances of the Black community was lucid, logical and explicit. It was heard with rapt attention by one and all. Dr. King said: "When we let freedom ring, when we let it ring from every village and every hamlet, from every state and every city, we will be able to speed up that day when all of God's children, black men and white men, Jews and Gentiles, Protestants and Catholics, will be able to join hands and sing, in the words of the old Negro spiritual — We Shall Overcome.

Hereafter integration and biracial approach through common committees to resolve local inequities became the SOP (Standard Operating Procedure). New job opportunities opened up almost everywhere. Various labour unions opened their doors to black workmen. Some clergymen welcomed Negroes to their white congregations. Some adoption agencies went so far as to seek white families for Negro children. There was backlash reaction here and there, in the western states in particular besides, of course, the South. States of Alabama and Mississippi continued to resist. So did the city of Danville, Va. which was notorious for its record of police brutalities comparable to Birmingham. But the kinks were resolved with the passage of time. However, it was in the field of integrated housing that maximum resistance was encountered. Perhaps, it still prevails even today, albeit at a much reduced scale.

The Negroes were proud of their new found status in mixed society. They became more sophisticated in their social etiquette and behaviour. The old inferiority and psychological complexes started giving way to

---

2. *Time* Magazine dated 3rd January 1964.

positive thinking self-image. They were no longer ashamed of their African roots; on the contrary they now considered Africa as their proud heritage. And who made this possible? Rev. Martin Luther King, Jr., who in little more than a year had 'risen from nowhere to become one of the nation's remarkable leaders of men'. Dr. King achieved this extraordinarily singular mass transformation through the Gandhian principle of nonviolence, a potent weapon indeed. For him: "The strong man is the man who can stand up for his rights and not hit back".[3]

3. *Time*, February 18, 1957.

Dr. King receiving Noble Peace Prize: December 1964

28

Noble Peace Price

Public Opinion alone can keep a society pure and healthy. Strength does not come from physical capacity. It comes from an indomitable will. Occasionally in life there are those moments of unutterable fulfillment which cannot be completely explained by those symbols called words. Their meaning can only be articulated by the inaudible language of the heart.

Unfortunately, 1963 was also a year of assassinations in the United States, the major casualty being The President himself. Edgar Evers in Jackson, Mississippi; William Moore in Alabama; and last but not the least, four Negro children in Birmingham. No doubt all these murders were politically motivated. The next year, 1964 was equally significant in the history of the U.S. in as much as the year started with Martin Luther King Jr. appearing on the cover of Time magazine as its 'Man of the Year'. He was called the Symbol of the Revolution. To cap it all, the news report that Dr. King had been selected for the award of 1964 Nobel Peace Prize came on 14th October. Martin realized that by this award he had been chosen as a symbol of the Black Freedom Struggle. History had thrust Martin into an historic position of leadership to a level much beyond Montgomery, Birmingham or the Washington March, and that he had to fulfill this moral responsibility at all costs. But having been deeply involved in the affairs of Selma, King was hospitalized due to fatigue and exhaustion. He was also emotionally drained as a result of the vilification campaign launched against him by the Director of FBI, J. Edgar Hoover. Since he was to go to Norway on 10th December to receive the Prize, the Selma march was temporarily placed in suspended animation.

Council of Federated Organizations (COFO) was composed of SCLC, CORE, NAACP, and SNCC and a number of local groups and small unions. Students were put through short orientation courses in non-violence and sent southwards. These youngsters were required to organize Black communities and persuade them to register to vote. The SNCC were already familiar with the police and 'crackers' and knew what they were up against. By the end of June these youngsters, blacks and whites, were familiar with the brutal methods employed by the Southern racists to suppress the deprived classes. They were beaten, harassed and humiliated during the mini-marches. Although the US District Court had issued an injunction against Sheriff David, it had no effect and the marchers were prevented from proceeding further through the use of physical force. Concurrently, President Johnson, in consultation with the Congressional leaders was giving finishing touches to the Civil Rights Act of 1964. Just as the Act was ready for Presidential signature, three prominent COFO leaders of the Movement were found missing. Later, their mutilated chain-whipped bodies were discovered sending shock waves throughout the nation.

In March 1964 Martin King and Dr. Hayling, a dental surgeon and local leader of NAACP in St. Augustine, had to suffer terribly under the Klan who ruled the countryside without fear of man or God, more so since it was Hayling who had encouraged the sit-ins of 1961. On Easter Sunday of 1964 an inter-racial group of eminent ladies including Mrs. Malcolm Peabody, the mother of Governor Endicott "Chub" Peabody of Massachusetts and Mrs. John Burgess whose husband was the first black bishop in the Episcopal Church, attempted to take communion at St. Augustine's Trinity Episcopal Church. They were not allowed to enter the Church and were arrested. Mrs. Peabody was then seventy-two. Naturally, tension mounted, and King arrived on the scene in May. The Sheriff and the local police chief, glove and hand relationship, informed that the marchers would be in serious danger if they tried to march through Klansmen land. While the leaders of the marchers obtained an injunction against the Sheriff and the police chief, but that did not help at all. The marchers were beaten up as never before. The two leaders were arrested and confined in the local jail for two days.

Meanwhile, the Civil Rights Act of 1964 was signed into law; but it had no effect on the situation in St. Augustine. However, when the Voting Rights Bill was signed on 6th August 1965, the two pieces of legislation were certainly a great advance inasmuch as they provided a high degree of basic legal protection for the Negroes. It was well known that the Southern States directly obstructed the Blacks from exercising their franchise. Even in areas where the Blacks outnumbered the whites, there was no black representation. It had been almost a century of white terrorism at the polls. So King undertook tour of the area to bolster support for the MFDP.

Economic Issues

That is alright as far as it goes; but laws do not fill a stomach. The real issue before the public, mostly the Blacks but some whites too, was the suffering and agony of poverty. Economic and political equality go hand in hand to achieve any degree of tangible progress. It was high time that the Black leadership faced the question of bread and butter, squarely and seriously to ameliorate the economic conditions of the oppressed classes. However, the frustration and disappointments with the authorities had caused King tremendous mental stress and strain. He needed a change badly. So King accepted the invitation of Mayor Willy Brandt of West Berlin and flew to Europe. Rome and Madrid were the next destinations. Moreover, King was more interested in influencing European leaders than those in Africa largely because, in his perception, the former were more influential in molding the world opinion and changing the course of global politics than those in the African continent. Concurrently, Malcolm X had told a rally that the Negroes required a "Mau Mau" — a revolutionary group of Africans in Kenya who were leading a revolt against the British imperialist colonial regime — to win freedom and equality for Negroes in the United States. At that time, the euphoria of Presidential elections was also in the air. King was of the opinion that a white Southern would make a better President than a white Northern. The former will do more good for the Blacks than the latter. King's subtle tilt towards Johnson, and Goldwater's thinly veiled apprehensions against the Blacks, brought the Blacks out into the hustings in exceptionally large numbers in favor of Johnson that resulted in his landslide victory. Most Negroes were quite happy about this outcome. However, through private sources, it was well known that "Nigger is a household word in Johnson's White House...."[1]

Dr. Martin Luther King, Jr. became the 14th American to receive the Nobel Peace Prize. Before Martin, only two other black men had been awarded the Nobel Peace Prize — Dr. Ralph Bunche in 1950 for arranging the Arab-Israeli peace after the partition of Palestine, and Chief Albert John Luthuli for his unrewarded search for racial peace in South Africa in 1961. Luthuli was under detention since 1958 after the "Treason Trials" that resulted in break-up of the African National Congress. There were difficulties about his leaving South Africa to receive the prize but the Government had to relent in the face of international pressure. While the international community rewarded Luthuli for his leadership of the African National Congress, he was arrested by his own Government for exactly

1. Williams A. John: op. cit. p. 73.

the same reason. So on return home, he was again placed under house arrest. Luthuli confessed that his 'greatest inspiration' had been Martin King's *Stride Towards Freedom.*[2] The United States retaliated against the white racist regime of apartheid by banning sale of all arms, ammunition and related defence equipment. Adlai Stevenson called upon all nations to follow the lead of United States in this regard. It was indeed an irony of international diplomacy and travesty of moral principles that the nation that was itself racist and was inflicting segregation on its minority, thought it fit to place an embargo on another country that was following in exactly the same footsteps. Incidentally, Dr. Nelson R. Mandela was also awarded the Nobel Peace Prize (1993) prior to his inauguration as the first democratically elected State President of the Republic of South Africa on May 10, 1994, which office he demitted in June 1999 on the expiry of his term bringing his political career to a voluntary end.

Martin King left the U.S. with a party of twenty-six people comprising of his parents, brother Reverend A.D. King, sister, secretaries, and of course Ralph David Abernathy. While en-route at London, Martin delivered a sermon in the celebrated St. Paul's Cathedral during which he announced that he would donate the entire amount of Prize money ($54,000/-) to civil rights causes. One of the notable newspapers editorialized: "... The Nobel-winner this year is not merely a leader within his own country, but also a symbol of the liberation movement involving hundreds of millions of the people..." Thus the summer of 1964 came to be known as the 'COFO summer'.

Besides the sermon, the high point of the ceremony was the Anglican ritual — "the priests in their vestments, the stately ceremony of the service, and the beautiful singing by the choir of men and the boys whose clear soprano voices were so pure." Martin preached one of his favorite sermons — "Three Dimensions of a Complete Life". In his clear rich resonant voice which filled the Cathedral, he said: "America is a great nation, offering the world the Declaration of Independence and enormous technological advances." However, it is incomplete because of its materialism. It has deprived twenty-two million Negroes of 'life, liberty, and the pursuit of happiness'. The individual should strive for self-fulfillment and completeness within himself. The second dimension of a complete life is "concern for and identification with one's fellow men." The third dimension is that "marvelous act of faith that will bring us to the true knowledge of God".[3]

2. Chief Luthuli died in 1967.
3. King Scott Coretta: op. cit. pp. 21-22.

London was beautiful. It is a unique metropolis, the only one of its kind on planet earth. But Martin was always conscious of the fact that it had been built through exploitation of African, Indian and other oppressed peoples. But the King family was also grateful to great God for His bountiful blessings. Martin's grandfather was a share-cropper. He bought his seed from the plantation owner, and also bought from him all the other necessities of life — all on credit. At harvest time, the entire crop was equally divided leaving nothing to clear the debts. It was the same story next year. The deeper he dug, the deeper he went into debt. That was the fate of the share-cropper.[4] Daddy King reminisced: "I came from nowhere. My Father was a sharecropper, and I didn't have the opportunity to get much formal training when I was growing up. In that sense, Martin Sr. must have been considered a "jackleg" which among the Negroes meant "unlettered, untrained but functioning on the brink. Moreover, the Kings lacked "colour" inasmuch as they were deficient of an adequate proportion of white blood in their veins that would have given them the status of what was considered a "pleasing brown".[5] It wasn't until I left the farm and went to Atlanta that I was able to get any real education. I was a man when I finished college, a grown man with my wife and three children. I wanted them to have all that I had missed. Martin became a minister, got a Ph.D. and eventually rose to what he is now." Martin was highly appreciative of what his Father had been through and, therefore, was 'amazingly respectful, thoughtful and considerate of Daddy King's feelings'.[6]

Martin received his Award on 10th December 1964. The hall was crowded to capacity with several thousands gathered outside who did not even get a glimpse of him since he was escorted in through a back entrance. King Olav and Prince Harold came in. The Orchestra played the Norwegian National Anthem. Dr. John read the citation: "... Dr. King has succeeded in keeping his followers to the principle of non-violence ... without his confirmed effectiveness of this principle, demonstrations and marches could easily have been violent and ended with the spilling of blood."

In his acceptance speech at Oslo on 11th December 1964, Martin said: "I feel as though this prize has been given to me for something that

---

4. Ibid, p. 89.
5. Black men generally preferred to marry girls having lighter skin colour than their own.
6. King Scott Coretta: op. cit. p. 82

really has not yet been achieved. It is a commission to go out and work even harder for the things in which we believe. ... I am mindful that only yesterday in Birmingham, Alabama, our children crying out for brotherhood, were answered with fire hoses, snarling dogs, and even death. ... were brutalized and murdered.

> "After contemplation, I conclude that this award which I receive on behalf of [the African-American] movement is profound recognition that non-violence is the answer to the crucial political and moral question of our time — the need for man to overcome oppression and violence without resorting to violence and oppression.
>
> Civilization and violence are antithetical concepts. Negroes of the United States of America, following the people of India, have demonstrated that non-violence is not sterile passivity, but a powerful moral force which makes for social transformation. Sooner or later, all the people of the world will have to discover a way to live together in peace and thereby transform this pending cosmic elegy into a creative psalm of brotherhood. ... Right temporarily defeated is stronger than evil triumphant."[7]

In his remarks, King connected the American civil rights movement with the entire planet's need for total disarmament. He emphasized M.K. Gandhi's technique of non-violence as a weapon of 'Truth-Force', 'Soul-Force', courage and self-suffering to achieve social justice and racial equality. Gandhi had proved beyond doubt that moral force can defeat machine guns, howsoever solitary example this may be. King went a step further to introduce nonviolence as a weapon for world peace. "I venture to suggest ... non-violence to become immediately a subject for study and for serious experimentation in every field of human conflict, by no means excluding relations between nations ... which (ultimately) make war."[8]

It is an unfortunate irony of fate that the Man from India who had propounded the great ideas of total non-violence, civil disobedience and peaceful resistance was not even mentioned in passing. Be that as it may, many 'whites were proud that a hometown man had won this great honour and felt a sense of identification with him' when black and white were indeed together, may be for a short-lived change only.[9]

---

7. *A Testament of Hope: The Essential Writings and Speeches of Martin Luther King Jr.*; ed. James Melvin Washington, San Francisco, 1986; pp. 224-226.
8. King M.L., Jr.: *The Quest for Peace and Justice*", Nobel Lectures, 1951-1970, Amsterdam, 1972, Vol. 3; pp. 338-43.
9. King Scott Coretta: op. cit. pp. 18, 26 and 31.

29

No Lie Can Live Forever

Morality is the basis of life and truth is the substance of all morality. All the religions of the world, while they may differ in other respects, unitedly proclaim that nothing lives in this world but the Truth. It stands even if there is no public support. Truth is self-sustaining.

Gandhi was revered by the people of India; so was Martin by the black people of America. Martin went to Selma shortly after returning from Oslo. It was right after New Year's Day 1965. Some days after that, a white man hit Martin on the head, as hard as he could. Fortunately, Martin was not seriously hurt. That is how white America treated its great son who had brought glory and honour to his country through the Nobel Prize. White rage was indeed senseless, like the communal riots of India where Hindus and Muslims, even though of the same blood and race, fall on each others throat like vicious animals now and then.

President Eisenhower and the attorney-general were invited to visit the South to learn about the situation, and to initiate suitable steps to curb the white violence. Of course there was no response from Washington. It was also decided to convene a much larger meeting in New Orleans on 14th February to give the expanded Movement a permanent shape. Meanwhile, Washington was informed that unless some effective remedial steps were undertaken immediately, "we shall be compelled to initiate a mighty Prayer Pilgrimage to Washington."[1]

The "Children's Crusade" was set for 2nd May 1963. The youngsters marched down from the Sixteenth Street Baptist Church, singing: "We Shall Overcome". They were all arrested. Wave after wave of young people followed; 959 youngsters were arrested that day and sent to jail

1 King Scott Coretta: op. cit. p. 166.

in school buses. The next day another one thousand "children and teen-agers" marched, singing freedom songs. The police chief ordered his men to open fire hoses. "Jets of water under a hundred pounds of pressure knocked the children flat, ripping the clothes off some of them. Then Connor (the Chief of Police in Birmingham) unleashed the police dogs — they ran wild, biting the children...." The Children's Crusade continued the whole of next week. The police could not cope with the pressure, more so since tremendous moral pressure was building up in the nation. One policeman asked an eight-year old child: What do you want?" She looked into his eyes, unafraid, and replied: "Freedom". The Third World was bewildered at the television pictures showing the cruelties inflicted on the Negroes, children in particular. Fire hoses under great pressure. Snarling dogs chasing and biting young children. A storm of telegrams protesting such uncivilized treatment of minorities in a proud democracy ... Martin proved his prophecy: "I hope to subpoena the conscience of the nation to the judgment seat of morality." Fearing a violent uprising, the White House sent in mediators who, in connivance with the local white moderates, tried for a compromise. The first prerequisite was to suspend the agitation as a cooling off measure. When Martin agreed to this, there was a dispute amongst the local black leadership who questioned King's right to take a unilateral decision like that. King pleaded for unity but Fred Shuttlesworth to whom the leadership of Birmingham agitation really belonged walked out of the meeting in a huff.

Militant Non-violence finally won the day. Yes, it did. 'Bull' Connor had lost to the extensive TV coverage of brutality of his methods. Peace was restored. President Kennedy was going through a crisis of conscience. He was sick after watching the images of snarling police-dogs attacking women and children, running helter-skelter. The political fallout from Birmingham forced the Kennedy Brothers to bring forward a civil-rights bill in 1963. He told the Congress that racial discrimination was morally wrong, besides being economically costly. That year proved to be a landmark year in the history of Negroes' freedom struggle, and Birmingham its focal point. Lest the momentum generated by the Birmingham Movement peter out, a conference of heads of all the affiliated organizations was held to chalk out the roadmap of future activities. Those who took part included A. Phillip Randolph, Roy Wilkins of NAACP, John Lewis of SNCC, Dorothy Height of the National Council of Negro Women, James Farmer of CORE, and Whitney Young of the Urban League. Concurrently, Robert Kennedy met with a group of Black intellectuals and artists. The meeting lasted almost three hours during which the Attorney General was grossly harassed. Indeed, he had a hard time and was totally at his wits ends.

By this time John F. Kennedy was in the third year of his Presidency. The mass movement launched by the Black leadership had raised passions to a boiling point. There were a number of other flash points all over the country besides Birmingham, threatening to burst into flames. King warned the Administration that they were at a 'historic crossroad'. It was high time that the Federal Government faced the reality of "its moral commitment and with it, its political (mis)fortunes. The Kennedy Brothers soon came to realize that repression or tokenism was not the answer to the crisis faced by the most powerful nation on earth. The word 'Freedom' was in the air, all over the country — freedom rides, freedom songs, freedom slogans, freedom schools, freedom movement, *et al.* It will thus be seen that the White House was merely reacting to the events as they unfolded, rather than playing a pro-active role as it should have done. At a White House conference on the proposed bill, President Kennedy said to Dr. Martin Luther King Jr. with a wry grin: "Bull Connor has done as much for civil rights as Abraham Lincoln." The Bill was eventually passed by the Congress in 1964.[2] Martin's faith in God and His will was like Gandhi's, whose religious and moral views were admirable and indeed were on a remarkably high altitude, though the British found it difficult to understand his practice of them in politics.

The workload on Martin had increased so very much that it had become virtually impossible for him to manage all the multifarious activities while in Montgomery. A move of the household to Atlanta appeared to be the only way out. The Board of Deacons was generous enough to offer him the post of co-pastor of the Ebenezer Baptist Church of Atlanta. Despite all the public pressure against his decision, on Sunday, 29th November 1959 Martin offered his resignation to move to Atlanta so that he could meet the increasing demands of civil rights work. The air was charged with emotion, so were the hearts of the congregation as well as of the out-going Pastor. "I would like to submit my resignation as pastor of the Dexter Avenue Baptist Church, to become effective on the fourth Sunday in January 1960." The congregation rose for the Benediction. They sang: "Blest be the Tie That Binds ..." Martin wept at the pulpit.

Two days later Martin declared: "The time has come for a broad, bold advance of the southern campaign for equality. After prayerful consideration I am convinced that the psychological moment has come

2. Coretta: op. cit. pp. 243-47.

when a concentrated drive against injustice can bring great tangible gains. ..." Stepped up campaign for voter registration; full-scale assault against discrimination and segregation; training of youth and adult leaders to work for social change through non-violent resistance. "We must employ new methods of struggle involving the masses of the people."[3] The enlarged scope of resistance made it necessary for the King family to move to Atlanta from where he could exercise better control and render guidance. On the last Sunday of January 1960 an elaborate ceremony was held at Dexter to honour, and to bid farewell to Martin. His parents as well as Coretta's parents made a surprise appearance. The Congregation presented a lovely silver tea service engraved with the inscription: "To Dr. and Mrs. Martin Luther King, Jr., in grateful appreciation. Dexter Avenue Baptist Church, Montgomery, Alabama, 1954-1960."

"The parting was so beautiful, so deeply touching; we felt exalted, yet unworthy of their admiration."[4] And King and the 'Queen' left Montgomery. Unfortunately, soon after they had settled down in a rented house in Atlanta, a serious attempt at character-assassination was made on Martin by the Montgomery Grand Jury on trumped-up charges — falsifying State income-tax returns for 1956 and 1958. By implication, Martin was charged with receiving money from Montgomery Improvement Association (MIA) and Southern Christian Leadership Conference (SCLC) that was unaccounted for. This attack on his personal integrity caused him deep anguish. The case went to the Jury on Saturday, 28th May. Verdict of 12-member southern jury of twelve white men: Not Guilty. "Truth crushed to earth will rise again. ... No lie can live for ever."

While the Selma march was underway, the President addressed the Congress: "The real hero in the struggle for equality was the Negro American. His actions and protests — his courage to risk safety and even life — have awakened the conscience of the Nation. His demonstrations have been designed to call attention to injustice. ... To ignore the Negro vote and Negro insistence on civil rights must be either an act of absolute folly — or one of absolute miscalculation."

While the Selma march was on and the Blacks were being beaten up on the Pettus Bridge, a delegation comprising of about twenty people had gone to White House to see President Johnson. The leader of the delegation had his statement written down and he passed on a copy to

---

3. Ibid, p. 197.
4. King Scott Coretta: op.cit. pp. 197-98.

the President. The President was 'arrogant as hell and mad'. He did not even look at the paper, let alone read it. He just threw it back across the table. The meeting ended with some of the Black leaders expressing their gratitude to the President for the opportunity he had given them to meet him, and how proud they were for this honour. But every one was not a bootlicker. John A. Williams spoke out: "We are interested in the lives of our people. Which side is the Federal Government on?"[5] Soon people realized that these White House meetings were a mere waste of time and that nothing was going to be achieved through them. Some of the black leaders even politely declined the invitations to the next conference at the White House.

30

Nehru's Fiasco

Friendship that insists upon agreement on all matters is not worth the name. Friendship to be real must ever sustain the weight of honest differences however sharp they are. The test of friendship is assistance in adversity, and that too unconditional assistance. Conditional cooperation is a commercial contract and not true friendship.

Out of all the so called 'neutral countries' President Kennedy was most interested in India. He regarded India as 'the key area' in Asia. In the President's opinion the future of Asia would be determined by the outcome of economic and political struggle between the two Asian giants. Leadership of Asia was at stake between communist China and democratic India. Joint American-European financial effort in support of India's Five-Year Plans for development was the need of the hour. "We want India to win that race with China. ... If China succeeds and India fails, the economic-development balance of power will shift against us. ... It is not enough to merely provide sufficient money. Equally important are our attitude and understanding", said the President. How very prophetic, besides depth of understanding of the geo-strategic considerations of long term significance. But — and it is a big 'but' — Kennedy was highly skeptical of the attitude and strategic commonality of thought, primarily because the Indian leadership lacked in understanding geo-politics and the strategic importance of Central Asia in the field of world power-politics. President Kennedy was discrete enough not to say so in so many words; but the personal chemistry between Indian Prime Minister Jawaharlal Nehru and JFK had gone sour right from the beginning when, in 1951, Nehru treated JFK with 'marked indifference' during the latter's visit to India.

President Kennedy had been informed that, when Nehru became bored, he would tap his fingers together and look at the ceiling. That is precisely what Nehru did just when JFK had been in his office for barely ten minutes! How very impolite! It seems Nehru was quite ignorant of the political power that Kennedy clan wielded in the United States of America. The cap-stone was Nehru's total lack of understanding of strategic and geo-political importance of Central Asian Republics in the context of defence and energy-resources development. Unfortunately, all other political leaders and most of the military brass were equally ignorant of the subject; otherwise there was no reason for India to have lost the Northern Areas (Gilgit Complex) in 1947-48. Ten years later, Nehru visited the United States in the first week of November 1961. In his remarks of welcome to Prime Minister Nehru at Andrews Air Force Base, Washington, D.C., on November 6, 1961, JFK said:

> India and America are separated by half the globe, but I think that you are aware, as you surely must have been aware, during the long days of your struggle for independence, of the great well of affection and regard for which your country and people are held in this country — a great affectionate regard which belongs to you particularly in these difficult days.

Instead of reciprocating the above gesture, during the state-dinner Nehru's daughter Indira Gandhi, who had no *locus standi* and whose understanding of geo-politics could be written on the back of a postage stamp, took an uncalled for liberty to assail President Kennedy about American policy towards India. And during the private meetings between the President and Prime Minister, "Nehru was terribly passive." And Kennedy was hard put to keep the conversation going. However, in conversations, Nehru "displayed interest and vivacity only with Jacqueline".[1] Nevertheless, Nehru's State visit to the States turned out to be a fiasco. The foundations of Indo-American future relations thus came to be laid in sand sans the binder, cement. Thus, it would not be far wrong to say that Nehru-Gandhi dynastic rule proved to be a disaster in so far as Indo-American relations were concerned.

In order to assuage hurt feelings on both sides, in November Nehru invited Jacqueline and the children to visit India during the winter. It took some time to finalize the itinerary, and Jacqueline accompanied by her sister Princess Lee Radziwill arrived in India only in March 1962. Nehru was at his best in graciousness. He did not raise any political or controversial issues. Both parties thoroughly enjoyed the trip. No doubt, Jacqueline's trip had been a great success. In keeping with the Washington policy of treating India and Pakistan on the same footing, Jacqueline and Lee then went to Pakistan.

1. Schlesinger M. Arthur, Jr.: op. cit. p. 456. It seems Nehru had a knack of hitting off well with charming beautiful ladies!

31

Selma-Montgomery March

Disenfranchisement of the Negro by white legislatures of the South was an act of total injustice inflicted through passing of unjust laws. While it is a legal and moral responsibility to obey just laws; disobeying the unjust laws is also a moral obligation. Denial of voting rights to the Blacks was the culmination of unjust laws.

Selma was a 'slave market' before the Civil War. It was first occupied by federal troops in the spring of 1865 after the Battle of Selma fought on April 02, 1865 when 1,500 Confederate troops and 2,500 civilians were defeated by a much stronger Union force. At one time it was also a military depot for the Confederacy. It was a centre of white supremacists, albeit less fundamentalists than the Ku-Klux Klan. It was predominantly a black town in the Dallas County Black Belt. The whites constituted less than half the population but almost all were registered voters. The Blacks were physically prevented from registering as voters and State Troopers used electric cattle-prods against potential voter registrants. The shock producing prods had actually been pressed under the women's dresses also. The news of award of the 1964 Nobel Peace Prize to King forced the Selma affair to take a back seat, at least for the time being. After his return from Norway, King was once again in the thick of Selma campaign along with the Students Non-violent Coordinating Committee (SNCC).

Despite the passage of Civil Rights Act of 1957, a large number of Negroes were being denied the right to vote on one pretext or the other. The Federal Government therefore decided to constitute a Commission on Civil Rights. It was all the more significant in the Southern States as was proved by the report of the Commission after it had held hearings in several cities. Consequentially, the Department of Justice instituted legal proceedings against the States of Alabama, Georgia and Louisiana charging that the Registrars had deliberately denied registration to qualified black voters. In the process, by the summer of 1960 the question of legal status of Negroes developed into a major national issue. The question of Negro vote assumed its legitimate importance, more so since there were more than one million registered Negro voters in the twelve Southern States. Neither Party, Republicans nor Democrats, could afford to ignore such a large chunk of vote bank without risking a setback.[1] All the Presidents had failed to put an end to discrimination against the Negroes in the matter of federally supported housing, which required a mere executive order from the White House. Even a liberal President like John F. Kennedy, who entered the White House on a wafer thin majority provided by the Negro tilt in his favour, did so only two years after assuming office whereas this should have been the first such order within a couple of days of his assuming the Presidency.

Johnson Takes Over Amidst Violence & Tension

The murder of Medgar Evers raised the black passions. And slaying of a Baltimore postal employee, William Moore while he was making a one-man freedom march further inflamed the black emotions leading to large crowds, about 20,000 strong, holding protest rallies in San Francisco and Los Angeles. The white segregationists resisted such rallies. The situation was indeed becoming volatile and the President or the Congress could no longer remain indifferent. President John F. Kennedy therefore sent a special message to the Congress followed by a more liberal and enlarged civil rights program in June.[2]

On the assassination of President John F. Kennedy on November 22, 1963, Vice President Lyndon B. Johnson succeeded him as the 36th President of the United States. He grasped the reigns of power firmly and made the passage of the Civil Rights Bill as his top priority.[3]

---

1. To ignore the Negro vote and Negro insistence on civil rights must be either an act of absolute folly — or one of absolute miscalculation — *The Making of the President* by Theodore Roosevelt.
2. We face a moral crisis as a country and as a people. It cannot be met by repressive police action. It cannot be left to more demonstrations in the streets. It cannot be quieted by token moves or talk. It is a time to act through positive affirmative action rather than indulge in rhetoric — extract from address to the Nation by President John F. Kennedy.
3. "We have talked for one hundred years or more. It is time now to write the next chapter, and to write it in the books of law." — Extract from address to Congress by the new President (Lyndon B. Johnson).

Concurrently, Nicholas Katzenbach assumed the appointment of acting Attorney General on 3rd September 1964. The new President directed him to redraft the next Civil Rights Bill to secure equal voting rights for all American citizens to close this chapter once and for all. The Black leaders were happy to hear these words although they least expected these from a man like Johnson as they had known him. Johnson got the peoples' mandate for the Presidency on 3rd November 1964 and Katzenbach became the Attorney General on 13th February 1965. The President discussed the new draft several times with Roy Wilkins, the Executive Director of the NAACP; Dr. Martin Luther King Jr., leader of the Southern Christian Leadership Conference; Whitney Young Jr., Executive Director of the National Urban League; Clarence Mitchell, Director of the Washington Bureau of the NAACP; A. Philip Randolph, and many others who had a finger in this large pie. "We all knew that the prospects for Congressional passage were rather dim, but we decided to go ahead. I would work within the Federal Government; the Black leadership would take their cause directly to the people."[4]

For the Negro minority, the passage of Civil Rights Act of 1964 was a turning point in their struggle for freedom. The right to vote became the basic issue, replacing all else for the time being. Hereafter, the emphasis shifted to political and economic tools to ameliorate the lot of the black populace. Organization of political parties and use of vote as a weapon for advancement in various spheres of life became the primary tools. Dr. King had already adopted Gandhi's term *constructive program* as a priority one item for future action. An important ingredient of this constructive program was an all out effort to get Negroes registered to vote. The Dallas County Voters League initiated the proposal in the first instance. In early January 1965 about one thousand volunteers, mostly white students, religious leaders and lawyers were deputed to serve in Freedom Schools and voter registration program in the State of Mississippi, the most-bitter Deep South stronghold of apartheid and segregation at its worst. This project was under overall supervision of Rev. James Bevel. The resentment amongst the white officials of the State machinery knew no bounds. They were prepared to go to any depth to thwart the black nationalists' efforts towards education and improvement of living standards of the Blacks. The white bureaucracy ensured disenfranchisement of the Negroes through the following tactics:

---

4. Johnson L.B.: op. cit. p. 161.

Dr. King and Rev. Abernathy in Albany Jail

Selma-Montgomery March to protest against restrictions on Black Voting rights: 1965

- The state police and troopers freely used guns, clubs and cattle prods to prevent the Blacks from registering in the first place. And if registered, same weapons were used to prevent casting of the ballot.
- City ordinances were specifically designed to ensure that Negroes could not act in unison, or give expression to their grievances.
- The number of days and hours during which the people could register to vote were restricted, and deliberately made inconvenient. To cap it all, the process of registration itself was kept at a slow pace.
- And last, but not he least, literacy test made sure that most Blacks were not qualified to register as voters.

The Beginning

Mrs. Amelia Boynton, an insurance agent, was already actively fighting for civil rights in Selma, almost single-handedly. The Brown's Chapel became the local headquarters from where Dr. King gave the clarion call: "We are going to bring a voting bill into being in the streets of Selma." Martin had chosen Selma as the focal point of protests after deliberate consideration. He believed that a confrontation at Selma was certain to be 'dramatic and dangerous', and thus assure media coverage at the national level, and to some extent internationally too.

Initially, the protests had a mild start. Blacks stood in orderly queues outside the court house for registering as voters. 1st February 1965 was the fifth anniversary of the start of sit-ins. Civil Rights workers were directed to assemble at Brown Chapel A.M.E. Church and were organized to march to the court house on the days that the county and the state designated as registration days. On that day, the Nobel Laureate along with about 250 other workers was jailed for 'seeking to go to the court house' in Selma, Alabama. The irony of fate was that King was jailed barely sixty days after the King of Norway had participated in the ceremony awarding him the Nobel Peace Prize. A crowd of about one thousand protested against this highhandedness, more so since President Lyndon Baines Johnson had announced that he would ensure implementation of the right to vote to everyone entitled to do so. But the State Government was all out to ensure that the Blacks would not be allowed to register. In all, about three thousand volunteers were jailed during this period. In one night-march, the State Troopers herded 165 demonstrators into a rural area at a forced pace, almost at run.[5]

---

5. Garrow David J.: *Bearing the Cross*, p.388.

Onwards to Montgomery

During the First World War a Negro unit in France had assumed the title of 'Black Panthers'. The SNCC in Lowndes County formed the Lowndes County Freedom Party which came to be popularly known as Black Panthers Party. The Whites united behind George Wallace and adopted the white fighting cock as their insignia. The Blacks in turn responded with Black Panthers. In another instance of brutality, on February 26 a State Trooper shot and killed a young black, Jimmy Lee Jackson, barely 25 years of age who was helping his grandparents who had been clubbed by the troopers during the night-march in Marion, Alabama. This was the proverbial last straw. On 1st March 1965 Martin King led a march through five Alabama Black Belt Counties including the Lowndes. The U.S. Attorney General Nicholas Katzenbach and the head of the Federal Community Relations Service, LeRoy Collins, were in contact with Martin King and the White House. Martin King announced a fifty-four miles long march from Selma to the State capital at Montgomery, with Sunday 7th March as D-Day.[6] The Governor George Wallace promptly imposed a ban on the proposed march through a temporary injunction issued by federal judge Frank Johnson forbidding the march. This was an added provocation to undertake the march since the injunction itself was a negation of the federal Constitution. In any case King had no intention of observing such an unjust law or decision, and decided that the march shall go ahead as scheduled. King emphasized: "And we march in the name of the Constitution, knowing that the Constitution is on our side. The right of the people peaceably to assemble and to petition the Government for a redress of grievances shall not be abridged. That is the First Amendment."

Sunday morning, March 7, 1965 was different from the other Sundays in as much as more than 500 marchers led by Hosa William John Lewis and James Forman headed for Highway 80. Most of them carried bags on their backs and wore heavy shoes. They walked quietly and uneasily past the State Troopers, crossed the Edmund Pettus Bridge and on the other side saw more State Troopers, Sheriff's Deputies and crackers *vigilantes*, with the usual media personnel without whom nothing would be news-worthy. Without any prior warning, all of a sudden there were galloping horses, stomping the marchers ahead, beating and shouting, shrieks of the wounded, resulting in close to seventy blacks and whites wounded altogether. These acts of police brutality attracted worldwide

---

6. On Tuesday, March 9, Judge Frank M. Johnson of the Federal District Court issued the ruling that Martin and his colleagues could not participate in the peaceful voting rights march to Montgomery.

attention. It was more of a scene from Russian history of the Czarist regime when the Czar's notorious Cossacks chased men, women and children using electric cattle prods. Martin's response: "We shall overcome."

In Atlanta King issued an urgent appeal for more marchers from Selma to Montgomery. His appeal was particularly directed to the clergy. Within hours a number of lay and clergy, black and white, collected at Selma to march to Montgomery. Jimmie Jackson was the first one to succumb to his injuries. Dr. Martin Luther King Jr. who had received the Nobel Peace Prize a few weeks earlier told the demonstrators in Montgomery: "No tide of racism can stop us." And they did march ahead, towards and over the same Edmund Pettus Bridge when a call came over the loud speakers to stop and disperse. And they stopped. The religious leaders took over. They led the protesters in prayer. Ralph Abernathy was the first to lead in singing "We Shall Overcome". The marchers then knelt on the pavement. As soon as the Methodist Bishop Lord of Washington, D.C., asked God to open the Red Sea for the Egyptians to pass through, the State Troopers pulled aside and the road to Montgomery was wide open before the protesters. But they did not take advantage of that situation. King did not wish to contravene the federal law. At the command of Dr. King, they turned back to the start point, the Brown Chapel, with King in the lead. No violence. No disturbances. The march through Selma and beyond the point of last violence on Sunday going, about 250 feet closer to Montgomery (!), had been the greatest civil rights demonstration ever in the Black Belt of the deep South.

The white majority could not reconcile to such an exuberant ending of the drama. That night Reverend James Reeb, a white Unitarian minister from Boston, Massachusetts, father of five children, was clubbed to death by white thugs, the 'crackers', on a street in Selma. He died two days later on March 11. They called him a 'white nigger'! The incident had wide reverberations. The Selma episode did stir the nation's conscience as had been anticipated by King. So was Lyndon B. Johnson, the first Southern to become President after the Civil War. However, it should be borne in mind that the very object of undertaking those protest marches was to dramatize injustice, to achieve justice through non-violence. But in the process if violence erupted, or violence was thrust on the Negroes, it was no deficiency in the doctrine of non-violence; instead, it was the backlash on the part of the perpetrators of injustice that led to violence. Certainly, one could not hold King responsible, by any stretch of imagination, for the violence of that 'Bloody Sunday'. Be that as it may, the evil of 'racism' had to be exposed, and if violence did occur in the process, it had to be accepted as a part of the total package.

Voting Rights Bill

By the morning of Sunday, 14th March, the Justice Department had completed most of the work on the draft of the Voting Rights Bill. Under the circumstances the President felt compelled to address the Congress stressing that the real hero in the struggle for equality was the Negro American. "His actions and protests — his courage to risk safety and even life — have awakened the conscience of the nation. His demonstrations have been designed to call attention to injustice, to provoke change and stir reform. ... We intend to fight this battle where it should be fought — in the courts, in the Congress, and in the hearts of men. And we shall overcome."

President Johnson addressed the joint session of the Congress the next evening, March 15, 1965:

> "I speak tonight for the dignity of man and the destiny of democracy. Rarely, in any time, does an issue lay bare the secret heart of America itself. The issue of equal rights for American Negroes is such an issue. And should we defeat every enemy, and should we double our wealth and conquer the stars and still be unequal to this issue, then we will have failed as a people and as a nation. ... At times, history and fate meet at a single time in a single place to shape a turning point in man's unending search for freedom. ... So it was last week in Selma, Alabama. There is no constitutional issue here. There is no issue of states' rights or national rights. There is only the struggle for human rights.... What happened in Selma is part of a far larger movement which reaches into every section and state of America. It is the effort of American Negroes to secure for themselves the full blessings of American life. Their cause must be our cause, too, because it is not just Negroes, but really it is all of us who must overcome the crippling legacy of bigotry and injustice. ... And ... We ... shall ... overcome."[7]

Thus the big man from Texas gave the ultimate commitment of federal support and moral leadership to the Negro cause.

The last three words of the President's address struck an emotional chord in the hearts of Blacks all over the country. A few seconds of "deafening silence" was soon followed by unprecedented overwhelming applause from all corners of the House. When he signed the Bill into law, the President announced:

---

7. Johnson L.B.: op. cit. p. 165.

"Today is a triumph for freedom as huge as any victory that's ever been won on any battlefield. Today we strike away the last major shackle of fierce and ancient bonds."

However, negotiations for an amicable settlement moved pretty fast. By Sunday, 21st March all differences between the State and Federal courts, between Governor Wallace and President Johnson, between King and SNCC, *et al*, appeared to have been sorted out. Meanwhile, Judge Johnson ruled that The Negroes had a constitutional right to march. Bur Governor Wallace was adamant. He threatened further resistance by the State Government whereupon President Johnson signed an Executive order federalizing the Alabama National Guard[8] and placed them under Deputy Attorney General, Ramsay Clark. In addition, four thousand regular troops were deployed to keep the peace. A fresh march was organized from Selma to Montgomery. It was the third and final attempt at the Selma-Montgomery March scheduled for Sunday, 21st March. More than ten thousand took part while another 25,000 joined them in the capital. Two weeks after the original date, 3,000 protest-marchers started on foot. They moved over the same Edmund Pettus Bridge in single file in an orderly manner. The SNCC leader John Lewis who had been badly beaten up on the 'Bloody Sunday' also joined the march, much against the advice of his rank and file. Members of the Congress came over by plane while entertainers from Hollywood and New York flew over. A number of religious leaders also came from across the country. The procession moved very slowly under tight security. They covered barely seven miles on the first day.

The whites were terribly upset. A number of them, flying Confederate flags and shouting and displaying obscenities at the marchers, crawled along the one open side of the main road, which was lined by Army Military Police to keep the traffic moving. The State Troopers who had inflicted severe atrocities on the marchers just two weeks earlier were also deployed in force, directing traffic and ensuring that no one stepped over the white dividing line. However, their cars carried the Confederate flag as their licence plate, and they kept shouting 'niggers' all the time. Air Force helicopters hovered above. But there was also a small plane dropping leaflet-messages "brought to you by the world's smallest air force — Confederate Air Force." The white resentment did not end there. They distributed hundreds of copies of *Alabama Journal* ridiculing the March vis-à-vis the "Salt March' in its editorial entitled "Dr. King's 'Gandhi' Humbug". There were water trucks and carriers for press and television crew. Portable mobile toilets followed in the rear. This march did cost the

8. Ibid, p.163.9.

federal exchequer a tidy sum of money which reminded Harris Wofford of the joke about Mahatma Gandhi by Sarojini Naidu: "If only Gandhi knew how much it costs us to keep the Mahatma in poverty"! Justice Department officials rode, and some walked, along side the marchers. So did the Deputy Secretary General of the United Nations, Nobel Peace Prize awardee Ralph Bunche; top civil rights leaders of America along with delegates from Canada and the United Kingdom; hundreds of clergymen of all denominations and sects — Protestants, Catholics and Jewish leaders. Of course, Coretta was also there. Martin was terribly fatigued and he looked so, with his feet blistered. He took time off. Meanwhile, the procession swelled to about 25,000. Hundreds more were on their way but the white train-crew at Atlanta refused to take them any further.

Meanwhile, King was back on Thursday, 25th to lead the multitude into Confederate Square in the middle of the town of Montgomery. The marchers were all praise for President Johnson. So was King himself. He told his people: "Never has a President spoken so eloquently or so sincerely on the question of civil rights." A grand rally was the ultimate climax. The crowd massed around the steps of the State Capitol where King gave a resounding speech. Nobel Laureate Ralph Bunche apologized for having to speak from the steps of the State Capitol over which fluttered the flag of the Confederacy. Coretta King then led the huge crowd in singing the national anthem. A number of speakers took turn followed by reading by Mrs. Amelia Boynton of a proposed petition to Governor Wallace. The crowd roared their approval. Mrs. Rosa Park, the harbinger of all that happened and was happening in Montgomery, was the last speaker of the evening. Within hours of conclusion of the Selma-Montgomery march, that night snipers shot and killed Viola Gregg Liuzzo, a white woman volunteer from Detroit, as she transported passengers from Montgomery back to Selma.[9] It was a dastardly cowardly act by the Ku Klux Klan night riders, one of whom was suspected to be an FBI agent. The irony of the situation was that her killers were exonerated from the murder charge! The following weeks were a period of tension all round.

The Voting Rights had come into being. Literacy tests were abolished. The U.S. Attorney General was empowered to appoint federal registrars to enforce the new laws. An overwhelming majority of Blacks soon registered as voters and over fifty per cent of them exercised their franchise the very first time. However, it was generally believed, and true, that Martin was getting justice for the Blacks at a slow pace. 'Justice delayed is justice denied' aptly applied to the plight of the Blacks. In the

9. Franklin John Hope: op. cit. p. 638.

South the Blacks were systematically excluded from participating in the political system, which in turn meant deprivation of economic power.

The Voting Rights Bill was not the end of the crusade: in fact, it was just the beginning of numerous problems, which were crying for immediate solution. The challenges of racial discrimination were many, but the solutions and resources limited, like untouchability in Indian social milieu was a mere symptom of deep rooted malady faced by Gandhi. Both India and America had to resolve the problems of poverty, filthy stinking slums without heating or plumbing, poor and inadequate schooling facilities, unemployment, violent gang-wars, drugs, *et al.* You name it, and the ghettos had it. So it was in Gandhi's India where corruption, inefficiency and nepotism were the order of the day.

On 21st June 1965 three civil rights workers — two white young men from New York and one black local youth — were murdered in cold blood. The worst part of this heinous crime was that it was committed by officers of the law in Neshoba County, Mississippi. The perpetrators of this hideous crime were not arrested for six months. At long last when the chief law officers including the Deputy Sheriff were arrested, they were not charged with murder; instead they were charged with denial of civil rights of non-violent workers under federal statutes, an offence of much lower degree calling for a rather mild sentence. The hand of FBI was suspected in these atrocious machinations. King's criticism of the Bureau irritated its Chief, J. Edgar Hoover. He had held the same job for nearly forty years and was instrumental in ruining the reputation and career of many prominent Americans by manipulating the powers of FBI, more so since the American Administration and public were paranoid about communism in the years of Cold War. Hoover was so irritated with King that he took upon himself to demolish King's reputation by calling Martin a "demagogue and the most notorious liar in the country". While referring to Stanley Levison, he cautioned Robert Kennedy, the Attorney General, that 'a major communist figure had penetrated King's inner cabinet'. Wiretaps on King's telephones were one of the aberrations of Kennedy Administration, perpetrated primarily by Robert Kennedy because of King's relationship with Levison.[10]

Insofar as a series of marches and demonstrations were concerned, the march from Selma to Montgomery held in 1965 was the last of the non-violent direct action by the Southern freedom movement. And most rewardingly successful too.

---

10. Wofford Harris: *Of Kennedys and Kings*, pp. 201-239. Also, Garrow David J.: *The FBI and Martin Luther King Jr.*; pp. 60-62.

32

Seeds of Conflict

Los Angeles Riots

The seeds of racial conflict were not restricted to the South only; they were germinating all over the North without being taken notice of. The shock and horror of Northern riots was an explosion of horrendous proportions. Fewer people had been killed in ten years of non-violent demonstrations across the South than were killed in 1965 in one night of rioting in Watts area of Los Angeles. The worse was yet to come!

WATTS!

The beginning of the 20th century witnessed the rise of conflict between the Negroes and the Whites. While the White majority was not willing to accept the Negro as their equal, the Blacks were not prepared to accept anything less than that. This was particularly true for the southern States, which were determined to delay, if not completely negate, the full implementation of Negro's legal and political rights. Although the Supreme Court of the United States of America had given a historic judgment in 1954 for integration of public schools, the southern States were loath to implement the same. Racial segregation in public schools in the South continued as heretofore. The Whites in the South were against the very idea of close, intimate, personal or prolonged relationship between the two races, like school children sitting side by side in a classroom, or using the same restrooms (toilets). The Negroes as a race were considered inferior in social and moral standards. For all practical purposes, the Negroes were considered second-class citizens in the Southern States. But the twenty million Negroes in America were not prepared to accept second-class citizenship at any price and demanded equal protection of the laws to which they are naturally entitled under the US Constitution.[1] The Supreme Court had accepted that "In view of the Constitution, in the eyes of the law, there is in this country no superior, dominant, ruling class of citizens. There is no caste here. Our Constitution is colour-blind, and neither knows nor tolerates classes among citizens."[2]

The legal victory was significant but it was a paper victory only. Racial and political equality was the aim of the movement. After all, three-fourths of the world's population is coloured. It therefore stands to reason that the coloured peoples — black, brown, red or yellow — should occupy the pride of place rather than the whites usurping the rights of the coloured. This certainly does not imply that the coloured people should dominate or humiliate the white man. Far from it. However, it does mean that the coloured people must have their rights and privileges, no less than those of the whites. The economic front was equally important. So the Negro leadership transferred their attention to these vital sectors. This took the form of boycott, 'picket lines', 'sit in' demonstrations, (*dharnas*), 'freedom rides', etc. Even before Martin Luther King Jr. was born, the concept of non-violence as a pacifist theory to be applied in the United States was developed by Richard Gregg, a white Southerner and a Quaker, a lawyer by profession, who was active in the local labour movement in the 1920s. He was greatly impressed by the Gandhian movement against the British domination in India so much so that he spent four years in India studying Gandhi's methods, the principles and practice of non-violence at first hand, when the Mahatma was alive and active. Martin was greatly influenced by his book, *The Power of Non-violence*, which he read and re-read. He wrote extensively on the subject and helped in popularizing the Gandhian philosophy in America. As a result of his untiring efforts to establish non-violence as the principal means of attaining freedom for the Blacks, a Committee for Non-violent Revolution was founded there in 1946. This Committee opposed the expansion of armament industry as well as development of nuclear weapons, and encouraged the people to refuse to serve in the armed forces, or in the armament industries.[3] Finally, non-violent civil resistance-

---

1. The United States Constitution which became effective in 1789 had a serious deficiency in that it did not guarantee personal liberty. A Bill of Rights was therefore added in 1791 through ten amendments passed simultaneous.
2. Supreme Court case; p. 404.
3. Richard B. Gregg: *The Psychology and Strategy of Gandhi's Non-violent Resistance*, Madras, 1929; *Gandhism and Socialism*, Madras, 1931; *The Power of Non-violence*, Philadelphia, 1934.

cum-disobedience movement was the outcome of all these efforts.[4] Another book that made a significant impression on Martin's mind was *War Without Violence* by Krishnalal Shridharani, a close associate of Gandhi, who had participated in the famous Dandi Salt March.

The Black Americans of the 1920's soon perceived that the Gandhian technique of struggle for Indian independence could be profitably employed to attain freedom for the Afro-American oppressed minority of the United States. Besides Richard Gregg, a number of Black young students of Gandhian strategy not only studied Gandhi but also visited India to observe at first hand how the Movement worked. In 1936 Dr. and Mrs. Howard Thurman visited Gandhi at his Ashram. Their interview was recorded. They requested Gandhi to visit America, not for the white America, but for the black oppressed people of America. While bidding the Thurmans goodbye, Gandhi concluded: "It may be through the Negroes that the unadulterated message of non-violence will be delivered to the world."[5] Next year Dr. Channing Tobias, Director of the Phelps-Stokes Fund, and Dr. Benjamin Mays, then President of the Morehouse College had a long interview with Gandhi which was published in Gandhi's paper *Harijan*. Prominent amongst other visitors to India to meet with Gandhi were James Farmer, James Lawson, *et al*, who established interaction between Afro-Americans and Indian independence movement well before Dr. Martin Luther King Jr., came on the scene.[6] Nevertheless, destiny had cast Martin to be the stalwart to lead and guide the mass movement, significantly between the Montgomery Bus Boycott in 1955 that commenced on Thursday, 1st December 1955 in Alabama and the passage of Voting Rights Act of 1965 — a fight for racial equality that created history for non-violent resistance to American apartheid and oppression. It is noteworthy that Montgomery Bus Boycott was not the first bus boycott as is often erroneously believed: Baton Rouge in Louisiana, Mobile in Alabama and Atlanta in Georgia had already successfully desegregated city bus seating on the basis of first-come, first-served.[7]

The original Negroes were imported from Africa to the United States of America as labour to work on the white-owned extensive plantations,

---

4. Ostergaard Geoffrey: *Non-violent Revolution in India*; Gandhi Peace Foundation, New Delhi, 1985.
5. Sudarshn Kapur: *Raising up a Prophet, The African-American Encounter with Gandhi*; Boston, 1922.
6. Fairclough Adam: op. cit. p. 12.
7. Garrow David J.: *Bearing the Cross: Martin Luther King, Jr., and the Southern Christian Leadership Conference;* New York, 1986, p. 439. Also, Cone James H.: op. cit. pp. 282, 286.

and for other odd jobs including domestic help. It was repetition of virtually the same story as that of the Indian indentured labour to South Africa, and subsequent historical catapulting of Mohandas Karmchand Gandhi to the top-slot of Indian leadership. This came about when Gandhi's Satyagraha began in South Africa in 1907 and climaxed in 1913 with an epic march by 5,000 Indian workers indentured to work in coal mines of Natal under inhuman working conditions. There was a massive response amongst the Indian women who coaxed their men-folk to join the strike. This was the beginning of what was then a novel method of protest demonstrations through 'freedom marches' and 'mass strikes'. The Defiance Campaign launched by the black population under the banner of African National Congress followed the pattern set by Gandhi.

During those early days there were hardly any blacks in the American urban centers. The two World Wars, recruitment of the Blacks in the defence services at whatever level, the economic depression of the 30's, the preponderance of the automobile, *et al*, altered the old pattern, besides awakening the Negroes to the realities of racial discrimination and inequality in the eyes of the law. A large number of Negroes moved out of the plantations to the ghettoes in the urban centres, thereby ending decades of isolation. Here they came face to face with the realities of two sets of rules: one for the Whites and the other for the Blacks. The former were the superior beings, supreme in the land they had grabbed from the American-Indians way back. The Negro was a second, if not the lowest class of citizen. His inferiority complex nurtured over a couple of centuries of slavery, segregation and racial discrimination, deprivation and denial of education, *et al*, erupted on the surface of social platform.

On August 1, 1965, racial violence erupted in Watts section of Los Angeles, a predominantly Black ghetto complex where sixty per cent of all adults were on welfare relief. It was the worst case of urban violence since 1943. The Watts riots resulted in the death of thirty-four persons and damage to property reached a staggering 200 million dollars. Race-riots started spreading their tentacles over a number of Northern Ghettos beating all previous records. The summer of 1966 saw the worst racial violence when Afro-American discontent led to race riots in twenty-two cities all across the United States. Chicago, Brooklyn, Cleveland were the worst hit. Dr. King totally rejected the culture of riots. He abhorred them, as nothing else, and deplored the 'immorality and impracticality' of the riots as a solution of the nation's or the Negroes' problems:

> The riots, North and South, involved mobs — not the disciplined, non-violent, direct-action demonstrators with whom I identify. We do

not condone lawlessness, looting and violence committed by the racists or the reckless of *any* colour. ... We are confronted primarily by a moral issue. It is as old as the scriptures and as clear as the American Constitution. The heart of the question is whether all Americans are to be afforded equal rights and equal opportunities.

The assassinations of Kennedy and King were not far off either. Violence and drug culture were taking America down the road into virulent anarchy.

While surveying the extensive devastation in the Watts section of Los Angeles, it came as a rude shock that many Negroes had not even heard of Martin Luther King — Sr. or Jr.! And when Martin addressed a small gathering of blacks at West Minister Community Centre and advised the people to abjure violence, follow the path of non-violence as practiced by Gandhi of India, some one from the audience shouted: "Get out of here Dr. King! We don't want you! The Watts riots coupled with this episode proved to be a turning point in King's perception of America and his role in the various movements. After all these years, King realized that there were "literally two Americas". One was an ocean of prosperity and plenty, beautiful, rich and predominantly white. The other was ugly, filthy, poor and essentially a set of black ghetto complexes. He told Bayard Rustin: "You know, Bayard, I worked to get these people the right to eat hamburgers, and now I have got to do something ... to help them to get to buy them."[7] After all, it did dawn on King and his colleagues that the economic problems of the class were far greater than those of racial segregation — the latter would automatically get resolved if the former situation was rectified. At this point of time King started reflecting seriously on socialism as a doctrine, on the same lines as Nehru of India had imbibed socialism as a panacea for solving the multitude of Indian ills. And poverty was not a problem restricted to the blacks only; whites suffered from it as much as the Negroes did. The reality that as America was becoming richer, stronger and more powerful as a nation day by day, the rich were becoming richer, and the poor poorer. "Economic Equality", and not merely social and racial equality, now came to be the major objectives of the Freedom Movement. The 1966-Gandhi Memorial Lecture at Howard University went a long way in clearing the cob webs from 'economic equality' and socialism as a doctrine. However, King and other leaders of the Movement were fully conscious of the danger of the new thinking lest they might be dubbed as communists, or as communist fellow-travellers. This is precisely what the Southerners and FBI were striving for all these years. It may be recalled that 'Christian Nationalist State Army' had issued death-threats against King on the occasion of fund-raising screening of *The Greatest Story Ever Told.* Hundreds of LAPD officers were deputed to guard King at the Hollywood Palladium and at the theatre on the Sunset Boulevard. It was feared that non-violence would suffer a tragic loss, and so would the American nation, if something ever happened to King as a result of such threats. Unfortunately, King dropped a brick, rather a huge stone, when he made a statement on TV that he would 'defend his family from attack in their home'. This led to banner headlines: "the biggest hypocrite alive" who "excluded his loved ones from danger that he constantly imposes on his followers." The death threats became all the more acute after King appeared on the cover of *Time* magazine as 'Man of the Year'. Consequentially, animosity towards Dr. King gained further momentum in the FBI circles. While Hoover was not at all inclined to give even an indirect impression that the Administration took the death threats seriously, President Johnson issued secret orders for King's security as a matter of national interest. However, King was unaware of the presidential concern or orders on the subject. He was equally unaware of the FBI wire-taps also, or the Neshoba County investigations for that matter.

After all, the Negro came to the realization that he too was part of the panorama of American kaleidoscope. His religion came to his rescue inasmuch as his belief that God loves all His children irrespective of the colour of their skin or the texture of their hair. In the ultimate analysis what mattered was his intrinsic and eternal worth as a person before God. The Negroes were thus inspired, determined to achieve parity with their white countrymen insofar as first class citizenship was concerned. At the same time the Negroes must be honest enough to accept that their standards often do lag behind. It was altogether a different matter that they feel short of the standards primarily on account of segregation.

33

Detroit Riots

There is something painfully sad about a riot. One sees screaming youngsters and angry adults fighting hopelessly and aimlessly against impossible odds. Deep down within them you perceive a desire for self-destruction, a suicidal longing. Rioting is the language of the oppressed and the have-nots.

Communal-race riots are not a phenomenon peculiar to the Indian sub-continent. It is the media hype that gives these episodes an altogether different dimension. The Western media derive a sadistic pleasure in blowing up odd episodes into full blown conflagrations, forgetting all the time as to what was the cause, and who caused it. The self-appointed guardians of minorities and human rights forget that the majority segment of India's population too cherish their human rights and cultural values. This is neither to belittle nor to justify the riots; but merely to highlight the travails of the majority, which are ignored by the western media. Democracy, cultural and religious freedoms are as much a right of the majority as these human values are of the minority, if not more! In the Indian riot scene the police open fire with live bullets to restore law and order. They opened fire on protesting crowds at Calcutta, Madras and Karachi. But that does not happen in the western world, except of course in the race riots of America where the Negroes were fired upon without compunction. The Western world must not forget their own recent past and the treatment they meted out to their own racial minorities. If in India the shadow of a low caste person was a sacrilege for the high caste, segregation of the blacks who were debarred from common public facilities like rest-rooms, buses and trains, cafeteria, dining rooms, service in restaurants, academic institutions, *et al*—the list is indeed endless — was a disgraceful blemish on the name of democracy and human rights there. And that too in the second half of the Twentieth Century! Who is more backward: the West or the East? Materialism alone does not constitute civilization.

The civil rights of the coloured people of the United States, the champions of human rights, were trampled *ad lib.* And segregationist policies had legal sanction. To overcome the legal lacunae, in 1960, the Congress passed another civil rights bill providing for legal action against the states concerned. But the same year also witnessed one of the largest mass migrations when almost one a half million Blacks left their homes and hearths in the South to seek peace and shelter in the already overcrowded ghettos of the North. By the end of 1950 the Blacks constituted nearly half the population of Washington D.C.—over a quarter of Philadelphia, Detroit, Cleveland, and Chicago. Houston and St. Louis.

It was not at all easy for the leaders, not even for Dr. Martin Luther King Jr., to keep control on the mobs. There were four days of serious rioting in Newark from 12th to 16th July followed by similar severe riots in Detroit that too lasted for four days. In both riots the police was on the side of the whites, and carrying out major portion of their task of suppressing the downtrodden. The casualties at both places were high. In Newark, twenty-one blacks and two whites were killed while in Detroit thirty-three blacks and ten whites died. The number of wounded was so high that a count could not be kept.[1] In order to prevent such riots in future more and more draconian laws were enacted, which only made the matters go from bad to worse. It became a vicious circle.

The events of 24-28th July 1967 — their extent, ferocity and resultant damage to life and property — proved to be the turning point. The Attorney General Ramsey Clark[2] rang up the President at 3:00 a.m. July 24th and informed him of large scale looting and arson in Detroit. Almost eighty fires were unattended at that early morning hour. "The Governor thinks he might need federal assistance." The President promptly agreed to put the army in Fort Bragg, North Carolina, on alert just in case. — The Attorney General and Governor Romney were in frequent contact but no decision could be reached till about 9:00 a.m. when the Governor called to read out a proposed statement recommending the use of federal troops. Clark explained the constitutional implications to Romney and told him that a specific request and certification had to be

1. Williams A. John: op. cit. p. 106.
2. Ramsay Clark had succeeded Nicholas Katzenbachas as Attorney General on 10th March 1967.

made by the Governor for deployment of federal troops before the President could send in the troops. The elaborate provisions in the Constitution were designed to prevent abuse of federal authority so as to safeguard democracy and rule of law.[3] No wonder therefore that Governor Romney continued to hedge the basic issue — certificate to the effect that there was a condition of insurrection or domestic violence necessitating deployment of federal troops. Since his request for federal troop assistance did not meet the constitutional prerequisites, the President could not, and did not want to send in federal troops. Nevertheless, he ordered airlift of troops from Fort Bragg, North Carolina, and Fort Campbell, Kentucky, to Selfridge Air Force Base in Michigan so as to be in a position to take effective action at short notice. Concurrently, the President deputed Cy Vance as his personal representative in Detroit. Meanwhile, as the situation continued to deteriorate further, the Governor declared a state of emergency; and Vance made a strong recommendation for federalizing the Michigan National Guard preparatory to deployment of 18th Airborne Corps under Lieutenant General John Throckmorton to restore order in the heavily riot-torn city of Detroit.

Having completed the urgent formalities, President Johnson addressed the nation from the White House at 11: 58 a.m. 24th July 1967 to explain the circumstances leading to federal intervention in the affairs of Michigan. This part was primarily a PR exercise to take the American people into confidence.

The main body of paratroopers reached the riot-torn area at 2:30 a.m. 25th July. Within hours of their patrolling 'the city saturated with fear', the situation started to quieten down. And normalcy was restored in another few days. The casualties: 43 persons killed, 324 injured and 7,231 arrested. The numbers of killed and wounded was much too high. The President therefore appointed the National Advisory Commission on Civil Disorders with Governor Otto Kerner of Illinois as the chairman and Mayor John Lindsay of New York as the member. The Commission completed its report in late February 1968 and made some far reaching recommendations that required $30 billion in addition to the more than $30 billion already earmarked for the poor of America. About a month after that, the assassination of Dr. Martin Luther King Jr. led to another bout of rioting all over the nation. The number of casualties and the damages to property were of staggering proportions. This part of the story is dealt elsewhere.

---

3. Till then, in the entire history of the United States the federal troops had been used only fifteen times to resolve domestic crises.

A Black Enterprise

The League of Revolutionary Black Workers rose from the ashes of the Detroit riots of 1967. Its primary objective was to organize Black workers for revolutionary changes. During its initial active period of four years, some enterprising Blacks were encouraged by the Nixon Administration to go into business towards betterment of their black brethren. Nixon established the office of Minority Business Enterprise whose primary objective was economic enticement of active black politicians to wean them from revolutionary movement(s). For instance: Floyd McKissick of CORE was sanctioned a government loan of fourteen million dollars to build a housing development complex in North Carolina. Nevertheless, in its totality, the Black business was mere peanuts. Just as a matter of comparison: the sales of the largest Black Corporation, Motown Industries, were $45 million in 1974 while that of Exxon Corporation amounted to $42 billion. Notwithstanding these palliatives, in 1977 the rate of unemployment amongst Black youths of America continued to be as high as 34.8 per cent; and six million Blacks were unemployed during the next year.[4]

Miami Riots

Detroit riots were not the last of the civil disturbances on account of race relations. However, industrial unrest had also created in as one of the factors along with the usual racial discrimination and high rate of unemployment, particularly amongst the Afro-Americans. And they were not the only poor unemployed, partially employed people in the United States. There were Latinos, Hispanics, Porto Ricans, Asians, and Red-Indians — all sorts of people in the nation of immigrants. During the Reagan presidency, the people had graduated from a 'frightened state' to an 'angry state' which did not bid well for the country. They started "acting out their frustrations in ways that will test the fabric of civil order." Reagan did not want to see the ruling white minority regime displaced by the radical African National Congress, a Black majority organization. His policies in South Africa alarmed the Afro-Americans and a majority of whites too so much so that Congress passed legislation imposing economic sanctions against the white South African Government overriding Reagan's veto.

The budget cuts effected by the Reagan administration spurred a series of strikes in the United States. The people were angered by

4. Zinn Howard: op. cit. pp. 456, 458-59.

layoffs, salary cuts, and uncertainty about job-security. Teachers in seven States went on strike idling more than 300,000 students for more than a week. There were a number of other class-actions due to financial difficulties resulting from economic policies of the Federal Government. When a 50-years old computer science teacher was sent to jail for leading a teachers' strike, about 2,000 people demonstrated in his support outside the jailhouse in Little Washington, Pennsylvania. In Pittsburgh area when unemployed or bankrupt houseowners faced foreclosures, sixty pickets demonstrated before the courthouse in protest against the auctions forcing the authorities to call off the proceedings. Again, 200 angry farmers had to be dispersed using tear gas and mace when a 320-acre wheat farm in Colorado State faced foreclosure.

With these background developments, when President Reagan arrived at Pittsburgh in April 1983 to make a speech, 3,000 unemployed steel workers demonstrated against him outside his hotel. Similar demonstrations by unemployed workers took place in Detroit, Flint, Chicago, Cleveland, Los Angeles, Washington and many more cities nationwide. That was the time when Miami witnessed serious rioting by the Afro-Americans. The unemployment rate amongst this section of the populace had exceeded fifty per cent and the Administration responded by severe police actions time and again besides building more jailhouses. The basic issues boiled down to guns versus children, guns versus butter, i.e., social welfare. President Reagan knew very well that the Blacks would not vote for him. Instead of resolving the basic issues of poverty and unemployment, Reagan approached Congress to eliminate a crucial portion of the Voting Rights Act of 1965!

The above was not all. 'Welfare' became a contentious issue during Reagan Presidency. "Aid to Families with Dependent Children' (AFDC), food stamps, healthcare through Medicaid were vital components of the overall welfare program. In most cases the program provided for $500-$700 per month, leaving the bulk of the poor recipients well below the 'poverty line' of $900 a month. The racial imbalance had come to the point where black children were four times as likely as white children to grow up on welfare. Here it needs to be borne in mind that this dismal state of affairs continued more than a decade and a half after the assassination of Martin Luther King Jr.

Ultimately, Reagan had to bow to the pressure of public opinion and withdrew most of the cutbacks while Congress eliminated the rest of them.[5]

5. Zinn Howard: op. cit. pp. 566, 597-98

34

Slum City Syndrome: Chicago

Segregated or Mixed Communities?

When the locomotive of history roared through the nineteenth century and the first half of the twentieth, it left the nation's black masses standing forlornly at dismal terminals. The scientific achievements came as a blessing to the American economy. But it came as a curse to the Negro because the skilled and semi-skilled jobs they filled disappeared under the magic of automation.

Shortage of semi-skilled and unskilled jobs was indeed a prominent facet of the basic Negro problem. The whites wanted to maintain segregation to ensure that their children did not come in close contact with Black children, while the Blacks were moving upward into the urban middle class and wanted their children to derive the benefits of public schools education. Moreover, while the White middle class had reached near the saturation point, the Black middle class were an ever-widening phenomenon. This in turn increased the pressure on public school education system in which the Whites did not feel comfortable. For example: In Chicago 25 per cent of pupils is Negro while in St. Louis the figure is as high as 40 per cent.[1] That holds good for the move of Negro middle class into predominantly white residential areas, as well as into development of new community centres. Robert Dishman cites the case study by the Philadelphia Redevelopment Commission: while 1730 Negro families had moved in during 1955, the figure for the Whites was 485. The point to note is that racial segregation amongst the middle class was giving way to mixed racial communities. Nonetheless, the presence and proportion of Negro middle class in a white neighbourhood

1. Dishman B. Robert: op. cit. p. 85.

continued to be a critical factor in decision making, and continues to be so even today, although it may be sacrilegious or even illegal, to say so in so many words. And of course it is not officially admitted, *per se*.

The SCLC decided to move the Movement out of its Southern confines to give it a national character. The Chicago campaign was the first step in that direction. It is not that the Negroes of Chicago were sitting on their haunches waiting for King; far from it. Chicago Coordinating Council of Community Organizations (CCCO), a coalition of local civil rights groups, was already active in the sprawling slums of the metropolis; what it required was strong leadership at the top to add fresh vigour, and to move ahead at a faster pace. A start was made by a march to the Chicago City Hall where King addressed a rally on July 26, 1965, sponsored by CCCO under the leadership of Al Raby, a former Chicago public school teacher turned a social activist. While the overall mission in Chicago was to redress the social ills generated by the 'ghetto pathology of the Northern Negro' in four successive stages of development:

- 'Quality Integrated Education' was chosen as the bill-board of Freedom Movement for Chicago, and so it became the first limited objective.
- To follow in the footsteps of Birmingham — the most segregated city in the South — 'integrated public accommodation' was designated as the symbol of desegregation in Chicago.
- The cap-stone for Chicago was to be the solution of the Northern Ghetto problems in all their ramifications throughout the nation.

Since drastic improvement of slum-life was the ultimate goal, Martin started living in, and working from, the very heart of the ghetto. The slum of Lawndale was a live 'island of extreme poverty surrounded by an ocean of plenty'. Martin chose Lawndale for his living and working quarters. While extreme poverty pervaded Lawndale, Chicago had higher per capita income than any city in the world. But it was here in the ghettos of Chicago that a baby was attacked by rats, murder and gang-wars were rife, drug-dealing was a source of employment and income, both parents worked to make ends meet, where the father held even two jobs at the same time resulting in total neglect of emotional needs of the children, social and environmental deprivation which in turn provided the raw material for various criminal activities by the youngsters — it was a vicious circle indeed. Economic deprivation, unemployment, nauseating living conditions, poor schooling — you name the social ill, and black Chicago boasted of it. The daily lives of inhabitants of these ghettos were dominated by welfare workers and the police. They just could not break out of the shackles of the 'captive island syndrome'. Indeed, the SCLC had taken on an uphill lifetime job. And Martin had placed his family in an "emotional pressure cooker" ready to explode at the slightest provocation![2]

The Chicago riots of July 1966 were symptomatic of the social upheaval for which the pressure was building over the past many decades. The official machinery of the government as well as the upper strata of society was primarily responsible for the eruption grown out of frustration and intolerable living conditions, more so when the next door neighbourhood is an oasis of prosperity. In one instance, eight policemen were observed beating one lad. Was that law and order? Harris Woodford, the celebrated author and journalist, had personally witnessed policemen beating protesters after their arrest — indeed a common daily occurrence in India even in the 21st century, and hardly any one raises a finger. The policemen swinging their clubs indiscriminately at one and sundry — called "lathi-charge" in Gandhi's India, a matter of routine police action. The police attacking reporters, cameramen, chasing bystanders into hotel lobbies, hitting victims till they fell unconscious — that was the plight of Negroes in the ghettoes. Some courageous Democrats like Harris Wofford, Bill Moyers and his wife Judith, Adam Yarmolinsky and a number of other delegates to the Democratic Convention then in progress in Chicago decided to expose the terrible extent of police brutalities heaped on the Negroes. They and many others held a silent vigil next noon, in front of the Conrad Central Hotel, standing on the edge of Michigan Avenue between the park protesters and the police.[3] Unfortunately, the concept and practice of non-violence was the immediate casualty. The slum-dwellers had lost faith in the technique and philosophy of Dr. Martin Luther King Jr. The fundamental issue of racial discrimination and subjugation was lost in the debris of racial riots. King launched his non-violent Chicago Freedom Movement whose marches met with a hail of bricks and bottles, jeers and jibes, unparalleled mob hostility decorated with Nazi flags and Swastikas on the roadsides and in parks. It was a clash of 'White Power' and 'Black Power', the powerful and powerless. Both sides indulged in racist catcalls spiced with the vilest of obscenities. Hatred soaked the air of Chicago. Tear gas, bayonets, machine guns, billy clubs and barbed — these were the tools of repression, of violence and hatred. But Martin and Company responded: "Our protests will be entirely peaceful. We will not return

2. King Martin Luther: op. cit. *Autobiography*, 302.
3. Wofford Harris: *Of Kennedys and Kings*, McGraw Hills, 1980; p. 427.

violence with violence. We call upon Mayor Daley and the citizens of Chicago to put an end to the use of armed force."

Once again the Executive head of the federal government did not uphold the Constitution. After one of the worst police beatings in front of the Hilton, President Humphrey defended the action by the police force, and instead criticized the non-violent protestors. He was on the side of Dick Daley, and not for justice to his people. Muriel Humphrey went a step further and said that the protestors were 'noisy and rude' and were getting too much attention.[4]

The primary issue before a number of delegates to the Convention was the inordinately excessive use of force by the police. When negotiations for peaceful end of the imbroglio failed, Dick Gregory had the Deputy Superintendent of Police address the gathering. He made it clear that the police will not permit obstruction of traffic by the marchers, and would therefore react to uphold the law, right or wrong, to prevent the march proceeding from the Hilton. Gregory informed the gathering that they had a legal right to accept his invitation to walk to his house with him on the side walk for dinner at his house. "We will stay on the sidewalks and cross streets only when the traffic lights let us..." The dignitaries, officials, all those with suits and tie, and the older people were requested to lead the procession. The Police was non-plussed. While on the march, the protestors were singing "Onward Christian Soldiers", "The Battle Hymn of the Republic", and "We shall Overcome." Nevertheless, the well suited and booted dinner guests were arrested down the road. But that is a different story altogether for most others except for Harris who had been taunted by the Gandhian Indian leader Rammanohar Lohia that Harris had never been to jail, and therefore how could he and the oppressed people of America hope to achieve freedom. Lohia[5] followed the footsteps of Mahatma Gandhi and, like the latter, strongly believed that a person fighting an oppressor must enter jail at least once, and enter the prison cheerfully "as a bridegroom enters the bridal chamber". The backlash from Chicago crusade increased to the point that even some conservative blacks became critical of King and his protest-marches and consequential racial tensions. However, King responded that if the Negroes were required to stop demonstrating, justice should prevail first. "If you want a moratorium on marches, put a moratorium on injustice."[6] In the same breath he also demanded

4. Ibid. p. 432.
5. Lohia had visited Mississippi sometime during 1964 and managed to go to jail there during one of the demonstrations of "Freedom Summer".
6. Schulke Flip and Penelope McPhee: *King Remembered*, New York, 1986, p. 234.

restraint on the police and other law enforcement agencies whose brutality had reached inhuman levels.

Ultimately, non-violence won the day. Peace was restored. But all said and done, the Chicago Convention episode came as a rude shock to many, particularly the younger generation. They were totally disillusioned by the politics of democratic system in America. The violence, street confrontations, nomination of Humphrey, defeat of peace platform, *et al*, added to a lingering feeling of defeatism. King was down and under. He had passed his zenith. Towards the end of his life, King himself recognized that he had been defeated by massive misunderstanding and outbreaks of violence. To some, it was now the return to violence as the sole panacea for equal rights and opportunities to attain first class citizenship in their own country. While commenting on the efficacy of non-violence in the post-Chicago period, one of the leaders of the Students for a Democratic Society said: "That whole Gandhi bag is broken, and the good old days of Martin Luther King are gone, and gone for ever, and a good riddance."[7]

On the other side of the coin, the writing was on the wall. Non-violence was still the only viable solution to the social ills from which America had suffered terribly. While he was the Defence Secretary, Robert McNamara, had watched an anti-war demonstration from his window in the Pentagon and had thought to himself: "If they stick to Gandhi, if they keep their discipline, they can stir the country and paralyze the prosecution of the war." But destiny had ordained otherwise. America was destined to suffer a humiliating defeat in Vietnam. But when some of the demonstrators below started throwing bottles and shouting obscene slogans, McNamara knew that the marchers had lost. In the process 'Free Speech' movement degenerated into 'Filthy Speech' movement.[8]

Nevertheless, the SCLC inspired by King launched a drive to make Chicago an open city for housing. A 'Freedom Sunday' rally was held on July 10 at Soldier's Field to mark the occasion. The Board of Realtors of the Real Estate Board of Chicago City made some peace-offerings leading to a ten-hour meeting on August 17. Finally, on August 26 King reached a 'summit agreement' with Mayor Daley and other Chicago leaders. 'Open Housing' in Chicago became a reality in black and white only, but not in concrete on the ground for which a couple of years' further effort was required. Meanwhile, 'Tenants Unions' formed on the lines of labour unions made remarkable progress in the quality of repairs,

---

7. Wofford Harris: op. cit. p. 447.
8. Ibid. p. 448.

rent freezes, regular janitorial and sanitation services, *et al*, went a long way in making a dent in the quality of life. Insofar as amount of rent[9] was concerned, CCCO-SCLC negotiated with the landlords who were mostly Jews, and in most cases amicable agreements were arrived at. "Operation Breadbasket" under which equitable employment opportunities were negotiated by SCLC with the industry-employer concerned gave a big boost to improve the economic life of the Negro. In Chicago three major industries — milk, soft drinks and chain grocery stores — joined the scheme even though some of the companies did so after short "Don't Buy" campaigns. By 1967 Operation Breadbasket was in force in some twelve major cities generating approximately seven million dollars in new annual income for Negro families.[10]

There is no doubt that the American Supreme Court and the White House had played a significant role in upward move of the Negroes to improve their standards, and to enable them attain the status of first-class citizenship. In this respect the First Amendment went a long way in protecting the rights of the people on an equal footing — freedom of speech, free press, freedom of peaceful assembly, freedom of religion, *et al*. Such rights had been enshrined in the Magna Carta and the Bill of Rights which was added to the American Constitution in 1791 through ten amendments passed simultaneously. The ten Rights guaranteed by the Constitution were:

- Freedom of Religion;
- Freedom of Speech;
- Right to assemble;
- Right to petition;
- Freedom from unreasonable searches;
- No illegal loss of liberty;
- Just compensation for property;
- Right to a public trial by jury;
- No excessive bail or fines;
- Right to summon witnesses.

---

9. Just to quote one instance: King was paying $94 for a four room ramshackle filthy apartment with no heating and broken down plumbing, while a white family in the next neighborhood was paying only $78 per month for a five rooms apartment in excellent sanitary condition with all facilities in working order. In other words, the Negro was paying a 'color tax' and that too for a shabby run down house. The Blacks had to resort to rent-strike in many cases to get fair rental agreement.

10. King Martin Luther: op. cit. *Autobiography*, p. 309

The same holds good for the Fourteenth Amendment also. Notwithstanding its passage, full and all-inclusive citizenship was not to be availed of by the Afro-Americans and other racial minorities, the Mexicans and Japanese in particular. It was an exercise in futility, at least for the initial decades.

The Workers Alliance of America with a membership as high as six hundred thousand was active in the field of organizing the poor working class of America into a strong, militant, powerful lobby. Those were the times of the so-called 'New Deal'. The workers demonstrated, agitated, protested; but the Roosevelt (F.D.) Administration was unmoved, and so was the President himself. The Alliance died a natural death. In the late 1960s, its place was taken by National Welfare Rights Organization (NWRO) composed mostly of Blacks, especially the black women. They staged hundreds of protest-demonstrations, marches and agitations under the leadership of George A. Wiley[11], a chemistry professor turned a civil rights activist. This organization too suffered an early death in 1973 due to policy differences amongst the leadership. However, another black civil rights worker active in the field of slum organization and amelioration work did achieve some notable success by way of rents and housing. But his work was much too insignificant to make a dent at the national level. It will thus be seen that the basic cause for failure of political advancement by the Blacks was poverty coupled with lack of education and job opportunities. Economic independence was *sine qua non* for climbing the political ladder. The black statistics of the time speak for themselves, loud and clear — forty per cent of children lived in homes without fathers; twenty-five per cent of black homes were affected by crime; the black unemployment rate had doubled since President Lyndon Johnson launched his poverty-eradication program; and so on.[12] It was an irony of fate that while the most affluent nation on planet earth was spending billions of dollars as aid to poor developing countries, it could not take care of its own poor. The American Administrations, one after the other, talked of democracy abroad but not at home; they lectured the world about human rights but denied the same to their own down-trodden; they were high on rhetoric but low on implementation; they shouted at the top of their voice that all men are created equal, but failed to put the principle into practice at home; and so on and so forth. The Blacks continued to be second class citizens in their own country for

11. Wiley died by drowning in the infamous Chesapeake Bay a few months after the failure of NWRO.

12. Burns M. James : op. cit. p. 571.

a couple of more decades, if not still much longer. The late President John F. Kennedy had aptly put this sentiment in memorable words: "If a free society cannot help the many who are poor, it cannot save the few who are rich." Unfortunately, his brother, Robert Kennedy, who had the potential to unite the poor, the blacks, the rich and the women's movements behind the Democratic Party suffered the same fate as the charismatic Black leader Dr. Martin Luther King Jr., who taught blacks and whites 'how to be both militant and non-violent'.

Yet another unfortunate aspect of working of American Constitution has been that the various Presidents, one and all, have been reluctant to use the powers vested in that august office for the benefit of the Negroes and other minority groups. The laws passed way back in the 1860s and 1870s together with the Fourteenth and Fifteenth Amendments gave enough executive powers to the President to wipe out racial discrimination and establish racial equality and balance. Every one of them failed the Afro-Americans. Discrimination in Inter-State transportation facilities could have been easily eliminated by a stroke of President's pen; but it was not to be. What could have been easily enforced through executive action was routed through legislative measures resulting in inordinate delay and considerable national damage in terms of life and property. Ultimately, it was the Supreme Court that resolved some of these ticklish problems while the Presidents abrogated their authority.

35

Black Power

The Negro has many pent-up resentments and latent frustrations, and he must release them. So let him march; let him make prayer pilgrimage to the city hall; let him go on freedom rides. If his repressed emotions are not released in nonviolent ways, they will seek expression through violence. The Negro needs the white man to free him from his fears. The white man needs the Negro to free him from his guilt. A doctrine of black supremacy is as evil as a doctrine of white supremacy.

Malcolm X was born Malcolm Little in Omaha, Nebraska, on May 19, 1925 as the seventh child of J. Early Little. It was a typical poor black family, a product of Northern ghettos, as opposed to Martin whose origins were in the Southern well-to-do black middle class. Malcolm spent his early years in Lansing, Michigan, working as a hustler in Boston and New York until his imprisonment in Charlestown State Prison on February 27, 1946. Like King Sr., Malcolm's father was also a Baptist preacher but he remained a 'jackleg' preacher, never called to a permanent pastorate. Nevertheless, Earl Little was seriously involved in Negroes' struggle for dignity and justice, as much as King Sr. was, if not more. Since Earl Little was president of UNIA, his views tilted heavily towards Marcus Garvey's philosophy of Black Nationalism. Malcolm's mother was a reporter and an active member in the 'Garvey Movement'. She was proud of her African heritage and inculcated a sense of pride and honor for the same in her children. Thus Malcolm imbibed Black Nationalism from his both parents, as did Martin too but in a different direction.

Both Martin and Malcolm were preachers, "men of cloth" as such professionals were called amongst the black community — one for the Christian faith and the other for Islam. While Martin earned a Ph.D. before completing his education, Malcolm's formal education ended at the eighth standard. His subsequent intellectual development took place in the school of life, in the ghettos of Boston and New York. Both men turned out to be charismatic leaders and ardent speakers who could keep their audiences captivated with their oratory. In his autobiography, Malcolm has described his childhood as a nightmare. His family was driven out of Omaha by the Ku Klux Klan while another white hate group, the "Black Legionnaires" burned down the family house in Lansing.

Malcolm was of the view that integration was a false solution to the problem of segregation. He was not advocating continued segregation; instead, he favoured *Separation.* When life and liberty of the black is regulated by the whites, it is segregation. It is forced on the inferiors by the superiors; but "Separation' is voluntary acceptance of what may otherwise tantamount to segregation. The distinction between the two concepts may be there; but it is much too subtle for an average white man to follow, let alone a Negro. Martin was almost forced by circumstances to acknowledge Malcolm's 'Separatism'. This happened with the rise of 'Black Power' as a dominant theme and slogan during the Memphis-Jackson march following the shooting of James Meredith in June 1966. King held on to his creed of non-violence declaring: "Today's despair is a poor chisel to carve out tomorrow's justice. Black Power is an implicit and often an explicit belief in black separatism. Yet behind Black Power's legitimate and necessary concern for group unity and black identity lies the belief that there can be a separate road to power and fulfillment. Few ideas are more unrealistic. There is no salvation for the Negro through isolation."[1]

All said and done, there was great commonality between Martin and Malcolm, the most important being their respective goals: they were the same though the paths, the methodology was different. Both sought 'unqualified liberation' of Afro-Americans, total desegregation and elimination of discrimination and oppression on racial grounds. Equal opportunity in education, training, honing of skills, and employment-incomes was the crux of economic independence. And both sought these objectives in their own way, although the significant differences in their historical and social origins led them to different tracks. Since the basic objectives of both were the same, their efforts did complement each other.

Both were respecters of human beings, each in his own way. Martin was eminently successful in galvanizing hundreds and thousands of blacks all over the United States not because of his intellectual advancement or

1. *Time* dated April 12, 1968.

academic qualifications, but because of his respect for the human personality for its own intrinsic value. Martin was a staunch follower of non-violence and the principles as enunciated by Gandhi, Thoreau and other liberal theologians, whose ideas he infused with Christian dogma and spirituality. However, the black masses that followed him as their leader did not, and most could not, understand the fine points of those philosophies; nevertheless they followed him through thick and thin, many risking their lives. The long and the short of it was that a "New Negro" — proud of what he was, his blackness, his African origins, his background as a descendent of slaves — was born, strong in spirit with a will to resist white bigotry.

So did Malcolm X.

White Morality

"Heads I win; tails you lose"! — This was the bottom line, the crux of white morality since the ages. Martin King was a man of morality, more or less pristine, and he spoke against the white morality. He was rather mild in his chastisement in the initial stages, but later came out strongly against this one way morality. Martin's views on the subject were moulded, at least partially, by Bayard Rustin. The latter generally remained in the background but still had a subtle influence on King's ideas regarding morality of violence and war. Rustin was a Quaker and believed: "... the law of violence is such that each side becomes equally vicious. To try to distinguish between which is more vicious is to fail to recognize the logic of war. It is war that is evil, not the Viet Cong, not the United States."[2]

Appearances can be deceptive. So they were in Vietnam. It came to be accepted that Blacks and Whites had found a "new brotherhood" while fighting shoulder to shoulder the 'common enemy' in Vietnam. This so called brotherhood was merely on the surface; it was only skin- deep. Many observers on the battlefield came to the conclusion that more racism was exercised by the white soldiers even on the battlefield. But back home, Martin King had built up a tremendous reputation. He had agreed to serve as a co-chairman of "Clergy and Laymen Concerned About Vietnam". The events connected with admission in 1962 of James Meredith, an Air Force veteran, in the White University of Mississippi had brought home the truth that the so called brotherhood of servicemen and women on the battlefield was only skin deep. Segregation and racial injustice was in the Southern white blood. And that took its toll on June 06, 1966, when James was shot and wounded in the back by a sniper while he was on his lonely 'March Against Fear' through the State of Mississippi.

---

2. Williams A. John: op. cit. p. 101.

The SCLC leadership immediately flew from Atlanta to Memphis to visit to visit Meredith. So did Floyd McKissick, national director of CORE. While in the hospital room, Stokely Carmichael and Cleveland Sellers of Students Non-violent Coordinating Committee also came in. The group left the patient alone with the assurance that they would continue the march in the same spirit as Meredith had begun. The group thereafter agreed that the march would be jointly sponsored by CORE, SNCC and SCLC with the understanding that other civil rights organizations would also be invited to join. After that they moved over to the desolate spot on Highway 51 where James Meredith had been shot the day before, and started the Freedom March as a continuation of Meredith's. While walking down the Highway, there was long discussion about the constituent units and members who would participate in the march and the conduct thereof, with particular reference to the slogan and placards announcing 'BLACK POWER' as the underlying theme. The new slogan supported by Malcolm X was an expression of distrust of any advantage conceded by the whites. In essence, it was a rejection of white paternalism, howsoever well meant it might have been. Of course, the Black masses were not aware of the famous saying of Aldous Huxley, "Liberties are not given; they are taken", but they wanted to be independent of white support to achieve their goal. This led to prolonged heated and emotionally charged discussions for the next day or two. Bayard Rustin, A. Philip Randolph, Roy Wilkins and Whitney Young were vehemently opposed to the new slogan. Wilkins was most emphatic when he said: Black Power is the father of hatred and mother of violence." Naturally, Martin was strongly opposed to the new theme. His view was that when you put 'Black' and 'Power' together, you mean 'Black Dominance'. He was strongly opposed to replacing the current Freedom Song "We Shall Overcome" by "We Shall Overrun".[3] However, a stage had been reached when Martin Luther King Jr., though still respected as the top leader of the Freedom Movement, his popularity was in the wane inasmuch as new heroes like Malcolm X, Huey Newton, *et al*, were posing a challenge to his leadership. Malcolm was a black revolutionary, but certainly not a Marxist revolutionary. The Panthers had guns and they believed in defending themselves. To many black-militants, non-violence seemed naïve, outmoded and even suicidal. "King was dangerously close to slipping from prophet to patsy."[4] In the process, Martin too fell in line with Malcolm in urging blacks to be proud of their blackness and African heritage. In fact, Martin went so far as to concede that 'racism was so deeply ingrained in America, especially in the

3. King Martin Luther: op. cit. (Autobiography), p. 316.
4. *Time* dated April 12, 1968.

North, that "temporary segregation'" was perhaps the only means by which a certain degree of power could be wielded by the Negroes. One may disagree with the extremism and religious fundamentalism of Malcolm, his untimely death at the hands of a fellow Black Muslim left a wide void in the black freedom struggle.

Gandhi too suffered the same fate. His frustratingly slow march towards independence, his idiosyncrasies and mild attitude towards the British, his 'unpredictable vagaries', etc. made the younger segment of the nationalist cadres start looking forward to the fire-brand leaders with a revolutionary bent of mind. Gandhi's popularity suffered a setback to that extent. Moreover, Gandhi was a dictator of sorts, even though his dictatorship was based on love. In the words of John Gunther, "he is a unique kind of dictator, one who rules by love." Be that as it may, there is no denying that during the last few years of his life, a big chunk of young Indians had become disenchanted with Gandhi's theory of non-violence and civil disobedience. In fact, John Gunther has listed what many Indians believed as 'Gandhi's defects':

- Dictatorial attitude was first on the list. "If you choose to follow my lead, you must accept my conditions." He insisted on going to the Round Table Conference alone and consequently was 'drowned in detail and outmaneuvered.
- Gandhi's medievalism and 'extravagant use of religious symbolism' was a pain in the neck to a large number of younger leaders and activists.
- Gandhi was alleged to be meek and masochist playing in the hands of the British.
- Gandhi's sense of proportion was thought to be off balance. His detractors cited a number of instances in support of this view.
- Gandhi was prone to compromise rather than keep up the fight. He 'preferred settlement to struggle'. And once a settlement was made, he 'cooperated with his enemies as vigorously as he fought them'.

Generally speaking, a revolution is based on hope and hate. Death and destruction invariably follow such upheavals. "What was new about Mahatma Gandhi's movement in India was that he mounted a revolution on hope and love, hope and non-violence", but not on hope and hate. King had followed this path with meticulous care, converting the traditional hate into 'positive non-violent power'. "Hate is just as injurious to the hater as it is to the hated".[5]

---

5. King: op. cit. (*Autobiography*) pp. 328, 332.

As they continued walking down the meandering Highway, the marchers were greeted by large crowds en route. It was a repetition of Gandhi's Salt Satyagraha Dandi March where the villagers in thousands welcomed the volunteers. Martin and his associates had similar experience and emotional upsurge. But the discussion regarding the slogan 'Black Power' continued off and on. After about ten days of marching the climax came at Greenwood, which was SNCC territory in that Car Michael and his associates had courageously worked there during the 'turbulent summer of 1964'. In the rally that followed, they roused the crowd to an emotional high pitch by repeating the slogan 'Black Power' again and again and again till it rose to a crescendo. It was not the first time that the phrase had been used — it had been used long before by Richard Wright and others, but as a crowd rousing slogan, it was used for the first time that night as an attempt to incorporate the slogan in the official lexicon of the Freedom Movement. Martin now faced a similar situation as the Frontier Gandhi also had way back in the 1930's, since the Muslim Pathans did not have the concept of Ahimsa, non-violence, and of *Tapasya,* self-suffering. The Pathan was used to establish his position in society through skilful and ruthless use of violent power. The proponents of Black Power wanted to follow the same path. The SNCC was hell bent on replacing 'Freedom Now' by 'Black Power', and Martin was not prepared to accept 'Black Power' as the official slogan of the Movement because of its offensive connotations, the pungent waft of violence that it carried in its wake. The manner, in which it was displayed, by placards as well as by shouting, was all the more offensive. Non-violence was also a form of force to reckon with, was not acceptable to young hot-headed minds. The discussions on the subject became so overheated and surcharged with emotions that the unity of the Movement appeared on the verge of being fractured. A slogan cannot be converted or implemented as a program. It was at that stage that Martin suggested a compromise: Neither 'Freedom Now' nor 'Black Power' will be chanted during the march, or used as slogans or placards by any participant in the Movement. The compromise solution was accepted by all the participating organizations. Nevertheless, the young black leadership soon fell in line like the Pathans of Frontier Gandhi. The Pathans appreciated that the British Government was so powerful that they could put down any degree of violence to which the Pathans may resort to; but no government in the world could put down the force of non-violence. The Black masses of America also came to the same conclusion and fell in line with Martin's exhortations to non-violence as a powerful weapon.

The proponents of 'Black Power' got a boost consequent of a tactless omission on the part of President Johnson — A brave young Negro,

Jimmy Lee Jackson, was killed in Alabama and a white Unitarian minister, James Reeb, was fatally clubbed to the ground by white hoodlums. President Johnson sent flowers to Mrs. Reeb and also mentioned his name amongst the martyrs during his "We Shall Overcome" eloquent speech. He did not mention the Negro nor sent flowers to his wife. The Black community in general and the SNCC leadership in particular, drew the obvious conclusion that Black life had no value in the eyes of the President, or the white community for that matter. They harped on this white attitude to no end, rightly so too. They strongly felt that the basic problem was lack of power in the hands of the Negro; hence the vital importance of the slogan: "Black Power". This made the task of reconciliation, and to follow the path of non-violence, by Martin all the more difficult. In fact, the crux of Black imbroglio was not so much political, but it was essentially economic coupled with financial insecurity.

It was during this period that many whites saw King as the next Presidential candidate for 1968, more so since a large number of Americans were bored stiff with Democratic politics.

During the same period Martin took the opportunity to remind both white and black America of some of the most significant and valuable contributions that the Negro had made towards white advancement and prosperity:[6]

- The first American to sacrifice his life in the American War of Independence to free the neo-colonists from British oppression was a Negro, Crispus Attucks.
- The first successful heart-operation performed in America was by a Negro, Dr. Daniel Hale Williams.
- The credit for devising a method to separate blood plasma, and storing it on a large sale goes to the Negro Dr. Charles Drew. This process led to saving of thousands of lives in the Second World War.
- The contributions of George Washington Carver in agricultural products went a long way in saving the economy of the Southern States.
- The invention of an evaporating pan by a Negro, Norbert Rillieux, revolutionized the sugar industry.
- It was a Negro, Granville T. Woods, whose inventions went a long way in improving performance of electric motors, which in turn boosted the growth and performance railroads in America.

---

6. King Martin Luther Jr.: op. cit. (*Autobiography*), p. 327.

And so on and so forth.

The Spring Mobilization Committee had scheduled a march for 15 April 1967 under the leadership of Reverend Dr. Martin Luther King Jr. and Dr. Benjamin Spock together with other religious and civil rights leaders. The march started from Central Park on a gray drizzling morning. Law and order was an important factor. However, insofar as the Whites were concerned, law and order simply meant repression of Blacks, poor people and political dissenters. By now the times had changed. It may be recalled that Rustin's 'Poor People's March' came towards the end of 1967 followed by another march by America's poor — the poor Mexican-Americans, poor Puerto Rican-Americans, poor black Americans, poor white Americans, and poor Red-Americans. This could well be the beginning of a grass-roots movement in the U.S. That is perhaps the reason why more Blacks re-enlisted in the army than the whites because "they find more democracy in the Army than in civilian life."

There are three major religions in the U.S. — Protestants, Catholics and Jews. All three are politically and economically powerful entities, all in their own peculiar ways. Martin King soon found out that all those who claimed to be true Christians were far from being Christians in true sense of the word. It is the Catholic community that started slave trade in Africa, and in course of time, that is what has been the basic cause of racial problems in the U.S. "From the beginning Catholicism has had an exploitative and dehumanizing relationship to black people. Priests went on the journeys to Africa, waiting beside the sandy, windswept barracoons of Badagry in Nigeria and Cape Coast in Ghana, blessed the slaves bound in chains for the New World."[7] Similar developments followed in Santo Domingo (Haiti). However, it would be wrong to lay the entire blame at the feet of the Catholics; the Protestants soon followed in their footsteps. Extra money and free labour was as welcome to Protestants as it was to the early Catholics. It would therefore not be wrong to conclude that practically the entire wealth of the New World was indeed Catholic wealth — and the slave was a commodity that added to the wealth of the white man.

Insofar as the Jews were concerned, anti-Semitism was a dominant sentiment all over the world. Notwithstanding that negative downward drag, the poor immigrant Jewish community prospered and attained the middle class status. They became an influential segment of society socially, economically, academically and politically, all within a single generation wielding influence much beyond their numbers. The Jews had attained

---

7. Williams A. John: op. cit. pp. 123-24.

such power and influence that if the Anglo-Saxon America found it necessary to rid itself of a minority group, it would be the Blacks and certainly not the Jews. However, Martin King's humanitarianism was a positive factor that immensely appealed to the U.S. Jews. As opposed to the Jews, the King's forefathers were way behind in education. And an uneducated or partially educated Black was held in contempt, especially so if he tried to move in a circle dominated by college graduates.[8]

Black Nationalism

In October 1966, two college-educated youngmen from Oakland in California, Huey Newton and Bobby Seale, formed the 'Black Panther Party for Self-Defence'.[9] The formation of BPP and 'Oakland Panthers' etc. was the direct result of despair, rejection and frustration born out of white violence and cruelty mercilessly perpetrated by the whites. The leaders of black groups were mostly college educated youngmen who would not let the whites continue their vicious treatment. In fact, SNCC leaders all came from the college educated middle class: Charles McDew, James Forman, John Lewis, Stokely Carmichael, Rap Brown, et al.[10] Initially these leaders were committed to non-violence, but they were met with violence and beaten up severely for no rhyme or reason. The 'Panthers' dressed in military attire carried arms for self-defence.[11] Their faith in non-violence soon evaporated, forcing them to the path of militancy, more so after Carmichael was briefly arrested in Greenwood along with numerous marchers on a flimsy charge of erecting sleeping-tents on the grounds of a black school in contravention of orders of state troopers. Following his release he addressed a protest rally of about 3,000 persons during which the theme was 'BLACK POWER',

8. In that sense, Martin Sr. must have been considered a "jackleg" which among the Negroes meant "unlettered, untrained but functioning on the brink. Moreover, the Kings lacked "colour" inasmuch as they were deficient of an adequate proportion of white blood in their veins that would have given them the status of what was considered a "pleasing brown". And black men generally preferred to marry girls having lighter skin colour than their own.
9. In 1970 the FBI reported to President Nixon that about twenty-five percent of the Black population of the country supported the Black Panther Party. Amongst the younger age group below twenty-one, the figure was as high as forty-three percent. It appeared that during the civil rights movement, on the one hand the government was making concessions through the Congress and on the other it was destroying the Movement through the medium of the FBI.
10. Williams A. John: op. cit. p. 161.
11. Under California law in force at that time, carrying guns and firearms was legal, if carried openly, unconcealed.

and the slogan was rhythmically repeated several times. In the days following the 'Meredith March Against Fear', this concept of Black Power and slogans thereof was condemned by many black leaders. Dr. King's reaction: "I happen to believe that a doctrine of Black Supremacy is as evil as White Supremacy. ..." Nevertheless, the concept of Black Power did bring about a significant cultural transformation in the black community. The blacks were now proud to be black. They came to accept their blackness as en inherent and essential element of their humanity. "I am Black and I am Proud" became the new watchword. Black became beautiful too. Curly Afro-hair came back in style. Hair straighteners went into garbage cans. Afro-history and writings came to be popular. 'Afro' became an outward sign of an inward transformation of the Negro psyche. The Negroes found their roots: they were Africans and that was their heritage, the legacy of their past. The achievements of Malcolm X and to some extent of Muhammad Ali (Cassius Clay) too, in furtherance of Black Movement could not be ignored or belittled. Notwithstanding the later break up between the two Black Muslim nationalist leaders, they had successfully provided a bright new identity to the Negro, howsoever limited in its scope.

Martin belonged to the middle class strata of society. He was well educated and quite successful in the white world. His emphasis on integration was therefore understandable, being the product of his exposure to the white world. On the other hand, Malcolm had very limited formal education and was self-taught. His exposure was limited to jam-packed filthy rat-infested ghettos of the North, largely Harlem and Chicago. Malcolm represented the slum dwellers who were struggling daily against unemployment, dope and police brutality. Malcolm therefore had no earthly reason to believe that integration with the whites was possible at all, nor could he bring himself to accept the view that white man would share power and privileges with those he was brutalizing and oppressing day in and day out. Thus there was a fundamental difference in approach to the solution of white-black conflict as far as these two leaders and their followers were concerned. The two were at a tangent and could not possibly reconcile to each other.

At this point we should not lose sight of the fact that leadership was thrust upon Martin soon after his assumption of the ministry when he was a very young man. On the other hand, Malcolm had a head-start in this respect, a definite advantage indeed. Martin barely had time to sort out his own ideas about the Black Movement, Freedom Struggle, Segregation and Separation, and host of other issues facing the Negro at that time. However, fate had destined to catapult Martin to an unprecedented level of leadership. And he was lucky in having a group of sincere competent advisers — Ella Baker, Stanley Levison, Bayard Rustin, and soon to be joined by Ralph David Abernathy. After some prodding by his advisers, Martin called a meeting of black ministers from all over the South to meet at Ebenezer Baptist Church at Atlanta on 10-11 January 1957 followed by another at New Orleans on February 14, leading to the founding of Southern Christian Leadership Conference (SCLC) with Martin Luther King Jr. as its founding President. The mission of the new organization was initially limited to eradication of segregation — "to redeem the soul of America" based on the principle of "All Men are Created Equal" endowed with inalienable rights of life, liberty and pursuit of happiness, amongst others— through non-violent direct action. Thus was born the "American Dream", a synthesis of American liberal democratic tradition as enshrined in the Declaration of Independence and the Protestant Baptist interpretation of Old and New Testaments. Religion was the essence of the new black movements: Christianity for Martin and Islam for Malcolm (and Muhammad Ali). The former was closely linked to political objectives. When Malcolm tried to follow suit by linking its religio-cultural philosophy with the objectives of civil rights movements almost in line with King's approach, Malcolm's followers objected. His confabulations with the integrationists like James Farmer, Kenneth Clark, Louis Lomax, James Baldwin, Bayard Rustin, *et al*, were tantamount to a radical departure from the basic tenets of the organization. The younger members, particularly the whites, led the revolt against the leader. Consequentially, Malcolm was expelled him from the 'Nation of Islam' in March 1964. That was the turning point in his political career and his subsequent trips to Africa and Middle East. Similarly, King's trip to Europe to receive the Peace Prize came to be a turning point in his career, when on return home he was faced with riots in Northern ghettos as well as the economic issues that ignited the riots.

During his last year Malcolm spent nearly six months abroad trying to convince African heads of states to pressurize the United Nations to charge the United States Government with human rights violations of twenty-two million Afro-Americans. He presented a Memorandum to this effect to the second meeting of Organization of African Unity (OAU) held in Cairo. Malcolm got appointments with several heads of states including Kwame Nkrumah of Ghana, Julius Nyerere of Tanzania, Jomo Kenyatta of Kenya and Gamal Abdel Nasser of Egypt, the host country.[12] But his intemperate severe criticism of Martin King's non-violent approach, and his proposal for a separate territory for the Blacks were rejected outright by the Negro community of America.

12. Cones James H.: op. cit. p. 255.

Black Equality

Life in the modern world is highly competitive. Success alone counts. And success is achieved over failure, or lack of success of others. Survival of the Fittest: that is the rule of the game. So King moved South. Meanwhile Ela Baker had moved from SCLC to SNCC (Student Non-violent Coordinating Committee) and then to the MFDP. She asked Martin King to undertake a tour of the voting centres to build up support for MFDP. Thus King got his biggest opportunity to enter the field of power politics, infinitely more valuable than moral preaching. The Mississippi voting restrictions against the Blacks were totally unconstitutional. These had no historical basis either. He could have mounted a nationwide protest. But King did not grab the opportunity and missed the bus of a life time. However, King's failure to make the best of the circumstances led to strengthening of black political groups in the South. The registration of Black voters received a big boost, leading to great success in the polls.

John Edgar Hoover had served ten Presidents. He never had any sympathy for the civil rights movements, nor was he expected to have any in the future. He had served so long in the same job, perhaps because he knew a lot about acts of omission and commission of a lot people in high places. Be that as it may, King and Hoover met, after all, even though King knew that Hoover had ordered bugging of his telephone, or general surveillance of King's activities.

King did not like the then new slogan "Black Power" in the same way as he did not appreciate the phrase 'White Power'. Both were enigma to King who was a firm believer in the Christian love. He therefore proposed "Black Equality", which was not acceptable to young black radicals. "Martin did not object to the concept of Black Power at all." He merely protested against the "violent context into which the slogan was being placed, and the deliberately provocative way in which it was being shouted."[13]

Detroit Riots

Materialism alone does not constitute civilization. And what is civilization after all? In the words of Will Durant: "Civilization is a stream with banks. The stream is sometimes filled with blood from people killing, stealing, shooting, and doing the things historians usually record, while on the banks, unnoticed, people build homes, make love, raise children, sing songs, write poetry ... The story of civilization is the story of what happened on the banks. ... The historians ignore the banks for the river."

---

13. King Scott Coretta: op. cit. p. 291.

The civil rights of the coloured people of the United States, the champions of human rights, were trampled *ad lib*. And segregationist policies had legal sanction. To overcome the legal lacunae, in 1960, the Congress passed another civil rights bill providing for legal action against the states concerned. But the same year also witnessed one of the largest mass migrations when almost one a half million Blacks left their homes and hearths in the South to seek peace and shelter in the already overcrowded ghettos of the North. By the end of 1950 the Blacks constituted nearly half the population of Washington D.C., over a quarter of Philadelphia, Detroit, Cleveland, and Chicago. Houston and St. Louis.

In the North there was no official segregation *per se*; but it was certainly virtual segregation inasmuch as a large metropolitan city like Chicago was teeming with slums and poverty of the worst kind. There were schools in black slum-areas but these were of an exceedingly poor quality as compared to the white schools which were out of reach of the black community. Dr. King and his associates in the SCLC and affiliated organizations like Albert Raby's Coordinating Council of Community Organizations decided that the time had come to launch a campaign against poverty and deprivation in the North for which the right place was Chicago. So be it: Chicago became the target city. However, many Black leaders realized that Martin did not fully understand in his guts the madness, despair, hopelessness and desperation induced by ghetto life. In order to have first hand experience of that type of life — in the footsteps of Mahatma Gandhi who travelled third class by rail to have first hand experience of the filth, congestion and degradation in boarding the train — in 1966, Martin King hired a slum apartment on the third floor of a dingy building in the Westside ghetto in Chicago. The entire family moved into the ghetto along with Martin. Coretta says she had never seen anything like that in her whole life. In fact, she could not even believe that such an apartment could possibly exist in a country like America! The building — if at all it could be called a building — had no lights in the hall. There was only one dim bulb at the head of the stairs. The front door of the house always stood open since it had no lock. For that very reason, the drunks came into the hallway off and on to use the premises as an open public toilet. To cap it all, the floor was not concrete but mere plain bare dust with the result that there was overpowering smell of urine pervading the entire building. The old refrigerator worked alright, but it did not keep the food cold or make ice for that matter, and one had to go through the bedrooms to reach the kitchen where there was a dilapidated gas stove which refused to heat the apartment since the outside temperature was at the low point of fifteen degrees Fahrenheit. The rent for this magnificent mansion? Ninety dollars per month, unfurnished! Exploitation of the poor at its worst.[14]

Whether Martin or any body else liked it or not, the new slogan "BLACK POWER" caught the mood of the black masses. The mask of black submission soon disintegrated. The Blacks were now on their own. And that, in one word meant: RIOTS. The 1967-riots in Newark, New Jersey, and Detroit, Michigan, were one of the worst episodes in race-relations in the United States.

Vietnam War

The war in Vietnam had taken on the dimensions of a national issue penetrating every facet of political activity all over the United States. Like every leader that mattered, Martin Luther King was also drawn into this controversy. In 1967 he came out openly against the unjust and evil war in Vietnam, loud and clear. He made no bones about the horrible acts of cruelty, death and destruction being wrought on the hapless Asians in the name of democracy and equality, while at home the same principles of humanitarianism and justice were being openly flouted by white racists against their own black countrymen. Coretta went to Washington to participate in a joint press conference held there on 28th March 1968. Dorothy Hutchinson, then international president of the Women's International League for Peace and Freedom, put forward proposals for "An Honorable Peace in Vietnam." Coretta spoke on the "relationship of our domestic policy and the urban crisis to our Vietnam involvement." Meanwhile, Martin had returned from New York to lead a march in Memphis. His plane was late and the march had already started. He managed to rush up to the head of the line when he realized that the march was not properly organized and that it was ill-disciplined. "Black Power" placards were openly displayed and same slogans were being shouted. Before Martin knew whether he was coming or going, some people from the rear started throwing rocks and bottles. Glass crashed all over. Mayor Loeb made the situation still worse. He let loose his police whose brutality was comparable to snarling dogs. There were numerous injuries and one fatality due to police shooting. "This was the first time violence had ever broken out in a march" that was being led by Martin."[15] Although Martin, and later President Johnson, did not like the sound of the word 'black power', there was no doubt

14. The Black leaders encouraged the people not to pay rent to the landlord. Instead, they should use the money to do the repairs. And the landlord sued the SCLC!

15. King Scott Coretta: op. cit. p. 322.

that "Black Power" had a different meaning to the black man ... To such a man, black power meant a great deal in areas that mattered the most — dignity, pride and self-awareness." [16]

Next morning Martin held a press 'briefing', as distinct from a press 'conference', in which he restated his total commitment to non-violence, giving out his principles of non-violence, as if Gandhi personified. Gandhi was convinced to a point almost bordering on fanaticism that non-violence and love would give India its independence and enable it to withstand the British Government. Martin drew a line for the benefit of the garbage workers for the amelioration of whose lot that protest-march was organized. He informed them what the Black movement was fighting for was neither a 'Race War', nor a 'Class War'. Racial equality, justice for all, and economic upliftment were the primary objectives He spoke in an 'eloquent, profound and moving' manner as if to obliterate the scars of violence of the day before. Meanwhile, it was decided to lead a march to Washington, beginning Monday, April 8th — an orderly, peaceful and totally non-violent demonstration. However, Mayor Loeb obtained a federal injunction against "non-residents" marching or demonstrating in Memphis. But later developments rendered all that unnecessary.

---

16. Johnson L.B.: op. cit. p. 167.

36

Mule Syndrome

The American Negro is neither totally African nor totally Western. He is Afro-American, a true hybrid, a combination of two cultures — the mule-plough culture of Africa came with him to America where they continued to work mule-ploughs in the white man's plantations. In the process they lost their 'Africanness', and could not imbibe Americanism for a few centuries.

Rev. Martin Luther King Sr. came from humble beginnings. His father James Albert King, Dr. Martin King's grandfather, was a poor sharecropper on a plantation in Stockbridge, a small town outside of Atlanta. His chances of making good in life were severely restricted by the stifling agricultural-plantation system that prevailed in the Southern States. The entire system was designed to work in favor of the white man who owned the plantation. The sharecropper had to buy the seed and almost all other home-supplies from the plantation owner, all on credit. Before the crop was equally divided at harvest time, the year's debt had to be cleared. And there was never enough money to get out from under. James King might work extremely hard for the whole year, but still end up owing the owner around four hundred dollars or so! What was so palpably unfair was that while James had to bear all the expenses from ploughing to sowing to reaping, he had to share the profits equally with the plantation owner. To cap it all, the bookkeeping was done directly by the plantation owner whose calculations always ended with 'you owe me so many hundred dollars'. It may be recalled that indigo plantation owners in the Champaran district of Bihar in India, the white Englishmen, treated the producers of their wealth in an equally bad, if not still worse manner. They were liberated from their bondage only when Gandhi was literally dragged there to see the situation. Once there, he could no tear himself from the place till imprisonment he got back the labourers their land and freedom, though he had to court imprisonment in their cause.

Once Daddy King happened to be present at annual reckoning between his father and the plantation owner. He told his father to take into account the cotton seeds and therefore, he owed nothing; instead he had to get some money from the plantation owner. This was not a pleasant interlude for the father and the son. In a similar incident, Daddy King went to fetch a pail of water for his mother. On the way back a white man demanded the water. Daddy King refused. The white man tore off the boy's clothes, made him naked, and then beat the hell out of him. These are the genes of which the Jr. was made of. And he proved more than worthy of his parental background.

James King had ten children, of whom Martin Luther was the second. The family's extreme poverty drove James King to the bottle, and Daddy King had a miserable youth. Perhaps watching his father's plight made Daddy King such a strong teetotaller. While Martin Luther was growing up, his main job was currying the mules. The other children in his school at Stockbridge used to poke fun at him since he generally smelled like a mule. That is how the other children used to tease him. And his response: "I may smell like a mule, but I don't think like a mule." Thus he became quite self-conscious of this mule-smell so much so that he used to avoid the company of girls. In later life he used to say: "You know, I've got a mule complex. I vowed when I left the countryside — I'm not going to be a slave, and I'm not going to plough another mule." While walking past the plantation owner's big brick house on his way to Atlanta, he said to himself: "Some day I'm going to have a brick house as big as that — bigger. Some day I'm even going to be a director of a bank like that man. ..." And this remarkable man did exactly that, plus a lot more, to make himself and his family great and proud of their heritage.

Thrifty by nature, Daddy King would drive across the town since the chicken there were ten cents cheaper, ignoring the cost of gasoline up and down the town. It was the pleasure of bargain that acted as the magnet. Even after Martin and Coretta were married, he would nit-pick on them for getting the cars washed. He would tell Martin to wash his car himself. But the clever son, who had a streak of socialism in him, would respond: "Daddy, I have a theory about that. You know the society is based on division of labour, and if I wash my own car it means somebody else doesn't have a job."

Mules proved quite handy during the desegregation movement too. In the aftermath of Rosa Parks's incident, the Black leadership unanimously decided to boycott the city bus service. Bayard Rustin who had long experience of such Gandhian inspired protests came over as adviser to the nascent boycott movement. The message of boycott was spread to Montgomery's 50,000 Blacks. Meetings of community leaders were held in various Baptist churches to organize alternative transportation. Montgomery Improvement Association was formed to coordinate the effort. However, it was for the mass meeting to decide whether to continue the boycott or not. Meanwhile, thousands were driven to work in black cabs at specially cut rates. Many hitchhiked in Black private cars while some rode mules, or just walked.

The mule complex came into play once again when mortal remains of Dr. Martin Luther King Jr. were to be taken in procession to the cemetery. Since the whites would not allow any military association with the funeral of a Negro howsoever great he might have been; the cortege was pulled by six mules.

Yet another occasion when mules were employed for transportation of men and materials was the move to, and construction of, the Resurrection City on the Mall in Washington D.C. This project was part of the Poor People's Campaign launched by Dr. Ralph David Abernathy soon after the assassination of Dr. King.

37

Negros' Psychological Complexes

One of the most damaging effects of past segregation on the personality of the Negro may well be that he has been victimized with the delusion that others should be more concerned than himself about his citizenship rights. Even where the polls are open to all, Negroes have shown themselves too slow to exercise their voting privileges. They suffer from pathetic indifference, a form of moral and political suicide.

Fear was the biggest problem faced by the Negroes, particularly in the South. It was not merely in the mind of the Negro; it was a physical entity in the form of Ku Klux Klan and racial hatred combined with segregation. The extent of their cruelty knew no bounds. In one case in Alabama, they castrated an African-American and dumped his mutilated body on the main highway giving rise to profound revulsion and sense of fear. The administrative machinery of the Southern States gave unflinching support to these disruptive elements and treated the Negroes as sub-human species whose life had no value or sanctity. One of the sermons Martin gave was on the subject of 'Fear' in its totality; its title: "Antidotes for Fear" for which he took as his text I John 4:18 — "There is no fear in love; but perfect love casteth out fear; because fear hath torment. He that feareth is not made perfect in love." Fear can be neutralized by:

- Firstly; a person can overcome fear by facing it squarely.
- Secondly; through courage of mind since 'courage is the power of the mind to overcome fear'.
- Thirdly; fear is mastered by true love.
- And finally; faith is the sure anti-dote to fear — faith in God, faith in one's cause and faith in the self.

The current designation, Afro-American, or African-American, correctly describes the American Negro. But it also signifies that the American Negro is the product, a synthesis, of two diverse cultures. It is not that he is racially schizophrenic; far from it. But it does mean that he is subject to pulls and pressures of divergent characteristics of which he needs to be conscious of, in that he is under a process of acculturation which needs to be balanced in the back of his mind. He has to avoid losing his psychological balance by over-tilting towards either of the two cultural traits. He is a hybrid, a combination of two cultures, and must retain a balanced outlook.

As a result of segregation and discrimination, the psychological scars on the black middle class children started showing up, more so after they and their parents had become aware of the inequalities of opportunity, social isolation and atrocities inflicted by the racist whites. The two instances of colour-bar to which King was subjected to during his impressionable years — the curtain in a restaurant and bus-ride for ninety miles standing in the aisle — left deep scars on Martin's mind. And he was not the only one to so suffer; every black man had some such tale of woe up his sleeve. The psychological scars on Martin were so troublesome that he even tried to commit suicide, twice before even he reached the age of 13 — once when his brother accidentally knocked down his grandmother unconscious while sliding down the banister. Martin thought that she had died and in despair he jumped out of the second floor window, only to land unhurt. He did the same thing a second time when his grandmother actually died. However, dame Fate saved him both times to thrust greatness on him in later life. Martin King became world famous when he made it to the cover page of *Time* magazine, February 18, 1957.

"When your first name becomes 'nigger', your middle name becomes 'boy' (however old you are), and your wife and mother are never given the respected title 'Mrs.'; when you are harried by day and haunted by night by the fact that you are a Negro ... when you are for ever fighting a degenerating sense of 'nobodiness'— then you will understand why we find it difficult to wait."[1] When one of the little boys told Marty that his father was the famous 'nigger', Marty retorted proudly; 'The word is Negro." This was the positive effect of the prevailing racial situation in so far as the black children were concerned. Negroes are by nature cohesive. They bind together easily thus putting up a joint front against oppression and injustice. There is a built-in sense of loyalty to each other, which goes a long way in creating solidarity in an organization. On the other hand,

1. King Martin Luther Jr.: *Companion*; p.7.

while passing playgrounds which were for white children only, the black children would cry out in anguish over the denial of such facilities to them since they could not play there much as they wanted to. This was all the more distressing when facilities like 'Fun town' did not exist at all for the blacks. However, down the road when the children discovered that they too could enjoy the 'Fun town' after Martin had achieved desegregation in that field, they were proud of black leaders of the community. Yet another field which caused severe disparity was the concept of beauty in the American society. It was totally based on white standards — 'Caucasian features, fair skin, straight hair, keen nose, thin lips' — these alone constituted beauty. If one did not fit the stereotype, well, one was not beautiful. And that explained the better treatment meted out to Mulatto children by the whites. "The emergence and gradual acceptance of the 'Black is Beautiful' concept is the most emotionally and psychologically constructive weapon with which the black child can be armed."[2]

A growing sense of self-respect has inspired the Negro to strive for, and look forward to, first class citizenship. The middle class elite amongst the Negroes were aware of certain inherent disabilities of their race. Their low moral standards were a drag in themselves. They were conscious of their crime rate being too high. For instance: Negroes constitute ten percent of the population of New York City but their crime rate is 35 per cent; and still worse, they form 76 per cent of the list for Aid to dependent children. In Missouri the Negroes are 26 per cent of the population but they commit almost twice the number of crimes. Their standards of cleanliness and hygiene were far too low. Their people were by nature boisterous. They drank too much, for whatever reason. The Negro was apathetic and indifferent to his fundamental rights and personal well being. He came to believe that others should be more concerned about his citizenship rights than he himself. These character-traits left behind a degree of inferiority complex so much so that the Negro really believed that he was an inferior being. Some of them therefore cooperated with their oppressors even against their own people, and avoided political activity of any nature whatsoever. However, this sense of guilt and inferiority complex was not a one-way traffic; the white man too suffered from a sense of guilt for the cruelties and injustice that they inflicted on the Black populace. Segregation was harmful to the Blacks; but it was harmful to the white psyche too albeit to a lesser degree.

Yet another contributory factor towards Afro-American psychological weakness was the centuries-old genetically induced after-effects of

---

2. King Coretta Scott: op. cit. p. 228.

sharecropping as a way of life for the African slaves. As has been brought out in an earlier chapter, white landowners used to lease plots of land to sharecroppers who were required to buy all the inputs from the master and receive payment, if at all any, after the crop was harvested and weighed. The poor Negro was cheated at every stage of the transaction. He was lucky if final accounts as maintained by the land owner did not show him in further debt to the master! A similar state of affairs prevailed in the Southwestern and western railroad projects where Chinese and Mexican labour crew were under total control of the construction-contractors who provided all necessities of life at rates and quality at their free will. The poor immigrant worker, a sort of indentured laborer, was cheated at every step, as had been discovered by M.K. Gandhi in South Africa where Indian indentured labour was imported by white contractors.

Imitating the whites, trying to behave and act like the whites, imbibe white culture and social norms, in short efforts made to achieve equality with the whites and the ill-consequences thereof, were a major factor in creating a sense of deficiency in the minds of the blacks. They were all the time conscious of not only their inferior status but also the effect of being spurned by the whites. None of these are material and need not be taken seriously. But their psychological results and denial of equal rights and facilities was bound to have an adverse effect, particularly on the impressionable minds. If a black frequently sees "Whites Only" signs, day in and day out, prominently painted all over the place, his psyche is naturally affected adversely. To cap it all, if he is treated in a sub-human manner, the mental scars would indeed be deeply etched.

The King children were deprived of the company of their Father. So were those of the Gandhi family. And that holds good for the Nelson Mandela family too. All of them suffered similar scars even though they reacted differently, for in the case of Dr. Nelson Mandela: "I was helped when preparing for my release (from 27-year long prison life) by the biography of Pandit Nehru, who wrote what happens when you leave jail. My daughter Zinzi says that she grew up without a father, who, when he returned, became a Father of the Nation." The children of these families had undergone the humiliation of colour-bar — Gandhi's had the sad experience of segregation and racial bias while in South Africa, and the Kings had plenty of the same in their own country from their own countrymen. Even after some of the American Blacks had fought for their country in some vicious wars under most intolerable conditions, the whites were far from appreciative; on the contrary, these patriotic Negroes continued to suffer the same fate as any other black person. The famous case of James Meredith and his achievement by way of integrating the 'whites only' Mississippi University needs no recounting here.

38

New Era of Social Change

History has thrust upon our generation an indescribably important destiny — to complete the process of democratization which our nation has developed too long too slowly. How we deal with this crucial situation will determine our moral health as individuals, our cultural health as a region, our political health as a nation, and our prestige as a leader of the free world.

Racial and political equality was the aim of the Freedom Movement launched by Dr. Martin Luther King Jr. The coloured people must have their rights and privileges, no less than those of the whites. The economic front was equally important, if not more. It was particularly so after a degree of desegregation had been achieved as a result of the Montgomery and Birmingham agitations. So the Negro leadership transferred their attention to these vital sectors, which directly affected the individual personally. The new approach followed the well trodden path of non-violent boycotts of business establishments, 'picket lines', 'sit in' demonstrations (*dharnas*), 'freedom rides', etc. provided the momentum for spread of this theory of pacifism as a means to achieve socio-political objectives. He was greatly impressed by the Gandhian movement against British domination in India. In order to study the principles and practice of non-violence at first hand, he stayed in India for nearly four years and discussed the American scene with Gandhi. In fact, he was instrumental in popularizing the Gandhian philosophy in America. In 1946 he founded a Committee for Non-violent Revolution to obtain freedom for the Blacks. This Committee opposed the expansion of armament industry as well as development of nuclear weapons, and encouraged the people to refuse to serve in the armed forces, or in the armament industries.[1] Finally, non-

1. Richard B. Gregg: The Psychology and Strategy of Gandhi's Non-violent Resistance, Madras, 1929; Gandhism and Socialism, Madras, 1931; The Power of Non-violence, Philadelphia, 1934.

violent civil resistance-cum-disobedience movement was the outcome of all these efforts.[2]

Christian Love and Gandhian Nonviolence

"Love your enemy", "turn your other cheek" — That is what Jesus Christ taught the world. In essence, that was the core of non-violence. And that was the philosophy of Reverend Dr. Martin Luther King, Jr. So far so good. But this concept was restricted to conflicts at the individual levels only. However, when nations and racial groups were in conflict against each other, this philosophy was considered inapplicable. That is what Martin, and the rest of the Christian world used to believe till Gandhi propagated his philosophy of total non-violence. Gandhi preached that love was a powerful instrument for 'social and collective transformation'. In the words of Dr. King, "Gandhi was probably the first person in history to lift the love ethic of Jesus above mere interaction between individuals to a powerful and effective social force on a large scale". King came to believe that the only practical and morally sound 'method open to oppressed people in their struggle for freedom' was the path shown by Gandhi through his technique of non-violent resistance. This brought Martin to the forefront of Freedom Struggle. Montgomery Bus Boycott further refined Gandhi's non-violence. It defined and removed the inherent contradiction between non-violence and 'militant non-violence'.[3] The fresh concept replaced militancy by 'dramatic confrontation' besides 'electrifying and educating the entire nation'. A new 'era of social change' had opened up new vistas for the entire United States, just the way the freedom movement under the inspiring leadership of Mahatma Gandhi had spread its roots all over the vast hinterland of India.

Reverend Fred Lee Shuttlesworth was a fearless man. He sent his children to public schools to desegregate them. Consequently, he was beaten up, his church and home were bombed. His wife was jailed and beaten. The entire family had suffered terribly in the cause of social justice, freedom and desegregation. Birmingham was Shuttlesworth's home-turf. He became Secretary of the south-wide movement for non-violent desegregation. In January 1962 the students of Miles College joined the SCLC to begin a boycott of segregated stores in Birmingham.

---

2. Ostergaard Geoffrey: op. cit.
3. The murder of President John F. Kennedy, his Brother Robert's on June 05, 1968 and that of Dr. King earlier in the same year, together with a spate of murders during the racial-riots as well as the vicious violence generated by the extremely unpopular Vietnam War had given rise to the famous quip that violence was as 'as American as apple pie'.

It was generally believed that if the campaign in Birmingham was successful, it would, perhaps, 'break the back of segregation all over the nation'. The similarity in methodology and system set by Mahatma Gandhi, and now imbibed by the SCLC leadership was much too pronounced to be overlooked.

After assuming the mantle of Presidency, Kennedy was no longer enthusiastic about the Negroes' civil rights. The Black leaders therefore made a fresh start with sit-ins at lunch counters, which commenced on 3rd April 1963. A number of demonstrators were arrested every day, so were Martin and Ralph. The President intervened on behalf of Martin, and that gave a big boost to the momentum of Birmingham Movement.

Dr. King was realistic enough to admit that many Negroes did not have the intellectual capacity to follow the highly spiritual path of non-violence. Not that the whites too could. Some may even consider it total nonsense, more so since many of them were going up the economic ladder thereby creating a niche for themselves in the American middle class. They saw no rational basis to give up what they had achieved through their hard work. In any case total unanimity is not a pre-requisite for every movement. Nor does nonviolent mass movement produce miracles overnight. It is essentially a positive concept. It requires non-cooperation with evil and simultaneously, cooperation with the positive constructive forces of the good. Love and sacrifice are its core elements. Malcolm X, a "Black Nationalist" in his own right, considered non-violence as rubbish. The Northern Blacks also felt that their problems were different from those of the South, inasmuch as they already had the vote and there was no segregation by law. As ill luck would have it, Gandhi, Malcolm X and Martin Luther King Jr., all three were assassinated for their moral and political convictions. However, Malcolm X and spirituality repelled each other like poles having similar polarity.

Economic Disparity

The major problem was poverty. The vast majority of the Blacks in the North lived in deplorable poverty, in squalid ghettos ruled by the slum-lords. Unemployment rate was high. The police treated every Negro as a criminal and they were victims of frequent police brutality. Race riots were a common feature. Dr. King therefore decided in 1966 to extend his movement to the North. King persuaded gang-leaders of Chicago to abjure violence, and adopt the path of non-violence as propounded by India's Gandhi. The Mayor of Chicago, Richard Daley, had strong local support. He mobilized his forces against King's movement.

By mid-1966 the Chicago campaign appeared to be petering out. "Black Power" was on the rise. Therefore, King had to devote major part of his efforts to counter the philosophy of Black Power. Non-violence cannot bring about social change overnight.

Gandhian-style non-violent civil resistance has had a much greater global impact on world politics than armed struggle and violent resistance. The large number of colonial countries that achieved their independence in the aftermath of Indian Independence is proof enough of the success of this methodology to fight the Imperialist powers. The Black masses in the North started imbibing the Gandhian political philosophy. The initial modus operandi to gain freedom and justice was non-cooperation. It was soon transformed into non-violent mass movement followed by 'militant non-violence', and then to the basic doctrine of *Satyagraha*. *Satyagraha* believes that the authority of the State is not unlimited. The tyranny of the majority is not necessarily to be tolerated merely because it is imposed by the majority. In fact, the State invariably tends to trample on the rights and privileges of the people, of minorities in particular. *Satyagraha* respects the moral worth of an individual and precludes cruder forms of coercion.

Desegregation through legal provisions is symbolic in that it is enforced through fear of the law. In a vibrant society intermingling of people of different races and creeds should come from the heart that brings about true unity, a state of "genuine inter-group and inter-personal living. Only through non-violence can this goal be attained, for the aftermath of non-violence is reconciliation and the creation of the beloved community." But this is easier said than done. Every legal victory of the Negro in federal courts brought in its wake angry passions and deep prejudices from the white race, the South in particular. The exceptions were indeed microscopic. City ordinances and State laws were enacted to counter the positive fallout from the Federal Courts. Negro leaders were continuously harassed and arrested under these local laws and their houses were bombed. The Police Commissioner and the Mayor apologized to Martin for what had happened in their city. But the people were furious, angry and excited. The tense situation could trigger the most awful riot in U.S. history. In a confident calm voice Martin told the crowd: "My wife and my baby are all right. I want you to go home and put down your weapons ... We must meet violence with non-violence. Remember the words of Jesus: 'He who lives by the sword will perish by the sword.' ... We must meet hate with love." It is as if Mahatma Gandhi was personified at that point of time, and inspired Martin to say what Gandhi too would himself have said. As the crowd started thinning out, a white policeman said: "If it hadn't been for that nigger preacher, we'd all be dead." They still called him a 'nigger'!

Dr. King charted out the following program for his people's emancipation:

- Non-violent resistance to all forms of racial injustice, including local laws and practices;
- Imaginative, bold, constructive action to end the demoralization caused by the legacy of slavery and segregation including schools, slums and second-class citizenship;
- Continue the struggle with dignity and courage to end the demoralization;
- A new frontal assault on poverty, disease and ignorance.

Consumer Prosperity

The twentieth century saw the United States successfully fight two World Wars, and at the threshold of a severe 'cold war' involving two super powers. On balance, the US was the stronger of the two but it was a question of mutually destructive balance of terror in which none would come out unscathed, and perhaps neither would survive. However, the US had an upper hand insofar as economic strength, industrial development and consumerism were concerned. From that point of view, there was none to challenge the Americans. They were the richest and most prosperous nation on planet earth. The beginning of the 1960's brought the standard of living of the average American to its highest level ever. It was also the highest in their own history too. Their prosperity was boundless. The variety, quality and availability of consumer goods exceeded all expectations, and further improvements were the order of the day. The market economy of the United States was the envy of the rest of the world, including the rival super power. This exceptional rise in the standard of living was not confined to whites only; it spilled over to the Negroes and American-Indians as well, albeit the Black communities, comparatively speaking, were not as well off as the whites. The rise in per capita income resulted in increased purchasing power of both the whites and blacks. They spent the additional funds to provide for luxuries, comforts and conveniences. Abundance of electric power made life more comfortable, and the car-industry made it more mobile. Three-fourths of the population of the United States had at least one automobile, and many had more than one. The supermarkets and grocery stores throughout the country were overflowing with a variety of goods and food products. The people of the United States were better housed, better clothed and better fed than at any time in their history. And they were better off than the people in the rest of the world. However, notwithstanding the high degree of prosperity, during the second half of the twentieth century the American nation faced serious domestic problems and severe internal challenges as never before in the past. Nevertheless, for the first time in the twentieth century there were as many as three Negroes in the Congress which number increased to six by 1964. It is noteworthy that Detroit sent a second Negro to the Congress in the same year. Similarly, by the end of 1956 there were some forty-six Negroes in the State legislature, albeit mostly in the Northern and Western States only. A significant event in this field was the election of a Negro, Hulan Jack, to the presidency of the borough of Manhattan of New York City.

That was not all. William H. Hastie became a Judge of the Third United States Circuit Court of Appeals as early as 1949. Similarly, Thurgood Marshal joined the Circuit Court in 1961 and became the Solicitor General of the United States in 1965. A number of other Negroes held high offices in the Federal Government including chairmanship of the United States Parole Board. But the situation in the South was quite dismal and distressing. Segregation was the rule in all spheres of activities and employment. However, in the North and West there was some light. Even then, many white workers threatened to quit if Negroes were employed or upgraded. Although such threats were rarely carried out, they certainly retarded the progress and promotion of Negroes in the bureaucracy. The colour-divide was as powerful in America as the communal-divide was in India. To mitigate the ill effects of communal-colour cancer, the Frontier Gandhi said: "To the Hindus and Muslims I would say that this fight for freedom is for the liberation of both. The Hindus are obliging none by taking part in the struggle, and the Muslims will oblige none by joining the Hindus. ... Remember this also that Musalmans alone are not the creatures of God. The Hindus, Sikhs, Musalmans, Jews, Christians and Parsis, in short, all the creatures that live in this world, are the creatures of God." Not only that, some Negroes holding high positions in the Administration were removed from senior executive positions all because they treated the Whites and Blacks at par, which was not liked by the white bosses. A case in point was: when a Louisiana registrar disqualified whites as well as Negroes who did not demonstrate their adequacy in understanding the Federal Constitution. She, the Registrar, was summarily relieved from the job. In other words, the North too wanted to discriminate against the Black minority and express their anger over equal treatment accorded to the Whites and Blacks.[4]

While the Southern States were suffering under severe segregationist constraints, the North and West were much better off. No wonder therefore that a significant number of Negroes migrated from the South to the North, notwithstanding the slum conditions prevailing in the Northern metropolises.

At the end of the Second World War the population of the United States was around 140 millions[5]. The post War baby boom, better health care and improved medical facilities resulted in a population explosion so much so that by 1963 it reached an estimated 189 million. The increased population required more homes, education, health care facilities, jobs, governance, *et al*, thereby increasing the pressure on available resources. The movement of population from rural areas to urban centers added to the complexities. While 18 per cent of Americans lived on the farms at the end of the War, by 1963 their number came down to a mere eight percent. Congestion and pollution in the urban environment were additional complications, besides the deterioration in law and order situation. The westward migration of population for more opportunities and better life was an additional complicating factor. California bore the brunt and became the nation's fastest growing State, as well as the richest. The rising cost of governance caused additional burden on local and state finances necessitating increased federal financial aid and consequent tax burden at all levels. Social security requirements sky rocketed, and so did the unemployment benefits leading to the evil of some citizens finding it more convenient to live on state charity rather than do useful work.

With the *de facto* emancipation of the Afro-American, America had undergone a sea-change in socio-politico-economic fields.

---

4. Franklin John Hope: *From Slavery to Freedom*; pp. 614-15.
5. According to US Census Bureau the total population of the United States as on July 01, 1945, was 139,682,000. It represented an increase of 8,330,725 over the 1940 census — "Facts on File" Year Book 1945, Vol. V, Person's Index, New York; Item reference 371G, and 269B.

39

Resurrection City

An Interlude[1]

The great tragedy was that our Government declared war on poverty, and yet it only financed a skirmish against poverty. This led to great despair, cynicism and discontent amongst the Negro community throughout the nation. There were islands of extreme poverty and deprivation surrounded by oceans of plenty all over the country. The disparity was far too glaring, and certainly not acceptable to the new generations of old slaves.

Resurrection City, Washington D.C. 20013

After a brief dedication ceremony on May 13, 1968, the Poor People of America started building their abodes of long cherished dreams. They managed to construct about one hundred 'houses' by night fall that day. It was easy indeed, more so since it belonged to them. These were A-frame huts, all prefabricated to the same design and specifications, each about eight by twenty eight feet, a fairly spacious bedroom! The Poor People continued overnight. Hammers pounded nails and saws bit into wood all night under spotlights. The next morning the Washingtonians were totally flabbergasted to see the equivalent of about six city blocks of raw plywood structures between the marble-edifice of Lincoln Memorial and Washington Monument covering the meticulously mowed green lawns along their beautiful Mall. An eye-sore indeed!

Although permit for temporary use of the land along the Mall had been issued by the City authorities for a limited period of one month,

1. This chapter is based on Chapter 15 of Autobiography of Ralph David Abernathy, Harper & Row, Publishers, New York; 1989, pp.494-539.

Dr. Ralph David Abernathy, the new head of the Southern Christian Leadership Conference after Dr. Martin Luther King's assassination on April 4, 1968, made a symbolic gesture of obtaining permission for use of the land from a Red-Indian girl since her ancestors were the original owners of all that land. She was delighted to grant permission. Plots of land were staked out along streets named after the heroes of the movement: King Boulevard, Abernathy Street, Fanny Lou Hamer Drive, and so on. The new residents of the new City were first registered at the City Hall and then taken to the site where they were allotted 'property' on first come first served basis. The first 'home' was built for Minnie Lee Hill and her eight children who had come from Marks, Mississippi, and "symbolized the need and deprivation that Martin had recognized and responded to in that community".

Resurrection City was an experiment in integrated living irrespective of caste, creed or race, in the true Gandhian style 'ashram', where everyone was treated equal, and provided food and clothing on a need-based system. Cooking and eating was centralized; so a large mess-tent was erected as the dining hall. Besides the individual shacks, tents for doctors, dentists and nursery were also provided. Barbers gave free hair-cuts in the open, weather permitting. Local police undertook policing duties. Many Congressmen, politicians and other VIPs including young George Bush, the future President, visited the City. Abernathy appointed Jesse Jackson as the Manager of Resurrection City, most appropriately named since the assassination of Dr. King, more so since the Poor People's March was part of Martin's protest marches to arouse the Congress to the plight of Blacks and other poor minorities including the whites.

It was a City where people just lived, ate and slept. No work, but no play also. Free food, shelter and clothing cannot last for ever. There was no commerce, no industry, and no work at all. The idle brains became the devil's workshops, particularly amongst the younger lot. Trouble started brewing. Some were shipped back home. But disturbances, extortion, thefts, and what have you, continued unabated. So was violence, sometimes against the police too. The 'Dream City' was on the verge of disintegration. The possibility of some of the hooligans from Washington's worst ghettoes having been planted in the City to disrupt the peace could not be ruled out either.

Language barriers were another major problem. Joint schooling added to parents' woes. People wanted to live in clusters of their own kind — Red-Indians in their own group housing, Puerto Ricans with their own kind, Mexican-Americans in a separate lot, whites with the whites only, and so on and so forth, thereby defeating the fundamental principle of integrated communal living, which was the concept on which the new City was established. Differences in food habits were another source of friction. So were differences in religious backgrounds. Political differences also started cropping up. The Puerto Ricans wanted independence from the United States; the Red Indians wanted at least part of their land restored to them. You name it, and they had the problem! To cap it all, money was in extremely short supply, not even enough to feed the whole lot. Sources of contributions had started drying up. Abernathy and Jesse Jackson were indeed in a very tight situation.

Poor People's Campaign

Well before Martin left for Memphis to assist the 'Garbage Strike' workers, Poor People's March to the nation's capital was already under planning. Unfortunately, King's assassination on April 4, 1968 completely upset the schedule of forthcoming events in the Negroes' struggle for freedom and equal rights. However, these rights have no substance or meaning if the people are not economically independent. Freedom, or slogans thereof, cannot fill hungry stomachs. Much as King and some leaders of the movement wished to change the focus to economic issues rather than abstract platitudes, the Black masses were intent upon fighting for their rights. The Negro middle class, being economically better off, were particularly outspoken in favour of civil rights. During the later years of the movement, Martin was often attacked by his own people for his strict adherence to non-violence. The criticism by advocates of violence and Black Power often caused him deep anguish, more so when they stooped low to personal level. And no doubt the King family was indeed economically well off.

Lest an impression be gathered that Memphis Garbage Strike was the first such labour union unrest, a digression from the main theme would be in order. It should be noted that labour movement was neither restricted to the Southern States only, nor was it limited to the Black workers. In 1873-74, railroad workers resorted to mass strikes and protests against working conditions and low wages. They tore up tracks, uprooted telegraph lines and uncoupled cars. In 1886, 1890 and 1891, a total of 1433, 1833 and 1717 work-stoppages respectively were recorded.[2] Furthermore, Blacks were not the first or the only ethnic minority that resorted to labour-action to assert their rights. Ethnic consciousness nurtured collective labour action by Mexicans-Americans, as well as Chinese and Japanese immigrant workers.

---

2. Glenn Nakano Evelyn: *Unequal Freedom*; London, 2002, p. 77.

With the departure of Martin from the scene, Ralph Abernathy promptly set the ball rolling to launch a campaign on behalf of the Poor of America, irrespective of colour, creed or race. It was not to be a mere march lasting a few hours or days; it was going to be a campaign for economic betterment on a long term basis. Job training and honing of skills were to be accorded a high priority in this campaign. In any case, a March to nation's capital with crowds pouring in from all parts of the country would have been prohibitively expensive,[3] besides it could not possibly achieve the level of success that the "I Have A Dream" march had already done. Abernathy was pragmatic enough not to follow Martin's initial plans for a Poor People's March to Washington, D.C. Instead, they decided to lease a strip of land along the Mall including fifteen acres of the most beautifully kept grass in the world. The Department of the Interior readily granted a temporary permit valid for slightly more than one month. Various charitable organizations volunteered generous quantities of gifts of food, clothing, and other necessities of life. AT&T donated some free telephones. But the various other essentials like electric lines, sewers, showers, toilets, medical supplies, *et al*, cost what turned out to be almost a fortune in those days — around thirty nine thousand dollars. It was going to be a fairly expensive camping trip, since the cost of transportation alone would come to a staggering sum. The financial position was so tight that the budget included a mere $1.30 per person per day.

A large tent was erected over the leased land in mid-May, 1968, to serve as the 'City Hall', the headquarters of the Resurrection City. Meanwhile arrangements for transportation of volunteers to come to live in the City had already been tied up. This was a momentous task by itself. Public transportation on normal payment was out of the question. Mules, wagons, trucks, trolleys, hitch-hiking — anything that could carry the people was collected and people started moving in from all corners of the vast hinterland. The two mules pulling Abernathy's wagon were named after Mississippi's two Senators, Eastland and Stennis, both of whom were viciously opposed to the Civil Rights legislation. Abernathy explained:

> The mule named Eastland is old and forgetful, and he doesn't even want to carry his part of the load. Although the mule named Stennis is still full of life, but he is stubborn and wants to get off the road to eat grass.

---

3. The guesstimate for the Poor People's March was around one million dollars whereas they had barely three hundred thousand in the kitty. So the idea of the march had to be abandoned in favor of creating a city of sorts where the poor could find shelter and free food.

Meanwhile Abernathy's entire family was arrested in Georgia under orders of Governor Lester Maddox on the charge of trespassing Georgia's highways. The federal courts soon intervened and the family was released. This outrageous behaviour by the white establishment brought additional publicity to the Movement as a bonus, besides sympathy from many quarters.

The Poor People's Campaign was officially inaugurated on May 12, 1968, with a rally in Cardozo High School Stadium located in the heart of Washington's worst black slum. The surrounding area had witnessed worst ever race-riots after King's assassination. There were signs of devastation all round. Mrs. Juanita Abernathy, Mrs. Robert Kennedy, Mrs. Harry Belafonte, Mrs. Phillip Hart and several other prominent ladies joined Mrs. Coretta King on the platform. People in their thousands came to the rally to hear Coretta King give a stirring speech:

> She called upon black women, white women, brown women and red women — all the women of this nation — to join in a campaign of conscience. She called for welfare reforms, and for restoration of benefits for women with children. "Our congress passes laws which subsidize corporation farms, oil companies, airlines and houses for suburbia, but when it turns its attention to the poor, it suddenly becomes concerned about balancing the budget."

On the one hand the United States Government paid the Mississippi planter, Senator James Eastland, more than thirteen thousand dollars a month not to grow food or fiber, but on the other it paid a starving child a paltry sum of nine dollars a month for its sustenance. This was the worst example of disparity and inequity practised by the democratic Government of the United States of America which made loud noises for human rights in other parts of the world, except its own backyard!

Solidarity Day Rally

The culmination of the Campaign was scheduled to be a giant rally fixed for June 19. A number of famous personalities were invited to attend the Rally. Meanwhile, the Department of the Interior readily acceded to the request for extension of permit by one week without which the rally would have been virtually impossible. This caused much consternation amongst many members of the Congress.

A couple of days before the appointed day, large crowds started pouring in the Capital from all parts of the country. They were milling around on the streets and coming over to Resurrection City to see for themselves what they had read and seen on the screen. Huge crowds jammed the Pennsylvania Avenue. The local police estimated that there were at least fifty thousand people to join the Rally. Abernathy and his staff were happy in that the number was about one thousand more than what they had hoped for, if not still more. A number of VIPs did not show up for the Rally, but quite a few prominent people did. Vice President Hubert Humphrey was one who did. Mrs. Robert Kennedy had been recently bereaved. She had suffered the same fate as Coretta. She could not come over but sent a touching message reading of which became the first item:

> "Today, on this most important day for all Americans, my heart and prayers are with you. The finest memorial to Dr. Martin Luther King would be the tangible action our country takes now to implement the programs he and my husband cared about so deeply."

Around this time, the Vietnam War was eating into the guts of America. It was at its bloodiest height snuffing put many young lives. The youth of America were up in arms against the War resulting in frequent clashes between the students and the police. They burnt their draft cards and many fled to Canada. Coretta set the tone for the rally when she remarked that this Campaign "may be the last opportunity to save the nation and the world from destruction."

Ralph Abernathy was the last speaker. He said:

> We will stay in Washington and fight non-violently until the nation rises up and demands real assurance that our needs will be met. ... I don't care for the permit. ... I intend to stay here until justice rolls out of the halls of Congress and righteousness falls from the Administration, and the rough places of the government agencies are made plain and the crooked deals of the military-industrial complex become straightforward. ... We will not bow down to the racist Congress. We will not bow down to an administration which refuses to administrate the blessings of this nation to the poor. ... "

Finally, Ralph listed the basic demands of the Poor of America:

- Elimination of hunger;
- Good housing;
- Jobs to all men;
- Adequate income to all citizens;
- Health care to one and all;
- Education to all, to the person's capacity and talent;
- Stop violence against Negroes, and to stop their murders;
- Equal justice to all, without prejudice.

Disintegration of Resurrection City

By this time the permit had expired. Inclement weather had set in. Heavy showers made life miserable. It was cold and muddy all over so much so that it was virtually impossible to walk in the 'City', let alone drive through it. Most people had left the city. Those left behind found life difficult. Moreover, they had responsibilities back home demanded their return. It was an outing; a camping trip cannot last for ever for an average citizen. The criminal gangs roamed the streets like they were used to doing in Chicago and Detroit. They made life quite impossible for the older people and women. The situation was fast deteriorating. To sort out this messy situation, police violence became a distinct possibility.

Violence in the 'City' had considerably increased. Several ugly incidents brought a bad name and poor publicity to the 'City'. A white man was attacked and robbed, and then shot, albeit not seriously. The gang-youngsters threw rocks and bottles at passing cars. The police reacted by firing tear gas into the camp. Finally, when the permit expired, bus loads of police arrived on the scene. They offered bus fare to all those who wanted to return home. Most did. Abernathy and a few who declined to move away were arrested. The camp was dismantled.

Resurrection City turned out to be an anti-climax.

40

Vote Bank Politics

The Southern States had contrived a classic ugly pattern of denial of voting rights to the Negroes even in the Southern Black Belt where the Blacks were in a majority. It was willful disenfranchisement of a large section of the population — a dirty game of vote bank politics designed to defeat the very purpose of federal legislation.

Nixon had refused to 'pander' to Martin Luther King Jr.; consequentially, he suffered a severe loss of black votes. In 1968 he had made a deliberate decision not to be under obligation of the Black community for their votes with the result that his share of Black votes dropped from a high of 32 percent in 1960 to 12 percent in 1968.[1] It is not that Nixon was openly following anti-black policies; it was sheer political calculations that guided his decisions. He appreciated that in any case Blacks would cast their ballot in favour of his opponent, as it had happened in 1960 when 'Martin elected Kennedy as the President'. He therefore made practically no effort to sway the Black votes in his favour. In fact, Nixon was of two minds insofar as desegregation was concerned. He wanted to have the cake, and eat it too. He was anti-segregationist and also anti-busing, both at the same time. The school-desegregation question turned out to be the most emotional and divisive issue in the early years of Nixon Administration. It was generally believed that Nixon would manage to carry the White South with him in his characteristic crafty way without having to lose ground on the desegregation issue.

Above all, 1968 was the year of murders in the United States — Robert Kennedy and Martin Luther King — besides the killings during the widespread nationwide riots, and the turmoil in Chicago. The FBI under Hoover went out of its way to concoct and make public derogatory information against

1. Wickers Tom: *One of Us*, p. 384.

Ralph Abernathy and his predecessor in the SCLC, the late Reverend Martin Luther King with reports of some imaginary sexual indiscretions. The student leaders, dissidents and intellectuals were deliberately targeted by Nixon Administration in which Henry Kissinger and Vice President Agnew played an active role in connivance with Hoover and his FBI.

The white racist regimes in the Southern States were ruling without let or hindrance. In the first place they placed a number of conditions and obstacles in the way of the Blacks that they could not even register to vote. The registrars were all whites; so denial of registration was a mere formality of turning down the black applicant. Even in the Southern Black Belt where the Negroes were in numerical majority, the number of registered voters was far less than the white numerical minority. It was all a game of manipulation by the white registrars. As long as the Blacks were denied the right to vote, political power would remain in the hands of the whites without any interference by the Negroes.

It is pertinent to point out that the question was not merely of the right of Afro-Americans to vote; equally, if not more, perplexing issue was female suffrage. The American opinion, both black and white, was divided on this matter. "Significantly, however, women were among those who voted on the issue, and they continued to vote at meetings even after negative decisions on a formal franchise for women." The irony of the situation was that the so-called educated and civilized protagonists of equal rights and democratic freedom, the whites, considered 'the very idea of female franchise as absurd', while the blacks were, by and large, in favour of granting full voting rights to the fair sex. In fact, Afro-American women were way ahead of their white counterparts in organizing political societies such as 'Richmond Rising Daughters of Liberty' and 'United Daughters of Liberty' to assert the rights of female suffrage.[2]

Voter Education Project (VEP)

During early 1960's there were more than five million blacks of voting age in the eleven Southern states; but in April 1962 when SNCC and other civil rights groups started the VEP, only 1,386,654 were registered to vote. This was a joint program in which NAACP, CORE groups, SCLC and SNCC field staff participated. By April 1964 they managed to add over half a million voters in the registered list thereby increasing the strength to 38.6 percent of those eligible. This increase was recorded from all the Southern

2. Rachleff J. Peter: *Black Labour in the South: Richmond, Virginia, 1865-1890*, Philadelphia, 1984, p. 32.

states with the sole exception of Mississippi. Two yeas of concerted drive yielded only 3,871 new black names leaving some 394,000 black adults unregistered. In contrast, in Florida, Tennessee and Texas the percentage of eligible blacks registered to vote was well over 50 percent — 57.7, 69.4 and 63.8 percent respectively. However, for the entire region only 40.8 percent of blacks eligible to vote were on the voting rolls, while in Alabama only 22.8 percent of the black voting-age population (about 500,000) or only 114,000 were registered at the end of 1964. In Dallas County of the same State, the blacks constituted 57 percent of the total population of which 15,115 were of voting age. But only 320 blacks were registered voters while 9,543 whites were on the rolls. To quote yet another instance of disenfranchisement: Registration of Negroes in Selma (Dallas County) was restricted to an average of 145 persons per year; at this rate it would have taken 103 years to register the 15,000 eligible Negro voters!

The above gross disparity gave rise to Mississippi Freedom Summer Project undertaken by COFO in the fall of 1963. The white community of Mississippi reacted violently to this simple and innocuous program of voters' registration. They burnt crosses on the night of April 24, 1964, in 64 of the State's 82 counties. Jackson, Mississippi Mayor Allen Thompson expanded the city's police force from 200 to 300 besides procuring an armoured personnel carrier, "Thompson's tank", having 12-gauge steel side plates, bulletproof windows and a sub-machine gun mounted on the turret.[3] A virtual martial law was enforced. The 'race war' seemed to have been set in motion by the all-white administration. Meanwhile, about 200 volunteers from Oxford, Ohio, pitched in for Mississippi. Three of these young men — 21-year old Andrew Goodman, 24-year old Michael Schwerner and 21-year old black James Chaney were arrested in a small town in Neshoba County for alleged over-speeding while returning to Meridian. They were released around 10:30 p.m. They were abducted and murdered in cold blood by KKK that very night. Their bodies were discovered in early August. On December 4, 1964, twenty-one men including Sheriff Lawrence Rainey and his Deputy Cecil Price were charged in connection with the murder of the three civil rights workers. The charges were subsequently dropped!

An interesting fallout from the Freedom Summer was the establishment by COFO of Mississippi Freedom Democratic Party (MFDP) as an alternative to Mississippi Jim Crow Democratic Party. About 6,000 disenfranchised blacks promptly enrolled in the new Party, MFDP. At the Democratic Party Convention, Fannie Lou Hamer of Ruleville, Mississippi, an MFDP delegate delivered the most moving address. She

3. Wexler Sanford: op. cit. pp. 199 and 215.

told the delegates how cruelly and unceremoniously she was fired from her 18-year job in a plantation on the very day that she registered as a voter. She described the violence she had suffered in retaliation for attending a civil rights meeting. Her closing remarks: "Is this America, the land of the free and the home of the brave, where we are threatened daily because we want to live as decent human beings?"[4]

The few Blacks who did manage to register as voters were indifferent to exercise their franchise. In the first place they were maltreated by the white law enforcement agencies while they stood in line to vote. And if at all they could cast their ballot, they became pawns in the political ploys of the white candidates. The Blacks constituted a 'vote bank' that was there for an artful candidate to dip into and get elected, by hook or crook. This was the crux of black vote bank politics. Poverty, economic deprivation, lack of education and ignorance of the political system added to the travails of the Negro who was deliberately kept out of the local and state political set-up.

"Martin Luther King elects John Kennedy as the President' is the classic case of vote-bank politics, albeit contrived by the Black leadership for the long term benefit of the Negro community — at least that was the intention!

The fight for ballot was not restricted to the King camp only. Malcolm X was equally, if not more, enthusiastic about black enfranchisement. His speech, "The Ballot or the Bullet" (April 12, 1964), which was one of his best talks rivaling his "Message to the Grass-roots", is almost at par with King's "I Have A Dream", albeit not as popular. Malcolm emphasized the plight of Negroes irrespective of their religious affiliations. Whether Baptist Christian or Muslim or a Nationalist, the Negro had the same problem. Again, education or absence thereof, place of residence whether in a ghetto or on a boulevard — "the consequences of being black in America were pretty much the same. ... They don't hang you because you are a Baptist; they hang you because you're black. ... They don't attack me because I'm a Muslim; they attack me because I'm black. ... We suffer political oppression, economic exploitation, and social degradation ..." Our enemy is the same, the white man. ... "We should form *rifle clubs* that can be used to defend our lives and our property in times of emergency." Notwithstanding the element of militancy in his speeches, Malcolm made sure that he worked within the bounds of law. He never advocated aggressive violence against the whites. However, the American Negro must fight back whenever he is unjustly attacked. But the whites refused to concede the right of self-defense to the blacks. And that became the primary reason why Malcolm could

4. Wexler Sanford: op. cit. p. 202.

never accept Martin's ideas of non-violence. While King and his colleagues were integrationists inasmuch as they tried to inculcate the spirit of Americanism as the basic identity, Malcolm insisted that "we are not Americans; we are Africans who happen to be in America. ... We were kidnapped and brought here against our will from Africa. We did not land on Plymouth Rock — that rock landed on us."[5] In the same vein Malcolm refused to refer to America as "my country". He compared being a citizen to being a diner. "Sitting at the table doesn't make you a diner, unless you eat some of what is on the plate. ... Likewise, being born in America doesn't make you aŋ American. ..."

Meanwhile, the Civil Rights Act of 1964 was signed into law; but it had no effect on the situation in St. Augustine. However, when the Voting Rights Bill was signed on 6th August 1965, the two pieces of legislation were certainly a great advance inasmuch as they provided a high degree of basic legal protection for the Negroes. It was well known that the Southern States directly obstructed the Blacks from exercising their franchise. Even in areas where the Blacks outnumbered the whites, there was no black representation. It had been almost a century of white terrorism at the polls. So King undertook tour of the area to bolster support for the MFDP.

From mid-1950s to his assassination in April 1968, Rev. Martin Luther King Jr., the eloquent Black Baptist Minister, led the first mass civil rights movement in US history. He applied principles of non-violent resistance patterned after Mahatma Gandhi. His leadership of the struggle for racial equality brought forth a sea-change in the racial balance in the United States. But the City ghettos remained almost unaffected. By then it became obvious that a large number of Blacks were getting frustrated, and losing their patience with their moderate leadership. Militant non-violence was on its way to turning into real militancy. Racial violence soon erupted. It soon spread to Harlem, New Jersey, Chicago and Philadelphia. According to the February-1968 National Advisory Commission Report on Civil Disorders, "the riots were spontaneous upheavals, chiefly caused by white racism and 'explosive mixture' it fostered — police brutality, slum housing, poverty and welfare dependency, job discrimination, unemployment and blighted opportunity. ... The Whites wanted not additional reforms but repression."[6] In the same vein the National Council of Churches claimed that "America was seen as a predominantly white nation using our overwhelming strength to kill more Asians".

5. Goldman Peter: *The Death and Life of Malcolm X*; Urbana, 1979, p. 157. Also Cones James H: op. cit. pp. 196-97.

6. Charles Sellers: op. cit. p. 422.

41

Campaign for Assured Jobs and Income

The Negro is struggling for concrete improvement in his way of life. How would it help him to send his children to an integrated school if the family income is insufficient to buy them school clothes? While most Americans are unaware of conditions in the ghettos, there are very few ghetto-dwellers who are unaware of life outside, thanks to the TV. The simplest approach to abolish poverty is to provide 'Assured Income' to the poor — black or white.

The Moynihan Report[1] (1965) on the black family came as an eye opener to black leaders. It was an unpleasant scathing attack on black manhood by a white man. Although the average Negro man was offended by what he read in the Report, most black men agreed that the black man was more victimized than the black woman, and that there was a definite need for them to assert their masculinity, more so since it was believed that many a black man was castrated by black women in the family circle. The primary reason for female domination was absence of male-jobs, and consequent inability of the black man to support his wife and children. Slavery, segregation and discrimination had deprived the black man of his manhood leading to a matriarchal society in a patriarchal sea. The need of the hour therefore was to provide a certain degree of economic independence to the man to be able to support his family so that black women alone working as domestic help were no longer the sole bread-earners for the family. King was now convinced that while equal rights, desegregation, integration, *et al*, had their own place in the agenda, economic issues had come to the fore requiring urgent attention. Jobs, equal employment opportunities, honing of skills had to be accorded a high priority.

1. U.S. Government Printing Office, Washington D.C.: *The Negro Family: The Case for National Action*; 1965

The ghetto-culture was not confined to the Northern metropolises only. High proportions of low-income Hispanic communities lived, and still do, in overcrowded sprawling ghettos in San Francisco, the East Bay and Los Angeles. The Second World War acted as a catalyst towards economic emancipation of the Blacks, albeit to a limited extent only. The War brought jobs and welfare programs in its wake. Since the Blacks generally proved to be better soldiers than the Whites — Eisenhower specifically asked for Blacks as reinforcements in the Battle of the Bulge — there was better appreciation of the Negro as a useful contributing member of the American democracy. However, these tangible benefits for the Negro were short lived. The collective memory of the public is proverbially short-lived. There is no denying that Theodore Roosevelt's 'Square Deal', FDR's 'New Deal' and Truman's 'Fair Deal', gave certain definite economic and psychological support to the Black community. However, it should not be lost sight of that these benefits accrued mainly to meet the needs of the Whites to fulfill their own international agenda. The end of the War brought home the realization that the economic benefits were 'mere crumbs'. However, the onset of the 'cold war' once again brought into focus the plight of Negro, and the need to struggle for equality in race relations and economic opportunities.

Racial Dilemma

The two World Wars brought out the glaring inconsistency of American approach to human rights in sharp focus. Woodrow Wilson in World War I and Franklin Roosevelt in World War II pompously proclaimed the rights of man, and their intention to defend and extend the same to one and all everywhere in the world; except of course in their own country where the Negro was treated a step lower than a second class citizen. In fact, they were not at all concerned with the plight of their own black minority while espousing the cause of oppressed minorities the world over. This state of what may be called America's internal cold war, particularly in the Southern States, prompted the Carnegie Corporation to sponsor a comprehensive analytical study of black-white relations in all their complexity. This onerous task was entrusted to a Swedish scholar, Gunnar Myrdal. His one thousand pages voluminous study was published in 1942 as *An American Dilemma*. While there was no doubt that the Black minority had to vigorously pursue their efforts to ameliorate their lot, it was virtually an impossible task in the face of white supremacy 'fortress syndrome' in the South. "No one made this point with such overwhelming intellectual authority, philosophical imagination and analytical skill" as Gunnar Myrdal who had so "immersed himself in the American racial dilemma as to become a citizen in thought if not in law."[2] He dissected the Black-White conflict with such clarity, and exposed the hypocrisy of White ideals of democracy and human rights in international relations with such intellectual force that the paradoxes of American cynicism at home proved a serious embarrassment to American diplomats all over the world. The hollowness of American ideals of liberty, justice, equality and democracy were exposed in clear focus side by side with gross injustice, inequality, cruelty and police brutality at home. However, his monumental work was so highly intellectual, and so voluminous, that it hardly made a dent on the average white psyche. The result: the Negro remained where he had been for the past more than three centuries. It was *status quo*, particularly in the South. Had the American Administration sincerely acted on Myrdal's report, there would have been no Martin Luther King Jr.!

Myrdal's updated study supported by historical data and sociological theories was published in 1962. It was now crystal clear that the Blacks must use all possible means at their disposal to achieve racial equality, desegregation in all walks of life, job opportunities and economic upliftment. They must fight for Civil Rights not only in the streets but also carry the same to the Federal and State capitols.

In the wake of police brutalities inflicted by 'Bull' Connor, the number of demonstrations in the North and West reached the same level as in the South. They were emphatic on increased job opportunities, provision of low-rent housing, and end of segregation in housing and educational facilities. An interesting point to note here is that they did not want new school construction in the ghetto areas; they wanted the additional schools to accommodate black children to be built outside the all-Negro neighborhood. Further, in New York and Philadelphia they demonstrated against tax-supported construction for the simple reason that the Negro derived no financial advantage from the same as he received little or no employment on such small scale dispersed construction. The Negroes resorted to sit-ins and demonstrations outside the offices of the Mayor, Robert Wagner and the Governor Nelson Rockefeller of New York. Similar sit-ins and school-strikes were resorted to in Boston, Chicago, New York, New Jersey and Englewood to protest against racial imbalance.

Operation 'Breadbasket"

This program was tried in the ghettos of Chicago where it proved most successful and effective. In essence, it meant the consumer industries

---

2. Burns M. James: op. cit. p. 359.

and their retail outlets were earning substantial profits from sales in the ghettos at prices higher than those prevailing in white neighborhoods, but they were not ploughing back any part of their profits for the welfare of the ghetto-residents. For instance: consumer items range from five to twelve cents higher in the ghetto stores than in the suburban stores, both run by the same super chain. This exploitation is possible because so many residents of the ghetto have no personal means of transportation.[3] Even if they were not charging higher prices, still they were making substantial profits. It therefore stood to reason that, in all fairness, those industries and their outlets should at least employ some ghetto-residents as part of fair hiring practice. The industries most affected were milk, soft drinks, chain grocery stores, etc. Negro leadership approached these industries and succeeded in getting them to employ a number of Blacks. SCLC took a leading part in negotiating fair hiring-practice agreements. By the end of 1967, "Operation Breadbasket" was in operation in more than twelve major cities, with remarkable results.

Dr. King was convinced that the panacea for abolishing poverty amongst the oppressed classes of Americans, especially the Negroes, was a system of "guaranteed income". The program of guaranteed income was not for the benefit of Blacks only; it was to benefit all the poor including two-thirds of them who were white. And that required combined effort of all the affected communities including the Hispanic and Red-Indians. But this was easier said than done. Nevertheless, a start had been made in that direction.

"The time has come for us to civilize ourselves by the total, direct and immediate abolition of poverty."[4]

---

3. King M.L., Jr.: *Companion*, pp. 68-69.
4. Ibid; p.70

42

White "Justice"

We must pray with unceasing passion for racial justice, but we must also use our minds to develop a program to bring an end to racial injustice. The decade of 1955 to 1965 with its constructive elements misled us. Everyone underestimated the violence and rage Negroes were suppressing and the amount of bigotry the white majority was disguising.

Frequent conferences were held at the White House to work out suitable measures to improve the lot of the Negro. Unfortunately, these were mere cosmetic exercises to gain time for doing nothing, or for passing the buck. While the President was often arrogant and hot-headed over the litany of grievances as well accusations about the failures of the Federal Government, there was no dearth of bootlickers who would thank him for the 'honour' of being invited to the White House. The cruel and extremely harsh treatment meted out to the volunteer activists at the Pettus Bridge (Selma March) was a classic case of apathy on the part of the federal authority, and the reaction of some of those who attended the meeting. Harping on violation of law by the black-activists was often the excuse for the atrocities meted out to the Negro in the name of maintenance of law and order. Is enforcement of unjust law(s) a legitimate function of a government? As recorded in *Gandhi Versus the Empire*[1], Gandhi was of the opinion that the "law that governs brute creation is not the law that should guide the human race. That law is inconsistent with human dignity." However, it goes without saying that every law cannot possibly be popular with the public at large. Some laws, of necessity, have to be harsh and unpopular. But they do work, are enforced under the authority of the State, and fulfill a specific

1. *Gandhi Versus the Empire*, published by Universal Publishing Company, New York, 1932.

purpose. Unfortunately, laws enacted for the benefit of the Negroes were 'so widely un-enforced that it is a mockery to call them laws.'

William Zantzinger, a wealthy tobacco farmer of Maryland was convicted of caning a black barmaid, Mrs. Hattie Carroll, to death. The formality of the so called 'due process of law' was gone through. But the punishment for the murder of a black woman employee? Six months imprisonment and fine of $625/-. His jail term was to commence after September 15 to enable him to finish gathering his tobacco crop. That was White justice delivered in the case of a Black victim! Nothing could be more shameful than that. It was a disgrace to high ideals of democracy and justice that the Great America lectured to the rest of the world. 'Injustice anywhere is a threat to justice everywhere.'

Some white racist-snipers shot and killed a white woman from Detroit as she transported some Black passengers from Montgomery back to Selma.[2] The accused were apprehended and they confessed to the murder. But they were not tried for murder! The killers were exonerated from the murder charge. White brand of justice tried them for violating the civil rights of another citizen. What a travesty of justice system — if at all it can be categorized as a system. The all-pervading white power structure made sure that justice was denied to the Negro whenever the culprits were whites. The white race was above the law of the land. In fact, interpretation of the same law was of one kind for the whites and of an altogether different kind for the poor oppressed blacks. Lynching of a Negro, twisting and cutting off his testicles, and hanging his body on a tree for target practice — that indeed was the white concept of justice in the South that the Negro had to face. The rules and their applications had double standards — one for the whites, and the other for the blacks. A Negro could be put to death for stealing a few dollars, while the same offence was a mere aberration when committed by a white.

In the Detroit riots of 1967 three black teenagers were killed in Algiers Motel. Three policemen and a black private guard were tried. The defence conceded that the four men had shot the two black youth. The jury exonerated them.

In 1970, the police laid down a barrage of twenty-eight seconds on the campus of Jackson State College, a Negro institution. Marks of four hundred shots were observed on the girls' dormitory. The Judge and Jury found the attack justified. In yet another case of police highhandedness, a black unarmed patient was killed by a policeman in

2. Franklin John Hope: op. cit. p. 638.

Boston City Hospital in April 1970. Five shots were fired. The judge exonerated the policeman.

In the course of these narratives innumerable cases of atrocities, unequal and highly anti-Negro 'white-justice' as meted out to the blacks have been mentioned in passing. It would serve no useful purpose to repeat the same here again. Suffice would be to say that the white governments adopted distinctly double standards in their judicial system — if at all one could call it a system. Of course they preached to the rest of world complete equality before the law!

43

The "Drum Major" Gone For Ever

America must seek its own ways of atonement for the injustices he has inflicted upon her Negro citizens. I do not suggest atonement for atonement's sake or because there is need for self-punishment. I suggest atonement as the moral and practical way to bring the Negro's standard up to a realistic level. If you lose hope, somehow you lose the vitality that keeps life moving, you lose that courage and quality that helps you to go on in spite of all.

AND TODAY I STILL HAVE A DREAM

Martin's first book was *Stride Towards Freedom* published by Harper, New York, in 1958. It was in the nature of an autobiography inasmuch it told the story of Montgomery Bus Boycott. While he was autographing the book in Harlem, he was stabbed by a Mrs. Izola Curry. The wound was indeed very serious, almost fatal, but Martin survived. That is when the newspapers published the news item that if Martin had coughed any time during those few critical hours, he would have died! When he had recovered fully, he along with his wife, Coretta, and Dr. Lawrence Reddick, a friend and Martin's first biographer who had authored a book on him, *Crusader Without Violence,* visited India, the country from which Martin had drawn so much inspiration and on which his entire political philosophy was founded. While travelling in India there was a pause for self-introspection. The desegregation ruling by the Supreme Court was passed more than five years ago. But the desegregation of bus system was implemented in barely forty towns out of a few hundreds southern towns and cities. It was as if the ruling was never passed and therefore shall never be implemented. The apparent failure of the Montgomery Boycotts made the Black population of the country thoroughly disappointed, frustrated and depressed, while the

Whites, particularly in the Southern States were full of joy and relief. The American socio-political system had successfully withstood the heavy battering that came from the pent up emotions of the Blacks. Soon thereafter occurred the unfortunate incident of lynching of Mack Parker in Poplarville, Mississippi. It was common practice with the whites to raid Monroe County, North Carolina and shoot up the Negro section at will. Robert Williams, an ex-Marine Corps man, organized an armed patrol for the area and used to exchange gun-fire with the whites almost every night. Thereafter the whites stopped harassing the blacks in that county.

Martin King was ever ready to jump into the fray for the benefit of the Blacks. His courage to stand for the Black man was boundless. He symbolized the courage, suffering and sacrifice of the struggling Negro. He had been arrested more than fifteen times, often physically assaulted, continually threatened, stabbed and his home bombed. There were frequent persistent demands on his time since his very presence was enough to electrify a movement anywhere, particularly in the South. His eloquence spiced with emotional appeal invariably carried the day. But in the process, he had hardly any family life, or respite. He went wherever people needed help. The garbage workers in Memphis, Tennessee, were on strike and requested Martin to come over to lead them, which he did. He marched with them, talked with them, sang with them and prayed with them. No religious leader has made a greater impact upon American society and its churches, white or black, than Dr. Martin Luther King Jr.

Assassination of Dr. Martin Luther King, Jr.[1]

Dr. Martin Luther King Jr. was shot and killed by a white man on Thursday, 4th April 1968, his second day in Memphis, Tennessee, plunging the nation in grief and darkness, particularly the Black people of America. Most whites were stunned and shocked by the news. The immediate official response was of horror and deep regret. And it was destined to happen in the Lenten season. The supreme sacrifice for the cause of Black people had to come in the Easter season. His assassination occurred on the eve of centenary celebrations of Gandhi's birth, and cast a deep gloom all over India also. Having given his life for the cause of Black People of America, for all the poor people of America, the Drum-Major for Justice, Peace, Non-violence, Righteousness and Brotherhood had gone, gone for ever! For Martin, the important thing was not for how long he lived, but how well he lived.

1. Memphis Garbage Strike and shooting of Dr. Martin Luther King has been partly covered in Chapter 11, Civil Rights and Civil Disobedience.

Free At Last, Free At Last
Thank God Almighty
I'm Free at Last

The Murder Scene

Hope and Horror had joined hands in America during one single week. The Vietnam War was sapping the American nation to its core. President Lyndon B. Jones declared a major peace offensive in Asia concurrently with his intention not to run for the Presidency for another term. His renunciation of power had an element of peculiar spiritualism. The good tidings had hardly set in when tragedy struck America once again, this time in Memphis, Tennessee, so soon after the assassination of President Kennedy. King had actually withdrawn his support to the garbage workers of Memphis after they had indulged in rioting during the earlier march led by him a fortnight ago. But fate had its quirks! He was prevailed upon to return to lead them again for another avowedly peaceful non-violent march. And return he did. When he had come for the first march he had stayed in the luxurious River Mont, a Holiday Inn property on the east bank of the Mississippi. His image suffered a blemish, made worse by the rioting that followed the march. As a measure of damage control, this time he and his entourage checked into the Negro-owned Lorraine, a two-storey motel near Memphis' renowned Beale Street, at $13 a night for their green-walled rust-spotted rooms.

There was a nameless tawdry rooming-house across Mulberry Street, on a slight rise, just about 205-feet from the Lorraine. It was conspicuous by its rusty metal awning painted red, green and yellow stripes. It was in fact a set of two adjacent interconnected cheap type ramshackle buildings, one portion for the whites and the other for blacks. It was located in a compound opposite the Lorraine. Mrs. Bessie Brewer was the manager of the establishment for whatever it was worth. She was rather surprised when a young dark haired white man in a neat business suit walked in for a room. She had never had a gentleman like him asking for a room in her shabby place. He gave his name as John Willard, carefully selected Room #5 which had a clear view of the Lorraine, and paid his $8.50 for the week with a crisp new $20 bill. This further enhanced her surprise. The image of the man therefore remained stuck in Brewer's mind.

Back at the Lorraine — After a day long hard work King washed, dressed for dinner and walked out of Room 306 down to the second floor balcony. He leaned casually on the railing, chatting with co-workers.

All of a sudden, there was a sound like a fire-cracker from the direction of the rooming-house. It was a high velocity heavy-calibre exploding-bullet fired from a window in the rooming-house. It smashed through King's neck and exploded against his lower right jaw, slamming him against the wall with his hands drawn towards his head. Blood started flowing all over his body and onto the floor. The Memphis police deputed for King's security swiftly converged on the motel in response to the sound of the shot. There were about thirty of them, but none made any attempt to rush towards the direction from which the shot had come. Later, the murder-weapon, a scope-sighted 30.06-caliber Remington pump rifle, binoculars and a suitcase were found near the rooming-house. Obviously, the murderer was not a very methodical person. He left behind unusually large amount of tell-tale evidence. Mrs. Brewer recalled that the killer was about 6-ft tall, 30-32 years old in appearance, of slender build roughly about 165 pounds. He was reported to have been seen running away from the rooming-house at the time of the shooting, 6:01 p.m. and leaping into a white Mustang with no front license plate and then "laid rubber" up the road. A reward of one hundred thousand dollars for the capture of the killer was announced. With all other available clues including a number of clear thumb and finger-prints it was thought that it would not take long to catch the murderer. However, there is no doubt that the Memphis police had missed their best chance of catching the killer within the first few minutes of the shooting. Why did the killer drop his murder-weapon and the overnight bag was indeed a mystery.

King was rushed to St. Joseph's Hospital, about 2½ km away and declared dead within an hour of the shooting. His death was the twelfth major assassination and most traumatic of all in the civil rights movement since 1963.

The U.S. Attorney General Ramsey Clark along with seventy-five federal law-men reached Memphis within fourteen hours of the Tragedy. The search for the killer was immediately spread to cover six-state area: Alabama, Arkansas, Kentucky, Mississippi, Missouri and Tennessee.

It was important that the assassin be identified and arrested as soon as possible. A maniac prowling free on the streets of America was indeed dangerous. The Memphis police was most upset and embarrassed that the assassin had slipped through an extremely tight security apparatus that had been put in place for King's protection. Since the threat perception to King's life was high, the security network was all the tighter. The various federal and state investigative agencies swung into action immediately after the most unfortunate incident. They already had substantial physical evidence in their possession and felt confident of nabbing the killer without much delay. The massive manhunt for the killer had already spread several hundred miles beyond the Tennessee-Mississippi borders. The Attorney General Ramsey Clark ruled out the conspiracy theory. His off the cuff remark was much too premature and could have put the investigating agencies off the trail. Be that as it may, two months later the 'two-bit criminal', James Earl Ray was captured at a London airport on June 8, 1968. He pleaded guilty to the charge of killing Dr. Martin Luther King Jr. and was sentenced to 99-years in prison. There were reports that he was part of a larger conspiracy. The House Select Committee on Assassinations chaired by Congressman Louis Stokes investigated these allegations. They came to the conclusion that the possibility of Ray being a part of an unidentified conspiracy to murder Dr. King cannot be ruled out.

The Aftermath

Much as President Johnson wanted to attend the funeral, he had no option but to accede to the unanimous advice of the Secret Service and FBI. "The situation in Atlanta was tense and dangerous; they recommended in the strongest terms that I not attend the funeral."[2]

President Johnson got the sad news at 8:20 p.m. April 4th, 1968. He called Mrs. Coretta King to convey the condolences of the Nation and tried to comfort her as best as he could. Shortly after 9 p.m. he went on nation-wide television and said:[3]

> "I ask every citizen to reject the blind violence that has struck Dr. King, who lived by non-violence. ... We can achieve nothing by lawlessness and divisiveness among the American people. It is only by joining together and only by working together that we can continue to move toward quality and fulfillment for all our people."

The President announced in the telecast that he was going to call an extraordinary joint session of Congress to put forward a program of action — "of constructive and not destructive action". He also proclaimed Sunday, 7th April, as a day of National Mourning. Senator Kennedy did his bit too. He sent a plane to fly Coretta and party to Memphis and got three more telephones installed in her house by the same evening to take care of the numerous telephone calls that were expected. Governor Nelson Rockefeller

---

2. Johnson L.B.: op. cit. p. 176.
3. Johnson L.B.: op. cit. p. 174.

sent his plane to be at the disposal of the King family. Numerous contributions started pouring in, the largest amongst the individual contributions, sixty two thousand dollars, came from Peter Fuller of Boston.

Soon after the Presidential telecast, trouble started building up in Washington D.C. At the first word of Martin's shooting, crowds had started gathering at 14th and U Streets, Northwest. There was an ominous hushed silence. People were anxiously awaiting further news of the tragedy. The news media reported Dr. King's death at 8:30 p.m. The crowds started moving north on 14th Street, asking stores to down shutters out of respect for Dr. King. Most complied. The general mood was one of sorrow, mourning and non-violence. But that changed within the hour. Anger, bitterness and inflammatory speeches filled the air. Wild rumours spread. Some windows were smashed. Some stores were looted; others were torched. Arson all over the place. Fires crackled just three blocks away from the White House and "from the air the Capital looked like a bombed city."[4] By next day entire blocks were up in smoke. Troops were patrolling the littered streets. Shock waves from Memphis soon engulfed the streets in Detroit, Nashville, Minneapolis, Chicago, Harlem, Boston, North Carolina, Mississippi, *et al.* But fortunately Memphis remained comparatively trouble free. For all one knows, that whole city could have been reduced to cinders. And Dr. Abernathy held an impromptu service in his chapel. Even such hard-core militants as Harlem Mau Mau Leader Charles 37X Kenyatta and Los Angeles Kon Karenga called for restraint and calm. The Vice President Hubert Humphrey declared: "This Nation of law and order, which has its President shot down, in cold murder, its spiritual leaders assassinated, and those who walk and speak and work for human rights beaten and killed — my fellow Americans, every one of us must resolve that we will never, never, never let it happen again."[5]

Numerous tributes have been paid to Dr. Martin Luther King Jr. But the one that Coretta likes most was written by his devoted and trusted friends, Harry Belafonte and Stanley Levison:

> In a nation tenaciously racist, a black man sensitized its somnolent conscience; in a nation sick with violence, a black man preached non-violence; in a nation corrosive with alienation, a black man preached love; in a world embroiled in three wars in twenty years, a black man preached peace. ... In only twelve years of public life he evoked

---

4. *Time* dated April 12, 1968.
5. Ibid.

more respect for black people than a preceding century had produced. ... He did not want to be idolized; he wanted only to be heard. ..."[6]

In a rare act of departure from traditional decorum insofar as a citizen of a foreign country was concerned, the Indian Parliament paid homage to Dr. Martin Luther King Jr. The Indian Prime Minister Indira Gandhi paid rich tributes to King for his services and sacrifices for the cause of the Negro minority of America, after which the members stood in silence for one minute. Subsequently, a specially designed postage stamp was issued in his Honour by the Government of India.

The President called a meeting of Civil Rights leaders[7] for 11:00 a.m. on Friday, less than seventeen hours after the fatal shooting. The emphasis in discussions was on perils of the situation and unity as the essential need of the hour. Bayard Rustin and Reverend Sullivan captured the essence of the discussions. They said: "The large majorities of the Negroes are not in favour of violence, but we need something to fight back with; we need something positive to carry to the people. Otherwise we will cough with nothing. And the people just won't behave in a vacuum." The President suggested "seizing the opportunity, and pressing for an open housing law". The proposal for an Executive Order to that end was turned down. "A new Executive Order might put more words in the books but it would not put more Negroes into decent houses." The murder of Dr. King brought about a positive change in the attitude of the Congress. Within twenty-four hours the full House gave its approval to the omnibus Civil Rights Act of 1968. The President put his signature on the Bill on 11th April 1968 in the presence of the Negro leaders who had made it possible.

Unfinished Agenda

The very first item on Dr. King's unfinished agenda included the march he had scheduled in Memphis for April 8, 1968 before his assassination. The Poor People's Campaign, economic issues, equitable housing, and a lot more were on hold. His widow, Mrs. Coretta Scott King considered it her moral duty — a sort of legacy to be fulfilled — and she arranged the Memphis-march to be carried out as scheduled

6. As recorded by Coretta; pp. 316-17.
7. The important ones among those invited were: Roy Wilkins; Whitney Young Jr.; Clarence Mitchell; Walter Washington, Mayor of Washington D.C.; Bayard Rustin, Executive Director of the A. Philip Randolph Institute; Leon Sullivan, Director of the Opportunities Industrialization Centre in Philadelphia; Judge Leon Higginbottham; Richard Hatcher, Mayor of Gary, Indiana; Walter Fauntroy of the Southern Christian Leadership Conference; and Bishop George Baber of Philadelphia. Martin's father was also invited but could not attend due to ill health.

by her late husband. Coretta along with her three eldest children led the march, silently and stoically, with dignity and fortitude writ large on their faces. It was indeed a memorial march in honour of Dr. King. More than fifteen thousand people from all over the United States joined in paying their homage to the departed leader, the like of whom was unlikely to appear ever again on the soil of America. Ralph Abernathy, who at King's request had succeeded him as head of the SCLC, accompanied Mrs. King.

Gandhi was a world leader, and so was King in his own right. Both were strong proponents of non-violence and both died a violent death by the assassin's bullets. Both came from average middle class families, and both were well educated. Of course both were coloured — brown or black was immaterial really. Both married and had four children except that Martin had two girls and two boys while Gandhi had all four boys. Both were charismatic leaders and both led massive political movements in their respective countries, albeit at widely different periods of history, using the method of non-violent non-retaliatory *Satyagraha*, the Truth-Force, whose basis was love. Neither of them held any public office but still both were powerful in their own characteristic way. In fact, Gandhi's rejection of power and refusal to hold any public office enhanced his authority.[8] Both were acknowledged in life as well in death as the greatest humanitarian leaders of their time. While Gandhi made a great impact on the life of others not only in his own country but in the world at large, Martin's impact on his fellow countrymen, mostly Blacks but some whites too, made him great in his own right. The whole world grieved at their passing away, and in Martin's case it was most untimely too. Martin was exactly half of Gandhi's age when he was assassinated — seventy-eight against thirty-nine. Since they were more than a generation apart, it was an unfortunate irony of fate that, in spite of so much of similarities, neither had they met nor did they correspond with each other. In fact, when Gandhi died he did not even know that any one like the 20-years old Martin Luther King Jr. existed, following in his foot-steps the teachings of *Satyagraha.*[9]

---

8. "Power tends to corrupt, and absolute power corrupts absolutely." Lord Aton, the celebrated English historian, has identified three men who defy this adage — Marcus Aurelius, Abraham Lincoln, and Mahatma Gandhi. And he says "the greatest of these is Gandhi". Indeed, Gandhi was a saint, not in the Vatican sense of course.

9. Jack A. Homer: Gandhi and Martin Luther King, in *Profiles of Gandhi*; ed. Norman Cousins, India Book Company, Delhi, 1969; p. 218.

After his return from India, Martin's life was in constant danger. King came to the conclusion that new and more radical methods were now required to carry on the struggle in a meaningful manner. Martin in consultation with the Southern Christian Leadership Conference (SCLC) decided that the next phase of protests will commence at North Carolina A & T College in Greensboro on 1st February 1960, and shall take the form of 'sit ins'. This 'sit in' attracted s good number of students including many whites. It was a success beyond expectations. Meanwhile the Kings were passing through tough times. Civil Rights Acts of 1957 and 1960 and the Emancipation Proclamation were welcome signs in that direction. But these positive changes were merely on paper. Words were spoken or written, but seldom implemented. And that was the crux of the problem. King not only preached non-violence but also practiced it. About his own security arrangements, he had said:

> "When I decided that, as a teacher of the philosophy of non-violence, I couldn't keep a gun, I came face to face with the question of death and I dealt with it. And from that point on, I no longer needed a gun nor have I been afraid. Ultimately, one's sense of manhood must come from within.

When Mahatma Gandhi was assassinated, his life's work had not been completed. Immediately after India attained Independence, his major task was to shut down the Indian National Congress as a political entity, and convert the organization into a creative social service for reconstruction, development and rural upliftment. Communal harmony amongst various sections of the new nation was on the top of his agenda; and he had totally failed in this direction. The assimilation of untouchables in Hindu polity was his most ambitious and difficult self-imposed assignment. But on his death the results were merely cosmetic while psychological integration of the low-castes in Hindu society remained a distant dream. They remained segregated from the mainstream Hindu 'Samaj', living in segregated slums away from the main village with separate wells and other facilities. The Indian situation was a mirror image of segregation as practised in the United States against the Negro minority. Similarly, when Dr. Martin Luther King Jr. was assassinated, his life's work was also unfinished. Civil Rights, Northern Ghettos, Vietnam War, and above all, inculcation of non-violence as the principal method of resolving grievances, *et al*, were some of the major unfinished tasks. It was indeed an unfortunate irony of fate that the man who abjured violence during his lifetime had to 'face' unprecedented acts of mass-violence by his people after his death, as a series of acts to avenge his murder by a white racist. In the process, more Blacks got killed than the whites! While both, the Mahatma and the 'King', departed from this world with a lot of their agenda unfulfilled, tasks incomplete, that of the 'Frontier Gandhi' was completely undone with the creation of Pakistan. Khan Abdul Ghaffar Khan had transformed the Frontier Province into an oasis of peace and non-violence in the midst of generations-old blood feuds, tribal wars and clan-hostility. All this good work came to naught through the kind courtesy of Jinnah in connivance with the British. In the bargain, Frontier Gandhi became more or less a stateless person, a *persona non grata*, since India was no longer his country, and Pakistan considered him a traitor to Islam. He belonged neither to India nor to Pakistan, but to jails of Pakistan. He spent another six years in various Pakistani jails.

Of course, there were a few pronounced dissimilarities too, the most obvious being their different religions — one a Christian, the other a Hindu with a strong streak of Jainism, and the third a Muslim of a secular bent of mind. Gandhi was a lawyer by profession, Martin was a clergyman, and the Frontier Gandhi started life as a military officer from which he took leave in a huff before he had even learnt the 'words of command'. Mahatma Gandhi was the leader of the majority community in his country while Martin belonged to the minority Negro race. And the Khan was a Pathan revered by the people of his tribe. While the first two had a countrywide national standing, the Frontier Gandhi's charisma was restricted to his own Province only. While Gandhi was a nineteenth century Asian, Martin was a twentieth century Afro-American. Even though Gandhi started his political career in Africa where he spent quite a few decades, their cultural backgrounds were oceans apart. Gandhi never visited America despite numerous pressing invitations, while Martin made it a point to visit India at the first available opportunity. Yet another irony of fate was that the person whose innovative technique of non-violent mass movement brought Martin the most prestigious Nobel Peace prize, Gandhi neither aspired nor received any such recognition even though he was revered the world over. Gandhi's immediate disciple groomed a Dynasty to rule over India — the Nehru-Gandhi Dynasty — but neither Gandhi nor Martin groomed any successors to their legacy. However, Dr. Ralph David Abernathy, the constant intellectual-spiritual companion of King, assumed the Presidency of SCLC immediately on Martin's death.

Ironically, the body of Gandhi, the apostle of peace and non-violence, was carried on a made-over weapon carrier. It was pulled to the cremation grounds by ropes by two hundred men of the Indian army, navy and air force, followed by about a million and a half persons. On the other hand, the Whites of America would not permit any military trappings to King's funeral cortege. His body was carried to its final resting place in South View Cemetery at Atlanta on a sharecropper's wagon. The caisson was pulled by two Georgian mules, followed by a multitude of 300,000 mourners. Scores of national dignitaries attended the funeral of the slain civil rights leader. The funeral services were conducted at the Ebenezer Baptist Church. The funeral procession then went on to the campus of Morehouse College where memorial services were held and the Morehouse Alma Mater was sung. On both occasions life in the two countries came to a standstill for about four to six hours during which the ceremonial processions were making their way to the last destination. "It is in death, if not in life, that Mohandas Karamchand Gandhi and Martin Luther King met."[10] In this context, words of Dr. Nelson Mandela appear as if the same were uttered by Dr. Martin Luther King, Jr. himself:

> Though separated in time, there remains a bond between us, in our shared prison experiences, our defiance of unjust laws and in the fact that violence threatens our aspirations for peace and reconciliation.

There are strong reasons to believe that King had premonition of his death, more so since, of late, the intensity and frequency of death-threats had multiplied considerably. As a matter of fact, about two months before his assassination, King had given a sermon on death to his congregation in Atlanta, in which he had alluded to his own death, funeral and the eulogy. He specifically forbade any reference to the Nobel Peace Prize and numerous other honours bestowed on him, nor to the academic institutions he had attended. Whoever was to give the eulogy was to say that Martin Luther king Jr. tried to feed the hungry, clothe the naked, help and love the poor, fight for justice, peace and righteousness. The basic theme of eulogy was to be agape, love for all men, and hatred towards none.

Mass Urban Rioting

King's murder flared into violence and hatred of unprecedented dimensions. The spark for that momentous fire of urban rioting was provided by the senseless murder of Reverend Martin Luther King Jr. on 4th April 1968 by a white man in Memphis, Tennessee, when the country witnessed its worst urban racial riots, anarchy and vandalism in which students played a significant role. Vicious police brutalities and savagery added fuel to the fire of hatred and violence. Martin's death triggered a great outpouring of grief and spontaneous epidemic of riots in almost 300 cities nationwide, out of which 125 cities suffered severe rioting, resulting in forty-six deaths, mostly Negroes, 5,117 fires, 23,987 arrests and $39 billion in damages, besides mobilization of 74,000

10. Jack A. Homer; op. cit. p. 222.

Army and National Guards troops. Dr. Martin Luther King, Jr. had become the canonized leader of his people. The initial outrage over his killing threatened the onslaught of a race war. "Rioting is the language of the unheard," "Temper tantrums" of the people who had lost hope in the future of America. Dr. King had said:

> "Violence may murder the murderer; but it doesn't murder murder. Violence may murder the liar; but it doesn't murder lie. It doesn't establish truth. Violence may even murder the dishonest man; but it doesn't murder dishonesty. Violence may go to the point of murdering the hater; but it doesn't murder hate. It may increase hate. It is always a descending spiral leading nowhere. This is the ultimate weakness of violence. It multiplies weakness and violence in the universe. It doesn't solve any problems."

And now the Black minority wanted to be heard, heard right and proper. The Whites feared that these developments portended 'race war', and the conservative elements amongst them were apprehensive that the "Negro Revolution" threatened to tear the nation apart while many liberals feared that the black activists, frustrated in their efforts to reform the American democratic system, sought its destruction instead. On the one hand burning, looting and killing terrified the populace irrespective of the colour of their skin; on the other it provided *raison d'etre* for the 'white backlash'. Looting went on as if it was "early Easter shopping". It gave an excuse to the white majority to psychologically rationalize their ill-treatment of the Blacks, and thereby an easy way out of the predicament. There was widespread panic amongst the Polish-American and Irish-American communities over the prospective inundation of their neighborhood and schools by Negroes. The popularity of the Democratic President and his administration had already nose-dived due to the civil rights issue. In fact, national approval of Kennedy Administration had fallen from 60 to 47 per cent. The year was further marked by the assassination of Presidential candidate Robert Kennedy on 5th June 1968 at Los Angeles by an Arab Muslim. It may be recalled that Attorney-general Robert Kennedy had authorized wiretaps on the Atlanta home of Reverend Martin Luther King Jr. since the Government believed that King was linked to the communists.[11] However, a positive outcome of the assassination-cum-rioting was the extraordinary speed with which the U.S. House of Representatives passed, and sent to President Johnson another Civil Rights Bill, an enlarged version. The story of the aftermath of Martin's murder is long. It transformed the entire social, economic and political structure of the United States of

11. Stearns N. Peter: op. cit. p. 920.

America. This Work is not the right medium to narrate it. However, some events stand out prominently:

January 08, 1970: Proclamation issued by Dr. Ralph David Abernathy in his capacity as the President, Southern Christian Leadership Conference, declaring January 15th a National People's Holiday in honour of Dr. Martin Luther King, Jr. (Copy in an appendix to this Chapter) On November 2, 1983, President Ronald Reagan signed the legislation establishing a national holiday in honour of Dr. Martin Luther King Jr. The only other persons so honoured in the history of the United States are Presidents George Washington and Abraham Lincoln. While signing this piece of legislation, Reagan recalled gunning down of Dr. King and quoted the American poet John Greenleaf Whittier: "Each Crisis brings its word and deed." Indeed, the crisis of racial discrimination in American life had brought about a historic change in the American Society. And Dr. King was primarily instrumental in this monumental transformation.[12] Under this legislation passed by the Congress, the third Monday in January of every year was declared a federal holiday as the Birthday of Dr. King. 20th January 1986 was officially observed as a national holiday for the first time as Dr. King's birthday. Since then it has become a regular feature of the American calendar.

19th October 1981: The Martin Luther King Jr. Center for Non-violent Change was opened in his home town, Atlanta, Georgia. It is popularly known as the 'King Centre'.

22nd November 1981: U.S. Senate approved the erection of a monument to Dr. King in the national capital, Washington, D.C. It was ceremoniously dedicated to him on 2nd November 1983.

13th April 1983: Congressman Harold Washington was elected Mayor of Chicago, Illinois, the first black to hold that office.

5th November 1989: Civil Rights Memorial in Montgomery, Alabama, designed by Vietnam Veterans Memorial artist Maya Lin was dedicated in honour of those who sacrificed their lives in the struggle for racial equality.

---

12. This Work does not permit the Author to make even a passing reference to the contribution of other Black leaders in emancipation of the Negro. All one can do is to merely list them: Paul Cuffe (1759-1817); Richard Allen (1760-1831); Frederick Douglas (1817-1895); Harriet Tubman (1823-1913); Ida B. Wells-Barnett (1869-1931). However, the part played in the Civil Rights Movement by Du Bois, Randolph, Roy Wilkins, Whitney Young, James Farmer, Andrew Young Jesse Jackson, *et al*, have been briefly covered.

Dr. King's coffin on a farm cart hauled by mules to its final resting place in Atlanta, Georgia

Grave Site of Dr. King in Atlanta

भारत INDIA

DR. MARTIN LUTHER KING

पै. P. 20

डा. मार्टिन लूथर किंग 1929-1968

Commemorative Indian Postage Stamp

Proclamation

by Dr. Ralph David Abernathy

Making Each January 15th a National People's Holiday

in Honor of

Dr. Martin Luther King, Jr.

WHEREAS, the late Dr. Martin Luther King, Jr. lived, worked and died for the cause of freedom, justice, equality and peace for all people; and

WHEREAS, Dr. King and the principles for which he stood should be suitably honored, commemorated, and carried out; and

WHEREAS, Black people, Poor people, and People of Good Will have a right to observe and celebrate Dr. King and his work;

THEREFORE, I Ralph David Abernathy, do hereby proclaim and designate each January 15th, the Birthday Anniversary of Dr. Martin Luther King, Jr., as a National People's Holiday in honor and in memory of Dr. King; and

I also encourage all Black People, Poor People, and People of Good Will to observe this National People's Holiday by taking the time they need each January 15th to engage in commemorative services, memorial and study assemblies, nonviolent demonstrations, and other activities which are consistent with Dr. King's philosophy and which will make life better for Poor People and all Mankind.

I issue this Proclamation through the powers vested in me as President of the Southern Christian Leadership Conference and leaders of the Poor People's Campaign.

Ralph David Abernathy

Washington, D.C., January 8, 1970

Bibliography

Abernathy David Ralph: *The Walls Came Tumbling Down*; Harper & Row, New York, 1989.

Adams Olive A: *Time Bomb: Mississippi Exposed and the Full Story of Emmett Till*; New York 1956.

Afaque, Khan Muhammad: *The Gandhian Approach to Communal Harmony*, Ajanta, Delhi, 1986.

Allen James S.: *Reconstruction: The Battle for Democracy, 1865-1876*; Int'l Publishers, New York, 1963.

Akbar M.J.: *Nehru: The Making of India*; Harmondsworth, Penguin, 1988.

Andrews C.F.: Ed. *Mahatma Gandhi*, His Own Story, Macmillan Company, New York, 1930.

Ansboro John J.: *Martin Luther King Jr.*; Orbis Books, New York, 1982.

Ashe Geoffrey: *Gandhi: A Study in Revolution*; Asia Publishing House, New Delhi, 1968.

Azad, Abul Kalam: *India Wins Freedom*, Orient Longman, Calcutta, 1959.

Baines Lee E.: Birmingham 1963; *Confrontation Over Civil Rights*, Harvard University, 1977.

Baker Ella: *Bigger than a Hamburger*, Southern Patriot, June 1960.

Baldwin V. Lewis, et al: *The Legacy of Martin Luther King Jr.*; University of Notre Dame Press, 2002.

Barrett George: *Montgomery: The Testing Ground*; The New York *Time Magazine*, December 16, 1956.

Barrett Russell: *Integration at Ole Miss*; Chicago, 1965.

Bates Daisy L.: *The Long Shadow of Little Rock*; David McKay, 1962.

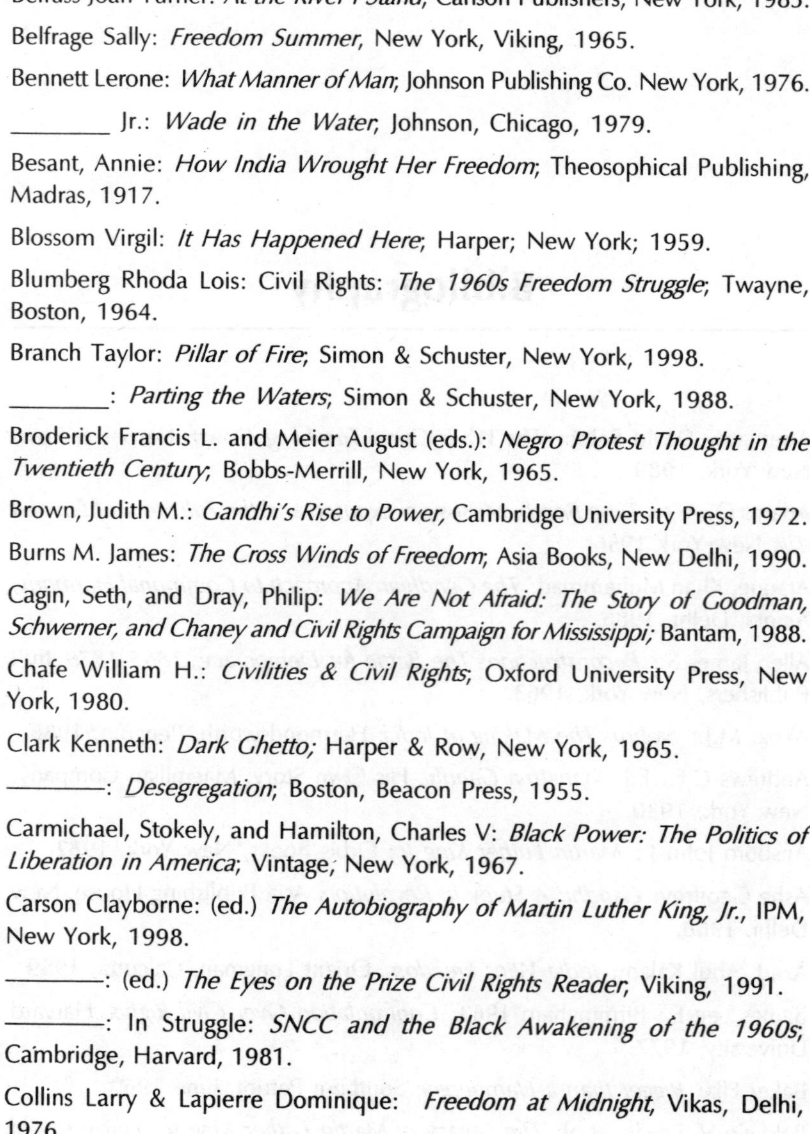

Beifuss Joan Turner: *At the River I Stand*; Carlson Publishers, New York, 1985.

Belfrage Sally: *Freedom Summer*, New York, Viking, 1965.

Bennett Lerone: *What Manner of Man*; Johnson Publishing Co. New York, 1976.

________ Jr.: *Wade in the Water*, Johnson, Chicago, 1979.

Besant, Annie: *How India Wrought Her Freedom*; Theosophical Publishing, Madras, 1917.

Blossom Virgil: *It Has Happened Here*; Harper; New York; 1959.

Blumberg Rhoda Lois: Civil Rights: *The 1960s Freedom Struggle*; Twayne, Boston, 1964.

Branch Taylor: *Pillar of Fire*; Simon & Schuster, New York, 1998.

________: *Parting the Waters*; Simon & Schuster, New York, 1988.

Broderick Francis L. and Meier August (eds.): *Negro Protest Thought in the Twentieth Century*, Bobbs-Merrill, New York, 1965.

Brown, Judith M.: *Gandhi's Rise to Power,* Cambridge University Press, 1972.

Burns M. James: *The Cross Winds of Freedom*; Asia Books, New Delhi, 1990.

Cagin, Seth, and Dray, Philip: *We Are Not Afraid: The Story of Goodman, Schwerner, and Chaney and Civil Rights Campaign for Mississippi;* Bantam, 1988.

Chafe William H.: *Civilities & Civil Rights*; Oxford University Press, New York, 1980.

Clark Kenneth: *Dark Ghetto;* Harper & Row, New York, 1965.

————: *Desegregation*; Boston, Beacon Press, 1955.

Carmichael, Stokely, and Hamilton, Charles V: *Black Power: The Politics of Liberation in America*; Vintage, New York, 1967.

Carson Clayborne: (ed.) *The Autobiography of Martin Luther King, Jr.*, IPM, New York, 1998.

————: (ed.) *The Eyes on the Prize Civil Rights Reader*, Viking, 1991.

————: In Struggle: *SNCC and the Black Awakening of the 1960s*; Cambridge, Harvard, 1981.

Collins Larry & Lapierre Dominique: *Freedom at Midnight*, Vikas, Delhi, 1976.

Cones James: *Martin & Malcolm & America*; Orbis Books, New York, 1991.

Cousins Norman: (ed.) *Profiles of Gandhi*, India Book Company, Delhi, 1969.

Cumming, Sir John: Ed. *Political India, 1832-1932*, Oxford University Press, New York, 1932.

Dalton Dennis: *Mahatma Gandhi; Nonviolent Power in Action*, Columbia University Press, New York, 1993.

Desai Mahadev: *Gandhi-Gita*; Navajivan Publishing House, Ahmedabad.

Desai Mahadev: *Gandhiji;* Navajivan, Ahmedabad.

Dishman B. Robert: *The State of the Union*, Charles Scribner's, New York, 1965.

Diwakar R.R.: *Satyagraha — Its Technique and History*, Bombay, 1946.

Dorman Michael: *We Shall Overcome*, New York, 1965.

DuBois, William Edward Burghardt: *Black Reconstruction in America*; Narcourt Brace, New York, 1936.

————: *Dusk of Dawn*: New York, 1940.

————: *The Souls of Black Folks*; McCurg, Chicago, 1903.

Evers Myrlie with William Peters: *For Us The Living*; Doubleday, New York, 1967.

Fager Charles E.: Selma 1965: *The March That Changed the South*; Beacon Pres, Boston, 1985.

Fairclough Adam: *To Redeem the Soul of America; The Southern Christian Leadership Conference and Martin Luther King Jr.*; University of Georgia, Athens, 1987.

Farmer James: *Lay Bare the Heart*; Arbor House, 1985.

Finch Minnie: *The NAACP: Its Fight For Justice*; Scarecrow Press, N.J., 1981.

Fischer Louis: *Life of Mahatma Gandhi*, Harper Brothers, New York, 1950.

Forman James: *Sammay Younge: The First Black College Student to Die in the Black Liberation Movement*; Grove Press, New York, 1968.

—————: *The Making of Black Revolutions*; Open Han, Seattle 1985.

Franklin John Hope: *From Slavery to Freedom: A History of the Negro Americans*; Chicago, 1961.

—————: *Reconstruction After the Civil War*, Chicago, 1961.

Frady Marshall: *Martin Luther King Jr.*; Penguin Group, 2002.

Frazier E. Franklin: *Black Bourgeoisie* ; Macmillan Company, New York, 1962.

Friedman Leon: *The Civil Rights Reader*, Walker, New York, 1967.

Garrow David J: *Bearing the Cross*; William Morrow & Co., 1986.

———— (ed.): *Birmingham, Alabama, 1956-63: The Black Struggle for Civil Rights*; Carlosn, New York, 1989.

———: *Protest at Selma: Martin Luther King Jr. and The Voting Rights Act of 1965*; New Haven, 1978

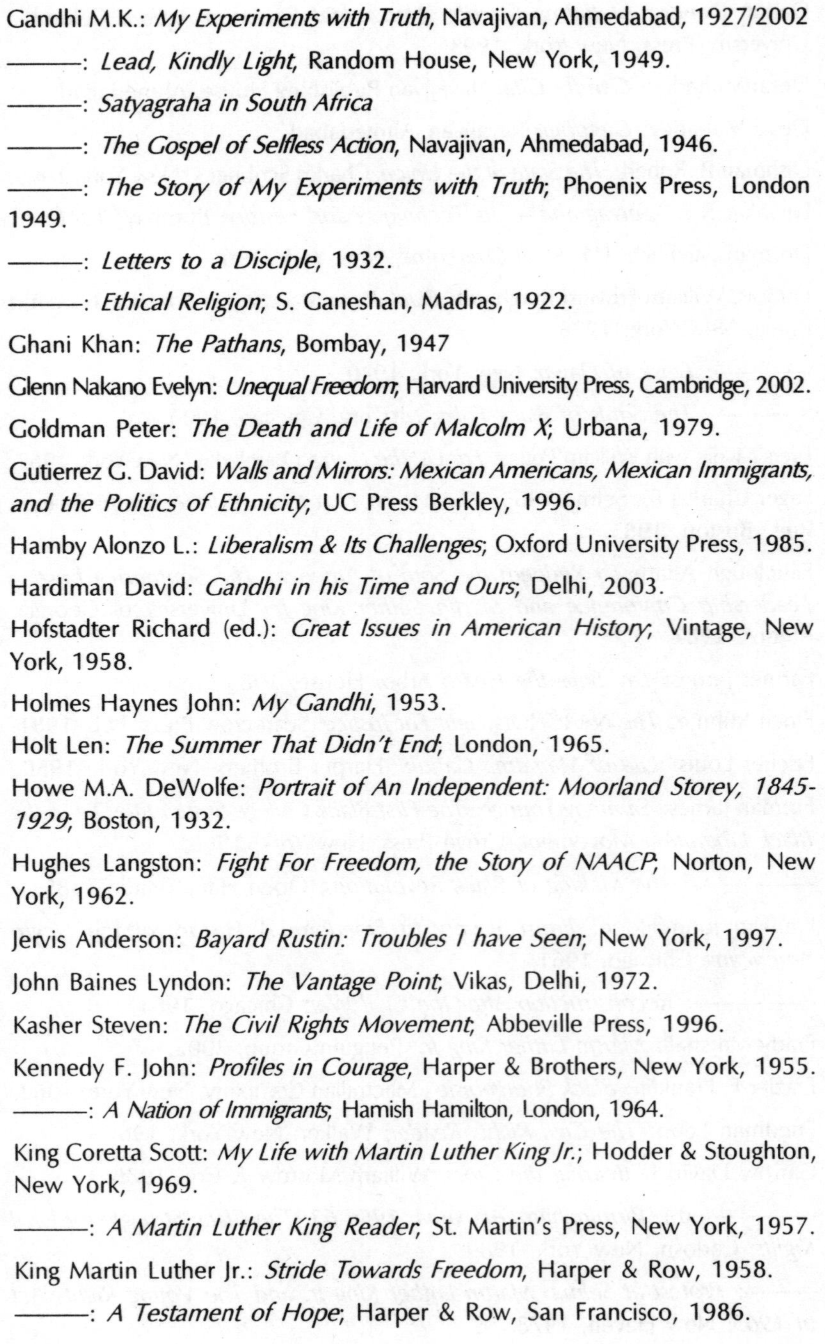

Gandhi M.K.: *My Experiments with Truth*, Navajivan, Ahmedabad, 1927/2002

———: *Lead, Kindly Light*, Random House, New York, 1949.

———: *Satyagraha in South Africa*

———: *The Gospel of Selfless Action*, Navajivan, Ahmedabad, 1946.

———: *The Story of My Experiments with Truth*; Phoenix Press, London 1949.

———: *Letters to a Disciple*, 1932.

———: *Ethical Religion*; S. Ganeshan, Madras, 1922.

Ghani Khan: *The Pathans*, Bombay, 1947

Glenn Nakano Evelyn: *Unequal Freedom*; Harvard University Press, Cambridge, 2002.

Goldman Peter: *The Death and Life of Malcolm X*; Urbana, 1979.

Gutierrez G. David: *Walls and Mirrors: Mexican Americans, Mexican Immigrants, and the Politics of Ethnicity*; UC Press Berkley, 1996.

Hamby Alonzo L.: *Liberalism & Its Challenges*; Oxford University Press, 1985.

Hardiman David: *Gandhi in his Time and Ours*; Delhi, 2003.

Hofstadter Richard (ed.): *Great Issues in American History*; Vintage, New York, 1958.

Holmes Haynes John: *My Gandhi*, 1953.

Holt Len: *The Summer That Didn't End*; London, 1965.

Howe M.A. DeWolfe: *Portrait of An Independent: Moorland Storey, 1845-1929*; Boston, 1932.

Hughes Langston: *Fight For Freedom, the Story of NAACP*; Norton, New York, 1962.

Jervis Anderson: *Bayard Rustin: Troubles I have Seen*; New York, 1997.

John Baines Lyndon: *The Vantage Point*; Vikas, Delhi, 1972.

Kasher Steven: *The Civil Rights Movement*; Abbeville Press, 1996.

Kennedy F. John: *Profiles in Courage*, Harper & Brothers, New York, 1955.

———: *A Nation of Immigrants*; Hamish Hamilton, London, 1964.

King Coretta Scott: *My Life with Martin Luther King Jr.*; Hodder & Stoughton, New York, 1969.

———: *A Martin Luther King Reader*; St. Martin's Press, New York, 1957.

King Martin Luther Jr.: *Stride Towards Freedom*, Harper & Row, 1958.

———: *A Testament of Hope*; Harper & Row, San Francisco, 1986.

———: *The Montgomery Story*, U.S. News & World Report, August 3, 1956.

———: *The Social Organization of Non-violence*, Liberation, August, 1959.

———: *Why We Can't Wait?* Harper & Row, New York, 1963.

———: *Strength to Love*; Harper, New York, 1963.

———: *Delhi Diary*, New Delhi, 1968.

———: *From Yeravada Mandir*, Navajivan Publishing Co., Ahmedabad, 1957.

King Mary: *Mahatma Gandhi and Martin Luther King Jr.*: New Delhi, 2002.

Lau James H.: *Direct Action and Desegregation*, ed. David G. Garrow, New York, 1989.

Lewis David L.: *King: A Critical Biography*; Praeger, New York, 1970.

Lincoln Charles Eric: *Martin Luther King Jr.*, Hill & Wang, 1970.

Lord Walter: *The Past That Would Not Die*, New York, 1965

Lynch John Roy: *Facts of Reconstruction*; Neale Publishing Co., New York, 1913.

Malcolm X: *Autobiography*; Grove Press, New York, 1965.

Mars Florence: *Witness in Philadelphia*; Baton Rouge, 1977.

Mazumdar T.H.: *Gandhi Triumphant! The Inside Story of the Historic Fast*, Universal Publishing Company, New York, 1939.

Mazumdar T. Haridas: *Gandhi versus the Empire*; Universal Publishing Co., New York, 1932.

McAdam Dough: *Freedom Summer*; Oxford University Press, New York, 1988.

McCord William: *Mississippi: The Long Hot Summer*; Norton, New York, 1965.

McKissick Floyd B.: *Three Fifths of A Man*; Macmillan, New York, 1969.

Meir August and Rudwick Elliot: *Core: A Study in the Civil Rights Movement, 1942-1986*; Oxford University Press, New York, 1973.

Menon K.P. Kesava: *The Great Trial of Mahatma Gandhi and Mr. Shankarlal Banker*, Ganeshan and Co., Madras, 1922.

Meredith James: *Three Years In Mississippi*; Indiana University Press, 1966.

Merriam S. George: *The Negro And the Nation*; Henry Holt, New York, 1906.

Mills Nicolaus: *Like A Holy Crusade: Mississippi, 1969. The Turning Point in the Civil Rights Movement in America*; Chicago, 1992.

Montejano David: *Anglos and Mexicans in the Making of Texas, 1836-1986*; Austin, 1987.

Moody Anne: *Coming of Age in Mississippi*; Dial Press, New York, 1968.

Moon Henry Lee: *Balance of Power: The Negro Vote*; Double Day, N.J., 1948.

Moon W. Glen and Don C. Cline: *Story of Our Land and People*, Holt, Rinehart & Winston Inc. New York, 1938/1964.

Myrdal Gunnar: *An American Dilemma;* New York.

Navajivan Publishing House: *Satyagraha in Champaran*; Ahmedabad.

Nehru Jawaharlal: *Indian Independence and Social Revolution*, Vikas, Delhi, 1984.

Nelson Mandela: *Long Walk to Freedom' The Autobiography of Nelson Mandela*; Little, Brown & Co., London, 1994.

Newfield Jack: *Robert Kennedy, A Memoir*, E.P. Dutton, 1969.

Oates Stephen B.: *Let The Trumpet Sound*; New American Library, 1982.

Newton Huey P.: *Revolutionary Suicide*; New York, 1973.

Ostergaard Geoffrey: *Nonviolent Revolution in India*; Gandhi Peace Foundation, New Delhi, 1985.

Peavy Charles D.: *Go Slow Now: Faulkner and The Race Question*; Eugene, 1971.

Peck James: *Freedom Ride*; Simon & Schuster, 1962.

Philips S. Foner (ed.): *Frderick Douglas: Selections from his Writings*; New York, 1964.

Powledge Fred: *Black Power/White Resistance*; New York 1967.

————: *Free At Last? The Civil Rights Movement and the People Who Made It*; Boston, 1991.

Pyarelal: *A Pilgrimage for Peace*, Navajivan Press, Ahmedabad, 1950.

Pyarelal: *Mahatma Gandhi: The Last Phase*, 2 vols. Navajivan Trust, Ahmedabad, 1958.

Rachleff J. Peter: *Labor in the South*: Richmond, Virginia, 1865-1890; Philadelphia, 1984.

Raman T.A.: *What Does Gandhi Want?* Oxford University Press, New York, 1942.

Randle Michael: *Civil Resistance*, Fontana Press, London, 1994.

Rau, Chalapathi M.: *Gandhi and Nehru*, Allied Publishers, New Delhi, 1967.

Ravoof A.A.: *Meet Mr. Jinnah*, Sheikh Muhammad Ashraf, Lahore, 1947.

Read Anthony & David Fisher: *The Proudest Day*, Jonathan Cape, London, 1997.

Record Wilson and Jane Cassels (eds.): *Little Rock, U.S.A.*; Chandler, San Francisco, 1960.

Reddick Lawrence.: *Crusader Without Violence*, Harper & Row, 1959.

Robinson Jo Ann Gibson: *The Montgomery Bus Boycott and the Woman Who Started It*; Garrow, Knoxville, 1987.

Rustin Bayard: *Down The Line: The Collected Writings of Bayard Rustin*; Quadrangle, New York, 1971.

———: *Even in the Face of Death: The Negro and Nonviolence*; Chicago, 1971.

Rolland Romain: *Mahatma Gandhi*, Paris, 1924.

Schlesinger Arthur M. Jr.: *A Thousand Days*; Andre Deutsch, London, 1965.

Schulke Flip: *King Remembered*; Penelope Ortner McPhee, Norton, 1986.

Seal Bobby: *Seize The Time: The Story of the Black Party Panther and Huey Newton*; Random House, New York, 1970.

Selby, Earl and Miriam: *Odyssey: Journey Through Black America*; Putnam's, New York, 1971.

Sharp Gene: *Dynamics of Nonviolent Action*; New York.

Sheean Vincent: *Mahatma Gandhi*, Publications Division, New Delhi, 1954.

Shridharani Krishanlal: *The Mahatma and the World*, John Day Company, New York, 1940.

Sitkoff Harvard: *The Struggle for Black Equality, 1954-1980*; Hill & Wang, New York, 1981.

Stearns N. Peters: *The Encyclopedia of World History*; Houghton Mifflin, Boston, 2001.

Stuckey Sterling: *The Ideological Origins of Black Nationalism*; Beacon Press, Boston, 1972.

Sugarman Tracy: *Stranger at the Gates: A Summer in Mississippi*; Hill Wang, New York, 1966.

Tara Chand; *History of the Freedom Movement in India,* New Delhi, 1977.

Tendulkar D.G.: *Abdul Ghaffar Khan: Faith is a Battle*; Bombay, 1967.

Tendulkar D.G.: *Mahatma: Life of Mohandas Karamchand Gandhi*, 8 vols. Jhaveri & Tendulkar, Bombay, 1952-54.

The Associated Press: *Triumph and Tragedy*, New York, 1968.

Torrance Ridgley: *The Story of John Hope*, Macmillan, New York, 1948.

Tuchman W. Barbara: *The March of Folly from Troy to Vietnam*, Michael Josep, London, 1984.

Viorst Milton W.: *Fire in the Streets: America in the 1960s*; Simon & Schuster, New York, 1979.

Washington Booker T.: *Up From Slavery: An Autobiography*; Doubleday, New York, 1901.

Watters Pat: *Down to Now: Reflections on the Southern Civil Rights Movement*; Pantheon, New York, 1971.

Weber J. David (ed.): *Foreigners in their Native land: Historical Roots of Mexican Americans*; University of New Mexico Press, Albuquerque, 1973.

Weisbrot Robert: *Freedom Bound: A History of America's Civil Rights Movement*; Norton, New York, 1991.

Wells-Barnett Ida B.: *Crusade For Justice*; ed. Alfreda Duster, Chicago, 1970.

Wexler Sanford: *The Civil Rights Movement*; Facts on File, New York, 1993.

White Walter F.: *A Man Called White*; Arno Press, New York, 1969.

Whitfield Stephen J.: *A Death in the Delta: Story of Emmett Till*; Free Press, New York, 1988.

Wicker Tom: *One of Us by Richard Nixon and the American Dream*;

Williams A. John: *The King God Didn't Save*; Eyre & Spottiswoode, London, 1971.

Wofford Harris: *Of Kennedys and Kings*; Farrar. Straus. Giroux. New York, 1980.

Wolff Miles: Lunch at the Five and Ten: The Greensboro Sit-ins: Stein Day, New York, 1970.

Wolpert S.: *Nehru*; New York.

Young Andrews: *An Easy Burden*; HarperCollins, 1996.

Young Whitney M: *Beyond Racism*; McGraw Hill, New York, 1969.

———: *To Be Equal*: McGraw Hill, New York 1964.

Yunus Mohammed: *Frontier Speaks*, Bombay, 1947.

Zamora Emilio: *The World of Mexican Worker in Texas*; A&M Press, Texas, 1993.

Zinn Howard: *Peoples' History of the United States*; 1492-Present, New York 1922/95.

———: Albany: *A Study in National Responsibility*; Atlanta, 1962.

———: *SNCC: The New Abolitionists*; Beacon Press, Boston, 1964.

Zutshi G.L.: *Frontier Gandhi*, National Publishing House, Delhi, 1970.

Index